# UKIP

# UKIP

## INSIDE THE CAMPAIGN TO REDRAW
## THE MAP OF BRITISH POLITICS

MATTHEW GOODWIN

AND

CAITLIN MILAZZO

**OXFORD**
UNIVERSITY PRESS

# OXFORD
## UNIVERSITY PRESS

Great Clarendon Street, Oxford, OX2 6DP,
United Kingdom

Oxford University Press is a department of the University of Oxford.
It furthers the University's objective of excellence in research, scholarship,
and education by publishing worldwide. Oxford is a registered trade mark of
Oxford University Press in the UK and in certain other countries

First Edition published in 2015

Impression: 1

Published in the United States of America by Oxford University Press
198 Madison Avenue, New York, NY 10016, United States of America

British Library Cataloguing in Publication Data

Data available

Library of Congress Control Number: 2015950968

ISBN 978-0-19-873611-0

Printed in Great Britain by
Clays Ltd, St Ives plc

# Contents

# List of Illustrations

# Cast of Characters

**Arron Banks**, major Ukip donor

**Roger Bird**, General Secretary, July–December 2014

**Chris Bruni-Lowe**, Head of Campaigns, 2014–2015; Head of Ukip Referendum Campaign, 2015–

**Douglas Carswell**, Ukip MP for Clacton, 2014–

**Steve Crowther**, Chairman of Ukip, 2010–

**Suzanne Evans**, Deputy Chairman of Ukip, 2014–

**Nigel Farage**, Leader of Ukip, 2010–; Ukip MEP 1999–

**Raheem Kassam**, Senior Adviser to Nigel Farage, October 2014–May 2015

**Paul 'Gobby' Lambert**, Director of Communications, December 2014–May 2015

**Paul Nuttall**, Deputy Leader of Ukip, 2010–

**Patrick O'Flynn**, Ukip MEP 2014–; Campaign Director March-May 2015

**Mark Reckless**, MP for Rochester and Strood, 2010–2015

**Matthew Richardson**, Party Secretary, 2013–

**David Soutter**, Head of Candidates, July 2014–May 2015

**Steve Stanbury**, Ukip Party Director, January–June 2015

**Paul Sykes**, Ukip donor, 2014 European Election Campaign

**Gawain Towler**, Ukip Press Officer

# Cast of Characters

# *Preface*

In the early 1990s, two academics sat down to write what would become the definitive account of an earlier challenge to Britain's established political parties. Founded in 1981, the Social Democratic Party (SDP) had set out on a quest to 'break the mould' of the country's two-party system—it wanted to redraw the map. Its rise was meteoric. The SDP, in alliance with the older Liberals, was soon polling ahead of *every* other party. At one point, its rating in the polls surpassed 50 per of the vote. 'Such an eruption of third-party support', observed its academic biographers, Ivor Crewe and Anthony King, 'is unprecedented: for speed, strength and duration there has been nothing to match it since Britain's modern party system emerged in the 1920s'. But, despite all of the excitement, the publicity, and talk of change, like almost every new party in British politics it did not last. While the SDP had shot up into the sky like a rocket, it had soon fallen down like a stick. Ultimately, concluded Crewe and King, as they put the finishing touches to their book, the party resembled somebody who had showed early promise but died young.[1]

Thirty years after the SDP peaked, Nigel Farage and the UK Independence Party (Ukip) were setting out on their own quest to try and redraw Britain's political map. In early 2014, and as the party braced for the European Parliament elections, it too had started to believe that it could overthrow the status quo. Over the eighteen months that followed, all eyes turned to Ukip as the party sought to mobilize the most important campaign in its history, planning to capture a handful of seats in the House of Commons and become a permanent force.

We wanted to tell the story of this campaign. As Sir David Butler, one of the founders of election studies in Britain, commented in 1952, while elections are hotly contested, the detail is soon forgotten and popular myths soon flourish. But, by studying election campaigns closely, or what Butler called the 'climaxes of politics', it is possible to challenge myths, throw light on how parties operate, and, for future historians, put on record what really happened.[2] So, just as Sir David had done more than sixty years before us, and Crewe and King a few decades later, we thought that somebody should be on hand to chronicle this particular campaign at this particular general election. And what a campaign it was.

The story that is told in the pages that follow commenced in the East India Club in Mayfair, London. In the early weeks of 2014, over lunch, we sat listening to Nigel Farage as he set out his plans for what lay ahead. He was in a good mood. Buoyed by rising support for Ukip in the polls, he talked of wanting to win the European Parliament elections and then lead his party on to a major breakthrough at the general election in 2015. We were not quite sure whether Farage and Ukip would fulfil their ambition by making it into the House of Commons. But we were certain that, win or lose, it had the makings of a compelling story. Both the party and its leader have generated serious amounts of publicity, but much of what happened during this campaign has yet to be told.

This is also inevitably a story about a particular moment in British politics, when young challengers to the main parties seemed to be all around and dominating the debate. The onward march of Ukip, the Scottish National Party (SNP), and even the Greens was watched with intrigue and fascination. Because insurgents have rarely mattered in Britain's political life, we tend to look at them as an antique collector might stare at an unexpected discovery in somebody's attic—with wonder and imagination. Like or loathe these parties, their rise has raised new and exciting questions about the health and direction of politics—about the strength of bonds between the older parties and the people, about the enduring viability of an electoral system that was only ever supposed to host two players, and about the overall representativeness of our politics. As we shall see, their rise reflects deeper changes that have been shaking the foundations of the party system and creating a more fragmented political landscape—and one that remains so, irrespective of the results in the general election of May 2015.

We also hoped that this story might teach us something about campaigns, elections, and voting more generally. In the study of politics, there are big debates about these topics—how parties campaign, how they win and lose, and how voters make up their minds.[3] Many of those who work in these areas tend to focus on developing theories about campaigns and elections in general. Developing theories is important, but it is also true that the richness of detail is often lost when party activists become 'actors' and parties become 'units of analysis'. Too often, academics tend to rely on journalists for information on what happens inside campaigns—people who are looking for a story, rather than an explanation. With this in mind, we set out to write a book that we hope will be of as much interest to those who watch political campaigns for fun as it is to those who study them.

Most of the material in the pages that follow has come from hundreds of interviews that were conducted between January 2014 and August 2015. Only by talking to those who were at the beating heart of the campaign could we hope to understand what happened—to see the campaign through what one journalist once described as 'an eye in the eye of a hurricane'.[4] Our interviewees include leaders, strategists, organizers, donors, and rank-and-file activists. Farage and his party did not need to provide us with an unprecedented level of access. But they did, and we are thankful. It is impossible to reduce all of the formal interviews and informal conversations to one number. On some days we talked to a handful of activists as they trudged their way around a seat, while on others we spent hours in the headquarters, talking to people as they came and went. Many of those whom we talked to were willing to go on the record, sometimes requesting that what they shared would not emerge until after the campaign. Others wanted the interviews to be conducted off the record or on a background basis, which as any researcher or journalist will tell you is often critical to obtaining honest insights. Some of those whom we talked to will never be named. One of the authors went to virtually every Ukip event during the campaign, including some that journalists were not allowed to attend. And not all our interviewees were in Ukip. Some were from the other parties that were feeling the effects of Ukip's campaign and trying to respond.

Our interviews came to an end almost nineteen months after we had first met Farage for lunch. Sitting in his living room, after the votes had been counted, we listened as the Ukip leader reflected on everything that had happened after Britain's latest general election had been and gone.

It is important to note that neither author is a member of any party, although we often find the people who commit their lives to politics to be fascinating. Parties like Ukip that campaign on emotive issues like immigration are divisive. By refusing to condemn without first consulting the evidence, we were often questioned. Throughout, we sought to treat all those whom we encountered, on all sides of the political battlefield, with respect—even if we did not always agree with their politics. We hope that what happened during this campaign makes for an interesting read.

This book follows an earlier study of Ukip. *Revolt on the Right* was written by Robert Ford and Matthew Goodwin and published shortly before the European Parliament elections in 2014.[5] That book examined Ukip as it was beginning to attract attention, drawing on data between 2004 and late 2013. This book is not an official sequel, but it does bring the picture (and the data) up to date. We are also focused on the question that brought that earlier book to a close, namely: could Ukip ever overcome the barriers to entry that are imposed by Britain's first-past-the-post system?

In the spirit of *Revolt*, we also strove to make this book as accessible as possible. That being said, the book is underpinned by our commitment to academic rigour. Extensive interviews with insiders are paired with comprehensive analysis of tens of thousands of voters to provide insight into the campaign, the election, and wider shifts in the loyalties of voters. For this reason, we include a detailed Appendix, where readers can find the more technical analysis that supports our arguments and observations.

Writing about a campaign as it unfolds is never easy. Events, stories, trends, results, and their significance must all be assessed quickly, and before the next chapter unfolds. During much of the campaign we followed the 'Crewe and King model', writing many of the chapters as events were unfolding or in the immediate aftermath. Some of the chapters are deliberately written to 'catch the mood of the time', significant not only for historical accuracy but because of the way in which this mood often impacted directly on the decisions that people made. Along the way we received help and interview material from numerous people. They include Tim Aker, Lord Ashcroft, Janice Atkinson, Tim Bale, Greg Beales, Roger Bird, Louise Bours, Paul Brothwood, Chris Bruni-Lowe, Sir David Butler, Douglas Carswell, Andrew Cooper, Matthew Cotton and the team at OUP, Lynton Crosby, Steve Crowther, David Cutts, Jack Duffin, Bill Etheridge, Geoff Evans and the participants of the Nuffield Political Science seminar, Suzanne Evans, Kirsten Farage, Nigel Farage, Stephen Fisher, Ameet Gill, John Gill, Zac Goldsmith, Paul Goodman, Neil Hamilton, John Healey, Michael Heaver, Philip Hollobone, Adam Holloway, Jamie Huntman, Diane James, Laurence Janta-Lipinski, Raheem Kassam, Eric Kaufmann, Paul Lambert, Damian Lyons Lowe, James Morris, Tim Montgomerie, Paul Nuttall, Patrick O'Flynn, Paul Oakden, Lord Pearson of Rannoch, Alex Phillips, Mark Reckless, Jacob Rees-Mogg, Adam Richardson, Matthew Richardson, Will Scobie, Paul Sykes, Gawain Towler, Lizzy Vaid, Hilary Walford, Anthony Wells, Steven Woolfe, and Ian Wright.

We would like to thank the former and current members of the British Election Study team for providing a unique and invaluable source of data. Colleagues at the polling firms Ipsos–MORI, Survation, and YouGov made various data available. Michael Thrasher and Colin Rallings at the Elections Centre at Plymouth University, as ever, made available to us their data on local elections. Our two Research Assistants, James Dennison and Albert Tapper, were extremely helpful throughout the project, meeting tight deadlines and contributing ideas along the way. Their involvement was made possible by a research grant from the British Academy (grant SG140319). Both of the authors would also like to thank their Schools and the Universities of Kent and Nottingham. Matthew Goodwin also thanks the Royal Institute of International Affairs at Chatham House. And last—but never least—we give special thanks to our families and our partners, Fiona and Siim, who had infinite patience as we devoted our nights and weekends to making this project a reality.

Kent and Nottingham
October 2015

# I

# Gateshead

On a mild spring evening in 2014, more than 1,000 people left their homes and offices and made their way to a public meeting about an election. It was in Gateshead, an old industrial town on the south bank of the River Tyne, in north-east England. Politics did not usually generate much interest there, but this felt different. The meeting was packed. It was standing room only. Many of those who had walked into the fading town hall were white pensioners who, over the years, had grown anxious about the direction of their town. They had watched their communities struggle to find ways to fill the void that had been left by the collapse of old industries. Somewhere along the way, officials in the council had decided to invest in the arts. Old tales about building ships and mining coal had made way for new claims about how the town was shaping national culture. Gateshead, read the leaflets for tourists, was home to the largest free-standing sculpture in the country, one of the largest shopping centres in Europe, and the world's first tilting bridge. But, like some of those at the meeting, not everybody had shared the new vision. When one tourist had visited England so that he could explore the town, he had been denied entry. It was just not credible, said the visa officials, that somebody would want to spend an entire week in Gateshead.[1]

They were not the first to criticize the town. During his famous tour of England in the 1930s, the writer J. B. Priestley had claimed that 'no true civilisation could have produced such a town', which must have been 'carefully planned by an enemy of the human race'.[2] But, despite such criticism, the people had pushed on. They were proud of their home town and their working-class roots. It was a background that had also shaped their approach to politics. Like voters in many other northern towns, they had traditionally voted for Labour, having been guided by a deep and tribal loyalty to the one party that had been founded to represent the working classes.

From one election to the next, this unwavering allegiance had made their town a Labour heartland, so much so that the results of elections had routinely felt like a foregone conclusion. Labour politicians had been sent down to Westminster at almost every election since the 1920s. They had controlled the local council for almost a century.[3]

But change was in the air. As in many other communities, the old bond between Labour and its traditional supporters, which had once felt so tight, was starting to fray. In Gateshead, though it could have been any one of a large number of towns, Labour no longer looked as though it had an automatic right to power. And in one month from this meeting, at elections to the European Parliament, these old loyalties would be tested again. It would be the last nationwide battle between the different parties before the 2015 general election. And now the people of Gateshead were turning out to listen to somebody from a very different political tradition. They had come to listen to Nigel Farage, leader of the UK Independence Party (Ukip).

Farage stood quietly at the back of the hall, reflecting on his surroundings. He felt that he thrived in environments like this. Ever since he had first joined Ukip in the early 1990s, the 50-year-old politician had always believed that he was at his best when he was out on the campaign trail—pounding pavements, knocking on doors, speaking at meetings, and making his case for why Britain should end its membership of the European Union (EU). There was no doubt that the campaigns were intense. The fight to win elections can be gruelling, relentless, and unforgiving, which is why the journalist Hunter S. Thompson had once compared them to a hurricane. But they were also where Farage felt most alive. He found them exhausting, but he also relished the opportunity for engaging in combat with his rivals. Behind closed doors, when he was alone among friends, he would often describe himself as a cavalry officer who was charging from the front, leading his small band of amateurs into a battle that would determine the future of Britain.

Ukip had joined the battle in 1993. The party had been formed by political amateurs who felt intensely anxious about Britain's integration into the EU—or what many saw as an undemocratic superstate that posed a fundamental threat to British sovereignty.[4] Many of the founders were former Conservatives who admired politicians like Margaret Thatcher but felt that their old party had failed to protect Britain's independence. They had been alarmed by the signing of the Single European Act in 1986, which created a single market and framework for European cooperation, and then the

Maastricht Treaty in 1992, which paved the way for a single currency and established the core pillars of the EU. Around the same time, the eruption of a financial crisis linked to Britain's membership of the Exchange Rate Mechanism, a precursor to the Euro single currency, appeared to underline to the activists the need for their country to stay out of the European project. Many of those who would later play leading roles had flocked to London think tanks like the Bruges Group that were campaigning for a less centralized European structure and waging an intellectual battle against the so-called Eurocrats in Brussels and Euro-federalists in Westminster. From these debates emerged the Anti-Federalist League, which in 1993 morphed into Ukip.

But, while the battle was over politics, for Farage it was also intensely personal. He had devoted more than twenty years of his life to fighting for Ukip, spending most of them as an irrelevant figure. He often joked that he was the 'Patron Saint of Lost Causes', but on many nights it had felt true. In 1994, when he had first put his head above the parapet to fight a by-election in Eastleigh, he won less than 2 per cent of the vote. Fewer than 200 votes separated him from Screaming Lord Sutch of the Monster Raving Loonies. In the years that followed, and with his family looking on, Farage was routinely ridiculed and dismissed. At best, he was seen as a bad political joke, a beer-swilling populist who wanted to drag Britain back to the 1950s. At worst, he was a racist, a would-be demagogue who secretly wanted to overhaul the country's proud tradition of liberalism and parliamentary democracy. Most commentators instinctively subscribed to a view of Farage and Ukip that was put forward by one of their colleagues—that, while the party postured as the protector of national sovereignty, it represented a reactionary brand of politics that was at odds with the pluralism of modern life.[5] Few ever thought that Farage and his party might actually get somewhere.

Fast-forward to the spring of 2014, and this picture had changed radically. Farage was feeling remarkably confident, and with good reason. His party was surging and he could feel it—the crowds were getting larger, his party's membership was growing, journalists were getting interested, and his speeches were sparking a reaction. In Gateshead, he was looking out at the largest meeting in Ukip's twenty-one-year history, a gathering that he saw as a symbol of its meteoric rise. What had started as a hobby had turned into the most significant new independent party in post-war English politics. In only four years, Ukip had swapped the wilderness for the centre stage, enjoying a string of record results and winning seats in the European

Parliament and local councils. Having polled ahead of the Liberal Democrats since early 2013, Farage was also now claiming with some credibility to be leading the third most popular party. The amateurs were on the verge of becoming a permanent feature on the landscape, or so it seemed.

As he prepared to take the stage, Farage was now pushing his party to make political history. He wanted to win the European elections outright. He knew that people were sceptical about the power of his revolt, and that most of the people who made their living commentating on politics saw Ukip as a flash-in-the-pan, a temporary rebellion that would soon be gone. Winning an election, he thought, would silence his critics, at least for a while. There was no doubt that it was an ambitious goal. The last time a group of politicians from outside the Conservative and Labour parties had won a nation-wide election was in 1906, when the Liberals had stormed to their famous (and last) majority government.

But Ukip was nothing like them, or the other main parties. From top to bottom it was filled with people who had little experience of how election campaigns were fought and won. They had never come close to winning an election. In fact, they had never won a single seat in the House of Commons.[6] And their movement was incredibly fragile. Ukip had no army of experienced campaigners, paid staff, pollsters, and donors. Behind the scenes, the party's entire operation relied on fewer than twenty people and a handful of elderly volunteers. One insider compared its internal life to people who were constantly spinning plates, or to a shambolic sky-diving team that was plummeting through the air as members struggled to get their hands to meet and their parachutes to open. The headquarters were in the affluent Mayfair district of London, tucked behind Claridge's hotel on Brooks Mews, but even that gave a false impression. The offices had been rented from a wealthy supporter at a discount rate. There were rarely more than six or seven activists present. Nor did Ukip have experience of power. Its excitable talk about redrawing the political map sat uncomfortably with the fact that, as the party braced for the biggest election in its history, it had only ever controlled one almost insignificant council on the outskirts of Cambridgeshire.[7]

It was no surprise, therefore, that they were written off. Farage offered a home for cranks, clowns, and misfits—people who did not belong in the mainstream. The general tone of coverage was best reflected in the instinctive reaction of David Cameron when he had been asked about Ukip a few years earlier. The party, he said, was 'a bunch of fruitcakes, loonies and closet racists'.

Farage had always preferred to listen to his instincts rather than dwell on the obstacles. He felt that he understood better than any of his advisers or opponents the mood of the people. Away from the headlines and the day-to-day battles in Westminster, he saw his party as a ship on the ocean—a vessel that was being pushed forward by deeper currents that lay hidden below the surface of British politics. And several currents were pushing him on.

There was the watering-down of traditional conservatism that had given rise to an army of disenchanted grass-roots Tories—angry, older social conservatives who wanted tough action on reducing immigration, to pull Britain out of the EU, and to halt the spread of liberal values that had produced same-sex marriage, all-women shortlists, and a seemingly endless celebration of ethnic diversity and cosmopolitanism. They were traditional Tories—people who did not see their own values reflected back in David Cameron and the modern Conservative Party. Their world was under assault, and they wanted somebody—anybody—to preserve it.

Meanwhile, at the other end of the spectrum Farage spotted another opening. There was a growing gulf between Labour and its traditional working-class base that was represented by a quiet but simmering anger among blue-collar Britons who felt marginalized by the onslaught of globalization, anxious about ways of life that seemed to be under threat, and cut adrift from a Labour movement that some felt had ceased to represent them. Long gone were the days of Ramsey Macdonald, Clement Attlee, and Neil Kinnock. They had been replaced by a new generation of Labour elites, middle-class and professional politicians who talked about economics over national belonging, appealed to the centre ground over class solidarity, and claimed to represent the workers while appearing to dismiss their concerns and mock their patriotism. If, Farage thought, he could find a way of mobilizing this distrust, then it could be potent. 'We're knocking at the door,' said one of his lieutenants, when asked about Ukip's growing interest in Labour areas, 'and sooner rather than later we are going to kick the door in'.[8]

But Britain was also changing in other ways that seemed to be creating new space for Farage's party. There was a resurgent English nationalism that mirrored its counterpart in Scotland and raised difficult questions for left-wing progressives who liked to argue that such ideas had been consigned to the dustbin of history. Then there was immigration—the continuing arrival into Britain of hundreds of thousands of EU migrant workers, which had unleashed a new wave of public concern about the impact of this rapid and unsettling change. And there was the emergence of what Farage saw as a new political and media class—members of a self-serving tribe who had gone to the same universities, inhabited the same Westminster laboratory, and knew little of life outside the London bubble. As he travelled across the country, from one meeting to the next, he felt that he was harnessing these trends, tapping into veins of frustration that cut across the old left–right divide. By the time that he had come to Gateshead, the same currents had allowed him to mobilize the most significant insurrection that English pol-itics had seen for a generation.

Farage had deliberately put public meetings at the heart of his strategy. He saw a meeting that was open to all as a symbol of traditional politics—of *real* politics. It was the oldest arena for political battle, a forum that had reigned supreme before the spin doctors had stripped the life out of cam-paigns, whittling them down to micro-managed photo shoots and bland speeches in front of the already converted. He had always wanted to cut out the middleman, to take his pitch direct to the people. Farage took pride in pointing out that he had learned his craft in the backwaters and had addressed more than 1,000 public meetings. He had counted them. During the wilderness years, while slogging around the country, he had refined his style in front of sleepy pensioners and half-empty rooms in smoky pubs and working men's clubs. Each event had provided a new opportunity to exper-iment with speech and posture. 'Nigel is like a stand-up comic,' said one of his closest advisers. 'He is constantly trying out new lines and perfect-ing old ones.'

By the time of his rise, he had developed a simple but effective routine. 'Get up, tell a story, make them laugh and make a series of points firmly.' He never struggled to remember his lines. 'His memory is second to none,' said one of his advisers. He would often remember phone numbers by memory rather than storing them in his phone, a habit that had led some in his party to call him 'Rain Man'. It had started during his earlier career working in the London Metal Exchange, where he had bought and sold metals. It meant that he never had to prepare speeches in detail. He had done so on only one occasion and hated the experience—the speech had felt dry, rigid, and wooden. And he had little interest in detailed intellectual arguments or setting out his political philosophy. Privately, Farage would often dismiss complex speeches or articles as 'PPE bollocks', a reference to the way in which many politicians and journalists had studied Politics, Philosophy, and Economics at the University of Oxford. His politics was different—it was instinctive, tribal, and emotional. He felt that something was wrong and he wanted to say so.

From one meeting to the next, he would deliver one of half-a-dozen stump speeches that had been cultivated over the years. Each was a variation of Ukip's three core messages—Britain should leave the EU, immigration was out of control, and the established politicians had failed to protect Britain's sovereignty and values. The message was delivered through a form of political entertainment, a style of communication that would be more familiar to an evangelical preacher than politicians. As his audiences had grown in size, he had stopped sitting on the stage with the other speakers. He would instead wait at the back of the room, have his arrival announced, and then pass triumphantly through the hall as part of what his advisers called the 'royal walk'. He had also swapped the traditional microphone for a headset, so that, when it was time, he could roam freely around the venue and engage fully with the audience. Somewhere along the way he had stopped calling them meetings and started to refer to them as 'the shows'.

Ukip had been formed to try and pull Britain away from Brussels, but Farage often began his routine by attacking politicians in Westminster. 'We have a career political class!' he declared. 'You know the people I'm talking about. They all go to the same schools. They all go to Oxford. They all study PPE. They leave at 22 and get a job as a researcher for one of the parties and then become MPs at age 27 or 28.' He took a long pause. 'We are run by a bunch of college kids who've never done a day of work in their lives!' The audience cheered. 'You have come to a meeting of a party that is unashamedly patriotic, proud to be who we are as a nation, sick to death of a career polit-ical class who have sold this country out to Brussels and we want our coun-try back!' He had not even mentioned the EU, but already most of the audience seemed to be on side.

Farage would often contrast his own background with that of other pol-iticians. He joked his way through the fact that he had performed poorly at school and then spent twenty years trading in the City—a destination that was not popular among voters in the wake of the financial crisis that had erupted in 2008. And he was open about the fact that he had worked hard but played harder. He had married, divorced, and then married again. He had fathered four children, battled financial problems, and survived a series of life-threatening events, including testicular cancer, a major car crash, and a plane crash for good measure. He saw himself as a survivor and would often say that he lived each day like it was his last. 'I love gambling,' he once said. 'I love saying and doing things that the others would never do.' It was an outlook that had also directly influenced his political strategy. 'Double or quits', he would say to his advisers. 'Double or quits.'

There was no doubt that events had taken their poll. The plane crash had left Farage with serious injuries that required ongoing treatment. Sometimes, as a result of the lingering physical trauma, he would suddenly flinch during interviews. Then there was the job of leading Ukip—the relentless and punishing schedule of interviews, the pile of papers that had to be read and digested, the weekly slogs to Brussels or Strasbourg, the seemingly never-ending disputes that had to be resolved, and the fact that, despite his constant requests for support, he felt as though he was carrying the entire movement on his back. And then there was the drinking—the endless cycle of long lunches, dinners with donors, talks in the City, and drinks with activists. Farage was leading the third most popular party in England, but so much of it must have felt like a blurry haze.

As the European elections approached, Ukip and its leader were now hoping that one specific gamble was about to pay off. Since 2010, he had calculated that Ukip could appeal simultaneously to disgruntled Eurosceptic Conservatives in the south while reaching into Labour's northern and industrial heartlands. 'It is no coincidence that we are here today,' he told the people of Gateshead, setting out a message that he was delivering from one Labour town to the next. 'We are going for the Labour heartlands. Labour and the trade unions used to stand up and represent the interests of ordinary working people but they have turned their backs on you in favour of the European project and big corporatism in the private sector. You are no longer represented by that party. We will stand up and fight for you!' The audience cheered. People who had spent much of their lives supporting Labour were now being invited to switch their loyalty to something else entirely, what Farage would call, 'our very English rebellion'.

Some insiders had been urging Ukip to target Labour for some time. They had argued that the Conservatives, unable or unwilling to shake off the toxicity of Thatcherism, were dying in the north. Labour had dominated the landscape for decades, but many of its branches looked like empty vessels that were filled with complacent activists who had not had to fend off serious competition for generations. Now, those who were unwilling to vote time and time again for Labour, who were angry about its failure to speak to their concerns about Europe, immigration, identity, and Englishness, were looking for an alternative. Farage had bought into the idea, arguing that Ukip was uniquely positioned to emerge as the main opposition in Labour heartlands. That the strategy had potential had been reflected in the results of by-elections where Ukip had come second to Labour. Farage was keenly aware that many in Westminster saw the stereotypical supporter as 'a retired half-colonel living on the edge of Salisbury Plain'. But he saw as much potential among a very different group of voters—patriotic, working-class Britons who had once upon a time voted for Labour—people who looked like those who were listening to him in Gateshead.[9]

He was now moving towards his core message. Drawing on his family history, he explained how, in a national referendum in 1975, his parents had voted for Britain to join the common market because they had believed that Britain's integration into Europe was just about trade. 'Nobody ever told them that it would morph into a European Union. We have been lied to!' Many in the audience were old enough to have voted in the referendum, and they were now cheering and clapping at the end of almost every line. 'And I'm married to a girl from Hamburg so nobody needs to tell me what it's like to live in a German-dominated project!' Between the jokes, Farage was focused fully on Ukip's *raison d'être*—the issue that had first led him to wander into one of its meetings.

Farage always sounded most passionate when talking about Britain's EU membership. 'I do not want the European Union passport!' he boomed. 'I do not want that flag! I do not want that anthem!' Some in the audience were now on their feet, clapping and cheering him on. 'I do not want 75 per cent of my laws made somewhere else! I do not want to pay £55 million a day! And I do not want a total open border to 485 million people!'

Yet it was his opposition to immigration that received the loudest cheer. Since 2010, and while trying to reach into the north, Farage had been trying to cast a wider net, fusing Ukip's traditional appeal to Eurosceptics with a message for the much larger number of voters who felt anxious about migration into Britain. It was deliberate. Europe dominated Ukip's entire world view, but the issue did not excite the people anywhere near to the same extent. It did not have enough power to propel Ukip from the margins to the mainstream. This was abundantly clear in the polls, which each month asked people to list the top issues facing Britain. Since 2005, Europe had appeared among the five most pressing issues on only one occasion and even then it had been ranked fifth.[10] But immigration was a different story. It was routinely among the top three. By the spring of 2014 it was second only to the economy and would soon be the most important issue of all.

'The fact', Farage declared, as he walked through the hall, 'is that in scores of our cities and market towns, this country, in a short space of time, has become unrecognizable! And in many parts of England you don't hear English any more. Is this the kind of community we want to leave our children and grandchildren?' He then paused. The room fell completely silent. 'You know,' he said quietly, 'we are three weeks away from what could and should be an earthquake in British politics. Ukip could win these European elections!'

# 2

# The Changing Landscape

By the spring of 2014, when Nigel Farage was speaking to the people of Gateshead, British politics had never looked so open to a new challenger. Compared to earlier years, it must have felt like another world to Farage and his party. Over the previous four years, Ukip's rating in the polls had jumped more than fourfold, surging from 3 to 13 per cent of the vote. The party's handful of staffers, who had become used to spending their days completing crosswords, were now being inundated with calls from inquisitive voters who wanted to find a Ukip meeting or join the party's rapidly growing membership, now a record 40,000 strong. Moreover, as Farage surveyed the landscape, he saw opportunities for further growth. Behind the newspaper headlines and daily battles in Westminster, deep-rooted changes had been eroding people's traditional loyalties to the two main parties. The old allegiances that had once given Britain one of the most stable and secure political systems in the world seemed to be breaking down. And, since the general election in 2010, other openings had appeared. Never before had there been as much room for a radical right and populist force that was working overtime to convert public anxieties over the social and cultural changes that were sweeping the nation into votes in the ballot box. In sum, Ukip could not have chosen a better moment to launch its campaign for serious power. And, ever the gambler, Farage knew when it was time to play a good hand.

But winning power would not be easy. British political history has shown how new parties routinely struggled to break through. So much works against them. Unlike many other democracies, Britain's had long been synonymous with a strong and stable party system, organized around only two political parties. People either voted for the Conservatives or they voted for Labour. Only rarely did they consider an alternative. When, in the 1950s and 1960s, academics like Sir David Butler sat down to look at how people voted, he noted how 'millions of British electors remain anchored to one of the parties for very long periods of time. Indeed, many electors have had the same party loyalties from the dawn of their political consciousness.'[1] The dominance of the 'big two' was overwhelming. Ten years after the end of war, in 1955, a striking 96 per cent of people had voted either for Anthony Eden and the Conservatives, or Clement Attlee and Labour. When the dust of that earlier election had settled, only 8 of the 630 Members of Parliament did not belong to the two main parties. Their monopoly owed much to the 'first-past-the-post' electoral system, which safeguards the dominance of the two main parties by stacking the deck against new challengers.

Farage had good reason to feel excited about Ukip's chances at a *European* election. The elections to Brussels and Strasbourg take place under a far more proportional electoral system, where the percentage of seats that parties receive more closely matches the share of the votes that they win. But *general* elections, which take place under first-past-the-post, are entirely different. They put two big hurdles in front of new challengers.

The first is mechanical. To win seats in the House of Commons parties need to build concentrated support within individual seats. Winning lots of votes that are spread across the country can deliver success in a more proportional system, but under first-past-the-post parties need to cultivate deep support within specific areas. At the general election in 2010, for example, the average politician who was elected into the House of Commons won more than 21,000 votes. Parties outside of the big two will struggle to reach these kinds of numbers in one seat, never mind repeating the achievement across a swathe of territory.

The second hurdle that parties like Ukip have to overcome is psychological. Because it is extremely difficult for new parties to mobilize this concentrated support, the system encourages people to avoid challengers who lack the history, support, and proven electoral credibility of the big two. Why vote for a party that is distinctly unlikely to win your seat? This psychological hurdle can have other effects. Wealthy people who want to donate and influence the agenda are unlikely to invest in parties that do not look like they can win. People who want to get active in politics are also unlikely to devote their time to parties that look destined to stay in the wilderness. And experienced campaigners, knowing how difficult it is to overcome first-past-the-post, are unlikely to commit to parties that will require a generation of work before they are in a position to win seats.

Parties that want to challenge Labour and the Conservatives typically lack the money and manpower to do so. But the very fact that they are not in a position to challenge the status quo discourages people from giving them these resources in the first place. Catch 22. It is a vicious cycle.

This is why challengers are often dismissed in Britain. Almost all of them have failed. Long before Ukip had even emerged, those who had set out with dreams of redrawing the map had often led their followers into a cul-de-sac. Challengers died as quickly as they emerged. In the 1970s, the neo-Nazi National Front attracted publicity but did not win a single seat. In the 1980s, the Social Democratic Party (SDP), in alliance with the older Liberals, did manage to win a couple of dozen seats, but it too proved unable to last the course. Then, in 1997, Sir James Goldsmith and the Referendum Party tried to mobilize anxieties over Britain's membership of the EU, but won less than 3 per cent of the vote and did not win a single seat. Thirteen years later, the far right British National Party (BNP) generated publicity, but never came within ten points of winning a seat. Meanwhile, though George Galloway and the Respect Party, who had opposed the Iraq War, captured one seat in 2005, and another at a by-election in 2012, they too collapsed under the weight of internal wrangling and a narrow platform. The unwritten law that insurgent parties never succeed in Britain remained very much in force.

Had Farage read up on these earlier challengers, then he might have concluded that his own revolt was similarly destined to fail. After the most recent effort to reform Britain's electoral system had failed in 2011, first-past-the-post continued to stand before his minnow party like an almost insurmountable mountain. Overcoming it was the equivalent of climbing Everest—only those with experience, money, and manpower stood a chance of making it to the top. Yet, while Farage knew that he too now faced the daunting challenge, he had more reasons than those before him to feel optimistic about the expedition that lay ahead.

This was partly because of the way in which longer-term trends had been chipping away at the foundations of British politics. In the sixty years since Sir David Butler had made his observation about the tribal loyalties that had once reigned supreme, deeper changes had been at work, making the system more open to challengers. While part of this was about how people *felt* about politics, it was also about how, consequently, people had started to *behave* at elections.

Like their counterparts in many other countries, the British public had already been moving away from the old monolithic allegiances that had more strongly guided their parents and grandparents.[2] In years gone by, such as when Anthony Eden and Clement Attlee had led the country, there had been incredibly strong links between the people and the two main parties. These created stability and continuity in politics. But, during the more than fifty years that separated the elections in 1964 and 2015, there had been a sharp decline in the number of people who identified strongly with a party. When Labour came to power in 1964, almost half of the population had felt a very strong connection to a party. But this soon plummeted. By 1974 the percentage of 'strong identifiers' in the electorate was down to 32 per cent. By 1992 it had reached a new low of 19 per cent, and by 2005 it had fallen to just 11 per cent. Meanwhile, the proportion of people who felt only *weakly* attached to the parties, or who did not identify with them at all, surged from less than one in five to more than one in two. As these ties began to fray, people became more open to persuasion, more indecisive about whom to support, more volatile at elections, and more likely to defect to a different party. This is not to say that they no longer felt *at all* connected to the two main parties but rather that their relationships with them, which had once been so strong, had become far weaker.

These changes in the way people felt about politics were increasingly reflected in how they behaved at elections. There were some fairly obvious signs that something had changed. A growing number of people were refusing to vote at all. In 1964, more than 75 per cent of the public had cast a

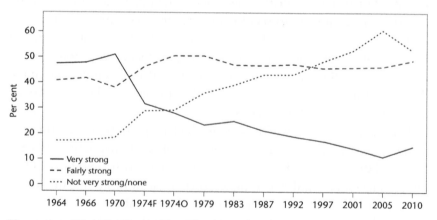

**Figure 2.1.** Strength of party identification, 1964–2010
*Source*: British Election Study, 1964–2010.

ballot. This meant that when Labour had won the general election with 44 per cent of the vote, it had secured support from more than one-third of those who were eligible to vote. But, fifty years later, it was a different story. When New Labour was re-elected in 2001, turnout had dwindled to 61 per cent, which meant that Tony Blair's 41 per cent of the vote translated into the support of just 25 per cent of the electorate.[3] First-past-the-post had given him another majority, but three-quarters of those who had been eligible to vote had not endorsed Blair.

For those who were still participating, meanwhile, their weakening sense of political identity and loyalty had started to influence how they were voting. In earlier decades, it was said that people would vote for the same party over and over again. It was a political ritual. 'Put a Labour or Conservative rosette on a pig around here and people would vote for it,' they would say. And it was true. The last time that England won the World Cup, in 1966, almost 90 per cent of the electorate had voted for the same party as the one they had supported at the election before that. But this fierce loyalty increasingly became a thing of the past. From one election to the next, larger numbers of voters were switching between the parties. By 2010, the percentage of voters who said they had voted for the same party as at the last election had dropped to 70 per cent. Make no mistake. There were still many loyal voters, which helps to explain why a large number of seats are considered 'safe' for the two main parties. Before the 2010 election had even taken place, for instance, the Electoral Reform Society was able to predict the outcome in more than 300 seats.[4] But the marked drop in the rate of loyalty among voters was nevertheless palpable. Something had changed.

Why had people become less loyal to Labour and the Conservatives? Many academics traced the breakdown of this loyalty to changes in the *social* foundations of support for the main parties—changes that have been discussed in greater depth elsewhere.[5] Traditionally, in the 1950s and 1960s, the social classes to which people belonged were a very good predictor of how they would vote. Working-class people tended to support Labour, while the more financially secure middle classes tended to vote Conservative. These predictable loyalties divided the electorate into two blocs, which could be relied upon to turn out in election after election to vote for the party that they saw as representing their class interests.[6] The outcome was a stable and secure political environment. But over time this relationship between class and voting weakened.

Much of this was because of how British society had changed. Unlike the days of Eden and Attlee, by the time that Ukip was trying to break through far more people were working in non-manual, service-sector, and non-unionized work, which diluted those feelings of class belonging and solidarity that had once kept them closely aligned to the main parties. Far more people had also benefited from a university education, which made them 'cognitively mobilized'—an academic way of saying that they were better able to process complex political information and so less dependent on the habitual loyalties that had guided their parents and grandparents.[7]

But the parties had changed, too. In response to how society was changing, both Labour and the Conservatives had overhauled their radical ideological appeals, moved towards the centre ground, where there were more votes to be had, and toned down their more explicit references to class-based interests. Along the way, the lines between class and voting became more blurred, while a growing number of voters struggled to identify clear differences between the big two.[8] In the 1990s, Tony Blair and New Labour had followed a 'third way' between traditional top-down socialism and unregulated neo-liberalism, and rescinded their commitment to the public ownership of key industries (the famous abolition of 'Clause Four' of the party's constitution). Blair was swept into power, but his move to the centre ground contributed to a loss of support for Labour among its core, working-class voters, who, in the past, had turned out for the party without question. This disconnect would become important for Farage, much as it was for radical-right politicians across Europe, for whom disgruntled manual workers were quickly becoming an important source of votes. Ukip's opportunity to reach out to this group was reflected in the numbers.

In 1997 Labour was still widely seen to represent the interests of the working class. Only 6 per cent of all voters and 7 per cent of working-class voters thought that Labour was *not* doing a good job of looking after this group. But from 1997, and as the reality of Blair's 'third way' was seen in action, the picture changed. By 2001 Labour was no longer overwhelmingly seen to be the party of the working classes—almost one in three people no longer believed that the party represented its core base. Even though more than 80 per cent of Labour voters continued to see their party as one for the working class, this feeling was shared by a shrinking proportion of actual working-class voters. By 2010, three years after Blair had stepped down, 30 per cent of all voters and the same percentage of *working-class* voters did not believe that Labour was doing a good job of looking after the working-class voters whom it had been founded to represent.

These changes once again fed through into the hard currency of votes. Unlike the days of Clement Attlee and Harold Wilson, in the early

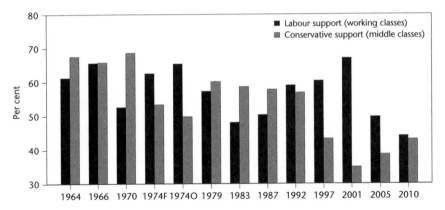

**Figure 2.2.** Class-based support for the Labour and Conservative parties,
1964–2010
*Source*: British Election Study, 1964–2010.

2000s the percentage of working-class voters who were turning out for
Labour had slumped. There was a particularly sharp drop between 2001 and
2005, when amid Blairism the number dropped by nearly twenty points,
from 67 to 49 per cent. By 2010, only 44 per cent of working-class voters
were supporting Labour. In the eyes of Farage, this disconnect between
Labour and its traditional base represented a major opportunity.

A similar trend could be seen on the other side of the divide. Support for
the Conservatives among middle-class voters had also begun to slide, particularly after 1992. By 2001, barely one in three of these more financially
secure voters were supporting the Conservatives, and there would be no
dramatic improvement. As Lord Ashcroft had warned the party in 2005, its
support among the middle class had shrunk at a time when the size of this
group had actually been on the rise, which left them with a difficult situation: the party was 'holding a shrinking share of an expanding market that
had once represented the bedrock of its electoral support'.[9] And although,
in 2010, middle-class voters would become more receptive to the Conservatives under Cameron, their support remained well below the levels that
his party had seen in the past.

These underlying shifts left more people open to considering alternatives. As they became less tribal, and less strongly influenced by the
blind loyalties of the past, more and more were unwilling to play by the
old rules of the two-party system. As an eminent political scientist once
observed, it is easier to vote against your class once loyalty to a party has
weakened, and to abandon your party once your loyalty to a class has

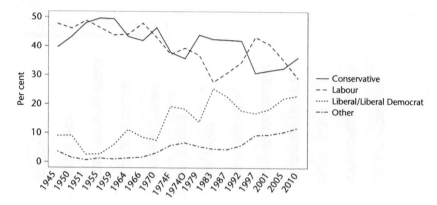

**Figure 2.3.** Vote share in UK general elections, 1945–2010
*Source*: UK Election Statistics, 1918–2012. House of Commons Library Research Paper 12/43.

withered.[10] So, even before Ukip was preparing to launch its own revolt, a system that had once been firmly closed off to challengers had started to fragment and open up. Amid this change, parties other than the big two began to break through. These surges of support would ebb and flow like the tide, each rising further up the shore than the last, but it was clear that more and more voters were turning elsewhere. As Figure 2.3 shows, in sharp contrast to earlier years, by 1983 30 per cent of the electorate had turned away from the main parties. And, over the next twenty-three years, this trend would continue.

The shaking foundations of British politics were reflected in other changes, which would soon pave the way for Ukip's challenge to Labour in the north and to the Tories in the south, as well as the rise of the Scottish and Welsh nationalists. In the 1950s, and excluding Northern Ireland, most of the battles over seats had been a straightforward contest between Labour and the Conservatives. The average share of the *votes* that were controlled by the two parties had ranged from nearly all of the votes in seats in the north-east of England to a low of 90 per cent in Wales. While there was a little evidence that the system was beginning to fracture in Scotland and Wales, where nationalists had started to attract support, they were not yet winning *seats*. But, by 2010, the picture looked very different.

As shown in Figure 2.4, by this time Labour and the Conservatives were averaging more than 70 per cent of votes in seats in only three regions—the Midlands, London, and the north-west of England. In the remainder, only around two-thirds of people had voted for the big two. In Scotland,

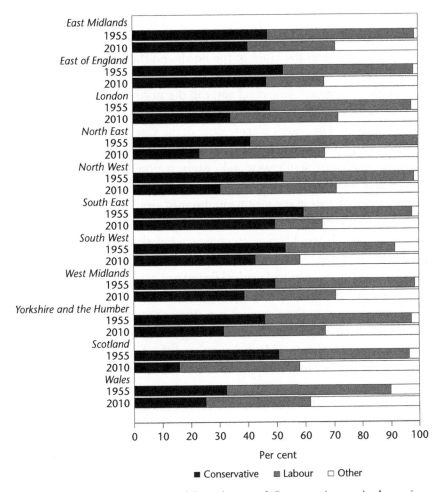

**Figure 2.4.** Average vote share of the Labour and Conservative parties by region in 1955 and 2010

which would soon witness its own insurgency, their share had fallen below 60 per cent. These regional variations in the relative strength of the main parties would soon present opportunities to other parties. Across northern England, while Labour's share of the *vote* had dropped by ten points, it still controlled the vast majority of *seats* in 2010. But support for the Conservatives had plummeted. Its share of the votes had dropped by twenty points, while the party averaged only around 30 per cent in the north-west, and 23 per cent in the north-east. The picture in terms of seats was even worse. By 2010

David Cameron and his party's share of the seats in the north-west had nearly halved to 29 per cent, and in the north-east had more than halved to just 7 per cent. Across the cities of the north and the Midlands, the Tories held only 20 out of 124 seats—a statistic that fuelled Farage's belief that his party could emerge as 'the second party in the north'.[11]

Across southern England, meanwhile, there had been more significant losses for Labour. The party's average share of the vote had slumped by more than twenty points. There was a particularly sharp fall outside London, across the south-east, south-west and eastern regions—all of which would soon attract significant attention from Ukip. Between 1951 and 2010, Labour's share of seats in the south-east dropped, from 13 to only 5 per cent, and in the south-west it slumped from 22 to 7 per cent. In eastern England, meanwhile, which would soon emerge as a heartland for Ukip, Labour's average share of the vote had more than halved from 46 to 20 per cent, while its share of the seats had crashed from 19 to 3 per cent. Here again was an opportunity for Farage. In the past, the Liberal Democrats had worked hard to fill the gaps in these regions, catering to more right-wing voters in northern Labour seats and more left-wing voters in typically southern Conservative seats.[12] But with the traditional third party now in government, Farage was hoping to capitalize and step into this space.

In the aftermath of the 2010 general election, the fragmentation of British politics became visible to all. Once again, neither David Cameron nor Gordon Brown and their parties had sparked widespread public enthusiasm. Together, their support had slumped to 65 per cent of the vote—the lowest on record. Meanwhile, more than one in three people had abandoned them. Cameron and the Conservatives were back in power, but they were forced to share it with Nick Clegg and the Liberal Democrats, a party that followed a very different philosophy. It was an outcome that reflected how, amid Britain's fragmenting politics, hung parliaments had become more likely. Unlike the years of Eden and Attlee, the number of MPs on the green benches who did not belong to either of the two main parties had rocketed more than tenfold to reach eighty-five.[13] Politics had also become even less representative, strengthening the populist critique being put forward by Farage and others. Because the main parties were struggling to inspire mass support, many MPs could no longer claim to hold a majority of votes in their seats. Back in 1955, nine in ten had recruited more than half of the votes in their local seats. But, by 2010, when voters were increasingly turning to other options, only one in three could claim such support, which meant that more than 400 MPs did not represent a majority of their voters. As constitutional expert Vernon Bogdanor observed, this was the largest number of MPs who had been elected on a minority vote since the 1920s.[14] The general concept of majority rule was also being directly challenged by the fact that no government since 2001 had managed to win support from more than two-fifths of the electorate. While parties continued to win parliamentary majorities, as more voters had moved away from the main parties, these majorities were lacking popular legitimacy.

While such changes had been a long time coming, after 2010 there also arrived other and more specific opportunities for Farage and his party. Ukip was spending much of its time pitching to economically disaffected and socially conservative Britons who felt intensely anxious about how their country was changing. Cameron's unsuccessful search for a majority had led him to present the electorate with a modernized and more socially liberal brand of Conservatism. But he had attracted only 36 per cent of the vote. This was more than his predecessors had won amid the seemingly never-ending dominance of New Labour. But it was also a long way from the levels of support that had been enjoyed during the Conservatives' glory years—the almost eighteen years of uninterrupted rule that commenced with the election of Margaret Thatcher in 1979 and ended with John Major bracing for defeat in 1997.[15] As Cameron stood in Downing Street next to Nick Clegg in May 2010, he looked pleased, but he must have felt disappointed. His share of the vote was, with only one exception, his party's lowest since 1918. Along the corridors of power, too, his MPs might have looked confident, but in the back of their minds they knew that their party had not secured a parliamentary majority since 1992. The traditional Conservative claim to be the 'natural party of government' was sounding increasingly hollow.

For Cameron and his followers, Coalition government meant that their dreams of implementing full-blown Conservative policy would have to be put on hold. While the failure to secure a majority reflected deeper changes, others saw it as a symptom of pressingly topical problems with the Conservative brand and their new leader. Cameron ultimately saw himself as a modernizer. He had spent much of his career watching Blair recast Labour and enjoy the spoils that came with three successive election victories. Perhaps he could do the same. Rather than focus on traditional right-wing themes such as immigration and Europe, which had failed his predecessors and damaged his party, he talked instead about tackling climate change, alleviating poverty, delivering overseas aid, legalizing same-sex marriage, celebrating Britain's rising ethnic diversity, and bringing more women and ethnic minorities into politics. His would be a Conservative Party that appeared at ease with modern Britain. But some within his camp had voiced concerns. Reaching out to new voters was all well and good, but there did not seem to be much of a strategy for keeping the loyalty of traditional social conservatives, who found the rapid social changes that Cameron was celebrating profoundly unsettling. 'Some Tory strategists', noted right-wing commentator Tim Montgomerie, shortly after Cameron's election as leader, 'only seem interested in the centre ground and they are leaving David Cameron's right flank dangerously exposed'.[16] Montgomerie was right, while others had also spotted the vulnerability.

After Cameron had become Prime Minister in 2010, Farage had spent much of the summer shuffling between hospitals and his bedroom, trying to recover from a plane crash that had left him with debilitating and painful injuries. If there had been any consolation at all, it was that the forced rest gave him time to plot a breakthrough. A few months later, he returned as Ukip's leader, replacing Lord Pearson of Rannoch, who was anxious to return to his Scottish estate for the start of the grouse-shooting season. Farage and his team now set off to try and fill the space on Cameron's radical right flank. The Conservative leader, he told disillusioned Tories from one meeting to the next, had let Britain down like a cheap pair of braces. He was met with a surge of support.

Meanwhile, though Labour and its new leader Ed Miliband were soon leading in the polls, their position looked far from convincing. Ever since Labour had left office in 2010, the party had been struggling to stage a comeback. Part of the problem was rooted in the longer-term pressures that were now constraining both of the main parties. But it was also wrapped up in the legacy of thirteen years in power. Under Tony Blair and then Gordon Brown, Labour governments had presided over a rapid upsurge in immigration into Britain and then, from 2008, a financial crisis that had fuelled the deepest recession since the war. By the time that Labour was packing up and leaving Downing Street, the country's annual budget deficit, the gap between the money going into government and the money going out, had jumped from around £40 billion in 2008 to over £145 billion. It was more than 10 per cent of the country's gross domestic product (GDP), the highest on record.[17] Meanwhile, Britain's public-sector debt, the amount of money that the government owed to creditors, had nearly doubled, rising from

36 per cent of GDP in 2008 to more than 60 per cent by 2010—or a debt of over £900 billion. Unemployment had also surged past 8 per cent, its highest level for seventeen years.

Even in 2010 it was clear that, in the eyes of most voters, Labour had lost credibility. As one of the party's own pollsters would later conclude, by the time that Miliband had become the new Labour leader in September of that year, the die was already cast. By that time, most voters thought that Labour should be ashamed rather than proud of its record in office—and by a striking margin of 50 to 28. Labour voters too wanted to see their party change direction.[18] And it was a problem that would not go away.

During the four years that followed, and while most people felt concerned about the state of the economy, most also thought that things would have been *worse* had Labour stayed in power. In their quest to reduce the deficit and national debt, Cameron and Clegg were now presiding over major spending cuts and fiscal austerity. But when people were asked whom they blamed for the cuts most pointed to Labour. It was certainly true that large numbers of people felt that the Coalition spending cuts were too deep and were happening too quickly. But, from 2013 onwards, as economic growth returned, employment rate hit its highest ever level, and unemployment dropped below 6 per cent, most people accepted that the cuts were necessary and believed that the deficit reduction strategy had been good for the economy.[19]

That the Conservatives held a key advantage, and one that Cameron intended to exploit ahead of the 2015 election, became increasingly clear. By 2014 the number of voters who thought that the government should 'stick to the current strategy' and believed that its policies had helped outnumbered those who thought otherwise. And, while nearly half of all voters could either see signs of a recovery or thought that the economy was definitely on the mend, less than one in five thought that it was still getting worse. Unsurprisingly, therefore, when people were asked whom they trusted to manage the nation's finances, they consistently put Cameron and his Chancellor George Osborne ahead of Miliband and his Shadow Chancellor Ed Balls.[20]

To some, it seemed as though Labour had failed to diagnose the problem. The party looked like a fading prize-fighter who was determined to recapture his glory days while not understanding why he was losing fights. That the public were unimpressed was reflected in the numbers. In early 2014, while Farage was targeting working-class Labour towns like Gateshead,

Labour had an average poll rating of 36 per cent. This was four points ahead of the Conservatives, who were some way from the support they would need if they were to secure a majority government in 2015. But while this poll rating was an increase of seven points on what Gordon Brown had won in 2010, when placed in historical perspective it should not have inspired confidence. As Miliband and his team would have known, when Labour had been in opposition in the past it had polled far more strongly.

At the same point in the cycle in 1984, under Neil Kinnock, Labour had averaged 38 per cent. Five years later it had held 42 per cent. Then, under the caretaker leadership of Margaret Beckett following the death of John Smith in 1994, the party had averaged 47 per cent.[21] Miliband was well behind these figures. More worryingly still, even these higher levels of support had not guaranteed success. Far from it. Only in the last instance, in the 1990s, had Labour actually gone on to win the general election. On the other occasions it had lost—and despite holding a vote share that exceeded Miliband's current level of support.

The weakness of Labour, and the opportunity for other parties, was evident from whichever angle one looked at the situation. In the year before general elections in the past, opposition parties that went on to form governments had almost always been in a stronger position. At the same point in 2009, for instance, Cameron and his party had enjoyed a poll rating of almost 40 per cent and a seventeen-point lead over Labour. In 1996, the year before New Labour had won its landslide, the party had held a rating of 52 per cent and a thirty-point lead. And in 1978, during the spring before the Winter of Discontent, Thatcher and the Conservatives had held a rating of almost 44 per cent and would soon push ahead of Labour. Even in 1973, the year before Labour came to power with a minority government, it had a rating of 45 per cent and a nine-point lead.[22] To number-crunchers who were watching Miliband closely, it was clear that something had gone wrong.

Like those frustrated Conservatives who blamed their lacklustre ratings on Cameron's more centrist strategy, when trying to diagnose Labour's problems many pointed at Miliband. In a political world where the old loyalties were breaking down, voters had come to rely far more heavily on the party leaders for cues. But Miliband, the former policy wonk, seemed to lack the leadership qualities that were required of a prime minister-in-waiting. There was certainly no doubt that, right from the start, he had failed to capture the public imagination. Within only one year of his election, the

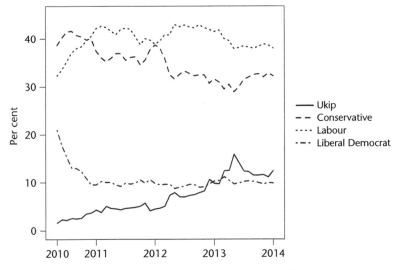

**Figure 2.5.** Support for the parties in national opinion polls, May 2010–January 2014

*Source*: Polling Observatory (monthly average).

number of voters who saw Miliband as 'strong', 'decisive', 'good in a crisis', 'a natural leader', or 'charismatic', had plummeted into the low single digits. On all of these attributes he was well behind Cameron and often by a wide margin. Meanwhile, when people were regularly asked between 2010 and 2014 whom they thought would make the best prime minister, not once was Miliband put ahead of Cameron. Instead, the Labour leader lagged behind by an average of at least thirteen points.[23]

A similar picture emerged when voters were asked about their overall feeling towards the party leaders. Miliband had quickly nosedived into negative scores, which meant that more people were dissatisfied with his performance than satisfied. By 2014 he was trailing Cameron by twelve points. But what should have rung even louder alarm bells was the reaction among his own *Labour* voters when asked whether they were satisfied or dissatisfied with his performance. Between 2010 and 2014, Miliband's net score plummeted from 44 to just 6 per cent. A leader who is unable to motivate his own troops is distinctly unlikely to attract defections from rival camps. Cameron was, again, in a far stronger position among his own voters, enjoying a lead over Miliband that never fell below thirty-five points and sometimes extended beyond fifty.[24] No party leader had ever become prime minister with ratings as low as Miliband's.

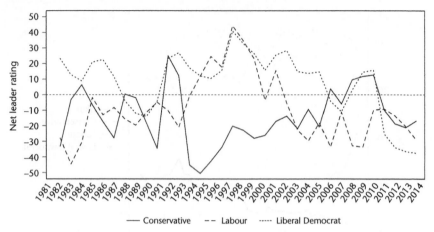

**Figure 2.6.** Net satisfaction rating of party leaders, 1981–2014
*Source*: Ipsos-MORI party leader satisfaction (annual average).

Farage, meanwhile, was attacking one just as much as the other. 'They are appalling people, truly appalling. These men are utterly hopeless. I judge everybody on the Farage Test. Number one, would I employ them? Number two, would I go for a drink with them?'[25] Out on the campaign trail, he was launching one grenade after another, claiming that Cameron, Miliband, and Clegg were all divorced from grass-roots opinion and failing to represent their traditional supporters. There was a receptive audience. When we look at the public ratings of party leaders over the past thirty-five years, none of the three who came to dominate politics after 2010 come off well. Unlike the days of Tony Blair and Paddy Ashdown, all three had plunged into negative ratings (see Figure 2.6). Their collective scores reached the lowest point for at least a generation. Voters were clearly not impressed, and Farage was determined to do everything that he could to capitalize.

Other changes were also opening up space for Ukip, adding to the deeper currents swirling below the surface that had gradually been eroding the foundations of the party system for some time. Since 2010, Nick Clegg and the Liberal Democrats had made the difficult transition from being a political outsider to being an insider party of government. The experience had been far from pleasant. Shortly before the birth of the Coalition, the Liberal Democrats had averaged an impressive 26 per cent in the polls. But after entering power Clegg and his party discovered just how quickly voters can turn their backs. Within one month, their rating had slumped by eight points and within three months it had more than halved to just 11 per cent. The dramatic slide continued, hastened by unpopular Coalition decisions, such as the increase in VAT and the cap on tuition fees. Within a few months, they had fallen below 10 per cent and reached levels that older Liberals had not seen since the 1980s. 'Clegg-mania' was soon a distant memory. The Liberal Democrat chief had become the most unpopular third-party leader since David Owen had led the renegade SDP in the late 1980s. It was a nightmare situation that seemed to confirm what Germany's Chancellor Angela Merkel had apparently told Cameron about coalition life: 'The little party always gets smashed!'[26] The collapse of the traditional third party created further room for Farage, who was now actively pitching to voters who felt politically dissatisfied and wanted 'none of the above', much as the Liberal Democrats had once done in opposition. These protestors no longer had a home, and Farage was planning to give them one.

But his was not the only party hoping to benefit from the growing willingness among voters to change sides. No longer focused solely on environmentalism, the Greens were now attracting new followers by dabbling in anti-establishment populism and reaching out to left-wing voters by opposing the government's austerity programme, bailouts for the banks, rising housing costs, and inequality. While hoping to emulate the success of radical left parties elsewhere in Europe, they were certainly drawing support from the same groups in society as their European sister parties—young graduates, the middle class, public-sector workers—as well as people who had once voted for the Liberal Democrats.[27]

In Scotland, meanwhile, another party had positioned itself to the left of Labour, opposing austerity, nuclear weapons, and inequality. By 2014 Alex Salmond, who would soon be replaced by Nicola Sturgeon, was readying the Scottish National Party (SNP) for a referendum on independence. Had Farage studied the Scottish nationalists, then he would have recognized many of the criticisms that they were firing at the established parties, not least Salmond's populist attacks on the 'bunch of incompetent Lord Snooties' in Westminster.[28] Such messages had resonated. Shortly before 2010, Labour had averaged 37 per cent of the vote in Scotland and been seventeen points clear of the SNP. But, while Farage was exploring Labour's heartlands in northern England, Salmond and Sturgeon were beginning to pull away in Scotland. By 2014 their average had surged to 40 per cent, and now they held the lead.[29] The SNP challenge to Labour would soon become one of the central talking points in British politics. It reflected the more chaotic nature of politics and how the market had become more crowded. 'Multi-party competition on this scale', noted one scholar, who had studied British politics for years, 'is quite unprecedented. We face a totally new electoral situation.'[30]

But while insurgents of various stripes appeared to be prospering, there had also emerged one other opportunity for Ukip, which was reflected in the issues that were dominating the minds of voters. The rise to prominence of one issue in particular was especially important and played directly to the party's strategy. It is no secret that the British public had never warmed to immigration. Since the 1960s, large majorities had always wanted the government to reduce immigration and voiced concern about the economic and social effects of this change. But, from 2004, and after the European Union had enlarged to include another ten nations, there emerged a new wave of public concern. Under the EU's principle of 'free movement', migrant workers from countries such as Poland and Lithuania were now free to work and settle in other member states. Concerned about the economic and wage differentials between old and new EU members, in 2004 most of the established EU countries imposed temporary restrictions on the inflow of migrants from the new states. Britain, Ireland, and Sweden were the only countries that did not. New Labour granted immediate and unrestricted access to the country's labour market. While free movement was obviously of benefit to many Britons, like those who had relocated to the coasts of Spain, the subsequent influx of migrants into Britain nevertheless began to generate unease among a broad swathe of the electorate. Nor was this anxiety calmed by the fact that official estimates proved to be wildly inaccurate. One early Home Office report predicted that the annual number of EU migrant workers entering Britain would be somewhere between 5,000 and 13,000. The numbers were much higher. Between 2005 and 2010 annual net migration ran consistently above 200,000.[31]

After the formation of the Coalition government in 2010, some voters might reasonably have expected to see a reduction in these figures. While in opposition, Cameron had promised to reduce net migration to the 'tens of thousands'. But, in the context of 'free movement', such a promise was always going to be impossible to deliver. In the early years of the Coalition net migration remained well above 200,000 and, after a short decline, remained above this level for the rest of the parliament. By 2014, as Farage planned to put the issue at the heart of Ukip's European election campaign, net migration stood at 318,000, compared to 244,000 when Cameron had first entered office. It was only 2,000 short of the highest number on record

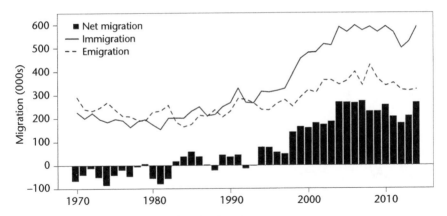

**Figure 2.7.** Long-term international migration, 1970–2013
*Source*: Office of National Statistics.

and more than three times the government's target (see Figure 2.7). With no way of stalling the arrival of mainly low-skilled migrants from within the EU, the government was forced to curb migration from elsewhere. This led to a cap on the number of sponsored skilled migrants and attempts to curb international students—ironically the two types of migration to which the electorate was less opposed.[32]

This significant social change pushed immigration to the fore of many people's minds and fuelled a wider feeling of dissatisfaction with the responsiveness of politicians.[33] Looking at Figure 2.8, we see that, in earlier years, issues such as the economy and National Health Service had dominated the list of priorities for voters.[34] But, in the following years, as Tony Blair campaigned to replace John Major, public concern over Britain's relationship with the EU heightened, having been triggered by the Maastricht Treaty of 1992 and a financial crisis that led to Britain's exit from the European Exchange Rate Mechanism. This concern peaked in 1997, by which time Ukip was emerging as a significant force. Two years later, at the European elections, the party won 7 per cent of the vote and its first three Members of the European Parliament (MEPs). But opposition to Britain's membership of the EU was not, on its own, enough for major success. Fears over Europe were on the decline, and at the 2001 general election Ukip attracted less than 2 per cent of the vote. Had the party continued to rely only on Europe, it would have remained firmly on the fringe.

Then, in the early 2000s, public concerns over immigration and its effects began to sharpen, coinciding with rising immigration and a toxic political

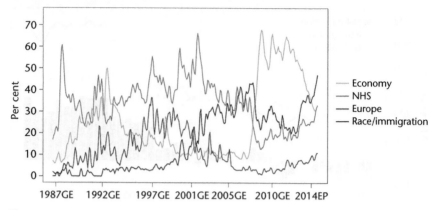

**Figure 2.8.** Most important issues facing Britain, 1987–2014
Source: Ipsos-MORI Issues Index.

debate. The Conservative leader at the time, William Hague, ventured into radical-right populism, devoting considerable attention to the issue and warning that Britain was becoming a 'foreign land'. By 2005 the issue was pushing ahead of the economy as a source of major concern. Three years later, and as the financial crisis erupted, the economy surged back onto the centre stage. But immigration remained firmly on the agenda. And, while the issue had temporarily taken a back seat, it soon regained momentum. By 2014 concern over immigration was again on the rise, with more than two-fifths of people identifying the issue as among the most important facing Britain. This shift presented a major opportunity to Ukip, and one that was underscored by a corresponding trend.

As people became more anxious over immigration, the perceived ability of the established parties to manage this issue began to wane seriously. In earlier decades, before the era of free movement, voters had felt broadly confident in the ability of the main parties to handle immigration. Traditionally, it was the Conservative Party that had benefited. Shortly before the arrival of Mrs Thatcher, for example, some 50 per cent of *all* voters had backed her party on immigration, which was more than twice the equivalent figure of 21 per cent for Labour.[35] Yet this picture would change. In 2010, when Cameron became prime minister, his party was still, by far, the favourite on this issue. The percentage who backed Labour, meanwhile, had dwindled to just 12 per cent. Labour would continue to suffer on immigration, with this figure never rising above 20 per cent. But this offered little consolation for Cameron and his team, as they too were

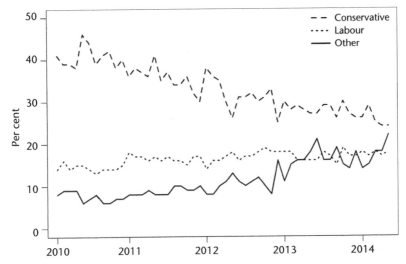

**Figure 2.9.** Perceived competence of parties on immigration, 2010–2014
*Source*: YouGov.

now struggling on an issue that they had historically owned. By the spring of 2014 fewer than three in ten of those polled felt confident in their approach. It was clear that both parties were being blamed by the people for failing to take hold of an issue about which they cared deeply. When, in 2014, pollsters asked voters whom they blamed for the failure to reduce immigration, they pointed the finger of accusation directly at the main parties.[36] As confidence in the ability of the two main parties to tackle the issue declined, so the number of voters who started to endorse 'other' parties on immigration increased. In 2010, less than 10 per cent of the electorate had felt that a party other than the big two was best able to manage immigration. Four years later, that figure had more than doubled.

A few months before the European election campaign in 2014, the Ukip faithful gathered in Central Hall, Westminster, for their twentieth anniversary. Somehow, they had managed to survive and were now attracting rising support. There was no doubt that the small party had come a long way. 'We've been on the march for twenty long years!' Farage reminded his mainly grey and elderly followers. 'There have been many failures, many disappointments, many ups and downs, lots of leaflets delivered and, over the years, many deposits lost. And, of course, we've been roundly abused, and laughed at, and mocked, and derided,' continued Farage. 'But despite that, over the course of the last eighteen months, something remarkable is happening! We are changing the face of British politics!'

Farage had good reason to feel optimistic. In only a few months he would be leading Ukip into the biggest campaign in its history—and all of the currents in British politics now seemed to be working in his party's favour. While first-past-the-post remained a very significant obstacle, the fragmentation of British politics had brought the absolute dominance of the two main parties to an end. What had once been a stable and completely secure two-party system had increasingly made way for a new environment that was characterized by weaker, fluctuating, and more volatile allegiances, where blind tribal loyalties to the Conservatives or Labour looked increasingly out of fashion. Britain's political climate and electorate, as a consequence, seemed more receptive than they had ever been to the idea of a revolt against the established parties. Such a breakthrough would still be difficult, but it now looked more possible than ever before, especially for a radical-right party that was actively tapping into the visible and growing disconnect between the people and the main parties, as well as widespread and often intense anxieties about how cultural and ethnic change was sweeping the nation. The approaching European Parliament elections offered an immediate opportunity to mobilize support under a different electoral system, one far more favourable to challenger parties such as Ukip. If all went according to plan, this would then provide the perfect backdrop to the much harder general election that would follow in 2015. For Farage, the moment to mobilize had arrived. If there was ever a moment to strike, this was it.

# 3

# Earthquake

It was a cold and bright morning in February 2014. Nick Clegg, leader of the Liberal Democrats and the country's deputy prime minister, was making his way through Leicester Square and into the studios of LBC Radio. He had arrived for one of his weekly phone-in discussions with voters. But this time he had a surprise—he was about to challenge Nigel Farage to a debate on whether or not Britain should remain as a member of the European Union. 'He is the leader of the party of out. I am the leader of the party of in. It's time for a proper debate so that the public can listen to the arguments and decide for themselves.' Clegg was rolling the dice. Like his weekly discussions with voters, the debate was part of a gamble to try and reverse his party's decline. In the polls, the Liberal Democrats were slumped well behind Ukip. They had fallen below 8 per cent, while Farage and his party were riding high on more than twice that.[1] And now the traditional third party was about to face an election that voters had often used to punish the governing parties. They were worried.

Clegg knew that he needed to take a risk. While he disagreed with almost everything that Farage said, he nevertheless thought that debating with the Ukip leader might—just might—help him mobilize the most committed Liberal Democrats who loved the EU but hated Ukip. 'I wasn't fussed about whether we won or not,' said one of his most senior advisers.

I wanted to use the debates to develop a sharper brand. The case for staying in the EU was not being made by anybody. We always thought that Farage and his party represented a strand of thought and feeling. There was a time when people dismissed Ukip, as if it wasn't real. But it was clear in our focus groups that it was real. So we wanted to take them on.

But not everybody had agreed. Another of Clegg's advisers had warned him against it, arguing that no good could come from debating with a populist who had spent most of his life discussing the costs and benefits of EU membership. 'It's very difficult to deal with someone like Farage. He acts as though he is bulletproof, as if things just bounce off him. It is hard to come up with the right strategy for someone like that.' But most conceded that there was little to lose. 'We knew it was a risk,' said another. 'But we were finding it difficult to stand out. One of our big problems was simply getting attention. The Euros gave us an opportunity to define ourselves, to insert ourselves into the debate and generate interest. Farage was a way of doing that.'

The first debate was held in front of a live audience on the evening of Wednesday, 26 March. Both leaders prepared thoroughly. In the Liberal Democrat camp, Farage had been played either by Tim Farron, who was then party President, or by a senior adviser. 'It is not very hard to play Farage,' said the latter. 'If you have a problem you just blame immigration.' Farage, meanwhile, was preparing with Gawain Towler, his colourful and long-serving press officer. Immediately before the debate they had continued to bounce questions over drinks in the Westminster Arms. Then, for one hour, the two party leaders jostled over questions from the audience— whether there should be a referendum on EU membership, had immigration been good or bad, would Britain suffer a skills shortage if it left the EU, and the percentage of British laws that were made in Brussels.

Much of the debate focused on the impact of migrants from Bulgaria and Romania, who could now work in Britain after transitional restrictions had been lifted at the beginning of the year. Clegg warned voters not to risk the hard-won economic recovery by cutting the country off from Europe and claimed that Ukip wanted to drag Britain back to the 1950s. Farage pushed on with his strategy of merging Europe with immigration, claiming that EU membership meant that voters were exposed to a 'total open door to 485 million people from poor countries'. The politicians, he claimed, had 'lost the ability to govern our country and control our borders'.

In the aftermath it seemed that some of Clegg's advisers had been right. A snapshot poll indicated that almost three-fifths of viewers, 57 per cent, thought that Farage had won. He held a twenty-one-point lead. While voters had been asked to forget their loyalties, it was clear that these had shaped their responses. Only one in five Liberal Democrats and fewer than half of Labour voters thought that Farage had won. In sharp contrast, seven in ten Conservatives and nine in ten Ukip voters saw him as the victor.[2] It was the first time that many voters would have taken a close look at Farage. Based on the polls at least, he had more than held his own.

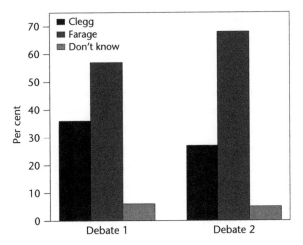

**Figure 3.1.** Public opinion on the Farage versus Clegg debates: Who performed better?

*Source*: YouGov/*Sun* post-debate polls.

The second debate was held one week later. Farage wanted a decisive victory. Conscious of the fact that during the first debate some had drawn attention to his 'sweaty' appearance, this time he prepared by going on long walks and avoiding alcohol. Once again, Clegg had set out to frame Farage as a man who felt uncomfortable in modern Britain, who wanted to return to the nineteenth century when the famous cricketer W. G. Grace had opened the batting for England. Farage pushed back, using a line that in months to come would influence Ukip's strategy for the 2015 general election. Clegg did not believe in Britain—he did not believe that the country could succeed as an independent nation. One of his advisers, liking the line, scribbled it down. In the aftermath the polls again presented Farage as the winner. But this time his lead had widened to between 38 and 41 points.[3] When it was all over, and as they walked out, the two men were briefly left alone. 'I suppose you are going to one of those private men's clubs to get drunk,' quipped Clegg. 'Yes,' replied Farage. 'The Reform Club. Where the Liberal Party was founded.'

The debates and the surrounding publicity provided Ukip with an ideal backdrop for the European elections, a contest that Farage was already predicting publicly his party would win. That evening, he and his team went to the Guinea Pub in Mayfair to celebrate. 'It was an amazing and euphoric atmosphere,' said one. 'Cabbies were tooting. Everybody was shaking Nigel's hand. Even in the context of London it just seemed that being with Ukip had become cool.' But as the campaign got underway the high would not last.

Three weeks after his debates with Clegg, Farage was in Sheffield to officially launch Ukip's campaign. It was Tuesday, 22 April, and the European election was little over one month away. In the polls, Ukip was in second place, trailing Labour by a few points. But Farage was trying not to dwell on the results. He knew from the past that support for his party tended to surge late on, during the final weeks of the campaign. And this time he had a different strategy, shaped by past experience and constraints.

Ukip was starting its campaign earlier than usual, anxious to win support from postal voters, who would be casting their votes from as early as three weeks before polling day. It was not a trivial consideration. The elections would see a record of more than seven million postal votes sent out. Almost three in ten of those who would cast a ballot in the election would do so by post.[4] By consciously targeting these voters, Farage was trying to learn from past mistakes. Two years earlier, at a by-election in the northern Labour seat of Rotherham, Ukip had won 22 per cent of the vote and come second. It had been a strong result. But Farage was convinced that it could have been stronger had his inexperienced campaigners only devised a strategy for winning over the postal voters. But they had not. Nor had Ukip's amateurs grasped some of the other basics of how to campaign successfully—how to collect and analyse data on voters, how to target them with literature that was tailored to their concerns, how to canvass a seat properly, and how to devise a 'get-out-the-vote' plan for mobilizing voters on polling day. These weaknesses, which would continue to haunt Ukip for months to come, had become abundantly clear to Farage, as he had watched the counting of the votes. 'We were neck-and-neck with Labour. But then the postal votes flooded in. They were 70 per cent Labour.'

Aside from starting early, Ukip had also decided to run a loud campaign. The idea was not complex. The party wanted to make as much noise as possible in a short period of time. 'The strategy was simple,' said one of Farage's advisers. 'We wanted to launch with a big bang and then dominate the news every day.' Farage had chosen Sheffield for the launch of the big bang. Surrounded by journalists and a few stray shoppers, he unveiled the first billboards that would soon appear on high streets, buildings, and roads up and down the country. They were big, imposing, and deliberately provocative. And they were focused squarely on Ukip's core supporters who had been pushing the party into the centre of British politics—struggling working-class and lower-middle-class voters who opposed Britain's EU membership, were intensely anxious over the cultural as well as economic effects of immigration, and felt completely cut adrift from politics in Westminster. Ukip was now offering them a simple but powerful message—'Take Back Control'.

The strategy had been orchestrated by a team of activists, most of whom would soon play leading roles in Ukip's quest to take its revolt into Westminster. Farage had assembled a handful of people who could bring to the table what his amateur party lacked and what he valued the most— experience, loyalty, and money. He needed people whom he could trust. Having spent most of his political life in the wilderness, he valued loyalty more than most. And he had a long memory. 'If Nigel likes you,' said one of his closest associates, 'he will trust you completely. But if you let him down, he will cut you off and never trust you again.' It was not unknown for Farage to ignore journalists who had insulted him years before. And he was careful about who was allowed into his inner circle. 'He is fiercely loyal,' reflected another. 'If you make it to the top and mess up then you are out. And if you are out then you are out. You are never coming back.' He was also demanding. Over the years, many of those who had worked for Farage had seen their marriages and relationships suffer as a result. 'I tell them', said Farage, 'there will be three people in your relationship. Are you ready for that?'

Farage brought four men in to help him run the campaign. The money-man was Paul Sykes, a multi-millionaire businessman who shared Ukip's hostility to the EU and its disdain of established politicians. In earlier years, Sykes had supported the Conservatives, including fellow Yorkshireman William Hague, and for a brief moment the Referendum Party. But he had never warmed to Cameron, whom he saw as a federalist, a prime minister who seemed determined to keep Britain in the EU and could not be trusted to restore its sovereignty. These views had led Sykes to channel serious money into Ukip. He would donate more than half of the £2.1 million that the party used to bankroll its European election campaign.[5]

But he was not a silent donor. Sykes wanted his money to be used to appeal to the types of voters he was meeting in Yorkshire—struggling, blue-collar work-ers who felt threatened by low-skilled EU migrant workers. He saw the EU principle of free movement as 'cruel and heartless' and thought that the work-ing class had been betrayed 'to the shame of Labour MPs and the trade union movement'.[6] 'Unusually', noted one senior official, 'for a very rich man Sykes understands the world as it appears to the working class. We decided to target Labour's working-class heartlands. Paul had a massive influence on that.' In fact, before the elections Sykes had already explored how to appeal to workers by running a campaign in his home county with a creative agency called Family. Now, in return for his money, he insisted that Ukip also use the agency and its director Ian Wright to help design its campaign for the European elections. 'The key question', recalled Wright, 'was how to take Ukip from what was in most people's minds a second- or third-division political party into one that could compete with the Conservatives and Labour'.

Sykes was not the only member of the team who was interested in Labour areas. Paul Nuttall, a Liverpudlian and budding historian, had joined Ukip in 2004 and from thereon had been urging the party to invade Labour's heartlands. Nuttall brought Farage loyalty. In return, he was fast tracked through the ranks, becoming Chairman and then deputy leader. There was often talk, an assumption even, that Nuttall would one day replace his mentor, a leader-in-waiting who could widen Ukip's appeal in northern England. Like Farage, Nuttall prided himself on being an active campaigner. He too would keep count of the number of meetings that he addressed. This commitment to the grass roots meant that he had strong support among activists and provided Farage with a direct line to his foot soldiers. From one meeting to the next, Nuttall would set out his belief that a reservoir of latent support lay waiting for Ukip in Labour's heartlands while also warning his party against an excessive focus on southern Conservative seats. In the coming months, he would have many chances to test the theory and demonstrate his loyalty to Farage.

Some of these ideas were shared by another member of Farage's team, who brought experience. Patrick O'Flynn had traded a successful career in journalism for an unpredictable life in Ukip. The 48-year-old was well known in Westminster, having spent years working for the *Daily Express*, a right-wing tabloid newspaper that ran populist campaigns against the EU and immigration. O'Flynn was talented, having risen to become its chief political correspondent and helping the paper launch a 'Get Britain out of Europe' campaign—which it published alongside an endorsement from Ukip.[7] The *Express* was the first newspaper to call for Britain to leave the EU and would soon provide direct support. Farage recruited O'Flynn, who was put at the top of Ukip's list of European election candidates in south-east England. It was a region where the party was strong, so that his election to Brussels was virtually guaranteed.

But, in a party that was bereft of experience, Farage wanted to get more out of O'Flynn. Throughout its history Ukip had never mastered political communication. Journalists were often fond of its press officers, such as Gawain Towler and Alex Phillips. But the party was renowned for leaking sensitive information and walking directly into public-relations disasters. Farage liked his press team, but he despaired at their inability to retain even a basic element of surprise. In an attempt to strengthen the operation, O'Flynn was appointed as the new Director of Communications. Within days, the journalist had brought a new sense of discipline to Brooks Mews, or what some insiders called the 'war room'. And it was not long until the former journalist was handed another promotion.

The director of Ukip's campaign had originally been Neil Hamilton, a former Conservative MP who in months to come would attract greater attention. But, when Hamilton publicly criticized Sykes, one of only a few big donors, his card was marked. It was only a matter of time until he was replaced.[8] The role fell to O'Flynn, which put the campaign in the hands of somebody who had no experience of fighting elections. 'Technically', said O'Flynn, 'this put me up against the Conservative Party's strategist, Lynton Crosby, a grizzled, highly experienced, tough nut campaigner'. The move entrenched his position and put him at the heart of the campaign. 'It was high paced, very demanding and people got exhausted. One or two bollock-ings but life was lived at great pace. I packed as much into the four-month campaign as in the previous four years at the *Express.*'

The last member of the team was Steve Crowther, Ukip's amiable Chairman. Crowther was a rare breed in Ukip, having been a former Conservative and Liberal Democrat. 'Some of them would describe me as a former Lib Dem, as a condemnation'. Seen by most as a safe pair of hands, the former marketing professional had been appointed by Farage, who saw him as a key ally. Having battled through the wilderness years, the leader knew just how quickly Ukip could implode without strong leadership. Crowther would spend his days shuttling back and forth between Devon and Mayfair, chairing meetings of the ruling body, the National Executive Committee (NEC), and resolving the latest crisis. He was at the very core of the party and would witness all of the fallout from the various scandals and storms.

If there was such a thing as a Ukip brain trust, then, for the European cam-paign, it was comprised of these five men—Farage, Sykes, Nuttall, O'Flynn, and Crowther, all of whom would now try and steer an inexperienced, small, and chaotic party to winning a nationwide election. And they were betting everything on a core-vote strategy. The party's message to the elec-torate had never been complicated. In earlier years, it had put all its gam-bling chips on setting out its opposition to the EU. But since 2010, the party had expanded its repertoire to develop a 'twin-track' message. 'The goal', Farage explained, 'was to get into people's heads that immigration and Europe are the same thing and that we are impotent'. He was gambling that, by fusing these two issues, he could appeal directly to a larger section of the electorate that felt under threat from either the rising numbers of migrants or the Eurocrats in Brussels, or from both. Little energy was spent on other issues or the question of how the party might widen its appeal.

The core-vote message was more a reflection of Farage's instincts than the results of detailed focus groups with a sample of voters. He had long believed that his party was strongest when it was offering a clear and direct message, pitching to people's tribal impulses and, like the gambler who would always bet on red, doubling down on its beliefs. It was neither a multi-layered nor a subtle appeal—Enough is Enough, Say No, Take Back Control, Be Independent. Now, by putting greater weight on immigration, Farage was trying to unlock the door to a much larger number of voters who felt worried about cultural changes that were sweeping the nation but cared less about the constitutional debates about EU membership. And, as we saw in the previous chapter, he was pitching to a receptive audience.

While Cameron had been failing to satisfy public appetite for a sharp reduction in net migration, the year before the European elections he had also launched an ambitious attempt to calm anxieties over the other plank of Farage's message. Since 2010, backbench Conservative MPs had been agitating for a referendum on Britain's EU membership, showcasing the intensity of their feeling by staging several rebellions in parliament. Meanwhile, outside Westminster the rise of Ukip had further convinced Cameron and his team of the need to offer something more than just rhetoric. In early 2013, in one of the most important speeches of his political life, the so-called Bloomberg speech, Cameron promised to deliver a referendum on EU membership by the end of 2017. Two months later, Cameron turned back to immigration, setting out plans to make it more difficult for migrants to access benefits and social housing and warning that the National Health Service was not a 'free international health service'.

But, if the goal had been to neutralize Ukip, there soon emerged evidence that it had failed. The next month, at a parliamentary by-election in Eastleigh, Hampshire, Ukip and its energetic candidate, Diane James, won almost 28 per cent of the vote. The party came second, within five points of taking the seat from the Liberal Democrats. Cameron and his party were pushed into third. Then, three months later, the Conservatives looked on as

Ukip staged another breakthrough in local elections, attracting disillusioned conservative voters in places such as Kent, Hampshire, and Buckinghamshire. The party captured more than 160 seats in local government, averaging 25 per cent of the vote where it had stood. That the electorate had not been won over by the Bloomberg promise was further reflected in the fact that Ukip had won the popular vote across nine constituencies, all of which were held by Conservative MPs.

Britain's wider political debate also seemed to be handing Farage more ammunition. Throughout the remainder of 2013 there emerged an even more strident debate over immigration. Some felt that Britain was rapidly descending into a toxic atmosphere of xenophobia and intimidation. It arrived as transitional restrictions on the rights of migrants from Bulgaria and Romania to work in Britain were about to be lifted. From January 2014 migrant workers from the two countries would be free to work and settle in the country. There was nothing that Cameron could do other than under-line his tough stance in areas where he had some room for manœuvre— much of which the media saw as an attempt to fend off Ukip.

First, over the summer a controversial government scheme saw billboard vans touring London boroughs, urging illegal migrants to leave Britain or face arrest. Amid a national outcry, even Farage, who had regularly opposed illegal migration, described the scheme as 'nasty' and further spot checks on migrants as 'not the British way of doing things'. Most voters, however, were not as opposed to the idea as some thought.[9] Then, in the autumn, Cameron called for a fundamental change to the principle of free movement and outlined measures to prevent new migrants from receiving out-of-work and housing benefits, deport those who were caught begging or sleeping rough, and bear down on companies who circumvented the minimum wage by employing cheap migrant labour.

A few weeks later, he joined police raids on illegal migrants and leant his support to a scheme that was sending text messages to around 60,000 peo-ple who were suspected of overstaying their visa. 'You are required to leave the UK as you no longer have the right to remain,' read the original texts, some of which were sent to the wrong people. Farage described it 'as the sort of behaviour one would expect from a fascistic police state, not a dem-ocratic and inclusive nation'. Cameron had then threatened to veto any future enlargement of the EU to include countries like Albania unless new laws were passed to prevent 'vast migrations'. Only days before the restric-tions on Bulgarian and Romanian migrants were due to be lifted, he also

brought forward measures that required EU migrants to wait three months
before they could apply for benefits. In a thinly veiled criticism of his colleagues, Vince Cable, the Business Secretary and Liberal Democrat, warned
of politicians resorting to panic and populist measures while referencing
Enoch Powell's 'Rivers of Blood' speech in 1968.

Farage might have complained, but the reality was that Ukip was campaigning just as hard on the issue. 'The seven-year period is up,' he told his
party's conference in the autumn of 2013,

and nearly thirty million of the good people of Bulgaria and Romania have open
access to our country, our welfare system, our jobs market. How many will take
advantage of that no one knows. The Home Office don't have any idea. The previous estimate was 13,000 in total. Migration Watch thinks 50,000 a year. It could be
many times that.

Over the next year, in 2014 an estimated 46,000 Bulgarians and Romanians
migrated to Britain, taking the total number to around 180,000, a significant
increase on the 23,000 who had come to work in the previous year.[10]

Amid this debate, and as an economic recovery was calming public concern about the state of Britain's finances, immigration moved to the forefront. By the time of the European elections, it was virtually neck-and-neck
with the economy.[11] And it dominated Ukip's pitch to the electorate. On
the party's billboards, EU migrants were presented as a source of crime and
pressure on housing, the welfare state, and the NHS. Farage, meanwhile,
sought to articulate public anxiety over the cultural as well as economic
effects of rising immigration by claiming that he felt 'slightly awkward'
when he did not hear English spoken on public transport.[12] His party also
traced the perceived problem to the post-1997 Labour governments, claiming that the unprecedented rise in net migration had been the result of a
'politically motivated attempt' under Tony Blair and Gordon Brown to
change Britain radically. Similar messages appeared on around twenty million election addresses that were landing on doormats. 'Our politicians have
allowed open-door immigration. Only UKIP will take back control.'[13]

There was no doubt that the billboards were polarizing. One featured an
image of a builder begging in the streets with the caption: 'EU policy at
work. British workers are hit hard by unlimited cheap labour.' Another contrasted struggling people on a bus with EU officials being chauffeur-driven
around in limousines. Another presented the national flag in flames against
the claim that 75 per cent of Britain's laws were made in Brussels and asked

voters: 'Who really runs this country?' Farage's favourite featured an escalator running from the sea to the top of the White Cliffs of Dover. 'No border. No control. The EU has opened our borders to 4,000 people every week.' He thought it was the best political poster since the Saatchi brothers had released their famous 'Labour Isn't Working' poster in 1979.

In some places there had been variations. Certain billboards that featured the Union Jack did not run in Scotland, while on others Clegg had been replaced by the SNP leader, Alex Salmond. Other ideas had also failed to see the light of day. One design tried to tap into public excitement about the forthcoming World Cup. It featured an image of the Royal Arms of England, but had replaced the three lions with three cats and asked voters: 'Why do we have three pussies these days?' Another idea was to distribute badges of the European flag with its blue background and circle of gold stars. But instead of the letters EU it had FU. 'It was like the [French Connection] FCUK campaign. Everybody would know what it meant but in the end it didn't happen.'

The billboards sparked a debate of their own. In Sheffield, the BBC's chief political editor Nick Robinson grilled Farage over the perceived hypocrisy of claiming that British workers were edged out of the market by EU migrants while the Ukip leader employed his German wife as his secretary. Farage objected, claiming that his wife earned a modest salary and worked unsociable hours, and questioning why the same accusations were not thrown at other politicians. 'That interview . . .', he said later. 'How I just didn't tell him to piss off and walk away I will never know. He would never have spoken to any other leader in those terms.' Farage tried to present the billboards as 'a hard-hitting reflection of reality as it is experienced by millions of British people struggling to earn a living outside the Westminster bubble'.[14] But, as Robinson and others were pointing out, some saw the billboards and Ukip's campaign more generally as a xenophobic if not openly racist attempt to mobilize votes. After pointing to the rise of Adolf Hitler, the Labour MP Mike Gapes said it was a 'racist, xenophobic campaign designed to win votes by whipping up animosity against foreigners living and working and contributing to this country'. Nor was he alone. Nicholas Soames, Conservative MP and grandson of Winston Churchill, said the campaign was 'deeply divisive, offensive and ignorant'.[15]

But others in the main parties were wary about attacking Ukip as racist. They included senior Labour strategists, who were watching the rise of Ukip with growing alarm. 'All of our opinion research', said one, suggested that the media campaign was helping them not hindering them. The racism row pushed views both ways. It hardened up people who were anti-Ukip into a 'we have to stop these people' outlook, and it encouraged anti-Ukip tactical voting in London. But it also hardened up a lot of people who were open to Ukip.

Labour's research had also thrown light on a challenge that would continue to influence how Miliband and his party tried to navigate Ukip.

We found that when the 'Ukip is racist' attack came from Labour it did far more to reinforce our negatives than it did to reinforce Ukip's negatives. This is because most of the people who were in play think that if you say 'Ukip is racist' you are saying that Labour does not understand immigration and thinks that anyone who is concerned about immigration is racist.

The message was clear: branding Ukip as a racist party would not work. Labour would need to find another and more fine-tuned response.

The view among voters, meanwhile, was more mixed. When pollsters at YouGov presented a sample of the population with two of Ukip's billboards, more than half, 59 per cent, disagreed that they were racist and more than half, 53 per cent, disagreed that they were offensive. Most voters, or 57 per cent, agreed with the suggestion that the billboards were a hard-hitting reflection of reality, while one in two supported the message. One-fifth of the sample said that they supported it strongly. But these views were not uniform across different groups in society. Older, working-class Britons were the least likely to find the billboards objectionable, while opposition had been strongest among the young, professionals, and people in London and Scotland. But even among these groups outright opposition was rarely a majority view.[16]

Ukip, which had deviated little from its core message, had also decided to build its entire campaign around Farage. Insiders shared a consensus that he was their main asset. His style of leadership was now hardwired into the party. Many at the top drew a straight line from their popular appeal and success to Farage. Some openly questioned whether Ukip was a party or a man. 'He has been a critical part in our success,' reflected one. 'I do believe that Ukip has a coherent political soul and I believe that Nigel is the thing that we need to get that across to people.' The campaign team was also aware that it had few if any other activists who could generate the same level of impact and interest. The result was a presidential-style campaign that put Farage at the centre of practically everything. 'To be frank,' said one, 'we

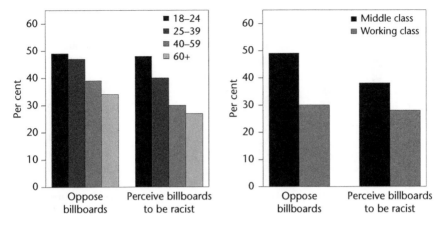

**Figure 3.2.** Public opinion towards Ukip billboards, April 2014
*Source*: YouGov.

just didn't have a cohort of well known people like the established parties. Nigel was the only one who could connect with a substantial section of the electorate. And we all felt that it was *his* time.'

Farage was handed almost every interview. He also embarked on an intensive two-week tour of England, taking the core-vote strategy into countless shopping centres, high streets, working men's clubs, and town halls. As in Gateshead, he addressed dozens of public meetings in places such as Bath, Dudley, Derby, Portsmouth, Manchester, and St Ives. 'It was one hell of a pace.' Farage was spending most days on the campaign trail surrounded by journalists and doing one interview after another. Then, in the evenings, he did 'the shows'. Most days finished in a pub or Indian restaurant, with Farage talking over the campaign with his team. He often did not get to bed until the early hours before waking at five and repeating the cycle. Some days he was so busy that he skipped meals entirely, surviving on Mars Bars. He often seemed to be running on fumes.

Yet the campaign did seem to be having an effect. In the polls, there was evidence that Ukip was not just benefiting from an anti-politics mood. When pollsters had asked a sample of the electorate to choose the party that had the 'best' policies on different issues, their responses had thrown light on Ukip's strengths and weaknesses. On issues such as the economy, health, education, taxation, and law and order, the party was nowhere to be seen. It lagged well behind the main parties. But on immigration and the EU it was beginning to push ahead of the others (see Figure 3.3). At least as far as

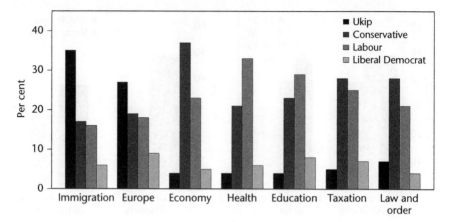

**Figure 3.3.** Public perceptions of 'best' policies on various issues, May 2014
*Source*: YouGov/*Sun* polls.

voters were concerned, the party had begun to take ownership of these issues, something that Ukip had never had before. Its revolt looked more durable than many thought.

The campaign was also having other effects. Before the campaign, only one poll had suggested that it could win the election. But by the end of April, Ukip was in the lead. Now, and with still almost one month until the election, a series of polls by YouGov, TNS, and ComRes suggested that it was on course to win. Its support peaked five days after its launch, when, on the final weekend in April, one poll put Ukip on 38 per cent, eleven points clear of Labour, its closest rival (see Figure 3.4).[17] But, while his party celebrated, Farage felt anxious. He was not used to being in front. He had never had to defend a lead and was worried that Ukip had peaked too soon. 'Everything was a dream,' he would later recall. 'It went beautifully. But it also left me perched on a rock with everyone firing at me for the last three weeks.' And, on several occasions, it looked as though he might fall off and Ukip's fragile lead would evaporate.

Farage and his party had long struggled to stop a wave of negative publicity about its eccentric and sometimes offensive supporters. But, as the election neared, that wave turned into a tsunami. Keeping count of the number of supporters who attracted negative coverage because of their offensive, racist, or embarrassing remarks had become an almost impossible task. The

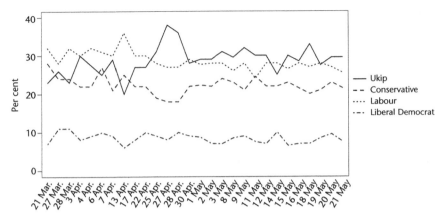

**Figure 3.4.** Average EU party support in national opinion polls, March to May 2014
*Source*: UK Polling Report.

problem was that, beyond the suspensions and expulsions, there was actually little that could be done. The party had grown quickly and simply did not have the resources that were needed to screen the hundreds of candidates who were standing in elections and the thousands of supporters who were trawling social media. All it could do was ask would-be candidates to sign a form and make a series of declarations—that they had never engaged in racist, violent, criminal, or anti-democratic behaviour, that they had never been a member of a group that the NEC thought might bring the party into disrepute, that they had never been convicted of an offence, and, lastly, that they did not have 'skeletons in the cupboard' that might cause Ukip embarrassment if they were to come out. If candidates were in doubt about the last point, they were invited to elaborate on another sheet of paper.

With no formal and properly resourced vetting procedures, Ukip was left seriously exposed. The vulnerability had not been missed by Neil Hamilton, who had overseen much of the campaign. 'There was no proper vetting procedure. They had to swear that there was no embarrassment lurking in their past life but it was beyond our means to vet 1,400 Facebook and Twitter accounts for idiotic posts.' Some insiders would later reveal their political naivety by complaining that the major parties had launched 'attack strategies', and that newspaper editors had 'put a lot of journalistic effort into social media archaeology'. But, under the strain of scrutiny, and the failure to impose party discipline, the party looked ill-equipped to deal with the onslaught. It was soon suffering from dozens, if not hundreds, of self-inflicted wounds that often looked as though they could derail the entire campaign.

There were countless examples, each serving to remind voters of wider claims that Ukip was a racist or extreme party that was filled with amateurs. There was the former official who had been imprisoned after a kidnap plot in Pakistan, the MEP who called for mosques to be banned and suggested that British Muslims should sign a code of conduct, the members with links to far-right groups, the councillor who had blamed bad flooding on same-sex marriage, the supporter who had described his own relatives as 'Mongols', the councillor who had suggested that shops should refuse to serve women and homosexuals, and the followers on social media who had suggested that Islam was similar to Nazi Germany and that the black comedian Lenny Henry should leave Britain. Nor was Ukip's image helped by stories about its headquarters on Brooks Mews. One claimed that officials brought a cat to work, wore an 'orgasmatron' headset, and used a whiteboard to list people whom they wanted to sleep with.[18]

Much of the coverage appeared in *The Times*, which during the campaign announced that it was launching a full investigation into the party. 'The time has arrived to take Ukip seriously and it is already clear that Ukip will not come out of the encounter well.'[19] It would later be claimed that the party had diverted taxpayers' money, that Farage had secret offshore accounts, and that Ukip MEPs enjoyed lavish dinners and first-class travel. 'They stay in smart Strasbourg hotels and dine in fine restaurants, slurping Château Margaux at taxpayers' expense while condemning the waste of money by the EU.'[20]

Farage would eventually be forced to make some concessions. The weak effort to vet the party's activists and candidates, he would later acknowledge in an interview, had gone 'catastrophically wrong' and 'collapsed'. Publicly, he also accepted that he would need to take action against those whom he called the 'Walter Mittys of Ukip'.[21] But, at the same time, it was also true that the coverage did not seem to be damaging his party's relatively stable position in the polls. On the contrary, there was evidence to suggest that it might even have been entrenching Ukip's status as a populist outsider. When asked whether media coverage of the different parties was biased or balanced, one poll suggested that almost half of all people thought that the media were biased against Ukip, more than twice the proportion who thought that journalists were biased towards the other parties. In another and more loaded question, which asked voters whether 'there is a political class, clubbing together, using their mates in the media and doing anything they can to stop the Ukip charge', 54 per cent of all voters agreed, which jumped to 92 per cent among Ukip voters.[22]

It was a concern that would surface regularly over the coming year. Some were anxious that the narrow focus on immigration was polarizing public attitudes towards Ukip. Even Nuttall, who was on the ultra right wing of the party, expressed concern. 'I think that we took it to the line and now need to move away from the EU and immigration for a while.' Others made similar observations. 'It was pretty close to the bone in terms of the narratives used on immigration,' said one. 'In the past people might have been ambivalent about Ukip. But now you've got 30 per cent who love us and 30 per cent who despise us. We ended up in that marmite situation where people either loved us or hated us more than we would have wanted.'

There was no doubt that a significant portion of the electorate felt negatively about Ukip. This could be seen in the surveys and polls. During the campaign, for example, the pollsters at YouGov ran two surveys to explore what people thought about the party and its supporters. The result was perhaps not as bad as some in the party had feared, but it still left a picture of a political brand that was highly divisive. While one-quarter felt that Ukip was racist *and* had racist supporters, the same proportion felt that they shared the views of ordinary people. Meanwhile, more than one-third felt that, while the party was not racist, its supporters did hold extreme views. Other explorations suggested that almost three-fifths of the electorate thought that Ukip was more likely than the others to have candidates who held racist and offensive views. While almost three in ten felt that the party was no different from other parties, only 3 per cent thought that Ukip was *less* likely to have offensive candidates (see Figure 3.5). Such results contributed to the feeling of unease inside the party. Whereas most of those around Farage felt that they were following the right strategy, particularly for a secondary election that tended to encourage people to protest against the establishment, some voiced their concern about the effects of this approach. 'We were rather upset when we discovered some people actually hated us. We went strong on immigration. It was always a risk. We knew it would be a risk. But we were upset we were characterized in that way.'

In the first week in May Farage arrived at the Emmanuel Centre in Westminster with a plan to push back against the negative publicity. The event had been briefed to the media as the 'Clause Four' moment in the history of Ukip—a reference to the pivotal moment when Tony Blair

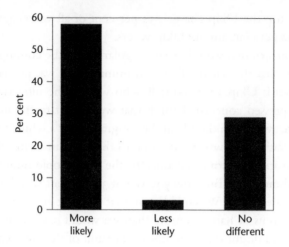

**Figure 3.5.** Ukip candidates more likely to have racist/offensive views?
*Source*: YouGov.

scrapped Labour's commitment to nationalization. Farage had long wanted to respond to the repeated claims that he was leading a racist party. Standing in front of a packed hall, and flanked by dozens of activists from ethnic-minority backgrounds, he tried to fight back. 'I'm addressing this comment to the press,' he said. 'I don't care if you disagree with us. I don't care if you think we are better off being governed by Cameron, Clegg and Miliband. I don't care if you think uncontrolled immigration is good for Britain.' With his headset on and arms stretched out he then looked directly at the section of the hall that had been reserved for journalists. 'You can call us right-wing, left-wing, small-minded, I don't care. But from this moment onwards please don't ever call us a racist party. We are *not* a racist party.'

Two weeks later, Farage and his team gathered at the Goring Hotel in Belgravia. Despite the attempt to defuse the growing backlash, they were deeply concerned about the direction of the campaign and what felt like a very fragile lead. Huddled around a table, they were looking at designs for new billboards that would try to shift the focus away from immigration and onto the financial costs of EU membership. They wanted to respond to Labour, which had deliberately sidelined immigration in favour of pushing arguments about the cost of living. Ukip's billboards claimed that household bills were £400 higher because of EU import controls and that fuel bills were £112 higher because of EU subsidies, carbon taxes, and climate-change measures. They were released in Doncaster, a Labour town in Yorkshire that would see a lot more of Ukip in months to come. Yet few voters would have noticed the shift in tone. Even if they had, the attempt to defuse the campaign was soon undermined.

On the morning of Friday, 16 May, Farage and O'Flynn walked through Leicester Square and into LBC Radio for an interview with talk show host James O'Brien. There were only six days until polling day. Farage had refused earlier invitations to appear on the show. It was only when O'Brien publicly ridiculed the Ukip leader for declining his requests that Farage finally agreed. There was little that he hated more than being called a coward. But what followed was seen as a disaster for Ukip and its leader. O'Brien had done his research. He repeatedly challenged Farage about his views on immigration, racist remarks that had been made by Ukip candidates, the party's association with far-right politicians in the European Parliament, and claims that Farage himself had used 'the N-word'. O'Brien then challenged Farage about his suggestion that people might not want to have Romanian migrants as their next-door neighbours. 'What if a group of German children moved in? What's the difference?' Farage, who was now visibly agitated, responded: 'You know what the difference is . . .'. O'Flynn walked into the studio and forced an end to the interview.

Individual interviews rarely impact on the outcome of an election, but the events at LBC Radio attracted another wave of negative publicity for the party. They also fuelled the concern among insiders about the growing public backlash to their campaign. 'We tried to have a very broad debate about the quality and volume of immigration,' said O'Flynn.

But as a result of that interview it got narrowed down to a far narrower debate, which was how would you feel if Romanian men moved next door? Then it became hard, aggressive, very sour and coloured the last days of the campaign in a way that a lot of us felt was regrettable. That was a low moment for me.

Others in the party, like the Chairman Steve Crowther, also voiced unease. 'I think Nigel would say that there were moments when he was overexposed in the media. I would not disagree with him. Nigel is not afraid to speak his mind. Sometimes he says things that he believes, which clearly are going to blow up on us.' The tone of the campaign had other consequences. Amid the negative coverage and rumours of threats to Farage's safety, he had taken on a security team. The man who had long cherished being a free spirit was now accompanied around the clock by between three and six bodyguards.

As the day of reckoning neared, Ukip's team had become very nervous. News had surfaced that a rival Eurosceptic party would also be standing in the election. Founded by Mike Nattrass, a long-serving but disgruntled Ukip activist, the new party was called 'An Independence from Europe'. It meant that it would appear above Ukip on the ballot papers. Moreover, the new party would appear with the tagline 'UK Independence Now'. It was a deliberate attempt to confuse voters and damage Nattrass's old party. With the race tightening, it was the last thing that Farage needed. In the polls, Ukip's lead had narrowed or disappeared altogether. In the first ten polls in May, Ukip had been in front with an average of more than 30 per cent of the vote. But its lead had started to wobble. On three consecutive days, the party opened newspapers to find that it had fallen behind Labour, and its support was down to around 25 per cent. Farage's fears about falling behind seemed to be coming true. 'It is as though the sand is slipping between our fingers,' he muttered in one meeting. One poll even put his party third, fueling fears among insiders that they were losing what felt like a once-in-a-lifetime opportunity to achieve a historic breakthrough and lay the foundation for a much bigger upset in 2015.[23] Then, only three days out, Ukip reached a new nadir. A poll put it on 24 per cent, four points behind Labour. Farage was shocked. Privately, he made a decision. If Ukip did not win, he would resign as its leader. Double or quits.

When all of the votes had been counted, Farage's gamble paid off. Ukip was first. It had caused its earthquake. With nearly 28 per cent of the national vote, the party had attracted support from more than one in four of those who had voted in the election. Farage and his band of amateurs had finished two points ahead of Labour and almost four points ahead of the Conservatives. Their prize was a new record number of twenty-four seats in the European Parliament, which in turn would bring more money, power, and influence. Farage had called on voters to join his self-anointed People's Army, to use his small party as a vehicle for expressing their concerns about immigration, national identity, the Eurocrats in Brussels, and the politicians in Westminster. He had been answered with more than four million votes.

Some were dismissive, arguing that elections to the European Parliament are not as important as general elections. There was certainly some truth to the claim that people vote differently in these secondary elections, where they often feel that less is at stake, are more likely to punish the parties in government, and back outsiders. But it has also been shown that people

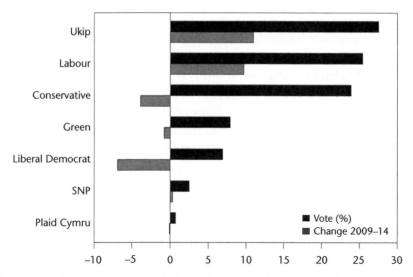

**Figure 3.6.** Vote percentage and change in support for parties at the 2014 European elections

approach these elections in an expressive way, that it is precisely because they are *not* electing a government that they vote with their heart over their head, taking the opportunity to express their loyalty to a group identity or concern about specific issues.[24] In this respect, and with less than one year until the 2015 general election, the campaign and results had shed light on the direction of deeper currents within British politics.

There was no doubt that Ukip's victory was remarkable. Its campaign had been run by only a handful of activists and had been repeatedly attacked by much of the political and media elite. But, even still, Farage and his party became the first new movement for almost a century to win a nationwide election. It was a rare moment in politics, when voters had put an outsider ahead of every established party. That the small party had even managed to top the poll had contributed to an uncomfortable fact for the two main parties—with less than twelve months until the general election, just over half of the electorate had not backed either of them. Meanwhile, on the same day, Ukip had also entrenched its presence in public office, capturing more than 160 seats in local elections and averaging more than 20 per cent of the vote. It was on its way.

The advance led some to ask whether the party was now part of the mainstream. As academic John Curtice observed, by winning the contest

Ukip had confirmed its status as the most serious challenge to established politics in post-war England.[25] Its performance had also raised deeper questions about British politics. Combined, public support for the three main parties had fallen to a new low. Whereas at the same elections in 1994 they had together polled almost 90 per cent of the vote, this had now dwindled to 56 per cent.[26] More than two-fifths of the electorate, or almost seven million people, had turned to parties outside the big three. It was further evidence of Britain's fragmenting political landscape.

For Ed Miliband and Labour, the result raised more uncomfortable questions. Even before the European elections Labour's position had looked far from convincing. Just prior to the contest, Labour had held a lead over the Conservatives of only around five or six points. And, as political historians would point out, with the single exception of 1972, every party in opposition that had held such a slim lead at this point had gone on to be defeated at the next general election.[27] Now, the result of the European election had underlined the problem. The results, said Shadow Chancellor Ed Balls, were not good enough. He was right. A small and untested party had pushed the official opposition into second place, making it the first opposition not to win a European Parliament election since Neil Kinnock and Labour had failed to beat Margaret Thatcher and the Conservatives in 1984. Kinnock had gone on to lose the general election three years later. That Miliband and his party had again failed to deliver a convincing performance was further reflected in the fact that their vote share was twenty points lower than what Labour had polled in 1994, the last time they had been the main opposition at the time of a European election.

Such observations fuelled anxieties about Ed Miliband's ability to connect with voters, including Labour's traditional working-class base. They also raised fresh questions about whether Labour had underestimated Farage and his revolt. As we will see in the next chapter, it was now clear that, rather than just dividing the right, the rise of Ukip was also stalling Labour's comeback in England. Meanwhile, further warning signs for Miliband and his party could be found in local elections, which had been held on the same day. Compared to its performance in 2012, Labour's support had slipped backwards by an average of eight points. To those who bothered to look at these less exciting results, more doubt was being poured over the claim that Miliband could lead his party back to power. In the Labour town of Gateshead, where Farage had set out his stall, more than one in four people had defected to Ukip. But it was far worse in many other Labour heartlands, as we shall soon see. Farage's revolt was taking on a distinctive pattern, and it was throwing up as many problems for Miliband as it was for Cameron.

The Conservatives, meanwhile, who had long been braced for defeat, had finished in third place. There were some obvious reasons for them to feel concerned. Their share of the national vote had fallen below 24 per cent, their lowest-ever at European elections. It was also well below the level of support that Cameron and his party would need if they were to fulfil their dream of a majority government in 2015. But there was something else, too. All of this had happened *after* Cameron's big offers to the social conservative voters who had been drifting away from his party since 2010—after his promise of a referendum on Britain's continuing EU membership, and after all the tough talk on immigration. If, despite all this, voters were *still* shifting over to Ukip, then what would bring them back?

But, at the same time, it was not quite as bad for Cameron as some in his team might have feared. In the polls, at least, the Conservatives were still only around four points below where they had been in 2009, before they had entered government. Labour's weakness and Miliband's dismal ratings had also been a welcome distraction. Farage, meanwhile, had not yet been seriously tested on the ground—in the cut-and-thrust trench warfare that took place under first-past-the-post. He might have won a secondary European election, but how would his fragile organization and divisive strategy hold up in a general election? There was clearly still a lot to do, but, as Cameron and his team looked ahead, at the mountain that stood in front of them, it did not look completely insurmountable.

The same, however, could not be said for their Coalition partners. It had been a truly disastrous night for the Liberal Democrats. While Nick Clegg and his team had clung to the hope that debating Farage might help them to fend off electoral annihilation, that hope had been completely shattered. They were nearly wiped out. Their share of the vote had been slashed in half, tumbling below 7 per cent, and they were now slumped in fifth place. While they had spent much of the past year behind Ukip, they now suffered the further humiliation of finishing behind the Greens as well, who had not only won a larger number of votes but were drawing many of them from disillusioned Liberal Democrats. Clegg and his party had lost ten seats, leaving just one lonely Liberal Democrat in the European Parliament. Since the last set of European elections, they had lost nearly one million voters. Those who had the courage to look at the local elections saw an even more depressing picture—the worst result since their party had been founded. 'It's as bad as I feared,' observed Tim Farron.[28]

In the aftermath of the contest, attention quickly began to drift towards the next major battle—the 2015 general election. According to the pollsters, it looked set to be one of the closest and most unpredictable battles for a generation. For the triumphant Ukip, the next twelve months offered an opportunity to entrench itself at the heart of British politics. Farage's earlier ideas about resigning as leader were now being quickly replaced by confident predictions that his party would capture enough seats at the election to hold the balance of power in a hung parliament. 'We will go on next year to the general election with a targeted strategy', he declared, 'and I promise you this—you haven't heard the last of us'.

# 4
# Left-behind Britain

A few weeks after the European elections, in June 2014, Nigel Farage was sitting alone in Ukip's headquarters on Brooks Mews. He had his mobile phone in one hand and a cigarette in the other. His eyes were fixed on his computer. He was looking at a spreadsheet that one of his party's number-crunchers had compiled. It was a list of Ukip's results at the European contest. With the general election less than a year away, Farage knew that the game had changed. After the earthquake his wildly optimistic followers were now expecting to win dozens of seats in the House of Commons. They had tasted success and wanted more of it. But the next contest would not be held under a proportional system. It would be held under first-past-the-post—a system that had brought down numerous challengers in the past. At this election, and unlike the last, simply throwing candidates at the contest and talking loudly about issues would not work. To stand a chance, Ukip would need to target its limited firepower in areas where it had concentrated support, and which might provide a springboard into Westminster. And it would need to fight toe-to-toe with the main parties.

But Ukip's appeal was not spread evenly throughout the regions, cities, towns and villages. Only certain types of areas had pushed it forward. What did these places have in common? What do they tell us about the appeal of this movement? Who, exactly, was supporting Ukip as the general election rapidly approached? And why were they doing so? In this chapter and the next we answer these questions, setting the stage for the general election campaign that would soon follow.

As Farage looked at his party's results he was often stunned by the numbers staring back at him. In some parts of England the scale of Ukip's support was striking. It had won the popular vote across six of Britain's regions, with its highest share of the vote at 34 per cent coming in eastern England, a large swathe of territory that covers Essex, Norfolk, Suffolk, Cambridgeshire,

Bedfordshire, and Hertfordshire, and that in earlier centuries had hosted other revolts against established authority.[1] Some had already noticed Ukip's eastern promise. Shortly before the election, journalist John Harris had set out to explore areas that looked more receptive than others to Farage's narrative of loss, threat, and abandonment. 'If Ukip has a heartland,' he wrote, 'it is the great stretch of eastern England that encompasses Suffolk, Norfolk, Cambridgeshire and Lincolnshire, whose people often seem to feel as remote from London as anyone in the north, Wales or Scotland'. From one town to the next, Harris had come across people who were voting for Ukip not because of blind prejudice but because of what he saw as intense feelings of anxiety about an 'insecure, unpredictable world whose governing logic they can no longer abide, least of all politically'. As he drove down the eastern roads, he reflected on what he saw around him.

The sky is so huge as to feel oppressive; villages pop up and disappear. There are no motorways and the mobile signal regularly goes dead. Not for the first time, a thought pops into my head: though a huge part of the national conversation remains devoted to the north/south divide, there is also a curious political gap between England's east and west, for which the rise of Ukip is a potent signifier.[2]

A few weeks later, after Harris had returned home, it was the same areas that gave Farage his strongest support. In 2009 Ukip had attracted more than 30 per cent of the vote in only three areas—and all of them were in the south-west county of Devon.[3] It had not breached the 40 per cent barrier anywhere. But now, five years later, it had won more than 30 per cent in over 200 areas and at least 40 per cent in 33 of them (see Figure 4.1). And many were along England's eastern flank, which hosted seventeen of the party's twenty strongest results.[4]

The strongest vote for Ukip in the entire country came in the small town and port of Boston in Lincolnshire, where 52 per cent of voters cast their ballot for the party. But this was not the only place where the party had almost doubled its vote to surge past the 40 per cent mark. Like Boston, most of its strongholds were small market towns or struggling working-class communities that were scattered along the east coast, from Lincolnshire to Norfolk, Essex, Kent, Suffolk, and round the coast to Sussex. They included South Holland in Lincolnshire, the small seaport and market town of King's Lynn in Norfolk, the blue-collar communities of Basildon, Rochford, and Thurrock in Essex, the commuter town of Broxbourne, the market towns of north-east Cambridgeshire, and a large swathe of territory in Kent that

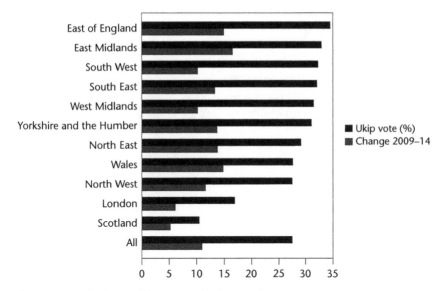

**Figure 4.1.** Ukip's 2014 European election results

*Source*: European Parliament Elections 2014 (June 2014). House of Commons Library Research Paper 14/32.

covered Gravesham, Medway, Shepway, and Swale. Some areas outside the east had also given strong support, including the industrial Labour towns of Mansfield in Nottinghamshire and Rotherham in south Yorkshire.

The party was growing quickly and not just because it was starting from a low level. In some areas that would soon play an important role in the general election, Ukip had already won between 20 and 30 per cent of the vote in 2009. In the seaside town of Clacton its support increased from 28 to 48 per cent. In Thurrock, where it was very active, support more than doubled from 22 to 46 per cent. In nearby Castle Point, which had a tradition of supporting independents, support rocketed from 28 to almost 50 per cent. In the traditional seaside resort of Great Yarmouth in Norfolk its support went from 25 to 45 per cent. And in Thanet, on the north-eastern tip of Kent, which had long felt the full force of invading forces, its support increased from 24 to 46 per cent (see Figure 4.2). As Farage looked at these numbers, he started to feel optimistic. His support had a distinctive pattern, which would be crucial under first-past-the-post. Without these concentrations he would never stand a chance of winning MPs. Things were looking good. Or so it seemed.[5]

Many of Ukip's strongest results had also come in Conservative territory. This had fuelled fears among Cameron's team that the crusade was cannibalizing their vote ahead of what looked to be one of the closest general

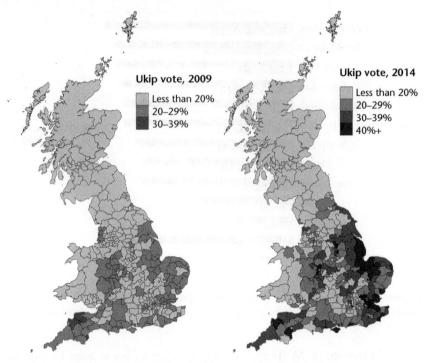

**Figure 4.2.** Ukip vote share by local authority in 2009 and 2014 European elections
*Source*: European Parliament Elections 2014. House of Commons Library Research Paper 14/32.

elections in living memory. Farage's victory had challenged a consensus that had emerged in the shadow of the Bloomberg speech and Cameron's tougher stance on immigration—that support for Ukip would soon melt like spring snow. On the contrary, it was stubbornly persistent. This was especially true in Conservative areas, where the party had averaged 32 per cent, compared to 26 per cent in Labour areas and 24 per cent in Liberal Democrat territory. When Cameron and his team looked at the numbers, they would have seen other sobering statistics. Of the thirty-three areas where Ukip had won over 40 per cent of the vote, only ten had not been under the control of Conservative-run councils. The insurgent army that was supposed to be running for the hills had finished in first place in more than half of almost 160 councils that the Conservatives had controlled before the election.[6] It might only have been a European election, but the results contained a clear message—unless Cameron could find a way of stalling the rebellion, then it threatened to advance into his core territory and ruin his hopes of a return to power.

The threat was certainly not lost on Cameron's chief strategist, Lynton Crosby. 'One thing I always used to say to Conservatives', said the campaigner, 'is that Farage is actually not a Conservative. His is another party. His ambition is only served by us [the Conservatives] doing badly. Our people came to understand that, which was important.' Nor was the threat lost on grass-roots Tories, who in the shadow of the European election result wrote to Cameron to warn of 'disastrous' losses unless he 'directly addressed' the problem.[7] But what was worrying his advisers was that Cameron had actually been far from passive. It was not as if he had been deaf to the concerns of traditional social conservatives. He had already met his Eurosceptic critics head-on by offering a referendum on Britain's continued EU membership. While his earlier pledge to reduce net migration dramatically could not be met, he had nonetheless cracked down on immigration in the few areas where action could be taken. Then, when Farage had broken through at the 2013 local elections, Cameron, who had once derided Ukip as being filled with fruit cakes, had modified his position a little more. 'It's no good insulting a political party that people have chosen to vote for.'[8]

The problem was not so much a failure of diagnosis but rather that the affliction was not responding to treatment. One person who had noticed the resistance of Ukip was commentator Paul Goodman, who, after scanning the results and new constituency polls, pushed back against the claim that Farage would soon fall off the radar. On the contrary, warned Goodman, he seemed to be entrenching his support in particular parts of England. The insights into what was happening on the ground had been provided by Lord Ashcroft, who, shortly after the European contest, had polled a series of seats that would be key battlegrounds between the main parties in 2015. Far from fading, Ukip was taking between 9 and 36 per cent of the vote. It was more than enough to damage Conservative prospects.

In four seats in the south-west, three of which had Conservative MPs, the polls had put Ukip in second place, with support from more than one in five voters. The party also looked set indirectly to cost Cameron some seats that, at a close general election, he could ill afford to lose—like the former mining area of Amber Valley, the struggling seaside seat of Morecambe and Lunesdale, and the working-class seat of Waveney on Suffolk's coast.[9] Farage had not yet decided where to stand himself, but the polls suggested that his party was running first in the Conservative-held seats of Thurrock in Essex and South Thanet in Kent, and was second in Great Yarmouth in Norfolk. That Ukip was advancing among voters whom Cameron needed to keep on side was reflected in another fact. Around one in five of the Conservative Party's voters in 2010 was now planning to vote for Ukip in 2015.[10]

But, while much of the debate was focused on what all of this meant for Cameron, Farage was also causing problems for Labour, too—although the threat would be diagnosed much later. Across a handful of marginal seats Lord Ashcroft had also found that Ukip's continued support was eroding the swing to Labour. In other words, by continuing to attract support, Farage was making life more difficult for Ed Miliband. That the insurgents were stalling Labour's comeback could be seen in struggling eastern seats such as Great Yarmouth and Thurrock, which Labour might otherwise have hoped to capture from the Conservatives, but where Ukip was drawing significant support—in some cases from around one in four of those who had voted for Labour in 2010.[11]

The challenge to Labour was also reflected in the European election results. Ukip had won the vote across a large chunk of Labour territory, an assault that some had once thought inconceivable. In the early days of Ukip's rise, some on the centre-left had cheered the party on, believing that its fierce Euroscepticism and critique of immigration would recruit social conservatives who loathed Cameron, create turmoil in the right-wing family, and ease Labour's return to power. 'Ukip emerged slowly,' said one of Ed Miliband's most senior advisers.

Our initial response was that it was dividing the right. If it was taking votes from us, then it was taking them in areas where we had more votes than we needed, while it was taking votes from the Tories in areas where they were weak. So it was beneficial. That was the initial view.

But some of Labour's analysts took a very different view. They were worried. Those who were watching the data closely did not view Farage and his party in isolation—they saw Ukip as a symptom of a much longer and broader problem that was staring Labour, and social democrats across Europe, in the face. Some put the new challenger alongside radical-right populists on the Continent, arguing that Ukip was a by-product of the left's weakened bond with its traditional, working-class supporters who felt economically left behind and culturally under threat. They traced the problem to research on voters who had abandoned Labour after Tony Blair's land-slide victory in 1997. The research had not made for a comfortable read. For every one voter that Labour had lost among more financially secure profes-sionals, it had lost three among the poorest, those on benefits and the low paid. And, if the net was widened to include skilled manual workers, then the picture had looked even worse—for every one professional voter that Labour had lost, it had lost six from struggling, lower-income groups. 'This was different from our problem in 1997,' said one of Miliband's advisers, who with others had been reflecting on the problem since 2010. 'Before 1997, Labour was a strong working-class party that was not reaching into a more female, middle class. Now, we were a middle-class party that was not keeping the working class. We could see that we were losing lots and lots of blue-collar voters.' By 2010, some of Labour's lost voters who had not left politics altogether had switched instead to the Conservatives, a point that was not lost on Miliband. 'The core Labour vote that some thought could be taken for granted', he wrote in 2010, 'became the swing vote that went Conservative'.[12]

Fast forward four years, and the situation had become even more difficult for Labour. In power, Cameron was failing to show that he could control net migration. Farage, meanwhile, was making hay—weaving anti-immigration appeals into his arguments about Europe, and delivering both alongside a critique of Cameron's brand of conservatism. 'He's not a Tory. He's a socialist. Tory voters feel much closer to me than their own leader. His priorities are gay marriage, foreign aid and wind farms. They're not mine.'[13] But, by this time, the Ukip leader had also turned up the volume on his attacks against Labour and was deliberately targeting the voters it had lost since Blair. As Labour's number-crunchers had been trying to point out, while Farage was drawing votes from the Conservative-leaning self-employed and lower mid-dle classes, he was also beginning to connect with the economically disaf-fected working class, which had once supported Labour or, amid austerity and economic hardship, might otherwise have considered doing so. By the time that many had cottoned on to the problem, Farage was already in blue-collar towns like Gateshead, relentlessly attacking the left, claiming that it had betrayed the working class through its support of EU migrant workers and big business. Labour, he told the party's traditional voters, had a vested interest in encouraging an influx of low-skilled migrants, which com-pressed their wages and damaged the fabric of their cherished communities. 'Patriotic Old Labour, working people, working families,' Farage said, from one Labour town to the next, 'these are the people that have been seriously impacted by the downturn in the economy. These are the people who have been hurt by uncontrolled mass immigration.'[14]

But few at the top of Labour seemed willing to listen. 'The annoying part', said one Labour analyst,

was that we were all too aware of Ukip, but it was not our job to build strategy. The political team ignored it for too long. There was a lack of confidence. It was easier to paint it as a Conservative problem than deal with it. Douglas Alexander [Labour's election strategist] kept saying it was more of a problem for the Tories. He had his head in the sand.

That Farage's message had resonated was now visible to all. In the European elections Ukip had recruited strong support across Labour territory and often in places where it had no local presence. In many areas where it did not come first, it typically came second, fuelling Farage's belief that his party could become the main opposition in Labour's northern heartlands, where the Liberal Democrats were rapidly disintegrating and voters saw the Conservative Party as a toxic Thatcherite force. The idea was not without potential. Across the three most northern regions of England the European elections had taken place across seventy-two council areas. Ukip had come first in twenty-five and second in all others.[15] Across the country, the party had finished first in one-third of all Labour-held councils—winning more than 40 per cent of the vote in places like Thurrock, Great Yarmouth, Gravesham, Mansfield, and north-east Lincolnshire. In eighteen other Labour-run areas, including many former industrial strongholds, Ukip had won support from more than one in three voters.[16]

The party's challenge to Miliband and his party was best reflected in the north-east, a historic Labour bastion, where Ukip won the highest vote in Darlington, Hartlepool, and Middlesbrough. In Yorkshire, the party finished first in Doncaster, the home of Ed Miliband's constituency, and Rotherham, where on the same day Ukip had won ten of twenty-one seats that were up for election on the council, winning more than 50 per cent of the vote in six wards. The idea that Farage would not win votes in Labour areas was being torn apart. Even in Wales, the party won the popular vote in six councils and finished second to Labour in left-wing strongholds such as Blaenau Gwent, Caerphilly, Cardiff, Rhondda, Swansea, and Torfaen. The sharpest increase in its support was recorded in Merthyr Tydfil, which had once fuelled the Industrial Revolution.

In these areas the decline of industry and once thriving communities had left fertile conditions for Ukip—a reservoir of angry, struggling workers who felt fed up with the managed decline of their areas, left behind by Britain's economic transformation, and cut adrift from Labour politicians, who no longer seemed to share their values. While they had often been slow to get there, some on the left had grasped the challenge. In the shadow of the results, Rachel Reeves, Shadow Work and Pensions Secretary, warned Labour that its traditional voters were 'abandoning' the party because they felt it had taken them for granted. The people whom Labour had been formed to defend in the first place were defecting to Ukip because they no longer 'see us as the answer'.[17]

Some traced the problem to representation. The disconnect between Labour elites and their voters was highlighted in research published by the *Guardian*, on people whom the party had selected to fight marginal seats in 2015. More than half had been political insiders, having worked in Westminster or Brussels, which seemed to confirm the populist critique from Farage and others—that Labour politicians were increasingly divorced from the everyday lives, experiences, and aspirations of their traditional voters.[18] This disconnect was best symbolized by the selection of Stephen Kinnock, son of former Labour leader Neil Kinnock, for the safe seat of Aberavon in south Wales. The seat had been held by Labour since the 1920s and once represented by the first Labour prime minister, Ramsay MacDonald. But few people in Aberavon would have seen their experiences and values reflected back in the march of the so-called Red Princes like Kinnock. Husband to the Danish Prime Minister, their new candidate was a Cambridge-educated, multi-lingual member of the political elite who divided his time between Brussels, Geneva, and Copenhagen. There was nothing necessarily wrong with Kinnock or his politics. But his selection for a traditional, working-class Labour bastion reflected a broader challenge that confronted the left, and that Farage was now routinely targeting—a view that Labour was hunkering down, turning in on itself, and no longer reflecting the groups of voters who it had been established to represent.

The significance of Ukip could also be seen at another level. On the first weekend after the European elections, Farage appeared on the *Andrew Marr Show*. His interview had followed Paddy Ashdown's, former leader of the Liberal Democrats, who in earlier years had also recognized the need for challenger parties to build support through secondary elections. With attention turning to the general election, Farage used the interview to underline his pitch to Britain's working class. He went further than usual—talking about wanting to tackle inequality, improve social mobility, remove tax on the minimum wage, and defend working families, who he said were finding their wages compressed and household bills on the rise. But when asked whether he could actually take his revolt into Westminster, Farage had also offered insight into his underlying strategy. Behind the hype that had surrounded the European elections, he said, it was at the local level where he was planting the seeds for what he hoped would be a much wider breakthrough.

In the spring of 2014, on the same day as the European poll, local elections had taken place across London, and northern and eastern England. The elections rarely capture public imagination but they provide a far more detailed picture of how the parties are performing. Much like Ashdown and his party had done in earlier years, Farage had been using these local battles as a stepping stone to national success. 'That changes the whole perception in a constituency and this is exactly what your previous guest Paddy Ashdown did in the 1990s. They built on local strength.' Though few had noticed, Ukip had become far more active. It had fielded more than 2,000 candidates across almost three-quarters of the wards that were up for election. It was a dramatic increase on earlier years. And, as the Liberal Democrats had mastered, the party was beginning to return to areas where it had stood before, trying to cement relationships with voters. In 2014 Ukip stood in 90 per cent of the seats that it had contested in 2010, the last time that they had been fought.[19]

The party was certainly not strong everywhere. But in some areas of England there was further evidence that it was beginning to cultivate the strongholds of support that would be needed if it was to have a chance of winning parliamentary seats. In areas that it had fought in the past, Ukip had averaged 26 per cent, compared to 22 per cent where it was standing for the first time. It was rewarded with more than 160 councillors, taking its total number of elected officials in local government to more than 300. This was still only a small proportion of the more than 18,000 councillors in England, and the party had still not taken control of an actual council. But in some areas it looked active and was on its way.

The pattern of this advance would become important. Ukip had particular momentum in eastern areas like Norfolk, where it had averaged 36 per cent and captured ten seats, and Essex, where it had won 30 per cent and

Table 4.1. Performance of Ukip in English wards, 2009–2014

| Year | No. of candidates | Wards contested (%) | Average vote (%) | Total Ukip votes | National vote (%) |
|------|-------------------|---------------------|-------------------|-------------------|-------------------|
| 2009 | 573 | 25.7 | 16.1 | 314,428 | 4.6 |
| 2010 | 624 | 20.9 | 7.9 | 226,569 | 1.6 |
| 2011 | 1,229 | 18.2 | 11.6 | 297,662 | 2.4 |
| 2012 | 692 | 30.5 | 13.6 | 216,119 | 3.8 |
| 2013 | 1,731 | 75.5 | 24.4 | 1,136,640 | 19.9 |
| 2014 | 2,193 | 71.0 | 23.1 | 1,277,521 | 15.7 |

Source: Elections Centre, University of Plymouth.

thirty-six seats. The breakthrough prompted columnist Simon Heffer to argue that Farage was connecting with the so-called Essex Man—aspirational, hard-working, traditional Conservatives who in earlier years had seen their values reflected back in Thatcherism. 'Today, most natural Tories, and quite a few long-time Labour supporters in Essex, have had enough of their views being ignored. That is why Essex Man is increasingly more likely to vote Ukip.'[20]

But the heavy focus on Essex was misleading. Ukip had won the same levels of support across Yorkshire and had turned heads in core working-class territory. In elections to Hull City Council, for instance, one-quarter of voters had switched to the party. In the working-class ward of Southcoates East it had polled 44 per cent, ousting a former Lord Mayor and Labour veteran who had served the area for twenty-six years. Ukip had also only narrowly missed out on taking a seat in the nearby working-class Bransholme estate, one of the largest estates in England. Its best result, a striking 63 per cent of the vote, came in Ramsey, a market town in Cambridgeshire where voters had once claimed John Major as their local MP and Ukip had been investing seriously in pavement politics (see Table 4.1).

Aside from showing where Ukip was strong, these results also allow us to gauge how the party's rise was impacting on other parties. Based on its performance in its breakthrough year of 2013, it may have been tempting to agree with those Labour figures who argued that Ukip was an exclusive problem for the Conservative Party. More than four-fifths of the seats that Ukip had captured came at the expense of Tories. But looking only at seats is misleading. A more fine-tuned analysis suggested that the Labour Party had suffered just as much. As observed by Stephen Fisher at the University of Oxford, one problem was that many people were comparing the results in

2013 to those in 2009, the last time that these elections had been fought. But it was not an accurate comparison. In 2009, the Conservatives had polled unusually strongly, Labour had polled unusually poorly, and Ukip had been largely absent. Instead, by comparing support in 2013 to 2012, Fisher showed how Labour was being hit as well. 'The pattern of the results across divisions suggests that relative to last year new UKIP votes have come as much from Labour as from the Tories.'[21]

We can update this picture. In 2014, Ukip's increased support in the local elections had cost David Cameron and the Conservatives control of councils such as Maidstone, Basildon, Castle Point, Peterborough, and Southend-on-Sea. But it had also cost Labour control of Thurrock and Great Yarmouth and led to the Liberal Democrats losing Portsmouth. Looking only at who controls the council, however, does not get at the impact in detail. In the Labour area of Rotherham, for example, Ukip captured ten seats, while Labour held onto the council. To paint a more detailed picture, we can explore the control of areas where Ukip polled strongest, over a five-year period. In 2009 the party fought an even percentage of seats that were being defended by the main parties (see Table 4.2). Its average support was also fairly evenly distributed—19 per cent in Labour areas, 17 per cent in Conservative, and 14 per cent in Liberal Democrat. Ukip captured eight seats, six from Labour and two from Conservatives. A similar pattern emerged in 2010 when Ukip stood more candidates in Conservative seats but averaged almost 7 per cent in Liberal Democrat wards, 8 per cent in Conservative ones, and 9 per cent in Labour ones. Before 2011 there was little evidence that the party was drawing its strongest support in Conservative areas. But then things change.

Between 2011 and 2013, and during the Coalition government, Ukip did win stronger support in Conservative territory—averaging 13 per cent in 2011, 15 per cent in 2012, and 27 per cent in 2013. During these years most of Farage's seats came from Conservatives—three in 2011, four in 2012, and ninety-seven during its breakthrough year in 2013. But it was continuing to attract significant support in Labour areas. The difference in the mean vote for Ukip in Conservative and Labour areas never exceeded five points and was often much smaller. Then, in 2014, when more elections were held in Labour areas, Ukip averaged almost 26 per cent in these areas compared to 23 per cent in Conservative ones. Ukip took most of its seats from Conservatives, but it was now having a broader impact on all parties than in earlier years—taking seventy-six seats from Conservatives, forty-eight from

Table 4.2. Performance of Ukip in local elections by political context, 2009–2014

| Incumbent | Seats defended | Seats contested by Ukip | Seats contested (%) | Mean vote (%) | No. of seats won | Success rate (%) |
|---|---|---|---|---|---|---|
| *Conservative* | | | | | | |
| 2009 | 984 | 271 | 27.5 | 16.8 | 2 | 0.7 |
| 2010 | 1,607 | 274 | 17.1 | 8.1 | 0 | 0.0 |
| 2011 | 4,285 | 568 | 13.3 | 12.8 | 3 | 0.5 |
| 2012 | 989 | 334 | 33.8 | 14.9 | 4 | 1.2 |
| 2013 | 1,082 | 843 | 77.9 | 26.6 | 97 | 11.5 |
| 2014 | 1,351 | 798 | 59.1 | 23.4 | 76 | 9.5 |
| *Labour* | | | | | | |
| 2009 | 442 | 73 | 16.5 | 18.8 | 6 | 8.2 |
| 2010 | 1,288 | 159 | 12.3 | 8.8 | 0 | 0.0 |
| 2011 | 1,330 | 206 | 15.5 | 10.9 | 0 | 0.0 |
| 2012 | 527 | 147 | 27.9 | 14.4 | 0 | 0.0 |
| 2013 | 92 | 57 | 62.0 | 21.4 | 0 | 0.0 |
| 2014 | 1,538 | 732 | 47.6 | 25.7 | 48 | 6.6 |
| *Liberal Democrat* | | | | | | |
| 2009 | 350 | 111 | 31.7 | 13.9 | 0 | 0.0 |
| 2010 | 789 | 128 | 16.2 | 6.5 | 1 | 0.8 |
| 2011 | 1,545 | 255 | 16.5 | 9.2 | 2 | 0.8 |
| 2012 | 508 | 159 | 31.3 | 9.9 | 0 | 0.0 |
| 2013 | 330 | 250 | 75.8 | 21.3 | 15 | 6.0 |
| 2014 | 607 | 369 | 60.8 | 19.2 | 25 | 6.8 |

*Source*: Elections Centre, University of Plymouth.

Labour, and twenty-five from Liberal Democrats. The more it grew, the more it was impacting on all the main parties.

Another way of exploring this is to look at how the presence of Ukip influenced support for the other parties. This can be done by calculating the change in the average share of the vote for each party where they had to compete with Ukip and then compare this to the change where they did not.[22] Almost all the parties performed worse where they had to compete with Ukip, but there were important differences. While the Liberal Democrats and Conservatives performed worse across the board, they suffered greater losses where they had to compete with Ukip. But the story is different for Labour. On average Labour improved on its performance in 2010, but made only modest gains when it was forced to compete with the insurgents, providing further evidence for just how Farage and his party

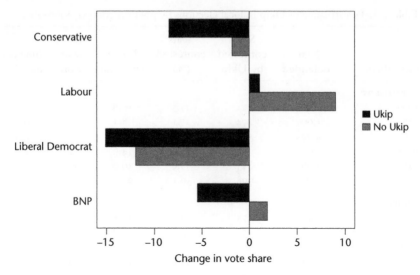

**Figure 4.3.** Change in vote share for parties in local election wards, 2010–2014
*Source*: Elections Centre, University of Plymouth.

were making it more difficult for Labour to stage a comeback. The insurgents were not just threatening Conservatives; it was the Labour Party that saw the largest difference in its vote share. When Labour did not have to face Ukip, it increased its share of the vote by an average of nine points compared to only one point in areas where Ukip was present. Meanwhile, the far right BNP fought fewer wards in 2014 than it had in 2010. But in these wards the BNP performed worse where it had to contend with Ukip. The BNP is the only party whose performance declined when it faced Ukip and then improved when it was free from this competition, revealing how Ukip was often benefiting from the collapse of the far-right party (see Figure 4.3).

But this does not answer *why* some areas were more receptive than others to Ukip. One useful starting point is Matthew Parris, a columnist at *The Times* and former Conservative MP who had once represented a safe seat in Derbyshire known for its rural and picturesque villages. Shortly after the European elections, on a day trip, Parris had swapped his London office for the fading coastal town of Clacton-on-Sea. He was researching the area for an article about the future of the Conservative Party and how it might fend off the threat from Ukip. Clacton was a good place to start. With only two exceptions, the Conservatives had controlled this part of Essex at every election since 1970.[23] But at the European elections Ukip had finished miles ahead, attracting 48 per cent of the vote and a twenty-three-point lead. The result had alarmed the local Conservative MP, Douglas Carswell, who watched his constituents give Ukip its strongest result in east England. The revolt was getting out of control. Parris was visiting to find out what was going on.

As his train pulled out of London and trundled eastwards he felt anxious. 'By the time you get to Clacton most passengers have fled at intermediate stops.' Parris was not sure what lay ahead. When he finally arrived, he took out his notepad and went on a stroll. He was not impressed. The once popular resort was grappling with numerous problems—entrenched deprivation, low social mobility, and lots of white pensioners who had few qualifications, low incomes, bad health, and bleak prospects. The ambitious, socially mobile graduates and young professionals who might otherwise have turned things around were few and far between. None of this should have been a surprise. Only a few years earlier the Office for National Statistics had ranked Clacton among the three most deprived seaside towns in England, while some of its neighbourhoods had extreme problems. One was Jaywick, a Labour-leaning community that was ranked the most deprived of more than 30,000 communities. When one newspaper ran a feature on Jaywick, it simply published pictures under the caption 'Welcome to Misery-by-Sea: Dilapidated homes, boarded-up shops and rubbish-strewn streets'.[24] Some locals called it Beirut. Parris was shocked. 'Clacton-on-Sea', he wrote, 'is a friendly resort trying not to die, inhabited by friendly people trying not to die'.

But did not stop there. The textile of choice among the people of Clacton, he continued, was Lycra. Almost no women wore dresses. Shops offered free shoes when you bought a suit. Pies were on sale for £1.50. Three-bedroom bungalows were available for less than £95,000. Health was poor. 'Only in Asmara after Eritrea's bloody war have I encountered a greater proportion of citizens on crutches or in wheelchairs.' The theatre was about to welcome Ken Dodd and the Bee Gees Story. 'There are ten tattoo parlours and no Waterstones.' As Parris looked down the high street, he saw a local population that was failing to adapt to Britain's new economic reality, never mind getting ahead. They were 'not getting where a 21st century Britain needs to be going'. He soon reached a conclusion. This was Britain on crutches. 'This is tracksuit-and-trainers Britain, tattoo-parlour Britain, all-our-yesterday's Britain.' Clacton was 'going nowhere. Its voters are going nowhere, it's rather sad, and there's nothing more to say.' And all this, he argued, mattered for Conservatives. Instead of trying to win over towns like

Clacton—'the disappointed, the angry, the nostalgic and the fearful'—they should redirect their energy to attracting other groups in society, like the socially liberal, middle-class graduates who admire immigrants, support gay marriage, travel in Europe, embrace diversity, and do not spend their days buying scratch-cards and their evenings smoking outside pubs. 'If you want to win Cambridge, you may have to let go of Clacton.'[25]

It was certainly an idea that would play well at Westminster dinner parties. But Parris was handing his party a recipe for electoral suicide. Clacton was not an exceptional place. It was merely one part of a much larger chunk of territory that was grappling with the same socio-economic problems. It was one of thirty-eight seats that were scattered along England's eastern and southern coasts, from Cleethorpes in north-east Lincolnshire down to Norfolk, Essex, and round to Portsmouth. Had Parris visited these other seats, such as Boston and Skegness, Great Yarmouth, or Louth and Horncastle, then he would have seen the same troubling cocktail of entrenched deprivation, elderly populations, and a lack of social mobility. And, while he patronized the locals, large numbers of them would have told him that, at the election in 2010, they had voted for the Conservatives.

These were voters who had helped Cameron and his party recover after the humiliation that had been imposed by Blair and New Labour. And they had done so while the Conservative Party had failed to connect with the young, professionals, and ethnic minorities whom Parris presumably saw as its future. Thirty-two of the thirty-eight coastal seats had chosen to elect Conservative MPs, compared to only nineteen in 1997. Over the same period the number of Labour MPs in these coastal seats had slumped, from fifteen to one. Only Austin Mitchell in Great Grimsby remained. It was this Conservative renaissance that prompted some on the centre-right to urge action rather than abandonment—to deliver better infrastructure, localism, investment, and reformed welfare that incentivized people into work.[26]

But Parris had been right about something. Clacton was incredibly receptive to Ukip, and it was not a coincidence. It had been receptive for a reason, and one that is found in many of other places that have been mentioned in this chapter. To understand why Farage and his party was attracting so much support in some areas but so little in others we need to look at the local population in these seats—or their demography.

If all the areas in the country are analysed according to the types of voters who live in them, and then considered alongside their levels of support for

Ukip, we are left with some very clear trends.[27] While Farage might have claimed that he had support across the country, this was not exactly true. His party's support was consistently strongest in areas where there were lots of older, white, and poor voters, while it was consistently weaker in areas that were younger, more ethnically and culturally diverse, and financially secure.

These differences are important to making sense of Ukip's appeal. For instance, in areas where more than 90 per cent of the population was white, or where more than one in four people had no qualifications, Ukip had averaged more than 30 per cent of the vote. But in areas where less than 80 per cent of the population was white, or where more than five in six people had qualifications, it had averaged closer to 20 per cent. Farage could attract support in slightly more prosperous areas, but the real source of his electoral strength was left-behind Britain—struggling, older, and marginalized communities where education levels are low, people have scant experience with ethnic diversity, and financial insecurity is rife.

But it is also important to consider how these conditions overlap, given that areas that have lots of people in insecure jobs also tend to have lots of people who have no qualifications. Because these conditions are individually associated with higher support for Ukip, we would expect to find that this support is amplified in areas that have both conditions. To explore this a little further we have created an overall measure of whether an area is favourable or not—which encompasses all the conditions that are displayed in Figures 4.4 and 4.5. This measure tells us whether or not areas are likely to be receptive to the party based on the concentration of Ukip-friendly voters.[28] The map below presents areas in England and Wales according to how favourable they are likely to be. As you can see, the favourable territory is by no means restricted to Clacton.

London and its surrounding areas offer little promise to Ukip. But as one moves away from the capital the climate becomes increasingly more favourable. The darkest and most favourable areas are spread along the eastern and south coasts, in parts of the south-west, and in Labour heartlands in northern England and also Wales. The most receptive populations are on the east coast, including Clacton, Great Yarmouth, and Boston and Skegness, which helps to explain why these areas provided the party with at least 40 per cent of the vote. These often have large numbers of people with little financial security and few qualifications. In the twenty-five most favourable areas, where Ukip averaged 38 per cent of the vote, one in three people works in an insecure job and has no qualifications. These areas are also

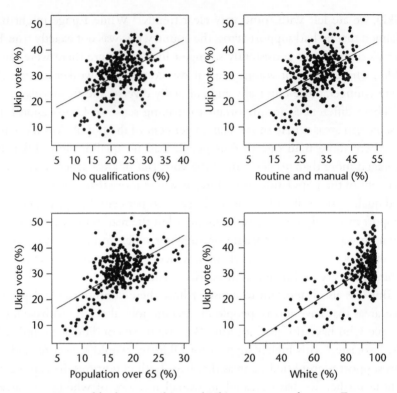

**Figure 4.4.** Favourable demographics and Ukip support at the 2014 European elections
*Source*: 2011 Census.

distinctive in other ways. They are almost exclusively white, with more than 95 per cent of people describing themselves this way. And they are older, often in the top quarter of areas in terms of their number of pensioners. Not all of the areas that we would expect to be receptive are so, however. Places such as Knowsley in Merseyside or Neath Port Talbot in Wales have lots of voters whom we would expect to find the party appealing. But they have not given strong support. This underscores the point that demography is not a perfect predictor of how people vote. But it is a major piece of the puzzle. Most of the highly favourable areas did provide Ukip with strong support. The most favourable included Boston, Clacton, and Great Yarmouth, which all gave the party upwards of 45 per cent of the vote (see Figure 4.6).

What about unfavourable areas? Perhaps, unsurprisingly, Ukip has struggled in younger urban areas and university towns such as Oxford, Cambridge,

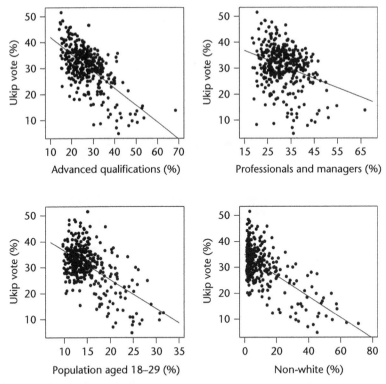

**Figure 4.5.** Unfavourable demographics and Ukip vote share at the 2014 European elections

*Source*: European Parliament Elections 2014 (June 2014), House of Commons Library Research Paper 14/32; 2011 Census.

Brighton, and Manchester, where professionals and graduates are a far more significant force. In such areas, fewer than one-fifth of the population have no qualifications, are pensioners, and work in insecure jobs, while around one quarter are non-white. But most of the unfavourable areas are actually elsewhere. Many are in London, such as Westminster, Camden, Hackney, and Kensington and Chelsea, which similarly have more-educated, diverse, secure, and socially mobile residents. These places look very different from the white, working-class, marginalized, and older communities that are scattered down the east coast. A typically unfavourable place for Ukip is Lambeth—a diverse area of London where almost half of the residents have a degree, compared to the national average of around one-quarter. It is also a young suburb, where only one in three people is a pensioner and people live on an average weekly pay of £645—20 per cent higher than the national

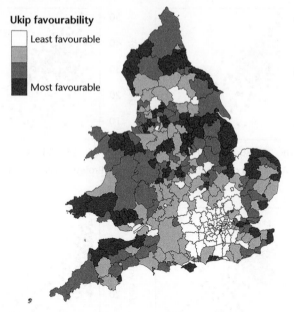

**Figure 4.6.** The most demographically favourable authorities for Ukip
*Source*: European Parliament Elections 2014 (June 2014), House of Commons Library
Research Paper 14/32; 2011 Census.

average and 30 per cent higher than what residents in Hull receive. Such
conditions are fairly typical in London and help explain why the capital
handed Farage fifteen of his twenty-five worst results.[29]

Some have attributed Ukip's poor performance in London to the idea
that its inhabitants are innately more tolerant by virtue of the much higher
diversity that they experience. The argument has been put forward by columnist Jonathan Freedland.

It's not just that the capital is uncongenial for someone who, like Farage, feels
uncomfortable hearing languages other than English. It also undermines Ukip's
entire argument about immigration and modernity. For if Ukip's core message is that
Britons cannot take too much diversity London stands as a rebuttal. It is the most
mixed, diverse place in Britain—but it is also the place apparently least troubled by
that variety, a sentiment eloquently expressed in its collective rejection of Ukip.

But this is not entirely accurate. It does not sit comfortably with research
by academic Eric Kaufmann, who provides evidence that white Britons
in London who do not have a degree are more likely than similarly educated white Britons outside the capital to support Ukip. Rather than being
because of some collective celebration of diversity, the party's lack of

success in London actually owes more to the fact that white Britons without degrees make up a lower proportion of the population there than other areas.[30]

Overall, then, these differences in demography help us to make sense of why Ukip was polling 40 per cent in Rotherham but only 14 per cent in Richmond-upon-Thames. As Farage travelled around England, he was encountering different communities that were reacting in different ways to how the country was changing. Support for Ukip had a distinctive geographical pattern. It was anchored in left-behind communities that had struggled to get by and had few good reasons to feel optimistic about the future. This map would also shape the party's quest to cause an upset at the 2015 election. But, before we turn to that campaign, we can first ask one other question that helps us to set the stage—who was following Farage and to what extent were these voters planning to stay with him as he led Ukip into the biggest election battle in its history?

# 5

# Farage's Followers

On an early summer's day, in 2014, the pollsters at YouGov were having some fun. As memories of the European election started to fade, they had devised a tool that could paint a detailed portrait of different people in society, including supporters of Britain's political parties.[1] Based on thousands of individuals, it could shed light, for example, on who was fuelling the so-called Green Surge, a reference to how public support for the Greens had more than doubled since the start of 2014. The portrait that it painted was fascinating. Green voters were far more likely than average to be under 24 years old, to live in the West Country, like Bristol, and to work for the civil service, a charity, or in media. They probably shopped at The Cooperative and made a point of buying fair-trade products. They enjoyed eating vegetarian bangers and mash, nut roasts, or lentil casserole, and in their spare time they probably played an instrument, badminton, read the *Guardian*, or listened to Björk.

But when the pollsters looked at Ukip's voters, they found the complete opposite. Farage's followers were more likely to be pensioners, to live in East Anglia or on the south coast, and to have worked in the military, transport, or construction industries. They shopped at the discount store Lidl, and if they could they would probably spend most evenings eating ham, eggs and chips, meat pie, and jam tarts. When they were not watching cricket or boxing, doing DIY or bird watching, they were probably reading the *Daily Mail* or listening to Cliff Richard, Roy Orbison, or Dolly Parton. While the Greens watched Louis Theroux and Professor Brian Cox talk about the solar system, Ukip's supporters watched *Dad's Army*, *Doc Martin*, *Top Gear* and basically anything that featured Jim Davidson, Jeremy Clarkson, or Les Dawson. And when it came to describing their personality, while the Greens saw themselves as ethical and imaginative people who could also come across as depressed and withdrawn, Ukip's followers saw themselves as firm-minded, unflappable, and individualistic while accepting that they could also appear intolerant and abrupt. While the personality of the average Green was reflected in sayings such as 'I wouldn't mind having a wind turbine in my area', or 'I only buy from companies that have ethics and values that I agree with', the outlook of the average Ukip voter was summarized in a rather different set of sayings—'people get far too easily offended these days', 'an eye for an eye and a tooth for a tooth', and 'this country is going to the dogs'.

The portraits are certainly entertaining, but there is also much more to discover about Farage's followers and their motives for supporting Ukip. In the aftermath of the European elections, it was clear that Ukip had the potential to attract widespread support. But who was actually supporting the party and why? Had the party's core-vote strategy, which had focused heavily on attracting working-class voters who felt concerned about immigration and opposed the EU, worked? And to what extent were these people planning on staying loyal to Farage as he readied his party for the biggest campaign in its history?

One way of answering these questions is to draw on the British Election Study (BES), a prestigious and impartial source of information on voters. It is extremely helpful, because it surveyed thousands of people before and after the European elections, and would return to them over the months to come. The surveys allow us to explore the backgrounds, loyalties, and beliefs of more than 30,000 voters, including around 6,000 who said that they had cast their ballot for Ukip.[2]

This information tells us that many of the core features that YouGov had identified were indeed accurate. If we compare Ukip's voters at the European elections to supporters of the other parties then we find that they were more likely to be older, white, and male, to have few qualifications, and little financial security (see Table 5.1). Farage's revolt was dominated by men and it was also very grey. He had the largest share of voters who were aged over 54 years old and the lowest share of 18–34 year olds. And his base was almost exclusively white. Fewer than one in twenty Ukip voters was non-white, a much lower proportion than the other parties. They were also the most likely to have left school before their seventeenth birthday. All this is consistent with past research.[3]

How was support for the parties spread across Britain's different social classes? As you can see in Table 5.1, all the parties drew most of their support from people in middle-class occupations. This is not surprising, given the

Table 5.1. Social background of party supporters and non-voters in the 2014 European elections

| Characteristic | Ukip | Conservative | Labour | Liberal Democrat | Non-voters | Full sample |
|---|---|---|---|---|---|---|
| **Social class** | | | | | | |
| Higher managerial/professional | 16 | 21 | 14 | 25 | 14 | 16 |
| Lower managerial/professional | 29 | 33 | 31 | 38 | 28 | 31 |
| Intermediate occupations | 20 | 21 | 26 | 16 | 25 | 23 |
| Small employers/self-employed | 8 | 7 | 4 | 7 | 6 | 6 |
| Lower supervisory/technical | 9 | 6 | 8 | 3 | 8 | 8 |
| Semi-routine | 11 | 8 | 11 | 7 | 12 | 11 |
| Routine | 8 | 4 | 6 | 4 | 7 | 6 |
| **Education (age left school)** | | | | | | |
| 16 or younger | 51 | 31 | 36 | 19 | 34 | 35 |
| 17–18 | 23 | 24 | 19 | 17 | 23 | 22 |
| 19 or older, still in school | 26 | 46 | 45 | 64 | 42 | 43 |
| **Gender** | | | | | | |
| Male | 57 | 49 | 49 | 53 | 43 | 49 |
| Female | 43 | 51 | 52 | 47 | 57 | 51 |
| **Age** | | | | | | |
| 18–34 | 12 | 24 | 26 | 28 | 39 | 29 |
| 35–54 | 31 | 29 | 35 | 30 | 32 | 32 |
| 55+ | 57 | 47 | 40 | 43 | 29 | 40 |
| **Ethnicity** | | | | | | |
| White | 97 | 94 | 88 | 94 | 90 | 92 |
| Non-white | 3 | 6 | 12 | 9 | 10 | 8 |

Note: Numbers in each column represent the weighted percentage of each party's 2014 European election voters who belong to a given group. For example, 57 per cent of Ukip voters are men and the same percentage are over 55 years old. By including the full sample, we can compare results to the population more generally.

Source: 2014–2017 British Election Study Internet Panel (Wave 2).

broader transformation of British society over recent decades. In only fifty years, the country has gone from a society where working-class voters with little education were the largest block in the electorate to one where the middle classes now dominate. Farage, however, had forged a particularly strong relationship with the working classes, whom he had been relentlessly appealing to in meetings like the one in Gateshead.

At the 2014 European elections, Ukip had been more likely than any other party to recruit support from people who worked in lower supervisory and skilled blue-collar jobs such as plumbers, electricians, and train-drivers, and those in routine jobs, such as labourers, cleaners, or drivers. It was also more likely than the Conservatives and Liberal Democrats, and just as likely as Labour, to have drawn support from people who worked in semi-routine jobs, such as bus drivers and shop assistants. While Ukip drew a large share of its support from people in more secure middle-class and professional jobs, it had a larger share of voters in its electorate from the lower social classes than Miliband, and significantly more than Cameron or Clegg. The party was also slightly more likely than the other parties to have drawn support from the more Conservative-leaning self-employed small-business owners and those who worked in lower supervisory and technical occupations. It was not a purely working-class revolt, therefore. Rather, Ukip tended to be more likely than the other parties to draw its votes from the more financially insecure working class, the lower middle class, and the self-employed—the same social groups that have fuelled many other radical-right revolts in Europe.

What was the political history of Ukip voters? Farage had long vented his frustration with the popular stereotype of his party as merely a second home for the disillusioned Conservatives who had been alienated by Cameron's more centrist appeals. He had long believed that his electorate was filled with people who had been recruited from across the spectrum and who had diverse political backgrounds. One way of exploring whether he was right is to look at how his supporters in 2014 had voted in past elections. Figure 5.1 shows their past loyalty. There is no doubt that many were disillusioned former Conservatives whose defections were raising problems for Cameron. In 2010, around one in two of those who would later defect to Farage had voted for the Conservatives. Moreover, if we look at how these defectors voted at an earlier election, in 2005, then we can see how three in four were *long-term* Conservative loyalists. Clearly, disillusioned Tories were an important source of strength for Farage. But the story does not end there.

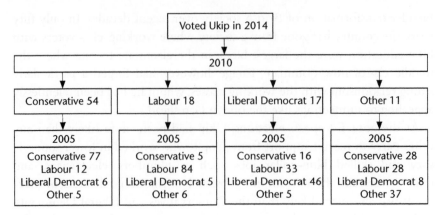

**Figure 5.1.** Vote choice of 2014 Ukip supporters in the 2010 and 2005 general elections

Source: 2014–2017 British Election Study Internet Panel (Wave 2).

There is far more churn among Ukip's base of support than is often acknowledged. In 2014, disaffected 2010 Conservative voters represented Farage's main source of support. But, at the same time, almost half of this support came from people who had *not* voted for the Conservative Party in 2010.[4] Ukip certainly picked up fewer voters from Miliband and Clegg than from Cameron, but the numbers are far from insignificant—more than one in three of those who helped Farage to cause his earthquake in 2014 had previously voted for Labour or the Liberal Democrats in 2010.

There were also interesting differences in the patterns of these defections. While Labour lost far fewer of its 2010 voters to Ukip than the Conservatives, more of the defectors from Labour to Ukip were *long-term* Labour voters. Of the 2010 Labour voters who switched to Ukip at the European elections, 84 per cent had voted for Labour in 2005. While they were less prominent in Ukip's electorate, these long-term Labour loyalists were slightly more likely than Conservative loyalists to defect. The opposite is true for the Liberal Democrats—of those who defected to Ukip, only one in two had been voting for his or her party over the longer term and so was unlikely to feel strongly attached to Clegg and his party.

It is worth noting that a significant number of the Conservative voters who defected to Ukip were *not* tribal Tories. Of those who voted Conservative in 2010 and then switched to Farage four years later, one-quarter had supported a different party in 2005. Almost one in eight who, based on their vote in 2010, might have been called 'Conservative defectors' had actually voted for Labour in the past. They had followed an interesting path to Ukip. They were people who tended to be working class, hostile towards immigration, and opposed to the EU, who had voted for Labour in the past and then switched to the Conservatives in 2010. Only in 2014, after this walk around the landscape, did they vote for Ukip.[5] Meanwhile, one in five of those who had voted for Ukip at the European elections had defected directly from Labour. By the time of its earthquake, one year before the 2015 election, Ukip was drawing most of its votes from disillusioned Conservatives but was also appealing to current and former Labour voters and disgruntled Liberal Democrats, some of whom had been switching around for some time.

These movements were not lost on Labour's strategists, who were well aware of the fact that, after thirteen years in power, their party had lost many of its traditional working-class voters. This had been clear in their internal research. 'You could see', said one of Miliband's most senior advisers, 'that the voters who had stuck with Labour saw it as the best of all evils rather than because of a deep conviction that Labour was going to do good things'. And, of those who had left, it was clear that one issue had played a particularly important role. 'They were chiefly concerned about immigration,' he continued. 'But there was also a heavy dose of anti-politics, a real antipathy towards the way the country was run. It was about elites and the poor, a sense that everyone feels that they've been ripped off.'

While Labour's research suggested that it had lost a large number of its traditional voters over immigration, it also indicated that lingering angst over how the party had handled the issue while in government was now also stalling its comeback. Others who had been crunching the numbers for Labour found that immigration was a bigger reason for doubting Labour than its approach to public spending. James Morris, who examined polling data for the party, consistently found that three-fifths of all voters were seriously concerned that Labour would be too soft on immigration—the same proportion who distrusted the party on the economy. Among voters who were considering Labour, concerns about how the party would handle immigration often ranked as their top reason for doubting the party.

And there was no doubt that immigration was at the core of Farage's appeal. In 2014, the British Election Study had asked voters to identify the single most important issue facing Britain. Among *all* voters, the top two issues were the economy and immigration. But, whereas supporters of the

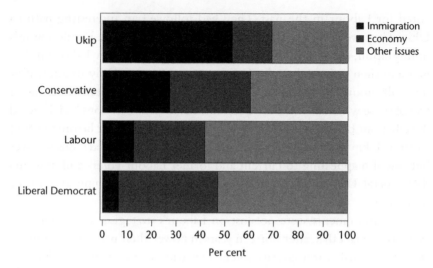

**Figure 5.2.** Most important issue facing Britain by party support, 2014
*Source*: 2014–2017 British Election Study Internet Panel (Wave 1).

other parties ranked the economy as their chief concern, those who were about to vote for Ukip put immigration ahead of everything. More than half of them, 53 per cent, saw it as the top issue. This was twice as high as the figure among Conservatives, revealing how Farage was winning over voters who felt intensely concerned about migration into Britain and how this was seen to be changing the country (see Figure 5.2).

Some in the Labour Party drew a straight line from these disaffected voters to events that had taken place long before the rise of Farage. Specifically, they pointed to how Tony Blair and New Labour had defeated the Conservative Party in 2005, when it was under the leadership of Michael Howard. 'For me,' said Miliband's senior adviser, 'that was the seed of what was to come with Ukip. That was when immigration first surged. The Tories went after public concerns with the poster "are you thinking what we are thinking?" Our strategy [in 2005] was to disable that campaign by basically calling it racist.' But New Labour's decision to prioritize political strategy over engagement with public anxiety about the actual, underlying issue would later be seen by some in Miliband's camp as having fuelled the growing disconnect between Labour, the working class, and immigration.

It had some electoral success but it also did two things. It set a tone for Labour for the next five years whereby the party did not feel that it should address immigration.

People thought we could win on immigration without addressing people's concerns about the issue. Second, it sent a clear signal to these voters that when they talked about immigration Labour thought they were racist. Those two things amplified the divide between Labour and its working-class support.

Five years later, against the backdrop of rising immigration, the perceived failure of the Labour Party to speak authentically to public discontent over immigration was then symbolically underlined, when Gordon Brown met Gillian Duffy, a lifelong Labour voter. Not realizing that he was being recorded, Brown appeared to dismiss Duffy's concerns over the free movement of EU migrant workers as bigotry and moved swiftly on.

The truth, however, was that Labour's problem could be traced back even further than 2005. As academic Geoff Evans at the University of Oxford had shown, traditional Labour voters had actually been moving away from the party since the 1990s, ever since it had joined the so-called liberal consensus on Europe and immigration. Whereas, in the 1970s, Labour had once been Eurosceptic, its new-found support for Britain's EU membership and liberal stance on immigration had begun to erode its appeal among traditional blue-collar Labour voters who did not share the outlook of Tony Blair and other Labour elites. 'In brief,' said Evans, 'the damage to Labour's core support had already been done by new Labour's focus on a pro-middle-class, pro-EU and, as it eventually turned out, pro-immigration agenda, before the arrival of UKIP as a plausible electoral choice in the years following the 2010 election'.[6] Other research added to this picture, showing how, increasingly, many working-class voters who had once loyally turned out for Labour had lost faith in the party and politics more generally. Whereas, in 2010, some of these disillusioned voters decided to switch to the Conservatives, others simply stopped turning out altogether. This loss of faith and the erosion of the left's traditional base would soon provide an opening for Farage, leaving a reservoir of disgruntled people who had once voted for Labour.[7]

In 2010, and after defeating his brother for the Labour leadership, Ed Miliband sought to revise Labour's position on immigration. 'David's line on immigration was New Labour,' reflected one insider. 'You know, "This is globalization so suck it up". But Ed was different. He made a point from the start by saying it was not prejudiced to worry about immigration.' From here on, and with his eyes fixed on returning Labour to power, Ed Miliband stressed how Labour had got things wrong on immigration, such as by not introducing transitional controls on EU migrant workers. He talked of

introducing stronger border controls and tougher measures on illegal immigration, enforcing the minimum wage to prevent businesses from using
cheaper workers from overseas, banning agencies that recruited only from
abroad, and making it more difficult for migrants to send benefits overseas.
While warning Labour that its working-class base should not be dismissed
as a 'core vote' and taken for granted, he also tried to address immigration
directly. Labour, he warned, had 'never had an answer for the people who
were worried about it'. He took a swipe at a tendency to smother these
identity-related anxieties in praise for globalization—'because it is a good
answer for economists but it is no answer for the people of Britain'.[8]

But, while Miliband tried to present a more empathetic response, some
of his advisers would later point to what they saw as a strategic blunder that
prevented him from closing down the space that would eventually be filled
by Farage, who was already starting to merge immigration with Europe. 'We
failed to land that major shift in the Labour position before Ukip went from
being a mass Europe party into being a mass immigration party,' said Morris.
'Our position was right but nobody really knew that we had changed the
position.' Labour's inability to land this clear shift was, in the eyes of people
like Morris, because of long-standing tensions inside the party over how to
handle this polarizing issue.

While there was a recognition that immigration was important, there was
a counter-view that, by talking tough on the issue, as Cameron and Farage
were now doing, Labour risked being seen as part of the right-wing response
and sparking a potentially damaging internal debate about the moral legitimacy of making such a move. It was a point that was raised by one senior
Labour insider.

Some in Ed's team recoiled when they realized they would need to make immigration central to the party's communications to show that the change in position
was authentic. They got the electoral argument for doing it, but they could not
face years of arguing that immigration was a central challenge facing the country
when they felt that, substantively, there were other bigger issues to deal with. They
didn't want political strategy to get in the way of focusing on what *they* believed
mattered more.

Another one of Miliband's senior advisers similarly observed how the
attempt to reposition Labour on an issue that was generating considerable
concern among its traditional base had been continually undermined by
internal tensions.

This led to the awkward compromise of getting into the right position but not really telling anyone about it. Right from the start there was a good understanding of the importance of immigration but a failure to do something about it. That created space for Ukip. Labour's reticence to sell its new position early on is for me the strategic mistake that allowed all of this to happen.

Whether a different narrative on immigration would ever have enabled Labour to win back its traditional voters is debatable. But what was undeniable was that, during the 2010–15 parliament, some of its lost voters were on the move, and their desertion was not lost on Labour insiders. 'By 2013 they were starting to be corralled around Ukip, which effectively came along and said "this is our space now". Then we found that attacking them [Ukip] on immigration was not helpful. It sounded like we were pro-immigration.'

But other aspects of Britain's immigration debate were also creating room for Farage. When both Labour and the Conservatives tried to address public anxieties about immigration, their narratives were often one-dimensional, focused narrowly on the contribution that migrants made to the British economy. Talk about immigration was often couched in a dry language that played down or completely avoided people's concerns about what they saw as broader challenges to national identity, culture, and their ways of life. This was especially true on the centre-left, where immigration has traditionally been viewed in terms of social class. 'Eastern European immigration', said Miliband, 'is a class issue because it increases competition for jobs, particularly those at lower wages'. The reluctance to move beyond this economic territory and address public concerns about the perceived *cultural* effects of how Britain was changing was especially pronounced within Labour, which also had a tendency of ignoring the issue altogether. This had been clearly on display during the European elections. Labour's campaign, observed one of Miliband's own advisers, had deliberately 'talked about housing and random cost of living stuff but not immigration'.

Farage, meanwhile, was focusing on the issue relentlessly, often employing arguments about the claimed economic threat from immigration. 'I don't blame those people from Eastern Europe for coming here,' he would say.

We are not against any of those people. What we are against are a British political class who through open door migration into Britain have given our own workers wage deflation over the course of the last ten years and led to a doubling of youth unemployment in this country since 2004.

From one speech to the next, the Ukip leader would draw a straight line from the impact of immigration to Britain's economically disaffected left-behind voters who were struggling financially and lacked the resources to get ahead.

I accept that open door immigration and mass cheap labour is good for rich people because it means cheaper nannies and cheaper chauffeurs and cheaper gardeners. And it is good for very big businesses and it is good for big landowners because it keeps their wage bills down. But it has been a disaster for millions of ordinary decent families in this country and surely it is the primary duty of a British government to put the interests of our own people first.

He was also talking increasingly about wanting to introduce a points-based system to prioritize high-skilled migrants over the mainly low-skilled workers who were arriving from Central and Eastern Europe, an argument to which many voters were strongly receptive.

I think Australia have got the right kind of immigration system and the kind of one we could have. Look at how they manage it. You've got to be under 45. You've got to be qualified. You've got to have a skill and a trade to bring. And you're not allowed to go to Australia if you have a criminal record, which is odd in a way as in the old days it used to be a prerequisite.

There was no doubt that most of Farage's supporters agreed with him. Whereas almost half of the electorate, 46 per cent, thought that immigration was bad for the economy, the figure among Ukip voters was much higher, at 75 per cent. And, whereas 28 per cent of voters thought that migrants were a burden on the welfare state, among Ukip voters it was almost twice as high, at 54 per cent. But crucially he was not only tapping economic worries.

Across Europe, there is now a large body of research on what drives public opposition to immigration and the EU. It shows that perceived conflicts over intangible social constructs such as national identity, national values, and ways of life are just as important, if not more so, than worries about economic self-interest. One of the most influential studies tested the relative importance of these feelings of economic and cultural threat. It found that prompting people to think about perceived threats to their culture—that immigrants did not speak their language, or were not expected to fit in culturally—evoked far stronger opposition to immigration than similar cues about the economic impact of migrants.[9]

While he might not have read these studies, Farage was spending much of his time appealing to the same feelings of cultural insecurity that they suggested were among the most powerful drivers of public concerns over immigration. 'I think', he would say, 'British market towns and cities have become far more divided communities over the course of the last fifteen years than they were before.' He talked frequently about the need for migrants to learn English and adopt British values, empathizing with voters who felt anxious about how their cultural surroundings seemed to be changing at a quick pace. 'They're worried about primary-school places. They're worried about the fact that in every city and market town in this country we've effectively opened up sections of those towns and cities where people don't speak English.' Farage was frequently denounced as a racist, but he was also talking directly to those feelings of cultural insecurity that had been fuelling radical right politicians across the continent.

This disconnect on immigration was visible to strategists in the main parties. 'The easier part is the economic part about exploiting workers, public services, and access to the NHS,' said one of Labour's senior advisers. 'The hardest bit is the cultural bit, the lack of a clear sense of what English identity is. It means it is hard to be unambiguously for it.' For social democrats who primarily see the world in terms of economic equality, financial redistribution, and cosmopolitanism, Farage's narrative of cultural loss, abandonment, and threatened ways of life posed a particular dilemma. 'Talking about things like a two-year welfare cap was limited because it is economic and does not engage with the cultural concerns,' said another adviser. 'Labour does not have an answer to that but it does have a good economic answer.'

Because of its long tradition of anti-racism, many in Labour were instinctively reluctant to engage in these more diffuse debates about identity and patriotism. 'The root back into these voters', reflected one strategist, 'goes through English identity and decent nationalism. But that is the most challenging bit for Labour because of the iconography of the flag being associated by some with the far right BNP.' Others voiced a similar view, pointing to how Labour's reluctance to move into this debate over identity had left Miliband and his party with little room for manoeuvre. 'If you accept that Labour is not going to do a good job at engaging in cultural concerns because it is a cosmopolitan party, then you are left in the economic, public service, and efficacy of government area.'

That Ukip's supporters were just as concerned about the cultural as the economic effects of this rapid social change was also clear in the data. Their concerns were clearly not one dimensional. Overall, among *all* voters, there was strong concern about the perceived cultural effects. Almost 50 per cent

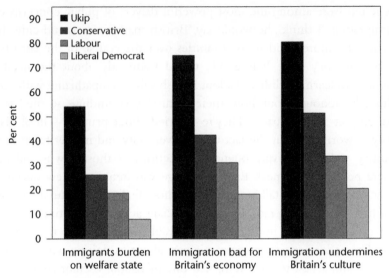

**Figure 5.3.** Attitudes towards immigration, 2014
*Source*: 2014–2017 British Election Study Internet Panel (Wave 2).

of the public thought that immigration undermined British culture. But among Ukip voters the figure was 81 per cent, even higher than the percentage of Ukip voters who thought that migrants were bad for the economy, or who saw them as a burden on the welfare state. In all these cases, the figures among Ukip voters were more than twenty points higher than their closest party, the Conservatives, and almost thirty points higher than the population at large. In fact, among Ukip's electorate, 48 per cent of them felt that immigration was bad for the economy *and* for Britain's culture, *and* that migrants were a burden on the welfare state. The next closest group was Conservative voters, but just 20 per cent of them expressed all three of these concerns (see Figure 5.3). By some margin, therefore, those who had switched their loyalty to Farage felt more concerned about this issue than all others in society.

Immigration was clearly not the only concern at the root of Ukip's appeal. Those who had turned to the party were also strongly Eurosceptic. It is not surprising to find that the people who had helped Farage to cause his earthquake in 2014 did not approve of Britain's EU membership. They were united by their strong dissatisfaction with the EU, their concerns about the scale of European integration, and their desire to keep Britain independent. When, in meetings in towns like Gateshead, Farage had called on Britain to leave the 'big club' in Brussels and become an independent

**Table 5.2.** Eurosceptic attitudes by 2014 party support

| Party | Britain should protect its independence | Unification 'gone too far' | Would vote to leave EU in a referendum? |
|---|---|---|---|
| Ukip | 90 | 86 | 93 |
| Conservative | 72 | 71 | 46 |
| Labour | 42 | 43 | 23 |
| Liberal Democrat | 29 | 39 | 9 |
| Non-voters | 59 | 58 | 45 |
| Full sample | 60 | 60 | 47 |

*Note*: Numbers in each column represent the weighted percentage of each party's supporters who indicated they agreed with the given statement.
*Source*: 2014–2017 British Election Study Internet Panel (Wave 2).

nation, building its economic future around trade-only deals with Europe and links with the Commonwealth, these voters would have strongly agreed. And so too would many Conservatives.

More than 90 per cent of those who turned out for Ukip at the European elections felt that European unification had 'gone too far'. The figure among Conservatives was 70 per cent, and among the public was 60 per cent—revealing how Britain is an instinctively sceptical nation when it comes to European integration. It was the same story when voters were asked whether or not Britain should protect its independence from the EU. More than 90 per cent of Ukip voters wanted to protect national sovereignty and independence (the remainder appear to have been motivated mainly by their dissatisfaction with Britain's political system). But only in Ukip and the Conservative Party were the Eurosceptics a dominant force. In both Labour and the Liberal Democrats they were a minority, outnumbered by those who felt more positive about the EU. And only in Ukip was there a large majority of people who would actually vote to pull Britain out of the EU, a point that we return to in the final chapter (see Table 5.2).

As Farage prepared for the 2015 general election, therefore, he had attracted followers who were driven mainly by intense concerns over immigration and Europe. But his followers also shared a number of other traits that are worth exploring. Many of them were far more likely than others in society to feel anxious about other issues—to feel that the protection of ethnic minorities, gay and lesbian people, and also women, had gone 'too far'. While the differences were less stark with regard to the protection of women, the percentage of Ukip's supporters who were dissatisfied with the

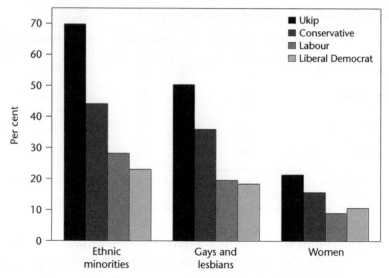

**Figure 5.4.** Protection of minority groups gone 'too far', 2014
Source: 2014–2017 British Election Study Internet Panel Survey (Waves 1–2).

protection of the other two groups further add to the picture of Ukip voters as feeling profoundly uneasy about the pace of social change in modern Britain (see Figure 5.4).

Pointing to such views, popular stereotypes often frame Ukip as a far-right party or present its voters as people who position themselves on the extreme right wing. But more of these voters actually identified themselves as being far more centrist or even left-leaning than we might expect. When asked to place themselves on the traditional 'left–right scale', 63 per cent of Ukip voters put themselves on the right wing of the continuum, lower than the percentage of Conservative voters who identify with the right wing. Moreover, more than one in three Ukip voters placed him or herself in the centre (22 per cent) or on the left (16 per cent) (see Figure 5.5). Other questions about ideology reveal a similar pattern.

British politics has long been organized around conflicts over the economy and the role of the state. Typically, those who identify with Labour favour higher taxation, the redistribution of wealth, and greater state intervention to encourage greater economic equality. Those who identify with conservatism, meanwhile, take a different view, favouring free markets, lower taxes, and a smaller state. This dividing line still exists today and was evident around the time of the European elections. Ed Miliband and Labour called for state regulation of electricity and gas prices, and showed an open distrust

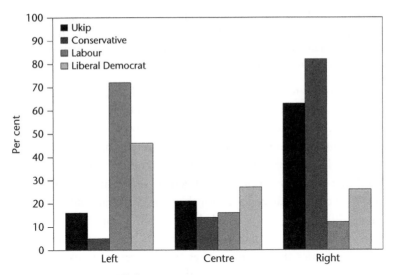

**Figure 5.5.** Left–right self-placement, 2014
*Source*: 2014–2017 British Election Study Internet Panel (Wave 2).

of big business, a desire for greater taxation of the rich, and using government and the state to help the financially disadvantaged in society. All this contrasts with the Conservatives, who have retained their historic faith in the power of the market and private enterprise. Many have seen Ukip as dividing the right and so its supporters must therefore fall on the Conservative side of this long-standing divide. Farage and his party, so the thinking goes, offer a stable for ultra-libertarian and Thatcherite voters who economically worship the free market, want to roll back the state, and embrace neo-liberalism. But, while some in Ukip's upper hierarchy do indeed hold these views, there was a big difference between the party's activists and voters.

That Farage had recruited support from the economically disaffected had certainly been noticed by the main parties. As one Labour insider reflected:

I think that Ukip supporters are economically, and in terms of public services, quite insecure about their position and future. Our challenge is to find ways that Labour can speak to that insecurity, to tell a story about that, which is partly about things like the economy like the minimum wage and public services like the NHS.

This underlines Labour's tendency to focus heavily on economic rather than cultural insecurity, although it also shed light on something else.

The other thing about the insecurity thing that is interesting is that it is a relative insecurity that amplifies it. They feel individually, and for their family, insecure *and* they think that both the top and bottom of society are not feeling that insecurity. You know, people on welfare are not feeling insecure and people in Starbucks are not paying their fair share of tax. So they feel anxiety but there is also a deep sense of unfairness that is attached to that anxiety.

When it comes to their economic outlook, Farage's followers actually looked more like Labour voters and the general public than diehard Conservatives. Almost eight in ten felt that big business takes advantage of ordinary people, and more than seven in ten felt that managers try to get the better of employees, that there is one law for the rich and another for the poor, and that ordinary people are not getting their fair share. Almost seven in ten also thought that privatization has gone too far, and that spending cuts in the NHS have also crossed the line. On all of these ideas Farage's followers looked more similar to Labour than Conservative voters. In fact, the survey indicates that in some cases the differences between Ukip and Conservative voters were more than thirty points. Those who turned to Farage tended to be more right wing than Labour but more left wing than Conservatives (see Table 5.3). This provides further evidence for how Ukip reflects a deeper divide in modern Britain—between the more financially secure and highly educated middle classes and the economically insecure, disaffected, and lower-income groups of voters who feel that society is not currently working for them.

There are two areas, however, where Ukip supporters were closer to their Tory counterparts—and these concern their attitudes to the idea of public spending cuts and redistributing income. Less than half of Ukip's electorate, 49 per cent, thought that public spending cuts had gone too far, while less than half, 45 per cent, backed the idea of income redistribution, the left's favoured method for trying to alleviate these disparities. Both of these figures are still between twenty and thirty points higher than those among Conservatives, underlining how these two groups of voters look at the economic world in very different ways. But they are also markedly lower than the figures among Labour voters, and the national average.

We can also see Farage's appeal to the economically disaffected when we probe people's past economic experiences and outlook as Britain moved towards the general election. Those who turned to Farage were among the most negative of all voters in 2014, often only a few points behind Labour voters. In the shadow of the European elections, 46 per cent said that their personal economic situation had worsened over the previous year and 41 per cent indicated that they expected this decline to continue over the next

Table 5.3. Left–right values by 2014 party support

| Left–right values | Ukip | Conservative | Labour | Liberal Democrat | Non-voters | Full sample |
|---|---|---|---|---|---|---|
| Big business takes advantage of ordinary people | 80 | 57 | 86 | 76 | 75 | 77 |
| There is one law for the rich and one for the poor | 75 | 42 | 86 | 65 | 71 | 71 |
| Management tries to get the better of employees | 73 | 52 | 79 | 59 | 68 | 69 |
| Ordinary working people do not get their fair share | 72 | 46 | 88 | 70 | 72 | 72 |
| Privatization has gone too far | 68 | 40 | 86 | 70 | 67 | 70 |
| Cuts to NHS have gone too far | 67 | 45 | 91 | 68 | 76 | 73 |
| Cuts to public spending have gone too far | 49 | 19 | 86 | 50 | 57 | 57 |
| Government should redistribute income | 45 | 25 | 74 | 59 | 50 | 53 |

*Note:* Numbers in each column represent the weighted percentage of each party's 2014 European election voters who indicated they agreed with the statement.

*Source:* 2014–2017 British Election Study Internet Panel (Waves 1 and 2).

year. Nearly one-third of the party's voters had a similar assessment of the situation in the country at large. Both Ukip and Labour were clearly attracting those who were not feeling—and did not expect to feel—Cameron's economic recovery (see Table 5.4).

A final area that is important to explore is the attitudes of these voters towards politics, an area that also emerges as a significant driver of Ukip support. Farage often pushed back against the argument that his party was a home for protestors. 'They are not voting for us just because they don't like the establishment as it is,' he would tell his party at conferences.

They are voting for us because the establishment has failed them, failed their families and failed their lives. They are voting for us and sticking with us because they believe that we are the party that most represents them in their lives, with their families, and with their thoughts, hopes and aspirations for the future. I think we are now in touch with a large segment of this country.

Previous books have already shown how Ukip has won over voters who have felt profoundly unhappy with how democracy is working in modern Britain—who feel that the government is not honest and trustworthy, that it is not treating them fairly, and that they do not have much political influence. Other researchers have added to this picture.

Around the time of the European elections, academics at the University of Southampton replicated research that had been carried out when Britain was at war, in 1944. The original poll asked voters their views about whether politicians were mainly out for themselves, their party, or the country. By asking the exact same question seventy years later they were able to explore the long-term trend. And there had been a clear shift. Overall, the percentage of voters who saw British politicians as 'out merely for themselves' had risen from 35 to 48 per cent, those who saw them as being 'out for their party' had risen from 22 to 30 per cent, while those who thought that politicians were out 'to do their best for the country' had fallen from 36 to 10 per cent. In other words, by 2014 only one in ten believed that his or her elected representatives were working to advance the interests of Britain. Aside from these findings, they also explored how disaffection with politics and politicians was driving Ukip's support. These voters, they concluded, 'are steadfastly negative about the political class'. The numbers were striking—74 per cent of Farage's followers believed that politicians were out for themselves, far higher than the figure for any other party and almost

Table 5.4. Economic situation 'getting worse' by 2014 party support

| Pessimistic economic evaluations | Ukip | Conservative | Labour | Liberal Democrat | Non-voters | Full sample |
|---|---|---|---|---|---|---|
| *Past twelve months* | | | | | | |
| Financial situation of your household | 46 | 22 | 51 | 32 | 38 | 41 |
| General economic situation in this country | 31 | 8 | 46 | 17 | 28 | 29 |
| *Next twelve months* | | | | | | |
| Financial situation of your household | 41 | 15 | 49 | 23 | 33 | 35 |
| General economic situation in this country | 30 | 8 | 46 | 18 | 30 | 30 |

*Note:* Numbers in each column represent the weighted percentage of each party's 2014 European election voters who said the economic situation had become/was going to get 'a lot worse' or 'a little worse'.

*Source:* 2014–2017 British Election Study Internet Panel (Wave 2).

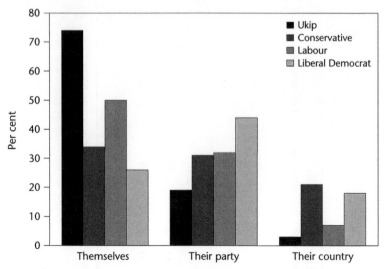

**Figure 5.6.** 'Do you think that British politicians are out merely for themselves, for their party, or to do their best for their country?'
*Source:* YouGov/University of Southampton.

thirty points higher than the average (see Figure 5.6). These views were also unambiguous and intense. Fewer than one in twenty Ukip supporters felt that he or she did not know what to think about the question, compared to more than one in ten of all respondents. 'They *know* that establishment politicians are serving themselves or their parties not the country,' observed the researchers.

There is no doubt that political dissatisfaction is central to explaining the rise of Ukip, and similar parties across Europe. That Ukip's rise is not simply about economic insecurity but encompasses a deeper and multifaceted sense of alienation and isolation from Britain's political and social mainstream is reflected in other work. Academic Eric Kaufmann, for example, found that support for Farage has been concentrated most strongly among voters who are less trusting of their neighbours, feel less strongly attached to their local communities, and express higher levels of anxiety about rising ethnic diversity in their neighbouring areas—traits that were also important to explaining support for other anti-establishment parties in Britain, like the BNP.[10]

We can add to this picture by comparing the views of voters across a wider range of questions, including those who did not vote at the European elections. On the one hand, this suggests that Ukip voters were certainly the

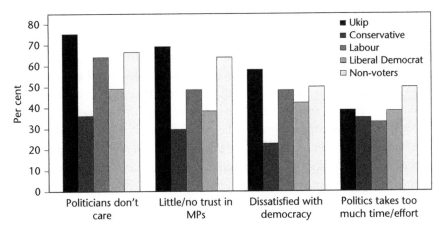

**Figure 5.7.** Political dissatisfaction and disengagement, 2014
*Source*: 2014–2017 British Election Study Internet Panel (Wave 2).

most dissatisfied with politics. Three in four did not believe that politicians listen to the people, almost seven in ten indicated that they have little or no trust in MPs, and almost six in ten were dissatisfied with the way that democracy is working. By including those who abstained from voting, we can see how Ukip supporters are actually closer to these non-voters than to supporters of the other parties, although Labour voters also feel very dissatisfied. Crucially, however, those who turned to Ukip are not completely disengaged from politics. As shown in Figure 5.7, most actually rejected the idea that it takes too much time or effort to participate in politics, and they were closer to supporters of the other parties than to abstainers.

The concerns of Ukip voters in 2014, then, were coherent and intense—they were motivated strongly by their scepticism towards European integration, and by their desire to see Britain leave the EU and return to being an independent nation, were strongly concerned about immigration, shared an intense anxiety about its cultural as well as its economic effects, and were profoundly dissatisfied with the political status quo. But, at the same time, they were not as distinctive as we might expect in terms of how they saw themselves on the ideological landscape, how they thought about economic and social equality, and how they thought about public spending and redistribution.

This story is confirmed in our more complex statistical analysis.[11] People who are white, older, male, have no qualifications, and work in more insecure routine or manual jobs were significantly more likely to have switched to Ukip ahead of the 2015 general election. Of all these characteristics, education and age were the strongest predictors of whether somebody had voted for Ukip. People between the ages of 55 and 64 years were three times more likely to support Ukip than those younger than 24 years old. And people who had left school at 16 were nearly twice as likely to have voted for Ukip than those who had stayed in school beyond their eighteenth birthday.

But, chiefly, it is attitudes that have driven this vote—how people feel about Europe and immigration are the strongest predictors of whether they defected to Ukip ahead of the 2015 general election, far outweighing the effects of their backgrounds and other characteristics. Eurosceptics who were also intensely opposed to immigration were eleven times more likely to support Ukip than someone who was favourable or neutral to Europe and not particularly worried about immigration. Eurosceptics who were not heavily anti-immigration were nearly five times more likely to vote for Ukip than somebody who was not particularly animated by concerns about European integration or immigration. Finally, those who expressed high levels of dissatisfaction with politics and the political system—who were not satisfied with democracy, did not trust their representatives, and did not think that politicians listen to what people think—overwhelmingly gravitated towards Ukip. They were nearly three times more likely to vote for the party than those who were more satisfied with politics. But, while Farage had mobilized distinctive followers, there remained a key question—were they going to stay with him until the general election?

In the aftermath of the 2014 European elections the widespread assumption was that Ukip would fall off the radar. Numerous journalists, commentators, and politicians subscribed to the idea. Some had already been dismissive of its staying power. 'Done with, finished, a footnote,' said journalist John Rentoul, a few weeks before the contest.

There will be a lot of fizz, smoke and carousel music, but in three weeks' time the Great Ukip Flying Circus will be in decline. Big social trends are against it. The economy is looking up, and people mind less about free movement of workers when they feel better off. Scepticism about the EU has ebbed.

The view was soon conventional wisdom. 'The Ukip threat', noted another commentator, 'doesn't exist. It's over. Farage's race is run. There will be lots of excitement. Lots of talk of revolutions and earthquakes. And then people's thoughts will turn away from registering a protest to electing a government.' Others in the corridors of power shared the same view. Craig

Oliver, Cameron's head of communications, reportedly compared Conservative voters who had defected to Farage to bridegrooms who were misbehaving on their stag night—who were looking for a 'last bit of fun' before settling down and returning to the party ahead of the general election. 'Ukip's so-called "political earthquake"', claimed the *Mirror*, 'is petering out with a whimper'. 'I don't think their appeal is one that is instinctively likely to continue,' said former prime minister John Major.[12]

The assumption was driven by the belief that Ukip had not attracted a group of loyalists, that it was a flash-in-the-pan party that would fall out of the sky as quickly as it had shot up. 'This political earthquake', noted journalist Tim Wigmore, 'may yet do no more than mildly shake the cutlery'. But, as Wigmore continued, this might not actually be the case. 'Farage will hope that the real legacy of this campaign is more than just a fleeting historical triumph for Ukip but the creation of a distinct brand of Ukip voters.'[13] It was also true that, ahead of the general election, Farage appeared to have recruited two distinct groups of voters—one that appeared far more loyal, and another that seemed markedly less so.

Ukip loyalists were people who had supported the party at the European elections and then said that they would stay with it in 2015. Defectors, on the other hand, were people who had voted for Ukip at the European elections but once it was over said they would switch to another party. These people were not identical. While they were similar in terms of their backgrounds, those who were planning to stay loyal to Farage were more strongly concerned about immigration and more dissatisfied with mainstream politics. In fact, Ukip supporters who expressed the highest levels of dissatisfaction with politics were almost twice as likely as people who did not feel dissatisfied to say that they would stay loyal to Ukip in 2015. Political dissatisfaction emerges as the strongest predictor of whether somebody was planning to stay committed to Farage at the general election.

But, while he had mobilized a hard core of politically dissatisfied voters who felt anxious over immigration, the Ukip leader also faced some risks. Figure 5.8 shows the percentages of each group of voters who were planning to stay loyal to their chosen party, or defect. Farage might have mobilized more than four million voters, but he now had lower rates of loyalty than his rivals. While around one in two of his voters was planning to stay with Ukip in 2015, both the Conservatives and Labour had retention rates of over 90 per cent, while the SNP was not far behind. Even two in three

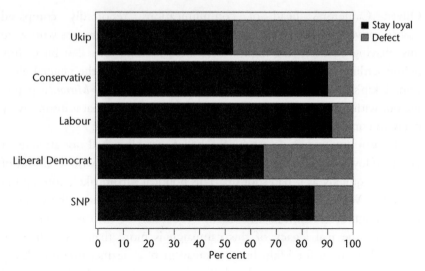

**Figure 5.8.** European election voters looking ahead to 2015
*Source*: 2014–2017 British Election Study Internet Panel (Wave 2).

Liberal Democrats said that they were planning to remain with their party until the bitter end. But Ukip's lower number suggested that problems might lay ahead.

Given that almost half of his followers were planning to defect, where were they planning to defect to? The largest number, by far, were planning to leave for the Conservatives. Almost one in four, or 23 per cent, said that he or should would return to Cameron's party in 2015. This makes sense, given that Ukip had picked up many Conservative defectors. A smaller percentage, 10 per cent, planned to defect to Labour. This means that between loyalists and the defectors we can account for the future choices of three-quarters of Ukip's voters at the European elections. The remaining defectors were undecided or intended to support other parties. This suggested that, while many Ukip voters felt a close connection to the party, other concerns might yet come into play when these voters were deciding how to vote. That being said, even if Ukip kept only half of its European election voters, this would still potentially put the party in a strong position in 2015. Assuming that the party picked up no extra voters between elections and that voters' intentions remained unchanged, this level of loyalty would mean that it could still expect to receive roughly 15 per cent of the national vote.[14]

A few weeks after the European elections, Farage was sitting alone in his office. He felt low. He had just led Ukip to its first election victory but he was far from jubilant. He knew what the success meant. He would now have to lead the party into the general election. While he relished the challenge of trying to make political history, he was also deeply apprehensive. 'I have got grave reservations about the next twelve months,' he said, perhaps thinking about the fact that he had never before led Ukip into a general election. 'I've been doing this job for seven days a week and fifteen years. You could say, "well you have got there now". Ok I have got there. But now that I am here I am not sure that I like it very much.' Farage was staring out of the window. 'It's not that I don't think that we can do it politically. I just think it's going to be hell. Life is going to be very miserable.'

Farage was certainly facing a difficult campaign. Never before had Ukip managed to hold onto its support at the European elections, and there was no guarantee that it could now. Moreover, as the general election rapidly approached, a significant number of his voters were already flirting with the idea of switching back to the main parties, most likely the Conservatives. If Farage was to keep them on board, then he would need to find ways to sustain his party's momentum. But it was not all doom and gloom for the Ukip leader. As we have seen, by the time of the general election campaign Farage had successfully mobilized a distinctive electorate of typically older, white, and economically struggling voters, who were more likely to be drawn from the working class and lower middle class. They also tended to be concentrated in particular parts of the country, where there was little affluence, ethnic diversity, and social mobility. And they were people who had responded positively to Farage's core-vote strategy—who often shared his fundamental concerns. They wanted passionately to leave the EU, to see Britain as an independent nation, and to end mass immigration, and they loathed politics in Westminster. They perhaps felt as though a world that they once knew was slipping away, and had turned to Farage as somebody who was offering them an opportunity to voice their grievances, and to express their support for a national identity that they cherished and for beliefs that they rarely saw expressed anywhere else in British media and politics. The question now was whether Farage could turn all this into a serious breakthrough at a general election.

# 6

# Sustaining Momentum

If Ukip was to take its revolt into Westminster, then it would have to change. Winning seats in the European Parliament under proportional representation was one thing, but winning seats in the House of Commons under first-past-the-post was a different prospect altogether. Farage was familiar with the challenge. In the past, he had twice watched Ukip poll strongly at European elections only then to run out of steam. In 2004 the party had won more than 16 per cent of the vote, but by the general election the next year this had fallen to 2 per cent. In 2009 it had polled more than 16 per cent at the European elections, but then, in 2010, this support had crashed to 3 per cent. The cycle had presented a difficult conclusion. As the attention of voters and journalists had drifted back to general elections, Ukip's support had collapsed. The party had no staying power.

But in the summer of 2014, Farage might have felt that there was more room for optimism. Aware of his party's weaknesses, he was pessimistic about the campaign to come. But he also knew that something had changed. Ukip had won a nationwide election, and both the party and its leader were now truly household names. Farage was finding it impossible to walk around or visit his favourite pubs without being stopped for people to take photographs or, sometimes, being harassed. Along the way, he had also forged what felt like a strong relationship with a section of the electorate—struggling, politically dissatisfied, older Britons who felt anxious about immigration and loathed the EU. There was no guarantee that they would stay loyal, but their votes had fuelled Ukip's confidence, so much so that the party was now demanding to have 'major' party status and threatening to sue if Farage was not included in debates between the main party leaders ahead of the general election. In a letter to the UK broadcasting watchdog Ofcom, Patrick O'Flynn argued that it was now 'unthinkable' to continue to regard Ukip as 'just as another minor party'.

One of the first opportunities to test whether Ukip could sustain its revolt under first-past-the-post arrived in the shadow of the European elections. A parliamentary by-election had been called in the market town of Newark, in Nottinghamshire. It had been triggered after the Conservative MP, Patrick Mercer, had resigned after being caught accepting money for lobbying. Both the scandal and the timing of the battle, coming shortly after Ukip's earthquake, fuelled speculation that Farage himself might stand. But Newark was far from ideal territory for his party. It looked nothing like the left-behind communities that had become the bedrock of Ukip's support. Newark was a fairly middle-of-the-road, rural seat that was neither especially deprived nor affluent. Its voters were more secure, middle class, and younger than Ukip's typical supporters. While the area was 97 per cent white, more than one in four of its residents had advanced qualifications and around one in three worked in professional and managerial jobs. That the local people were not especially receptive to Ukip's politics had already become clear. Only a few weeks earlier, in the European elections, they had given Ukip a lower level of support than their surrounding areas.[1] Nor did the seat look politically vulnerable. While Cameron and his party were trying to contain a scandal, they were also defending a large majority of more than 16,000 votes and, with only one exception, had won Newark at every election since 1979. But there was another fundamental problem, and one that would continually undermine its quest to break through—when it came to first-past-the-post elections, Ukip did not know how to campaign.

The weakness had been concealed by Ukip's success at the European elections. That campaign had been about making as much noise as possible, attracting voters through an 'air war', and exploiting a proportional electoral system. But constituency campaigns that took place under first-past-the-post demanded an altogether different approach. It was winner-takes-all. They were about fighting a ground war, street-to-street, going door-to-door, and mobilizing support in the face of sustained opposition from the other parties. To win, parties needed to work hard, target their voters, and, carefully, cultivate concentrated support.

Ukip's traditional approach to campaigns had been like that of the part-time athlete who represented a small nation at the Olympics. After turning up, looking pleased with itself, and hoping for the best, the party would be left in the dust by its far more professional competitors. There was little training beforehand and little reflection afterwards about what had gone wrong. This weakness was a by-product of history. Ukip had not been founded to fight elections. It had been born into a room full of amateurs and academics who saw themselves as constitutional experts, not electoral campaigners. The original plan had been to launch a pressure group that would influence other parties through debate and detailed policy documents, not to build a disciplined fighting force that could take seats off the main parties and use electoral victories to extract concessions. These origins mattered because now, as the party started to fight elections, few if any of its activists knew how to win them.

Farage might have seen himself as a cavalry officer, leading his troops from the front, but few of his foot soldiers had been trained. Ukip's veterans, who had loyally followed the party from one election disaster to the next, even took pride in their amateur approach. Seen through their eyes, the tactics that the main parties used to win elections represented everything that was wrong with modern politics—the way that they carefully canvassed a constituency to identify and target their voters, their ruthless mobilization of postal votes, their endless use of constituency polls and focus groups to develop tailored messages for swing voters, and their professional 'get-out-the-vote' operations, where busloads of activists would descend onto a seat to get voters out of their armchairs and into polling stations. If this was how elections were fought and won, thought the veterans, then they did not want to play the game. This pushed Ukip down a different road.

'Our typical plan', recalled one, 'was to turn up, make lots of noise, release a few balloons, give out a few leaflets and go home, thinking we'd be lucky if we saved our deposit. In most cases we didn't.' The results were almost always embarrassing. Between its birth in 1993 and the 2010 general election, Ukip had thrown itself at thirty-five by-elections. But it had averaged 2.3 per cent of the vote and lost its deposits by failing to reach 5 per cent in thirty-one of them. In nine, it failed to attract 1 per cent. At one election in Uxbridge, the party won only thirty-nine votes and finished behind the Monster Raving Loonies.[2]

The inexperienced veterans even struggled with the most basic procedures. As late as 2012, their amateurism had been laid bare when they filed incorrect nomination papers for elections in London. After failing to note limitations on the word length, their candidates had appeared on the ballot under 'Fresh Choice for London'. Ukip, the name of the party, was nowhere to be seen. 'It is a lesson hard learned,' sighed Farage, who could barely disguise his frustration with his veterans. But, while grappling with these problems, he had spotted an opportunity. If the party *could* get its act together, then Ukip was well positioned to take advantage of some broader changes in English politics, especially in the Labour heartlands.

In many areas where Labour was strong it had held power for generations. With its roots in a strong and tribal relationship with industrial Britain, the Labour Party's strength had been cemented by Thatcherism, which had cast a long shadow over these areas. Voting Tory was often not an option. Blue-collar voters who held socially conservative views on immigration or Europe would often stay with Labour or abstain, rather than throw in their lot with the Conservatives. When, during the New Labour era, some of these voters became disillusioned with Blair, they had turned to the Liberal Democrats, who were often seen as the most viable opposition in Labour seats.[3] By 2010, Clegg and his party had become the second force in no less than 243 seats, many of which were held by Labour. This left many Conservative associations moribund and hollow vessels, lacking the activists, voters, or will to mount a comeback.

When, after the 2010 general election, the Liberal Democrats joined the Conservatives in the Coalition, Ukip was handed an opportunity to reshuffle the opposition and, if it moved quickly, to emerge as the second force in these seats. Despite its internal weaknesses, the party was now being helped by broader trends, and its ability to supplant the governing parties in Labour seats had become increasingly clear. Between January 2011 and February 2014, there were fifteen by-elections, and all but two were in Labour seats where there were often large numbers of older, blue-collar voters.[4] This time, Ukip averaged a more respectable 12.3 per cent of the vote and finished second in six of the seats, five of which were held by Labour.

As Ukip fought its way through the succession of by-elections, from Oldham East and Saddleworth to Wythenshawe and Sale East, it began to consolidate support not just from disaffected Tories but from a wider coalition of voters. It was now emerging as the main opposition to the winning party, which was often Labour. One example was the seat of Barnsley Central, where, since the 1980s, support for Labour and turnout more generally had declined. Whereas in earlier years Labour could count on more than 65 per cent of the vote, by 2010 the figure had fallen by almost twenty points. At a by-election in 2011 Labour had easily retained the seat. But Ukip was now offering a new home for voters who opposed Labour. While its support increased by almost eight points, support for the Liberal Democrats and Conservatives slumped, as did support for the far-right BNP. Farage and his party were still almost fifty points behind Labour, but they had displaced the Liberal Democrats as the second force and could claim to be laying a stronger foundation (see Table 6.1). It was a sign of things to come.

Table 6.1. Party support at parliamentary by-elections, 2011–2014

| Constituency | Ukip | Conservative | Labour | Liberal Democrat | Other radical right |
|---|---|---|---|---|---|
| Oldham East and Saddleworth (Jan. 2011), Labour Held (%) | 5.8 | 12.8 | 42.1 | 31.9 | 4.9 |
| *Change since 2010* | +1.9 | −13.6 | +10.2 | +0.3 | −1.2 |
| Barnsley Central (Mar. 2011), Labour held (%) | 12.2 | 8.3 | 60.8 | 4.2 | 8.2 |
| *Change since 2010* | +7.5 | −9.0 | +13.5 | −13.1 | −2.9 |
| Leicester South (May 2011), Labour held (%) | 2.9 | 15.1 | 57.8 | 22.5 | — |
| *Change since 2010* | +1.4 | −6.3 | +12.2 | −4.4 | — |
| Feltham and Heston (Dec. 2011), Labour held (%) | 5.5 | 27.7 | 54.4 | 5.9 | 3.7 |
| *Change since 2010* | +3.5 | −6.3 | +10.8 | −7.8 | −1.2 |
| Cardiff South and Penarth, Labour held (%) | 6.1 | 19.9 | 47.3 | 10.8 | — |
| *Change since 2010* | +3.5 | −8.4 | +8.4 | −11.5 | — |
| Corby (Nov. 2012), Conservative held (%) | 14.3 | 26.6 | 48.4 | 5.0 | 2.9 |
| *Change since 2010* | +14.3 | −15.6 | +9.8 | −9.5 | −3.0 |
| Manchester Central (Nov. 2012), Labour held (%) | 4.5 | 4.5 | 69.1 | 9.4 | 3.0 |
| *Change since 2010* | +3.0 | −7.3 | +16.4 | −17.2 | −1.1 |
| Croydon North (Nov. 2012), Labour held (%) | 5.7 | 16.8 | 64.7 | 3.5 | 0.7 |
| *Change since 2010* | +4.0 | −7.3 | +8.7 | −10.5 | — |

| | | | | | |
|---|---|---|---|---|---|
| Middlesbrough (Nov. 2012), Labour held (%) | 11.8 | 6.3 | 60.5 | 9.9 | 1.9 |
| *Change since 2010* | +8.1 | −12.5 | 14.6 | −10.0 | −3.9 |
| Rotherham (Nov. 2012), Labour held (%) | 21.7 | 5.4 | 46.5 | 2.1 | 11.7 |
| *Change since 2010* | +15.8 | −11.4 | 1.8 | −13.9 | −2.0 |
| Eastleigh (Feb. 2013), Liberal Democrat held (%) | 27.8 | 25.4 | 9.8 | 32.1 | 0.1 |
| *Change since 2010* | +24.2 | −13.9 | +0.2 | −14.4 | −0.3 |
| South Shields (May 2013), Labour held (%) | 24.2 | 11.5 | 50.4 | 1.4 | 2.9 |
| *Change since 2010* | +24.2 | −10.1 | −1.6 | −12.8 | −3.6 |
| Wythenshawe and Sale East (Feb. 2014), Labour held (%) | 18 | 14.5 | 55.3 | 4.9 | 3.0 |
| *Change since 2010* | +14.5 | −11.0 | +11.2 | −17.4 | −0.9 |

*Notes:* Other radical-right parties refer to the British National Party (BNP), English Democrats, or National Front (NF). We also exclude by-elections in Scotland and Bradford West, owing to the unique circumstances surrounding Respect's success.

*Source:* By-elections 2010–15 (June 2015). House of Commons Library, Research Briefing SN05833.

Three years later, the party arrived in Wythenshawe and Sale East. By this time, and after a string of by-elections, Ukip had established itself as the main opposition in five seats. Labour again retained the seat, but Ukip had benefited from a sharp decline in support for the other parties and leap-frogged into second. As in other seats, disparate strands of opposition to Labour had begun to consolidate behind Ukip and its working-class candidate, John Bickley. The result allowed Farage to claim, once again, that the Tories were a 'dying brand' in the north and that Ukip was on its way to becoming the main opposition in Labour heartlands. In fact, across all these battles in Labour seats both the Liberal Democrats and the Conservatives, on average, saw their support fall by nine points while Ukip's jumped by eight. That the Conservatives had a problem had also been reflected in the European elections, when Ukip had pushed them into third across every northern region, fuelling hopes among Farage and his team that they could replace the centre-right in areas where memories of Thatcherism remained vivid. But these early advances also arguably owed more to the unique by-election context than to any increased professionalism on the part of Ukip. While the party was trying harder, its campaigns remained amateur. And this was nowhere more evident than in Newark, where the Conservatives were determined to stop Farage.

While Cameron and his team had been forced to accept an embarrassing defeat in the European elections, they now looked determined to crush the revolt once and for all. They flooded Newark, sending close to 300 MPs, many of whom were ordered to visit the seat at least three times. Some locals quipped that it was the largest presence of parliamentarians since the seventeenth century, when the area had served as an important battlefield in the English Civil War.[5] The local climate and campaign were reflected in three polls from Newark, which were released in quick succession (see Figure 6.1). The Conservatives looked set to retain the seat easily with an average of 40 per cent of the vote. Ukip was second but well behind, on 27 per cent. It was an increase of twenty-three points on its 2010 result, but it was nowhere near enough.

While the unfavourable terrain was one part of the explanation for why Ukip was struggling, its campaign was another. The effort had been plagued by numerous problems. When Farage ruled himself out from standing, Ukip's ruling body had ignored suggestions from organizers to stand a 'young and feisty female', such as Diane James, who had attracted almost

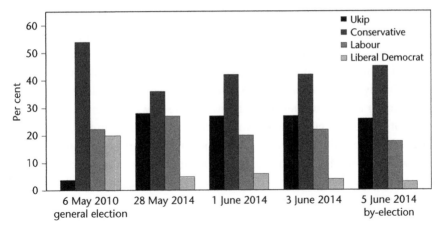

**Figure 6.1.** Party support in Newark, 2010–2014

*Sources*: 2010 general election result, Survation and Lord Ashcroft polls, by-election result.

28 per cent of the vote in Eastleigh. Instead, the party selected Roger
Helmer, a former Conservative and pensioner who embodied the stereotype of Ukip activists as old white men who held offensive views. Within
hours of his selection, journalists were noting Helmer's long record of
remarks, including the suggestion that women who are date-raped 'share
part of the responsibility', and that homosexuality is 'abnormal'.[6] The tone
of coverage was reflected in the title of an article that appeared in the *New
Statesman*: 'Meet Ukip's Seal-Hating, Gay-Baiting, Victim-Blaming Newark
Candidate, Roger Helmer'.[7]

But Helmer was not the only problem. During the European elections
Ukip had invested heavily in its air war, communicating its core-vote
strategy in media interviews, billboards, and mass leafleting, all of which
were controlled centrally. The stream of activity that had taken place in
the skies above the electorate had been supported by Farage's tour of
the country, again run by the central office. The strategy had worked. But
in a by-election its weaknesses were quickly being laid bare. Ukip was
still not a functioning, nationwide, and well-oiled party. Prior to the
by-election it had not even had an active branch in Newark. Meanwhile,
many of its activists were still visibly exhausted from the European elections,
which had thrown light on the party's lack of manpower. Such limitations
raised serious questions about whether Ukip really could wage battles across
multiple fronts, fighting for southern Conservative seats while invading
northern Labour territory.

Meanwhile, on the ground the party lacked many of the weapons that had become standard tools in election warfare. Ukip had no computer system for collecting information about voters, which left it unable to target and mobilize support. Whereas activists from the main parties were meticulously noting down the responses of voters on the doorstep, Ukip was sending its foot soldiers into the streets to scrawl random observations on disorganized sheets of paper. And because so few of them had ever campaigned before, they often wrote down the wrong information—something that would come back to haunt later campaigns. The inability to paint an accurate and detailed picture of what was happening on the ground was compounded by another bad habit.

Ukip's veterans had long argued that they should contact every voter in a seat—that only by knocking on the door of every household could they find people who might not be on the electoral register and who might want to vote for the party. It was known as the 'every door policy'. But it suffered from a fundamental flaw. By knocking on every door, activists risked the very real possibility that they would also mobilize their opponents, reminding those who disliked Ukip that it might be worth turning out on polling day. And there were problems with the message, too. In Newark, as in many past campaigns, Ukip focused heavily on abstract macro-messages about immigration and Europe. This had worked at a European election, but in a constituency campaign you need to link these issues to the local environment, to the concerns of ordinary people in the seat.

Even if Ukip had remedied these problems, it had no way of mobilizing its voters on polling day. Unlike supporters of the main parties, the people who wanted to vote for Ukip typically received no telephone call or letter reminding them to vote. There had rarely been a strategy for winning over postal voters, and there was almost never any transport or help to get people into the polling stations on the day of the election. The absence of a 'get-out-the-vote' operation was reflected in the complaint of one demoralized activist as he returned to the office after a long day of campaigning. 'What can we do when a voters says that a Conservative Shadow Minister just knocked on their door and offered to take them to the polling station?' Farage was aware of the problem. When he had arrived in Newark on the day of the election, he found that he had little to do. 'I walked around the town square, tried to look cheerful and then headed for a pub crawl.' The dire state of Ukip's ground game was reflected in the polls. Research from

Newark painted a picture of an amateur party that was out of its depth and being heavily outgunned. According to research by Lord Ashcroft, compared to the other parties, the party had fewer billboards, made fewer phone calls, delivered fewer leaflets, sent fewer emails, and knocked on fewer doors.[8] And, when the election was over, it was revealed that Ukip had also spent less money. They were being bulldozed aside.

The Conservatives easily retained Newark, receiving 45 per cent of the vote and finishing nineteen points clear of Ukip. Farage and his team of amateurs had added twenty-two points to their share of the vote, finishing second and once again reshuffling the opposition—the Liberal Democrats were down seventeen points and Labour were down by five. Nonetheless, Ukip had failed to keep pace. Suddenly, the earthquake that had been caused only a few weeks earlier felt like a distant memory.

In the aftermath of the battle Ukip was written off. The 'Great Ukip Flying Circus', declared political commentator John Rentoul, is in decline—the party was 'finished'. Columnist Dan Hodges voiced a similar view. 'Can we drop this ludicrous fiction that Ukip is a real political force?' The party, he continued, 'is over'.[9]

But, contrary to such claims, the result in Newark had not been a complete disaster. The result reflected the broader trend of Ukip emerging as the second-placed party and reordering the opposition. Aside from adding more than twenty points to its vote, the party had collected its sixth second-place finish at a by-election and the fourth in a row. Though it was not evident at the time, Newark would also help Ukip in other ways. The result fuelled a sense of complacency among Conservatives about the Ukip threat, encouraging those in Cameron's team who had long argued that the party would collapse by the time of the 2015 general election. And for Farage, if not his veteran organizers, the loss had made something abundantly clear. If he was serious about breaking into Westminster, then he would need to find somebody who knew how to campaign.

Compared to the storm of publicity that had surrounded Ukip in the spring, the summer of 2014 was relatively quiet. Only a few events put the party in the news. One of the first was in Brussels. Ukip now had twenty-four seats in the European Parliament, but to have real influence it needed to form an alliance with other parties. Farage loathed the institution, but he knew how it worked—it rewarded pan-European cooperation. Only by working together could the various political parties from different EU member states gain access to money, jobs, and speaking time in the chamber, which Farage had been using to cultivate an international following on YouTube. To get hold of these benefits he would need to forge an alliance between at least twenty-five MEPs from seven member states.

Ukip had needed to choose its allies carefully. The party had already been damaged by its past associations with toxic parties. During the European elections these links had been highlighted by interviewers like James O'Brien on LBC radio, who had pointed to Farage's dubious allies in the previous European Parliament while questioning his commitment to human rights. After the elections in 2009, Ukip had joined twelve parties to form the 'Europe of Freedom and Democracy' group, on which Farage served as co-president. Members had included Morten Messerschmidt of the Danish People's Party and Timo Soini, leader of a populist Eurosceptic party in Finland called the True Finns. Soini became a close friend of Farage and Paul Nuttall. But the group had also absorbed some other controversial figures who would later attract O'Brien's attention.

One was Mario Borghezio from the Italian Northern League. In the summer of 2011, and while a member of the alliance, Borghezio had appeared to endorse the ideas of Anders Behring Breivik, a right-wing extremist who murdered more than seventy fellow Norwegians. Borghezio had been supported by another member of the group, Franceso Speroni, who had also seemed to support Breivik's Islamophobia. 'Breivik's ideas', said the Italian politician, 'are in defence of Western civilization'.[10] Speroni served alongside Farage as co-president. Nor was this the first time that his ally, Borghezio, had courted controversy. The Italian politician had already joined protests against the 'Islamification' of Europe and described Serbian General Mladic, who had been indicted for war crimes that included the mass murder of Muslims, as a 'true patriot'. Borghezio's suggestion that politicians had covered up information about unidentified flying objects had also raised eyebrows. While his comments about Breivik had led to him being temporarily suspended from his own party, he would not be expelled from the European group until two years later when he abused Italy's first black cabinet minister, claiming that she had made the government 'bonga bonga'.[11]

Nor had these been Farage's only problems in Brussels. During the same post-2009 parliament his own MEPs had repeatedly failed to establish basic discipline. By the end of the parliament in 2014 five of Ukip's thirteen MEPs had abandoned the alliance or left the party altogether, generating damaging headlines along the way.[12]

This time, and with his eyes on the 2015 general election, Farage needed things to be different. For much of the past year he had been repeatedly pushed onto the defensive, forced to rebut accusations that Ukip was racist and associated with extremists. Meanwhile, the party's campaign had focused relentlessly on immigration, fuelling allegations that it was indulging in xenophobia and anxieties among insiders that the strategy had damaged their longer-term prospects. Steering clear of anything that might fuel such claims was now the priority.

However, at the same time as Ukip's earthquake, the European elections had seen a plethora of radical right, populist, and extremist parties make gains. And not all of them respected democracy. Ukip had not been the only outsider to break through. The radical right Danish People's Party and the National Front in France, led by Marine Le Pen, had also won their own European elections. Elsewhere, an assortment of similar parties that had railed against immigration, the EU, and established parties had either retained their existing seats or broken into Brussels for the first time. While the British debated the rise of Ukip, their neighbours across the Channel debated the appeal of parties such as the Austrian Freedom Party, the Italian Northern League, Geert Wilders's Party for Freedom in the Netherlands, the Sweden Democrats, Alternative for Germany, and Five Star Movement in Italy, an Internet-based populist movement. But even more toxic parties had also made gains.

Amid a financial crisis in Greece, the neo-Nazi Golden Dawn had won three seats, in spite of the fact that members of the party were linked to racist violence and murder and that many of its leaders had been imprisoned.[13] There were other disturbing parallels with the past in Germany, where a party linked to neo-Nazism, the National Democratic Party, won one seat. In Hungary, meanwhile, the anti-Semitic and anti-Roma Jobbik saved its three seats. Such results prompted the *New York Times* to talk of an angry eruption of populist insurgency that had sent ripples across the continent, 'unnerving the political establishment and calling into question the very institutions and assumptions at the heart of Europe's post-World War II order'.[14]

Ukip was not in the same ideological camp as many of these parties. It was rooted in a long British tradition of Euroscepticism rather than anti-Semitism, ethnic nationalism, Nazism, or Islamophobia. Farage had certainly started to use more strident language when addressing immigration, and there was no doubt that some individual supporters of Ukip held xenophobic, racist, and Islamophobic views. But neither Farage nor his party subscribed to the conspiratorial anti-Semitism that was espoused by some members of the French National Front, the crude anti-Islam rhetoric of Geert Wilders in the Netherlands, or the open hostility towards democracy that dominated the fascist right. The same could not be said for many parties that were now looking for allies in the European Parliament. Farage now faced the task of trying to build an alliance while avoiding these more extreme parties that would undermine his claim to be leading a legitimate and credible alternative in Britain.

The task was further complicated by the fact that some of Ukip's older allies had decided to switch sides. Only one week after the European elections it was revealed that the True Finns and Danish People's Party had defected to the Conservative Party's rival group. The exit of Denmark's Messerschmidt had been expected and confirmed by a source in the group who had been leaking information to Ukip. But the defection of Soini, Farage's friend, was a blow. The Ukip leader had felt 'badly let down', while Nuttall felt 'devastated' on hearing the news. Some insiders claimed that the defections had been orchestrated by Conservatives in the European Parliament who were trying to halt Ukip's revolt before the general election. Whether or not this was true, figures like Soini were also clearly trying to wield greater influence at the European level. Farage, who needed allies from seven countries, now faced the prospect of not having any group at all.

One party that agreed to do business with Farage was Five Star in Italy, an anti-establishment movement led by a comedian-turned-politician, Beppe Grillo. By harnessing the power of populist rhetoric, Internet technology, and old-fashioned grass-roots rallies, Grillo had built a formidable movement that had support from around one in four voters. At the European elections his party had won almost six million votes and seventeen seats. The model impressed Farage. 'If I was starting Ukip today,' he later said, 'would I spend twenty years speaking to people in village halls, or would I base it on the Grillo model? I know exactly what I would do.' When Grillo had been asked to join with Ukip, he had remained true to his beliefs in direct democracy and put the decision to his members. After assuring them that their British allies rejected xenophobia, were democratic, and opposed foreign conflict, and that Farage, who had worked in the London Metal Exchange, had 'never been a banker and has nothing to do with banks and financial services', almost four in five of the Five Starrers endorsed the alliance.[15]

Farage and Nuttall, meanwhile, had been negotiating with other potential partners. Anxious to avoid damaging headlines, they had quickly ruled out controversial organizations like the Austrian Freedom Party, because of its past links to anti-Semitism and nostalgia for the Third Reich. One of Ukip's new MEPs, the British-born Muslim Amjad Bashir, had also made it clear that he would leave the group if it contained Islamophobes like Geert Wilders. Even before the elections Farage had rejected repeated invitations from Marine Le Pen and Wilders to join a new group, which they claimed would 'liberate Europe from the monster of Brussels'.[16] Despite intense media interest, Farage had never seriously entertained the idea. Though he was potentially receptive to Le Pen, he was conscious of the extremist baggage that came with the older generation of National Front leaders, like her father Jean-Marie Le Pen and stalwarts like Bruno Gollnisch. To distance himself from the proposed alliance, Farage had publicly endorsed a smaller centre-right party in France that in the end failed to win seats. In a thinly disguised criticism of the baggage within Marine Le Pen's movement, he later talked about wanting to find allies who had 'views that are consistent with classical liberal democracy'.[17]

Farage would actually sit down with Le Pen, face to face, after the election. 'I was annoyed with the continual invites to join, which were dominating the press. I told her it was not going to happen.' Farage and Nuttall had also initially vetoed the idea of joining up with a party in Poland called the Polish Congress of the New Right (KNP). Of concern was the KNP's eccentric leader, Janusz Korwin-Mikke, who had a long record of offensive remarks. They included suggestions that women should not have the vote, that women are not as intelligent as men, that there is only a small difference between rape and consensual sex, and that Adolf Hitler had not known about the Holocaust.[18] 'We just could not allow this man anywhere near us,' observed Nuttall, who during one meeting with the KNP's chief of staff read aloud eight statements that had been attributed to Korwin-Mikke. When the chief of staff claimed that the comments had been taken out of context, Nuttall replied, 'How many times can you be taken out of context?'

After further negotiations Ukip eventually forged an alliance with Grillo's Five Star Movement, an anti-immigration and Eurosceptic party called the Sweden Democrats, a social conservative party from Lithuania called Order and Justice, and a liberal Eurosceptic movement from the Czech Republic, the Party of Free Citizens. Farage managed to fulfil the criteria only when he also recruited one MEP from a Latvian farmer's movement and a rebel

MEP from Le Pen's party, who had been thrown out after suggesting that migrants should be given the right to vote. Together, the assortment of mainly Eurosceptic and anti-establishment politicians forged a group called Europe of Freedom and Direct Democracy, gaining access to additional money and resources. But it would not be smooth sailing.

A few months later, the Latvian MEP defected to another group, threatening the alliance with the risk of collapse. Ukip filled the gap by recruiting one member from Korwin-Mikke's controversial party in Poland, Robert Iwaszkiewicz, whom some around Farage called 'Bob the Pole'. While some pointed to the irony of Ukip relying on somebody from Poland to keep its alliance together, the addition of the new member was followed by the backlash in the press that the party had feared. Farage's new ally, observed the Board of Deputies of British Jews, 'belongs to an extremist party whose leader has a history of Holocaust denial, racist remarks and misogynistic comments'.[19]

After the alliance had been formed, attention remained fixed on Brussels. The prime ministers and presidents of the EU member states were nominating the next President of the European Commission. Cameron had tried to prevent the appointment of the favourite, Jean-Claude Juncker, who was the former prime minister of Luxembourg and was seen by many as an arch-federalist. The Conservative Party leader had initially described the proposed nomination as 'totally unacceptable' and warned that Juncker would stifle reforms that were needed to convince sceptical British voters to support continued EU membership.[20] But he was outnumbered. Twenty-six states endorsed Juncker, leaving Britain and Hungary as the only dissenting voices. For Cameron, it was a humiliating defeat. Farage, meanwhile, was busily claiming that the Conservatives would no longer be able to achieve reforms that the British public wanted to see ahead of any referendum on their continuing EU membership—not least an end to the free movement of EU migrant workers. To underline his party's hard-line Euroscepticism, a few days later Farage led his MEPs in turning their backs on the ceremonial opening of the new session of the European Parliament. But, by this time, events were also taking place away from Brussels.

Ukip's decision to follow a presidential-style campaign for the European elections may have contributed to its success, but it had also come with costs. Farage was exhausted, while some insiders felt concerned that the strategy had fuelled an image of their party as a one-man band. 'The ratio in other parties is completely different,' said one. 'You might say that Ed Miliband is twice as well known as Ed Balls, or David Cameron is three times as well known as Philip Hammond. But in Ukip Nigel is *twenty times* as well known as everybody else.' The fortunes of the party and its leader were now intimately entwined. The distinction between the two had become less clear by the day. 'If he went under a bus tomorrow, we'd be buggered,' whispered one member to a journalist.[21] If Ukip was serious about mounting a long-term revolt, then it would need to present a broader front.

The response was the launch of a 'front bench', which was a shadow cabinet of sorts. Eleven carefully selected activists were given portfolios and pushed gently towards the media spotlight. The party was deliberately cautious. All but one of the activists had already been elected to the European Parliament. They included Farage loyalists such as Nuttall, O'Flynn, and Ray Finch, and others who reflected an attempt to push back more forcefully against accusations of racism and male chauvinism.

Steven Woolfe was an ambitious and mixed-race activist who had been raised by his Jamaican mother in the deprived Manchester suburb of Moss Side. During his teenage years, Woolfe had joined Labour, before working in the City of London and then defecting to become a Conservative councillor. He had then joined Ukip in 2010 and made an impression, rising quickly through the ranks to become its spokesman for financial affairs and being elected to sit on its National Executive Committee, the ruling body. In the European elections Woolfe had stood on the stage at the 'Clause Four Conference' at which Farage had repudiated claims that his party was racist. When anti-fascists in the audience had heckled Woolfe as a 'fake' and 'coconut', his reply had drawn on his childhood experiences. 'A five year-old child having to go home and tell his mum he was called a nigger all day at school—that's not a fake.'[22] Shortly afterwards, Woolfe was made spokesman for migration and during interviews would often reference his mixed-race heritage when discussing Ukip policy. Meanwhile, Amjad Bashir became the spokesman for communities—a British Muslim whose father had left Pakistan in the 1950s to work in Bradford's textile mills. The party also promoted five women, including the MEPs Diane James, who had helped to put Ukip on the map at a by-election in Eastleigh, and Jane Collins, who was trying to build the party in south Yorkshire towns like Rotherham. Another activist who was pushed forward but did not hold elected office was Suzanne Evans, a former Conservative councillor and competent media performer. Evans would increasingly be seen as a possible successor to Farage.[23] Whether these activists could improve Ukip's appeal remained to be seen, but they would now play a central role in communicating its message.

Yet, while the front bench had been designed to inject a sense of professionalism, it was soon undermined by yet another wave of embarrassing revelations. At the height of the summer it was revealed that one of Ukip's fundraisers, a former madam, had been jailed for running brothels. Shortly later, one of the newly elected MEPs, Janice Atkinson, found herself at the centre of a scandal after describing a Thai supporter of Ukip as a 'ting tong'. Farage, who was now determined to take a more assertive approach, personally visited the supporter to make a televised apology. Atkinson, despite the protests of some in the party, would not be expelled. David Soutter, who had been brought in to help the party manage its growing number of candidates ahead of the general election, had argued for a tougher line. 'I said she should go. Every time she appeared the questions would be about ting tong. But the NEC refused.' Shortly afterwards, Farage was again pushed on the defensive. Speaking to the party's youth conference, Ukip MEP Bill Etheridge was reported to have described Adolf Hitler as a 'magnetic and forceful' personality who could provide the activists with a model for public speaking. 'I'm not saying direct copy,' he advised; 'pick up little moments'.[24]

While it was more of the self-inflicted negative coverage that had undermined Ukip earlier in the year, there was also little evidence that the publicity was leading to a sustained loss of support in the polls. Around the time of the European elections, 14 per cent of voters had said that they were planning to support Ukip at the 2015 general election. This was notably lower than the almost 28 per cent who had supported the party at the European elections, but it was still more than enough to inflict a real impact on the election. Contrary to the arguments that had surfaced in the aftermath of Newark, Ukip's support had then stayed fairly stable throughout the summer, averaging 14 per cent and hovering between a low of 10 and a high of 18 per cent. Ukip's Teflon nature had also been underlined by the Atkinson and Etheridge scandals. In the days that followed Etheridge's remarks, support for the party dropped to 10 per cent—the only point in the entire year when the Liberal Democrats moved ahead of Ukip. But the party recovered almost immediately. The next day it was back to 12 per cent and within one week had returned to its average levels of support (see Figure 6.2). The revolt was proving to be stubbornly resilient. And in the coming weeks it would experience an upsurge of support.

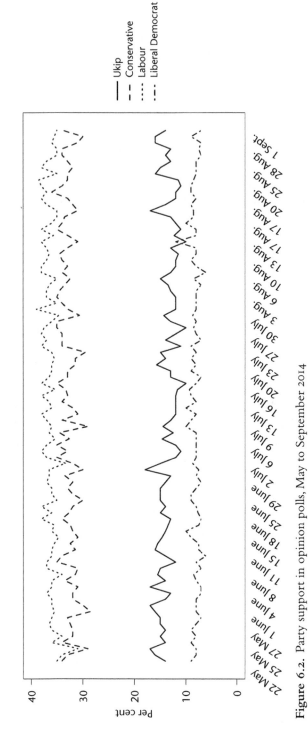

**Figure 6.2.** Party support in opinion polls, May to September 2014

*Source:* UK Polling Report.

As the latest wave of public-relations bombshells went off around him, Farage also found himself at the centre of a media storm. It arrived when an unknown elderly secretary from one of Ukip's branches unwittingly revealed the seat that the Ukip leader was planning to contest at the general election—a piece of news that journalists had been pursuing and one that Farage had wanted to hold back. 'It is the worst-kept secret in town,' said the secretary, laughing as a journalist from the *Financial Times* stood in her office. 'We now have two names on the list and one of them is Mr Farage.'[25] Within hours the news was all over the Internet.

Farage had only ever considered one seat. South Thanet is located on the eastern tip of Kent in south-east England, beyond Canterbury and to the north of Dover. Traditionally it is safe Conservative territory. Conservative politicians had held the earlier Isle of Thanet seat since the 1800s and controlled much of the area until the 1990s, by which time it had been reorganized into North and South Thanet. But in the mid-1990s the political winds had changed. In 1995 Labour took control of the local council. Then, two years later, and while North Thanet stayed Conservative, Labour took South Thanet as Blair's landslide swept the country. While more affluent neighbourhoods like Sandwich stayed Conservative, Labour had been pushed forward by struggling, low-income areas that were close to the seaside and among the most deprived in Kent—places such as Cliftonville, Margate, Newington, and Ramsgate.[26] The Conservatives had then staged a comeback in 2010. After retaking the council, its candidate Laura Sandys then took back South Thanet. But they were soon faced with renewed pressure and a new competitor. Labour had continued to poll strongly, while a few local Conservatives broke rank, defecting to Ukip, and another was imprisoned after misconduct.[27] Then, at elections to the local county council in 2013, Ukip achieved a real breakthrough, winning 39 per cent of the vote, taking seven seats in Thanet and seventeen across Kent. On the same day, a largely unknown Labour activist named Will Scobie also won a seat—in the deprived Margate and Cliftonville area.

By 2014, therefore, South Thanet had become a marginal seat where the vote was divided fairly evenly between Labour and the Conservatives. This provided a potential opening to a popular third-party candidate who might run through the middle. Farage's prospects had also been helped by other factors. Sandys, the Conservative MP, had decided to stand down in 2015, which had removed the incumbency advantage that is often an obstacle for challengers. Furthermore, the new Conservative Party candidate was Craig

MacKinlay, a former leading Ukip member whose selection some thought might alienate swing voters and moderate Conservatives who wanted to support an anti-Ukip ticket.

There were other considerations, too. Farage had been born in Kent, and from 1999 had represented the South East in the European Parliament. And he had fought the seat before. In 2005 he had finished fourth with 5 per cent of the vote, a battle that had come before Ukip's rise in the polls. Now, he was confident that he could deliver a much stronger performance. In the European elections Ukip had taken 46 per cent of the vote across Thanet, twenty-four points ahead of the second-place Conservatives. It was the party's strongest result in the South East. Insiders felt that the Conservative vote in Kent was melting away. Two months later a constituency poll from South Thanet had put Ukip in first place, with 33 per cent, four points clear of the main parties. And all this, as Farage pointed out, had come before news of his decision to fight the seat. The results fuelled his belief that—with his profile and a bit of work—the seat could propel him into Westminster.

In the coming months, the race for South Thanet would become one of the classic battles in the general election and one that would profoundly influence Ukip. But the news about Farage's candidacy was soon eclipsed by an announcement of an altogether different magnitude. Only a handful of activists had known what was coming. One was Paul Nuttall, who had been given a clue while he had spent part of August touring the battlefields of the First World War with Farage. The two men had followed the retreat of the British army in August 1914 from Mons to the outskirts of Paris. On their last night they had sat around drinking, talking about the general election campaign that lay ahead. 'I told Nigel that if we got 10 per cent of the vote and four seats I would take it. He thought that it would be more.' Later on, Farage had suddenly turned to Nuttall. 'I need you in London on Thursday,' he said. Nuttall asked why. 'Just trust me. It's something big,'

On the morning of Thursday, 28 August, two days after Farage had been officially selected to stand for Ukip in South Thanet, he summoned some of his most loyal followers to Ukip's headquarters on Brooks Mews. The relative calm that had descended over the summer was about to come to an abrupt end. None of those who gathered in the small office knew why they were there, including the press team. Farage, who knew that his party could not keep a secret, had decided to work alone. 'It's not that I don't trust you,' he said to the activists who were now circled around him. 'It's just that nothing in politics is a surprise any more.' Then, the most important people in Ukip made their way to a hastily organized conference in the heart of Westminster, speculating en route about what was about to unfold. 'Perhaps Elton John is coming out as a major donor,' said one, referring to a recent newspaper report that Farage had attended a dinner party with the pop star and former press baron Lord (Conrad) Black.[28] Nor did the journalists who were waiting at the venue have any information. All they had been told was that it was going to be 'a very good story'.

The man who would soon be at the centre of the national story was sitting on a park bench, only a few hundred yards away. Douglas Carswell, the Conservative MP for Clacton, was squeezed between Patrick O'Flynn and a few tourists. The 43-year-old was quietly reflecting on the events that had led him to this day—or to what he and his wife had come to call 'D-Day'. Carswell was thinking about when he had first joined the Conservative Party. It had been in 1989, when Thatcher was in power and he was only 18 years old. He remembered his excitement, his unwavering belief in Conservative ideology, and how he had always wanted to be more than just a member. The opportunity to progress to the next level would not arrive for another ten years, when Carswell had a chance to be selected as the Conservative Party candidate for The Wrekin, a Labour-held marginal in Shropshire. He had made it to the shortlist but so too had one of his close friends—an economist in the City named Mark Reckless. They agreed to break with convention and help each other through the process, passing along information and offering advice before the interviews. 'Alan Clark once said that there is no such thing in politics as true friends', recalled Carswell, 'only sharks that are circling and waiting for traces of blood to appear in the water. But that is not true. Mark and I were always true friends.'

But, in the end, politics trumped friendship, and they both lost. United by disappointment, they looked on as Jacob Rees-Mogg was selected. While he would fail to win the seat, the two allies pushed ahead. In 2001 Carswell was given an opportunity to stand in the northern Labour seat of Sedgefield, against then-Prime Minister Tony Blair. It was an impossible political baptism, but his loyal friend Reckless urged him on, encouraging Carswell to raise his profile and make contacts. Carswell agreed and in the end added three points to his party's share of the vote, impressing the people who mattered. The next year he was rewarded by being selected as the candidate for the Labour seat of Harwich, in Essex—soon to be renamed Clacton. It was a far more promising prospect. Unlike Blair, the local Labour MP held a majority of less than 3,000 votes. Carswell seized the opportunity and threw himself into the campaign. He worked hard and won the seat in 2005. He was finally in the House of Commons. Over the next five years he cemented his position in Clacton, holding regular fish-and-chip suppers in the disadvantaged coastal seat and cultivating his local brand as a man of the people. Many voters simply called him Douglas. In 2010 Carswell transformed a majority of 920 votes into a commanding lead of more than 12,000. But, while his seat was safe, somewhere along the way Carswell had begun to feel disillusioned with his party. He had begun to question Cameron's leadership and the direction of British Conservatism.

Carswell ultimately saw himself as a reformer. On one level he talked about being a radical Gladstonian liberal who believed passionately in the free market and the power of individuals over the state. On another he saw himself as a modern innovator, who wanted to harness the power of the Internet and the digital revolution to overhaul how we 'do' politics—ideas that he set out in a book that talked about the 'birth of iDemocracy'.[29] Carswell wanted to roll back the state and make politics more accountable, and was deeply sceptical of the EU. Like other Eurosceptics, he saw the EU as a distant, centralized, and undemocratic structure—something that was anathema to those who believed in direct democracy. He also contrasted himself with many of his fellow Conservative MPs, whom he saw as part of the old Tory elite—a patrician brand of conservatism that had failed to modernize and move on from the 'barren Tory script of the 1990s'.[30] Some saw him as a genuine, maverick intellectual whose unorthodox and radical ideas meant that he would never make it into the inner sanctum of the Conservative Party. Others saw him as a confused man who would move seamlessly from quoting Ghandi to Steve Jobs, firing out ideas that lacked any unifying philosophy or intellectual coherence. Even some of Carswell's own sympathizers painted a picture of a man who advocated admirable ideas but appeared as an odd political creature. 'He is uncomfortable and serious,' noted Charles Moore,

rather like the sort of crank who stalks the streets carrying plastic bags bursting with documents which prove that UFOs are beaming radiation into the water supply. His weird idea is that voters should be able to make MPs genuinely answerable to them. For this reason, many of his colleagues regard him as a lunatic.[31]

There was no doubt, however, that Carswell had increasingly felt out of place in his chosen political home. In this respect his experience of campaigning in the Labour bastion of Sedgefield and struggling Labour-leaning areas in Clacton, like Jaywick, had been formative. Carswell's relationship with Labour voters, he would later claim, had opened his eyes to the need for a different brand of centre-right politics—'neither reheated Thatcherism, nor patrician Toryism. Something more grass roots, authentic and rooted in the tradition of English radicalism.' He had already begun to develop his ideas with a close friend—Daniel Hannan, a fellow Eurosceptic and Conservative MEP. Together, the men articulated a clear vision of what they wanted—for decisions to be taken as closely as possible to the people, for decision-makers to be made more accountable, and for citizens to be as free as possible from state coercion. The unifying theme was direct democracy, and from this flowed more specific ideas about how to reform Westminster—an end to perks for MPs, reductions in the ministerial payroll, a directly elected House of Lords, the use of open primaries to select parliamentary candidates, locally elected sheriffs, greater use of referendums, and the withdrawal of Britain from the EU.[32]

It had been partly in response to the pressure from Eurosceptic back-benchers like Carswell that Cameron had given his Bloomberg speech in 2013, in which he had pledged to renegotiate the terms of Britain's EU membership and hold an 'in or out' referendum by the end of 2017. The speech had been intended to pacify Eurosceptics and the growing army of voters who were defecting to Farage. The two currents had complemented one another, squeezing Cameron from inside and outside parliament. Searching for possible alternatives, Carswell had then travelled to the Eastleigh by-election to watch Ukip poll 28 per cent of the vote. He saw it as a symbol of the Conservative Party's decline and shared his views publicly. 'The Conservative Party is run a bit like HMV and if it does not change, it will go the way of HMV.'[33]

It was not long until frustration turned into anger. Zac Goldsmith was a Conservative MP and close friend of Carswell's. He was also the son of the late Sir James Goldsmith, a billionaire who through the Referendum Party had tried to force a national referendum on EU membership at the 1997 general election. After his election in 2010, Zac Goldsmith tried to provide voters with a mechanism that would allow them to remove their MP if the representative had engaged in wrongdoing. The idea behind 'recall' was straightforward. If at least 20 per cent of voters in a seat signed a petition within a certain timeframe, then they could trigger a local referendum on whether the MP should be recalled from parliament. If more than half of voters thought that the MP should be recalled, then a by-election would be held. For its advocates, recall was a crucial step towards strengthening accountability and restoring public faith in a politics that was still limping on in the shadow of the expenses scandal of 2009. But in early 2014 the version of recall that was being proposed by the Coalition government fell well short of what Goldsmith and others had envisaged. Instead of handing power to the electorate, the proposed system put the final decision in the hands of a committee that was comprised of MPs. 'It was not recall,' said an angry Goldsmith, 'it was an insult to voters'.[34] Carswell, who supported Goldsmith, was furious. But he was even more dismayed when he was called by a government whip, asking him to help block further attempts by Goldsmith to revive the debate.

A few weeks later the demoralized Carswell attended the annual gathering of a centre-right blog, Conservative Home. As he sat in the audience pondering his future, he listened as researchers set out the most Ukip-friendly seats in the country. Clacton, filled with blue-collar, poorly educated, and struggling white voters, was the most receptive of all.[35] Perhaps conscious of the discontent among Conservative backbenchers like Carswell, Farage gave a filmed speech to civil servants at the Institute for Government, setting out his support for ideas on political reform. He talked of ending an 'unhealthy relationship' between big business and big government, embracing direct democracy, and making greater use of referenda, which he saw as a 'valuable safety net' for when politicians become disconnected from the people. Farage also underlined his support for recall, citing the work of Carswell. The ideas did not mark a radical departure for Ukip, which in both 2005 and 2010 had flagged the principle of direct democracy in its election manifestos, calling for locally elected sheriffs, police, education, and health boards and the right to recall MPs.[36] But Farage was sending a clear message to disillusioned politicians like Carswell that he was thinking along the same lines. Around this time Carswell had also sat in a meeting of the 1922 Committee, an influential forum for backbench MPs, listening to Cameron set out his views on Britain's relationship with Europe. The initial enthusiasm that he had felt on hearing the prime minister's Bloomberg speech was withering away. Cameron was now dismissive of Ukip and appeared to rule out a trade-only agreement with Europe, which some like Carswell had wanted to see. 'For a while', he recalled, 'I thought that Cameron wanted fundamental change in our relationship with

Europe. But it then became obvious that with this guy you need to read the small print.' Cameron's relationship with his party, thought Carswell, was like that of a rider to a horse. 'He was just kicking us in the ribs.' He began to think about defecting.

After a short stroll around St James's Park with a member of the House of Lords who had long acted as an intermediary between the Conservative Party and Ukip, Carswell attended a secret meeting with Farage. Before he would change sides, however, he wanted two assurances—that Ukip would deal more effectively with activists who voiced racist or extreme views, and that he would be able to appoint whomever he wanted as his agent and chief campaigner in Clacton. Like others, Carswell worried about Ukip's electoral amateurism and felt anxious about the divisive campaign that the party had run during the European elections—concerns that would only sharpen in the coming months. But, for now, Carswell felt that he was making the right decision and headed home. For much of the summer he would struggle to sleep. At one point he even went on holiday with a member of the Cabinet, unable to breathe a word about the looming defection. Now, he was sitting on a park bench with O'Flynn who had spent two days preparing the MP for the storm of publicity that was about to erupt. 'This is probably the moment of no return,' Carswell murmured out loud.

'I am today leaving the Conservative Party and joining Ukip,' announced the disgruntled MP to a room full of journalists and Ukip activists. Over the next twenty minutes Carswll set out his reasons for defecting. The Conservative Party had failed to deliver real change. It had failed to reform Westminster and the banks. It had failed to curb the national debt and immigration. And it had failed to deliver a referendum on Britain's EU membership. But this was also about more than just British conservatism. 'All three of the older parties seem the same,' continued Carswell. 'They've swathes of safe seats. They're run by those who became MPs by working in the offices of MPs. They use pollsters to tell them what to tell us. Politics to them is about politicians like them.' Carswell finished with another surprise. Rather than simply change allegiance, he would put his decision before the people in Clacton—he would trigger a by-election.

The defection was a major coup for Farage. For more than fifteen years he had been trying to translate speculation about possible defections into actual reality. Now, with less than nine months until the general election, he had given his revolt fresh momentum and put Ukip back in the headlines. The party had never won a by-election before. But insiders knew that their prospects looked good. If there was such a thing as perfect territory for Ukip, then it was Clacton. After a round of interviews Farage left the conference and headed to one of his favourite restaurants in Mayfair. He was celebrating over what insiders called a 'PFL'—a Proper Fucking Lunch. The celebrations spilled into an even longer dinner with an assortment of donors and celebrity supporters at the Goring hotel, where Farage and his team had met for their crisis meetings during the European elections. One figure, however, was noticeably absent. Carswell, the defector, had never been a big drinker and often seemed uncomfortable in social situations. His mind was elsewhere. With one of his closest aides, who in the coming months would rise to the very top of Ukip, he was already planning his re-election campaign in Clacton. And one thing was clear. He did not want it to be anything like the typical Ukip campaign.

# 7

# The Deal that Never Was

On the last weekend in September 2014, around 2,000 Ukip supporters descended on Doncaster for their annual conference. It was bright and sunny, and the party faithful were feeling confident. It had been only four months since Ukip had caused an earthquake by winning the European Parliament elections and only four weeks since Douglas Carswell had left the Conservative Party to join them. In the days that followed there had been two constituency polls from Clacton, where Carswell was already fighting for re-election under the purple banner. Both suggested that he and Ukip were about to score a comfortable and possibly historic victory— the party was averaging 60 per cent of the vote and was a striking thirty-eight points ahead of the Conservatives.[1] Farage and his party looked set to capture their first elected seat in the House of Commons.

Other events also seemed to be working in Ukip's favour. Newspapers were filled with rumours that at least two more Conservative MPs were about to defect and that a secretive Ukip official was stalking pubs in Westminster, urging others to do the same. As the summer came to a close, it was also clear that the received wisdom that Ukip's support would wither away had been incorrect. In the polls the party was on 14 per cent of the vote, a picture that had remained fairly constant throughout the summer. Almost one in eight voters were still planning to back Ukip at the 2015 general election. Furthermore, there had also emerged another opportunity for the party to enter Westminster. The sudden death of Labour MP Jim Dobbin had put a second parliamentary by-election on the horizon—and it would be nothing like Clacton.

The northern seat of Heywood and Middleton was traditional Labour territory. Labour had held the seat since its creation in 1983, often with large majorities, and had represented much of this part of Greater Manchester since the 1960s. At the last set of local elections before Dobbin's death Labour had won forty-six of the sixty seats on the council.[2] Farage, who had been claiming for months that Ukip could damage Labour, now had another chance to test the thesis. The two battles in a southern Conservative seat and a northern Labour heartland were less than two weeks away. It was going to be a busy autumn. 'No one', observed the *Guardian* as Ukip's conference got under way, 'can pretend that Ukip doesn't matter any longer'.[3]

Ukip had chosen Doncaster for a reason. Once one of the largest coal-mining areas in the country, the south Yorkshire town was home to Ed Miliband's constituency. It was surrounded by other traditionally safe Labour seats, including Barnsley East, Don Valley, Rother Valley, and Wentworth and Dearne, which were filled with struggling, older, and white working-class voters who looked receptive to a new opposition. Farage saw Doncaster and south Yorkshire as central to what he had started to call the '2020 Strategy', a plan for entrenching Ukip as the main opposition in scores of Labour seats at the 2015 general election. The idea had been fuelled by results at the by-elections and was intended to lay a foundation for a more significant breakthrough in years to come. By emerging as the second force in Labour seats, Farage also hoped to pile pressure on Miliband to match Cameron's commitment to hold a referendum on Britain's EU membership. Once Labour had made the commitment, Farage calculated, then Eurosceptic Conservatives who had defected to Ukip would have no incentive for returning to Cameron, who claimed that only he could make a referendum possible. Or at least that was the theory.

The 2020 strategy had also been shaped by other factors that insiders saw as paving the way for a more impressive revolt. One week before Ukip's conference in Doncaster, Scotland had voted by a 55–45 margin against becoming an independent country. But, despite losing, there soon emerged evidence that the Scottish National Party (SNP) was enjoying a surge of support, which Farage hoped might fuel feelings of nationalism among English voters. Ukip and its leader had never got on particularly well with voters in Scotland. In 2013 Farage had been chased out of Edinburgh by pro-independence protestors, whom he had later described as a 'feral mob of subsidized students', while at the European elections in Scotland Ukip had finished fourth with 10 per cent of the vote.[4] But in the aftermath of the referendum a profound shift was taking place. Membership of the SNP had reportedly increased by 70 per cent in only four days, while opinion polls would continue to track a sharp rise in support for the party as the general election neared.[5] Farage saw the SNP as fuelling anti-English sentiment in Scotland and was now hopeful that anxious voters in England, especially in Labour seats where centre-left politicians struggled to address concerns over national belonging, would give Ukip a second look. The idea that his party could emerge as a serious force in northern England was also encouraged by the fact that support for the Liberal Democrats in urban Labour areas was in decline, leaving voters who wanted to protest against the big two tribes with nowhere to go. Meanwhile, Farage also believed that many northern Labour branches were weak, having not had to fend off serious competition for generations. Ukip saw Doncaster as a symbol for all of this, and highlighting one other factor that had caught Farage's attention.

Less than twenty miles from Doncaster is the town of Rotherham, another Labour-held town that had seen a large number of voters defect to Ukip. The town was struggling with an array of social and economic problems, but one issue in particular had been simmering below the surface of Britain's political debate. It had been brought into the open only weeks before the Ukip conference. There had long been rumours about the sexual exploitation of children in England's northern towns. In 2001 *The Times* had reported that the head teacher of a school in Rotherham had written to parents to express his fears about 'the systematic sexual exploitation' of teenage girls in the school's care. Soon after the *Yorkshire Post* published the harrowing account of a mother who detailed how her 13-year-old daughter had been repeatedly raped by a gang of Asian men. It was one of the first articles to talk of a 'web of sex gangs' across the country. But it was not until 2011 that an investigation by *The Times* brought the issue to a national audience, sparking an official inquiry. The findings, which emerged three years later, attracted widespread publicity. They included the 'conservative estimate' that during sixteen years 1,400 children had been raped, abducted, and abused. Girls as young as 11 had been raped by multiple perpetrators. One had been doused in petrol and threatened with being set alight. Parents who had tried to remove their children from houses where the abuse was taking place had been arrested. Most victims, the report noted, described their abusers as 'Asian males'.[6]

The inquiry was strongly critical of the authorities in Rotherham, pointing to a repeated failure among politicians, police, and social workers to acknowledge and address the problem. The Labour-run council had failed to engage with the Pakistani-heritage community, not least because of an anxiety that it would be seen as racist. Social workers had also underplayed the problem, while police had failed to take complaints seriously, even suppressing reports about the abuse. A subsequent inspection in 2015 would conclude that the local authority had failed to accept responsibility and was 'not fit for purpose'.[7] This time the criticism was far stronger. The council had been in denial and was shrouded in an archaic culture of sexism, bullying, discomfort about race, and the covering-up of uncomfortable truths. It also criticized a history of weak leadership. Before the inquiry the council was comprised of sixty-three members, fifty-seven of whom represented Labour. Shortly afterwards the government intervened and took over the local authority.[8]

To Farage, a perfect storm seemed to gathering over south Yorkshire, an area of the country where his party was already bearing down on Labour. In 2012 Rotherham council had taken three children from a minority background away from foster parents because the carers were members of Ukip. One week later Ukip had finished second to Labour at a parliamentary by-election in the town, taking 22 per cent of the vote. Then, at the European elections, Ukip won more votes than Labour in Doncaster and Rotherham. It had also made gains in local elections, capturing one seat in Doncaster and finishing second to Labour in another fifteen wards. Shortly afterwards, and just before its conference, the party took another local seat at a by-election and on a 21 per cent swing away from Labour. Meanwhile, in Rotherham Ukip had won ten seats, finished second to Labour in eleven wards and won a higher average share of the vote.[9] As the party arrived in Doncaster, its strategy of targeting Labour heartlands seemed to be bearing fruit.

At the conference, Farage's speech to his followers revealed how he was trying to position Ukip ahead of the general election. He devoted much of his time to underlining the attacks against Labour. He drew a straight line from child sexual exploitation to Labour's support for multiculturalism and political correctness, arguing that Labour's 'one-party state' in northern England had contributed to the problem. 'We want to signal to the world', he declared, 'that we are now parking our tanks on the Labour Party's lawn'. Whether Ukip, with its campaigning problems, could ever challenge the Labour machine in its stronghold areas remained to be seen. But Farage had left no doubt that he saw the northern heartlands as a reservoir of potential votes. He proceeded to outline Ukip's offer to the electorate, which was reported widely as a pitch to struggling blue-collar workers.

That Farage had not liked Ukip's message at the 2010 general election was no secret. He had publicly disowned the manifesto, which had included bizarre ideas—that people should wear 'proper dress' to the theatre, that the Circle line on London's underground should be made circular, and that taxi drivers should wear uniforms.[10] But in Doncaster Ukip set out a different message and one that was focused clearly on its core voters—reducing immigration, leaving the EU, scrapping inheritance tax, curbing foreign aid, taking minimum-wage-earners out of tax, allowing employers to discriminate in favour of British workers, introducing compulsory medical insurance for migrants, insisting that only English MPs can vote on laws affecting England, opposing the 'multicultural experiment', and being more assertive in the promotion of British values.

Farage had also made a point of trying to push back against Labour's strategy for dealing with Ukip, which ever since the European elections had focused on portraying his party as an ultra-right-wing movement that wanted to privatize the National Health Service. Ukip, claimed Farage, would keep the NHS free at the point of delivery and oppose plans to charge patients for visiting their local doctor. The targeting of lower-income voters had also been underlined by another idea that had been floated by Patrick O'Flynn. Ukip, he suggested, would implement a luxury goods tax on expensive shoes, handbags, and cars—or what some called a 'wag tax'.

However, while some journalists saw it as the most eye-catching offer to disillusioned Labour voters, Farage quickly vetoed the idea. 'It isn't going to happen,' he said. Further insight into Farage's inner thoughts was provided when a journalist stumbled across the Ukip leader's notes for his speech, which he had left on the lectern. As usual Farage had not written his speech but listed a few points. The document provided an interesting insight into the issues that the Ukip leader considered most important as his party prepared for the general election: 'We will be opposition in the north... whatever points—immigration no.1 issue...NHS...Deficit...War home front...need fight...5th column...radicalisation schools and prisons...Sharia Law.'[11] Farage had also made a point of mentioning Carswell, who, some of those around the UKIP leader had noticed, was absent on the first day of conference. The Ukip leader would return to the stage the following day and with an announcement that would reverberate around British politics. 'The most exciting phase of Ukip's story', he told the audience, 'is about to begin'.

One year before Ukip's conference in Doncaster, Farage was standing outside the Savoy Hotel on the Strand in London. He was alone and having a smoke. Inside, an assortment of Westminster-types were attending the annual awards of the *Spectator* magazine. It had been a mixed night for Farage. He had been crowned 'Insurgent of the Year', but was not enjoying himself. Over the years he had been mocked by many of those at the event and he did not feel as though he was among friends. One person who did venture outside to speak to him, however, was a Conservative MP who was also from Kent—Mark Reckless. The men had known each other for years. In many respects Reckless was a typical politician. Before entering the House of Commons he had studied PPE at the University of Oxford, gone to work in the City of London, and then joined his friend Carswell in the Conservative Party. Along the way he became a committed Eurosceptic, having been influenced by a crisis in the financial markets in 1992, when on 'Black Wednesday' Britain was forced to suspend its membership of the Exchange Rate Mechanism, a precursor to joining the single European currency. It was around this time that Reckless had first met Farage at a meeting of a group called the Campaign for an Independent Britain. A few years later, he was selected as the Conservative candidate in the Kent seat of Medway, which he failed to win in 2001 and 2005. He was eventually elected into the House of Commons in 2010, by which time the seat had been renamed Rochester and Strood. In his maiden speech to parliament, Reckless compared his desire to make authorities more accountable to the ideas of the Levellers, a movement in the seventeenth century that had campaigned against an abuse of power and for the extension of the suffrage.

Like other backbench MPs, Reckless soon became disillusioned with Cameron's stance on Europe. He was convinced that the Conservative leader wanted only minor changes to Britain's relationship with Europe and wanted the country to stay in. Reckless wanted to do more than just 'carp from the sidelines'. Towards the end of 2013 he began to think seriously about defecting. One of his early ideas had been to capitalize on public anger in his Kent seat about an unpopular proposal for an airport on the Thames Estuary. He thought about defecting and holding a by-election on the same day as the European elections—which would boost turnout and improve his prospects. But other factors held him back. He was new to parliament, had a young family, and was unconvinced by research on the breadth of Ukip's appeal. 'They were cannibalizing the Conservative vote', he thought, after reading one analysis of the Ukip vote, 'but not bringing new people into the anti-EU camp'. Perhaps, like other MPs, Reckless was working on the assumption that, if he defected, then he would need to attract a more diverse coalition of voters than that which had first elected him to parliament. He would need to win over Labour and other voters to offset the loss of some Conservatives who would most likely feel angry about his defection. This would be especially important for Reckless, whose seat contained significant numbers of Labour voters in disadvantaged areas like Strood. But the MP was not convinced that he would be able to win over a sufficient number of Labour voters under the Ukip banner. 'Mark needed to understand that Ukip was seriously able to win Labour votes,' noted one of his advisers.

But that was not the case in January 2014 because the evidence just wasn't there. But as each month went by it became apparent that the higher Ukip went in the polls the more they were reaching into the Labour vote. That mattered to Mark in a seat like Rochester and Strood where Labour voters could make the difference.

While Reckless called off the defection, a few months later two factors collided and led the wavering MP to change his mind once again.

The European election results provided clear evidence of Ukip's ability to win support in Labour as well as Conservative areas. Reckless had watched the party win more votes than Labour across a swathe of England, including Medway in Kent, where Ukip finished almost twenty points ahead of the Conservatives. Then a working paper arrived on his desk. It had been written by one of his closest advisers and contained the answer to a question that had long been debated on Britain's centre-right—whether there could ever be a deal between Ukip and the Conservatives.

Chris Bruni-Lowe was only 28 years old but was already an experienced campaigner. Raised in south London, he had studied politics at university and become a Eurosceptic along the way. After earning his stripes as a Conservative Party agent, Bruni-Lowe had then launched his own political consultancy, helping politicians to run their campaigns. He specialized in organizing local referendums. The plan was simple but effective. Bruni-Lowe would immerse himself in a constituency and organize a public vote, asking people whether they wanted a referendum on Britain's EU membership. Once he had shown the scale of public support, he would try to convince the MP to work for a referendum nationally. Or, if the MP was already Eurosceptic, he would hand him or her the highly valuable data on the local electorate, which could be used to mobilize voters at elections. The campaigns provided the activist with experience, a reputation, and networks that reached across Westminster.

One of his contacts was especially important. In the early 1990s Lord (Malcolm) Pearson had been one of Margaret Thatcher's last appointments to the House of Lords. Pearson was a committed Eurosceptic. But over the years he had grown disillusioned with the Conservative Party's stance on Europe and in 2007 defected to Ukip, promising to help its advance from the upper chamber. 'The only thing that Conservatives understand is brute force, and brute force through the ballot box. Nothing else.' Three years later, the lord was temporarily thrust into the spotlight when he agreed temporarily to replace Farage as the leader of Ukip and take the party into the 2010 general election. While the official reason was that Farage wanted to focus on winning the constituency of Buckingham at the election, and on ousting the Speaker John Bercow, the real reason was that he was fed up with the lack of support that he had received from his amateur party and needed a break.[12] Lord Pearson might have been a multi-millionaire businessman, but he was soon out of his depth. While he knew what he wanted to do, he would need help, and so he turned to his adviser—Bruni-Lowe.

Lord Pearson did not have much interest in trying to win seats in Westminster, which he had always considered an unlikely prospect. Like many Ukip donors, he saw little point in standing against Eurosceptic politicians from the main parties—people who had already been elected into the House of Commons, or who would have a better chance of winning than Ukip. If Eurosceptics were ever to secure a referendum and achieve their dream of seeing Britain leave the EU, then they would need to 'put country before party'. For Ukip, this meant forging a series of non-aggression pacts with reliable Eurosceptics in the main parties—people who could be trusted to work for a referendum in parliament and so should be given a free run. By not taking votes away from Eurosceptics while leaning on others who supported Britain's EU membership, Pearson wanted to contribute in his own way to making the House of Commons as Eurosceptic as possible.

Bruni-Lowe helped to organize the pacts from behind the scenes. Ahead of the 2010 general election thirty-five Conservatives approached Ukip for a pact, but only seven were formed. Many of those who asked for help were not proven Eurosceptics, or 'come outers', and had not earned their stripes in campaign groups, such as Better Off Out. 'All of these people were suddenly ringing us up during the campaign saying they were Eurosceptic but they didn't have a good enough case.' Lord Pearson and Bruni-Lowe also struggled to convince rank-and-file Ukip activists to stand aside for established Conservatives—people who represented everything that they thought was wrong with Britain. In the end, Ukip stood aside for only three Conservative MPs and four candidates—namely Douglas Carswell in Clacton, Mark Reckless in Rochester and Strood, Philip Hollobone in Kettering, Philip Davies in Shipley, Janice Atkinson (then Small) in Batley and Spen, Alex Story in Wakefield, and an independent in Castle Point. The election saw Ukip attract only 3.1 per cent of the national vote, but the pacts were considered a success. Four of the seven candidates won their seats and three would later defect to Ukip.[13]

More generally, the 2010 campaign had helped to establish Bruni-Lowe as an intermediary between Eurosceptic Conservatives and Ukip. Many in Britain's Eurosceptic movement saw him as one of their own—as someone who could be trusted to handle delicate conversations between the rival camps. He was also discreet, actively avoiding the endless cycle of parties and spin rooms that dominated the Westminster village. When bloggers and journalists walked into an event, Bruni-Lowe walked out. And he had made an impression on Ukip. In 2012 Farage had asked the organizer to become his Campaign Director. But, like others on the centre-right, Bruni-Lowe was sceptical that Ukip could become a serious campaigning force and win seats under first-past-the-post.[14] He refused, and instead went to work for Mark Reckless, who was beginning to think about joining the radical right party. Reckless asked the young campaigner to organize one of his local referendums in Rochester and Strood. Officially, the disgruntled Conservative MP was exploring what his constituents thought about EU membership and also proposals to build a local airport. Unofficially, he was collecting as much data as possible about his electorate that could be used to maximize his chances at a by-election that would follow his defection. As part of a last-ditch attempt to avoid conflict, Reckless also asked Bruni-Lowe to use his contacts to write a paper on whether there could ever be an alliance between the two right-wing parties.

Many had suggested the idea. Since 2010, and while anxiously watching the rise of Ukip, Conservatives had become concerned about its potential to thwart their hopes for a majority government in 2015. But this was about more than electoral arithmetic. To Eurosceptics, Ukip was also threatening a once-in-a-generation opportunity to secure a referendum on

EU membership, which Cameron had now promised to deliver should he secure a majority. So long as the two parties and their supporters were split into warring camps, so the thinking went, an instinctively Eurosceptic public would most likely return Labour governments that had no desire to hold a referendum and wanted to keep Britain in the EU. Some of those who called for an alliance, such as Conservative MEP Daniel Hannan, had been particularly influenced by events in Canada.

In the late 1980s, the Progressive Conservatives had faced a similar threat from a radical right-wing insurgent called the Reform Party. Reform, which loathed the more socially liberal brand of mainstream conservatism, advocated a different political vision—tax cuts, greater use of referendums, decentralization, a tougher approach to tackling crime, and opposition to progressive ideas such as multiculturalism and same-sex marriage. Reform candidates were often in the news for making offensive statements, but their party continued to grow. At elections in 1988 Reform began to lay a foundation by standing a few dozen candidates and achieving some strong results, mainly in western Canada. But it would soon make political history. Five years later the party achieved a dramatic breakthrough—it gained fifty-two seats and won almost 19 per cent of the national vote, much of which came at the expense of the Progressive Conservatives, who had been engulfed by scandals and failed to manage the revolt effectively. The mainstream centre-right party watched in horror as its share of the vote plummeted from 43 to 16 per cent, and its number of seats crashed from 156 to only 2. It was the worst defeat for an incumbent party in the history of Canadian politics, and one of the most humiliating defeats for a governing party in the history of democracy. It had also taken place under first-past-the-post. As Hannan pointed out to his British colleagues, so long as the right-wing parties were divided, the Canadian liberals had dominated. It was only in 2006, when the two right-wing parties had been reconciled and merged to form the Conservative Party of Canada, that they returned to power, remaining in office for at least the next nine years.[15]

The idea that Ukip might replicate the trajectory of Reform looked unlikely, but in 2013 its impressive local election results had underlined its potential to jeopardize Conservative hopes in 2015. Fearing the worst, Hannan and others began to call for an alliance between the two camps— urging the parties to find unity around the offer of a referendum on EU membership.[16] Nor was he alone. Others, like Conservative MP Michael Fabricant, had circulated a paper on the prospect of 'a final rapprochement between warring brothers', suggesting that Ukip should stand down in certain areas in return for a referendum and a role in government for Farage. The idea, however, was quickly ruled out by the Conservative Party Chairman and Number 10. Around the same time Ukip's multi-millionaire treasurer, Stuart Wheeler, claimed that he had held a series of 'secret lunches' with eight Conservative MPs, urging them to switch sides. Farage denied that he had called for a pact between the two parties. 'I would not do a deal that compromised the party for short-term political gain,' he told journalists,

but if something was on the table that meant we could more easily walk through a door marked independence we'd be crazy not to consider it. But we could not negotiate anything until we absolutely knew that this country was going to get a full, free and fair referendum on our EU membership.[17]

Ideas continued to be circulated. While the leaderships of both parties ruled out a pact, this did not stop others from proposing alternative ways forward. In the spring of 2014, and with Ukip gaining pace, the Conservative Toby Young suggested that supporters of the two parties could come together in an online forum and exchange their votes. The idea suffered from numerous problems and was soon vetoed by the parties. But, while trying to find common ground, Young had stumbled across something interesting. In the inner sanctum of both parties, he observed, was an instinctive and tribal antipathy towards the other side. 'Farage and Cameron', he noted, 'have a mutual loathing that's rooted in their identity as members of their respective parties, and which is echoed lower down the ranks'. Deep animosity and suspicion ran through the lifeblood of both parties, fuelling a belief from top to bottom that each was hell-bent on the other's destruction. 'They regard each other not as estranged members of the same family but as bitter enemies.'[18]

Bruni-Lowe, meanwhile, was reaching similar conclusions. After holding secret meetings with Ukip leaders and Conservative MPs, he outlined the reasons why a pact would not work. Ukip, he noted, had turned into a different beast. Encouraged by its success and angered by insults from Cameron and other Conservatives, the party now seemed determined to head out on its own. 'I reported back to the MPs that nothing could be done,' recalled the campaigner. 'Ukip had simply become too big a beast for a pact to work. A deal would now never be possible.' Forging an alliance with the Conservatives would also undermine the 2020 strategy, which Farage would soon be setting out in Doncaster. It was ultimately a plan that identified Ukip's future as lying not in the southern Conservative shires but in the industrial Labour north.

Desperate to find some kind of accommodation, one Conservative MP pitched a last-minute idea. Prior to the 2015 general election, Conservative MPs who were contemplating defecting to Ukip would gather nomination papers from both parties—they would have one set of forms from the Conservatives, and another from Ukip. Then, at the last minute, they would switch their affiliation and put themselves forward as a Ukip rather than a Conservative candidate. It was not clear whether the plan could even work. Either way it was immediately vetoed by Farage. 'No. Not doing it. It is not Marquess of Queensberry rules.' Farage held a firm view—if people wanted to change sides, then they would have to defect, out in the open and avoiding anything that looked like trickery. It was not long afterwards that Reckless arranged a secret meeting with Farage. Standing in a private apartment in Pimlico he pledged his allegiance to the Ukip leader. 'I want to join,' he said. 'You have kept the Eurosceptic movement alive.'

A few months later Reckless was standing behind a curtain on a stage in Doncaster. He was thinking about how his career—and life—were about to change. His friends in the Conservative Party family would publicly disown him. There was no guarantee that Ukip would even be able to win a parliamentary by-election in his seat of Rochester and Strood, which he warned Farage would be a far more difficult battle than the one in Clacton. And Ukip's future looked uncertain, even if its prospects in the autumn of 2014 looked positive. As Reckless waited to be called on to the stage, Farage was at the podium presenting results from a recent wave of polls, some of which had been funded by a Ukip donor. They suggested that, in 2015, the party was on course to win Boston and Skegness, South Thanet, Eastleigh, and Thurrock, was within one point of the Conservative Party in North Thanet and also Great Yarmouth, and within nine points of Labour in Rotherham. 'There is no such thing as a safe safe,' Farage told his excited activists. 'We have got the potential, if we get the campaign right, to win virtually anywhere.'

Reckless's defection had been meticulously planned. It had been timed to coincide with the arrival of postal vote forms in Clacton, putting the party back in the news at the exact moment when the voters in Essex would be deciding whether or not to give Ukip its first seat in the House of Commons. Bruni-Lowe had already prepared a wave of literature to be distributed in

Reckless's seat of Rochester and Strood and had also helped prepare his speech. On the way to conference he had warned Reckless that he would need to pause between lines, pointing to his speech as he offered guidance. 'The Kippers will be delirious. You will need to stop here, here and there to let them clap and applause.' When Farage's latest defector was invited on to the stage, he was not even able to finish his first line. 'Today I am leaving the Conservative Party...'. The crowed instantly jumped to their feet and cheered him down. 'U-kip! U-kip! U-kip!'

As the party packed up and left Doncaster, it faced a busy autumn. For the first time in its history the small band of amateurs would be fighting simultaneously on multiple fronts—for a safe Conservative seat in Essex, a safe Labour stronghold in northern England, and another safe Conservative seat in Kent. The first two by-elections were scheduled for 9 October— which also happened to be Cameron's birthday. The battle for Rochester and Strood would follow in November. All three battles would test Ukip's claim to be a serious force that could prosper under first-past-the-post, capturing votes in both Conservative and Labour territory. And all three would see Ukip learn valuable lessons about election campaigns, in turn shaping how the party approached the general election.

1. Paul Nuttall, Paul Sykes, Nigel Farage, Patrick O'Flynn, and security

2. Ukip Billboard, European Parliament Elections 2014

3. Ukip Billboard, European Parliament Elections 2014

4. Ukip Billboard, European Parliament Elections 2014

5. Douglas Carswell, Nigel Farage, and Mark Reckless

6. Nigel Farage and John Bickley, Heywood and Middleton, October 2014

7. Douglas Carswell and Nigel Farage (centre), Clacton, 2014

8. Mark Reckless, Nigel Farage, and Douglas Carswell in Rochester and Strood, with Gawain Towler looking on

9. Nigel Farage and Douglas Carswell

10. Nigel Farage launches Ukip's campaign, Canvey Island, 12 February 2015

11. Nigel Farage launches Ukip's general election campaign

12. Nigel Farage on the campaign trail

13. Raheem Kassam and Chris Bruni-Lowe, February 2014

14. The party leader debates, 2 April 2015

15. Michael Heaver (left), Nigel Farage (centre), and Chris Bruni-Lowe (right)

16. Nigel Farage resigning as Ukip leader, with Raheem Kassam looking on, 8 May 2015

17. Nigel Farage contemplates his future

# 8

# Learning Lessons

Only two days after Mark Reckless had followed Douglas Carswell into Ukip, the Conservatives were assembling in Birmingham for their last gathering before the general election. It was conference time. The sky was filled with dark clouds. There was a palpable feeling of anger about the latest defection. The loss of Carswell had been a disappointment, but it had been bearable. He was respected by his old party. But Reckless was different. He had needed constant support to win election, which he had managed only on his third attempt. Now, before one of the most important moments in the political calendar, he had repaid their loyalty with betrayal. It was for this reason that, while some in Cameron's team accepted that the defection was damaging, they also saw it as a unifying moment. 'The defection was, psychologically, quite good for us,' said one of Cameron's former advisers. 'It united us. We felt that we were betrayed in a way that we had not been by Carswell.' The revelation had sparked a renewed determination to stall Ukip, as well as personal attacks on its latest recruit. 'Even late last night', said Grant Schapps, the Conservative Party Chairman, 'he was leaving voicemails for people saying how much he looked forward to coming to a campaign day . . . People will come to their own conclusions about whether this is a trustworthy individual.'[1]

But hidden behind the unity and the anger was a growing anxiety. The Conservatives were deeply worried that the defections might begin to spiral out of control. As gloomy activists huddled on autumn evenings, it was not clear when, or with whom, the desertions would end. The election was rapidly closing in, and there were rumours that Farage was planning to unveil one defection each month, dropping shock announcements like a sustained bombing raid until polling day. The fear was reinforced on the morning of Cameron's conference speech, when news broke that a Conservative donor had given Farage serious firepower. Arron Banks, a millionaire businessman, had donated £100,000. 'I've never heard of him,' retorted William Hague. Within hours the sensitive donor had increased his commitment to £1 million.

Other factors were fuelling a growing sense of panic. When the Conservatives looked at the polls, their support was moving in the wrong direction. As news of the defection hung in the air, their support was down to 30 per cent, four points behind Labour. And, contrary to what some in Cameron's team had predicted, their other rival was not running out of steam. Ukip held steady at 14 per cent. It was not supposed to be like this. On these numbers, it was thought, the Conservatives could kiss goodbye to the idea of staying in power, never mind securing a majority.

Meanwhile, within the inner sanctum of the Conservative Party, there was also an awareness that, when it came to squashing the revolt, Cameron and his team were quickly running out of options. 'It seemed to me', said one of Cameron's former advisers, who had worked directly on the Ukip problem,

that in the second half of 2014 they ran out of ideas on how to win back Ukip votes. All the way through they'd assumed that people would turn back because of Miliband. They'd hoped that the referendum pledge would bring people back, but it didn't. Then they hoped that toughening talk on immigration would bring people back, but it didn't.

Unless something changed, and quickly, then the natural party of government would soon be back in opposition, facing the fact that it had not won a majority for nearly thirty years. 'If you'd told the Conservatives', continued the adviser, 'that on the eve of their final conference before the general election two MPs had defected and Ukip was still polling 14 per cent, the idea that they would recover *and* end up in government would have been astonishing. It felt like a very, *very* damaging set of events.'

This is not to say that Cameron and his team were blind to the appeal of Ukip, however. They knew that most of those who had deserted them for Farage were older, white men who were struggling to get by and pessimistic about the future. They knew that they were driven by deep-rooted concerns about immigration, social liberalism, and perceived threats to national identity. They knew that Farage was tapping direct into these intense feelings of anxiety. And they knew that Cameron was part of the problem. 'In Downing Street, we often quoted a line from a book on Ukip, that Cameron was their chief recruiting sergeant.' But they also knew that the problem would be hard to resolve, especially when it came to immigration. In the era of free movement across EU member states, there was little that they could do to curb net migration. Unlike in the days of Margaret Thatcher and John Major, controlling the number of immigrants entering the country had become almost impossible. Some around Cameron began to refer to the problem as the 'boulder in the road'—a major obstacle that lay before their party, and one that they knew was driving people into the arms of Farage.

It was these observations that now informed their broader strategic response to Ukip. If they could not satisfy public opinion on these issues, then they could at least provide the army of disgruntled Tories with answers, even if they were not necessarily the ones that people wanted to hear. 'Our whole approach,' said one of Cameron's current advisers,

since our pledge to offer a referendum, was to make sure that we had answers, so we were not exposed—answers on Europe and immigration. We did not want to talk about those issues, but we wanted at least to have answers so we could tell voters what we were doing.

As their leader walked onto the stage in Birmingham, looking out at anxious supporters, he was about to underline some of the answers.

Cameron was good in a crisis. He knew that he needed to calm nerves and reassert his authority. In a rousing speech, one of his strongest, he proceeded to set out the battle lines that would guide their strategy for winning the general election. The policies were built around his core narrative of economic competence. He talked about making another £25 billion in spending cuts, achieving full employment, taking low-wage-earners out of tax, creating millions of apprenticeships, and delivering tax cuts by raising the threshold at which people entered the 40 per cent tax bracket. And there was a pitch to the disaffected and mainly older Tories who were thinking of defecting to Farage. Cameron would abolish an unpopular tax on inherited pensions savings, scrap human rights legislation, and put free movement at the heart of his renegotiation strategy with the EU. 'I will not take no for an answer, and when it comes to free movement,' he said, 'I will get what Britain needs'. And he underlined the tactical squeeze that Conservatives were hoping would be enough to thwart Farage as voters turned their minds to the implications of their vote. 'If you vote for Ukip,' warned Cameron, 'that's really a vote for Labour. Here's a thought: on 7th May you could go to bed with Nigel Farage and wake up with Ed Miliband.'

The speech was seen as a resounding success. It was, noted one commentator, polished and relentless in its political intent. 'The Prime Minister's pitch to the voters was wide-ranging: an attempt to shore up the Tory vote, win back Ukip switchers, reach out to swing Labour voters while stealing the Liberal Democrats' most popular policy: tax cuts for the low paid.'[2] But it at its heart was the guiding message of economic competence. It was an appeal to the head—to prioritize security amid an era of economic turmoil. From here on, with discipline and vigour, references to the long-term economic plan and stability would be deployed over and over again. Repeatedly, almost religiously, Conservative MPs would contrast their claims of sound financial management and leadership with the alleged 'chaos' that would follow the election of an Ed Miliband-led Labour government. It was neither complicated nor nuanced. As Winston Churchill once said: 'If you have an important to make, don't try to be subtle or clever. Use a pile driver. Hit the point once. Then come back and hit it again. Then hit it a third time—a tremendous whack.'

But whether or not this pile driver would cut through into Ukip's support was unclear. Cameron and his party were investing heavily in claims about a recovery that a large chunk of Farage's supporters was neither feeling nor expecting to feel in the future. Meanwhile, it was difficult to see how, if at all, the government could demonstrate competence on the chief issue that was dominating the minds of these voters—immigration. Nor was the task of winning them back helped by some of the other, less-disciplined messages that surfaced from the conference.

Within hours of his speech, it was reported that Cameron had shared a more personal view about the latest defection. 'Rumour is rife', said one, 'that the words "effing Reckless", "fat arse", and "dick head" were blurted out in various versions of a tub-thumping turn by Cameron'. Nor was the effort to charm Ukip voters helped by comments from other senior Conservatives, which soon made their way into newspapers. After describing Ukip supporters as 'grumpy old men' who had experienced a 'hard time in life', former Chancellor Ken Clarke compared Farage's followers to a mob of racist thugs who in earlier centuries had run riot in London, hanging people from France. Boris Johnson, meanwhile, offered a different view—they liked to have sex with vacuum cleaners.[3]

There was some hope for Cameron, however. At another event at the conference Lord Ashcroft was quietly unpacking the challenge presented by Ukip. If the Conservatives were to secure a majority or remain as the largest party, he argued, they would need to make inroads into four groups of voters: *joiners*, who had not voted Conservative at the last election but were planning to; *considerers*, who might think about offering support but had neither done so in the past nor planned to; *defectors*, who had voted Conservative but would not do so again; and the *loyalists*, who had voted Conservative in 2010 and planned to again, in 2015. It was the last two, also the largest, the loyalists and the defectors, who could make or break Cameron's hopes.[4]

The loyalists represented one-fifth of the overall electorate. These were the ultra-committed Conservatives who would have loved Cameron's speech. They were satisfied with their leader, preferred him over Miliband, felt that the Conservative Party shared their values, and were among the most likely to think that it had the best policies for the long term. 'This', said the pollster, 'is the real core vote and it is not going anywhere.' Ashcroft was right. In the autumn, data from the British Election Study told a similar story: 83 per cent of Conservative loyalists were highly certain about their decision to support the party and 87 per cent liked Cameron. And they had faith in the recovery: three in four felt that the economy was on the mend. They looked happy and they felt at home. But others had gone someplace else and were not yet coming back.

Between 2010 and the conference in Birmingham, the Conservatives seemed to have haemorrhaged support. As Ashcroft pointed out, only 63 per cent of their 2010 voters were now planning to support the party in 2015. Of those who were not, just over one-quarter, or 27 per cent, were planning to support a different party. And of the voters who had moved elsewhere, more than half had gone to Ukip. They outnumbered defectors to Labour by four to one. Farage had given them a second home.[5]

If these deserters were to be won back, then some big challenges would have to be overcome. Those who had left for Ukip were not feeling what Cameron was now trying to force home—the recovery. As Ashcroft pointed out, whereas nine in ten of the loyalists felt the changing economic winds, only four in ten of the defectors felt better off, or expected to. Those who had left for Ukip were among the most likely to believe that the recovery was passing them by. And three in four said that immigration was the most important issue of all. But the news was not quite as bleak as it might have sounded.

Hidden in the numbers was good news for Cameron and bad news for Farage. Many of those who had defected to Ukip did not look like committed rebels. They had certainly pledged their allegiance to the insurgents, but more than half, 56 per cent, said they would still consider voting Conservative in 2015. It suggested that they could be won back. This was underlined by

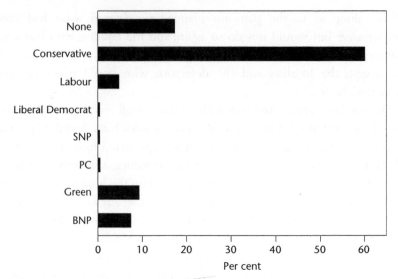

**Figure 8.1.** Second preferences of Conservative defectors to Ukip, September 2014

*Source*: 2014–2017 British Election Study Internet Panel (Wave 3).

another point. Almost two-thirds of them, or 65 per cent, preferred the idea of a Conservative to a Labour government. Fewer than one in five wanted Miliband in power. Perhaps, as the battle neared, Cameron could use a tactical squeeze to turn the screws on these voters—underlining a binary choice. Forget about Farage. It was Cameron or the other guy.

That Cameron faced an opportunity, and Farage was vulnerable, becomes clearer still when we explore the second choice among those who had defected to Ukip—the party that they would probably vote for if their first choice was unavailable or, as Cameron hoped, they had changed their minds. There was mixed news for Cameron, but the good outweighed the bad. Almost two-fifths of those who had left the Conservatives since 2010 now looked off limits to Cameron. They either had no second preference at all (17 per cent) or their second choice was a party other than the Tories (22 per cent) (see Figure 8.1).[6] But, crucially, a large majority of those who had switched from the Conservatives to Ukip, 60 per cent, still saw their old party as a viable alternative. The question now was whether Cameron and his team could win them back in time.

While the Tories continued to grapple with the dilemma, the Labour Party, which had been slower to react to the rise of Ukip, was still struggling to diagnose the actual problem. Its fumbling response was best reflected in Miliband's speech to the party faithful in Manchester, which offered a sharp contrast to Cameron's polished performance. While the Conservatives had been working to provide Ukip defectors with answers on immigration and the deficit, Miliband forgot to *mention* the issues entirely, leaving out whole sections of his speech. It was, noted *The Economist*, one of the worst speeches of his career, and it happened to coincide with one of Cameron's best.[7] Amid widespread ridicule, Miliband also attracted another intervention from Boris Johnson. 'His subconscious rebelled. The baggage handlers in his memory went on strike—as they would under a Labour government—and refused to load the word deficit onto the conveyor belt of his tongue.' In the aftermath, and with the battle rapidly approaching, Blairites would sound out former home secretary Alan Johnson about whether he intended to stand against Miliband—but the coup would never materialize.[8]

By this time, those in Labour who had been advocating a more assertive approach to Ukip felt sidelined and frustrated. One example was John Healey, an MP from the Yorkshire seat of Wentworth and Dearne. Healey had experience with Ukip. In 2012 he had helped organize Labour's by-election campaign in Rotherham, watching Farage and his party finish second with almost one in four votes. 'It was clear even then', noted the MP, 'that some people felt that their town no longer had a place in modern Britain'. But Labour had been slow to respond, even in the face of mounting evidence that Ukip was slowing its comeback in parts of England. It was only now, within a few months of the general election, and after Ukip had already won serious support in Labour areas, that the party finally sprang into action.

Labour had been exploring its dwindling support among the working class since 2010, but it did not establish a stream of work on Ukip until the summer of 2014. The formation of a working group, comprised of Healey, Yvette Cooper, Caroline Flint, and Jon Trickett, who was a close confidant of Miliband, was designed to improve understanding about the threat. But some in Labour saw it more as an exercise in political party management than as a genuine attempt to take on Ukip and the underlying issues. 'The group was about getting the Parliamentary Labour Party [PLP] into the process rather than strategy,' reflected one insider. 'It was about making sure that MPs were not running around complaining, demanding resources for seats that would not decide the general election.'

Working with the number-crunchers, some of whom had been warning about Ukip's rise for some time, the group produced materials and risk reports that MPs could use to inform their work in seats where Ukip was surging. But some had doubts about the quality. 'Most reports', said one insider,

were for MPs with big majorities. It was a complete waste of time. Whilst the PLP felt it was important, I don't think it had an impact at all. A lot of people were in massively safe seats that were not under threat. It was driven by political reasons, to keep people happy.

Another analyst who was brought in to work directly on Ukip was especially critical.

The risk report was the first thing that was put on my desk. I had three days until it was going to be signed off. I was not happy with it at all. I thought it was flaky in terms of the evidence, the recommendations were not strong, and there was not a lot that could be used on the ground actually to deal with Ukip.

But Labour trundled on, delivering one-on-one briefings to around fifty MPs over the autumn. 'The ones that I spoke to', said the analyst, 'got my briefings not Labour's briefings. Mine were blunter. They were not driven by a desire to put people's minds at ease.' When one MP was presented with evidence about the scale of public support for Ukip in his seat, he went silent for ten minutes. Others were criticized for failing to have enough contact with their voters. 'I modelled contact rates against support for non-mainstream parties and it was crystal clear', continued the analyst, 'the relationship between contact rates falling off and insurgent parties taking off. We had MPs whose contact rates were through the floor.'

Some of the documentation was soon leaked and offered a glimpse into the response. It explained that the voters Labour was most vulnerable to losing to Ukip were older men, from the lower social grades, who had few qualifications. Working-class men over 47 years old were four times as likely as upper- and middle-class women who were younger than 46 to defect. To win them back, the party urged campaigners to focus on issues on which Labour was strong, such as the health service and housing. Where activists had to address immigration, they should do so in tandem with other issues on which Labour was competing with the Conservatives. 'The purpose of this is to raise the salience of those issues in which Labour has a much clearer lead and stands to benefit more from their prominence with the electorate.'[9]

Yet the advice was arguably ducking the core concerns—the deep-rooted anxieties over perceived threats to identity that Labour had long struggled to resolve. According to data from the British Election Study, among Labour's loyal voters who had supported the party in 2010 and planned to do so again in 2015, only around one in ten, or 9 per cent, felt that immigration was the most important problem facing Britain. But among those who were now planning to defect to Farage in 2015, almost two-fifths, or 40 per cent, identified this as their greatest concern. Meanwhile, Labour voters who would have been leaning towards Ukip, who rated the party as their second choice, were also far more likely than Labour loyalists to point to immigration. And, while some in the party were urging it to twin these concerns with issues like the NHS, in these data neither those who were defecting to Ukip, nor those who were thinking about doing so, were particularly animated by public services.

While Labour was certainly facing fewer defections to Ukip than the Conservatives, its strategy of linking public anxieties over immigration and its effects to resource-based issues, such as housing, was unlikely to lure these voters back. Many would probably have been motivated far more strongly by identity-related anxieties—feelings of threat to British or English identity, long-held values, a sense of belonging, and ways of life (see Figure 8.2). But, even still, there was also a feeling at the heart of the Labour campaign that the work should have started sooner.

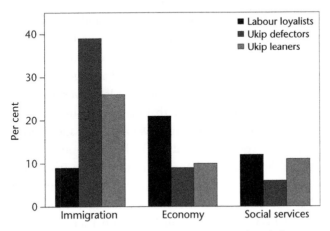

**Figure 8.2.** Most important issue for Labour loyalists, Ukip defectors, and Ukip leaners, September 2014

*Note:* Social services includes references to education, housing, the NHS, pensions, poverty, and spending on social services.

*Source:* 2014–2017 British Election Study Internet Panel.

It was too late for messages and narratives. The [anti-Ukip] work started in November. The election was in May. The majority of voters who were going to Ukip had gone. So any amount of messaging on the doorstep was just not going to work. Getting voters back is not a doorstep conversation. It takes a long time, years, and they might never come back.

Whether Labour could make an impression remained to be seen. But what was clear in the autumn of 2014 was that, before the main war that was the general election, both Labour and the Conservatives first had an opportunity to face their new competitor in three battles. While each offered a chance to win back deserters, they also offered Farage and his team a chance to learn how finally to conquer first-past-the-post.

Douglas Carswell had always wanted his campaign for re-election to be different from the typical Ukip campaign. He wanted nothing to do with the amateurism that had been on display in places like Newark. To circumvent the problem he would need to find a campaigner—somebody who was experienced and could put his ideas into practice. He turned to Bruni-Lowe, who by this time had become convinced of Ukip's potential and agreed to become Carswell's agent and organizer. Together, the two newcomers would try to bring the party its first elected seat in the House of Commons.

It would not be difficult. As Matthew Parris had observed, Clacton was full to the brim with the blue-collar workers and nostalgic pensioners who had pushed Ukip on. Carswell was also an incumbent who had a large majority. The favourable terrain was soon reflected in two polls that had emerged in the days after his defection. Ukip had averaged 60 per cent of the vote and held a commanding thirty-eight point lead over the second-placed Tories. Nor was there much evidence that Carswell could be neutralized by rallying local anger about his defection. When asked about his decision, a majority of Clacton voters felt that he had acted honourably, including more than half of those who had voted for the Conservatives in 2010. Only a minority saw him as a selfish opportunist. The numbers in these polls instantly killed any weak wind that was gathering behind Tory sails and cemented expectations of a Ukip win. 'Cameron Faces Ukip By-Election Bloodbath', read one front page.[10]

The sheer scale of Carswell's popularity had also startled Ukip. Before the defection, the party's internal polls certainly suggested that he held a strong lead and irrespective of whether he was a Ukip, Conservative, or Independent candidate. But many of those around Farage, who had never really known political superstardom, were still shocked by the reaction on the ground. Carswell could not walk around without being constantly stopped and cheered on by locals. 'The first day of campaigning was like a religious experience,' said one activist. 'I have campaigned alongside Boris Johnson and other major politicians. But I have never seen a reaction like it. People were jumping off the bus, including the bus driver, rushing across the street to meet Douglas, and then rushing back across the street to meet Nigel.' One voter said that he would vote for Carswell even if the politician was standing for the Teddy Bear's Picnic Party. Farage was stunned. 'This Carswell–Ukip combo is like nothing we have ever seen!' he said after a long day of campaigning. 'It is truly remarkable!'

But to mobilize support into votes, Carswell and Bruni-Lowe would need to run a more professional campaign than those their new party had delivered in the past. They did not believe that Ukip's inexperienced veterans could outflank the established parties, even in an ideal seat like Clacton. So they took full control. Having managed to keep the defection a secret, they hit the ground early, eager to capitalize on what campaigners call 'first-mover' advantage. They were also helped by the Conservatives' decision to select a candidate through what was claimed to be a US-style open primary, whereby local residents and not just Conservative Party members would be able to vote for their favoured candidate. Open primaries are designed to bring a large number of voters into the process and thereby bolster the chance of selecting a popular local candidate. It was a specific rejoinder to Carswell, who had spent years talking about the need to implement 'direct democracy'. But there were problems. It meant that a whole fortnight would pass between Carswell's defection and the selection of a candidate. And, as commentator Mark Wallace pointed out, in the end the selection process consisted of a meeting that fell well short of a true open primary. 'The point of holding a full postal primary', said Wallace, 'was to seize the initiative and involve the whole electorate—a town hall meeting will reach a few hundred people at best. Better than nothing, but well short of the best possible scenario.'[11] Bruni-Lowe used the time to entrench Carswell's dominance.

But they were still operating within an amateur party, something that became clear to Carswell during one early day of campaigning. After promptly issuing his activists with a long list of instructions, he was pulled to one side. 'Listen Douglas,' said Farage. 'A lot of these people have come a long way for you. They are volunteers. You need to thank them individually.' The former MP went quiet. 'That's when I knew I was not in a big corporate party any more.'

But, with Bruni-Lowe by his side, Carswell had acquired an experienced campaigner who made immediate improvements to his ground game. Even before the defection, the activist, who had spent years mobilizing support at the constituency level, made full use of data on Carswell's 'pledges'—people who, over the years, had already pledged their support to the MP. Thousands were sent a personalized letter from Carswell, setting out why he had decided to join Ukip and urging them to follow him. 'People have a right to expect a competent government that answers to them. Instead, Westminster is run by a cosy clique, who aren't on our side, but in politics for themselves'. Single pieces of literature seldom make a difference, and such tactics are routinely used by the main parties. But the letter symbolized a more professional campaigning approach that was now underway within Ukip. For the first time in more than twenty years the party was deploying some of the standard weapons in election warfare.

Carswell also had ideas about messaging. He wanted to avoid his new party's relentless and divisive focus on immigration. He thought it was unnecessarily polarizing. Ukip had already established ownership over immigration and Europe. People who felt anxious about these issues would probably support the party regardless, he thought. So, rather than spend its energy on attracting its already committed core voters, the party should reach out—beyond its core base. He talked repeatedly about the need to anchor campaigns in the 'local space', to target issues that mattered to people on the doorsteps, and not just to deliver abstract talk about Europe and immigration. His literature was focused heavily on local issues: youth delinquency, a fading seafront, and claims that Carswell had helped save a local maternity unit. 'The people of Clacton knew they had been left behind,' he said. 'The narrative of our campaign was to tell that story through local examples.' It was an idea he would continue to push, and one that would soon cause tension.

On his party's core issue, meanwhile, he talked about wanting 'fair, ethical immigration that does not discriminate against anyone, wherever they come from in the world'. On the street, when asked about the issue, he would talk in vague terms about wanting to 'control borders' but stress the need to offer a more positive and optimistic message. When cornered by journalists, he would refuse to endorse calls by Farage to ban migrants who have HIV from entering Britain. He also made it clear that he did not share his leader's view that he felt uncomfortable when he did not hear English spoken on public transport. 'I have no difficulty with Britain as Britain is today,' he said, fuelling speculation within only weeks of his defection that there would soon be a rift between the two men, if there was not one already.[12]

There was also change in terms of how the party was delivering this message. For the first time it was now using a computer database to collect information about voters, which could then be used to mobilize them nearer the election. The software was basic and did not always work. But it was a start for a party that had only ever used paper and pens and had become used to being pushed aside by the micro-targeted campaigns of the main parties. 'Until Clacton', said one insider, 'the missing ingredient was a database to go with the grass-roots work. We met people, had volunteers and publicity that was financed. But now we could use canvassing data so we knew where our voters lived.'

The software meant that the party could tentatively begin to target different areas of the seat with different messages. It could experiment with 'squeeze messaging'—a technique for trying to win over supporters of other parties by giving them reasons for defecting. In Clacton, this was organized by area, but in the future it would become more sophisticated and precise. In more Conservative areas of the seat the party targeted concerns about a shortage of GPs and a dislike of Cameron, while in Labour areas it outlined its opposition to the bedroom tax. While Carswell pushed arguments in Conservative suburbs, Farage was sent into working-class pubs in struggling neighbourhoods like Jaywick to speak to disillusioned Labour voters. The double act was on display at a public meeting towards the end of the campaign, which attracted more than 800 residents. It was only after Carswell had addressed local concerns, speaking directly to parents whose children had been the victims of knife crime, that Farage took the stage, setting out Ukip's opposition to immigration, the EU, and Westminster. On that evening, the approaches seemed to complement one another, but the two men's different ideas about messaging and strategy would soon create major problems.

What was driving support for Carswell and Ukip? While it was difficult to know which of the messages had cut through, it was clear that policy rather than protest was at the heart of their appeal. That their campaign was not just capitalizing on an anti-politics mood was clear in the polls. More than half, or 57 per cent, of those who were planning to vote for Ukip said

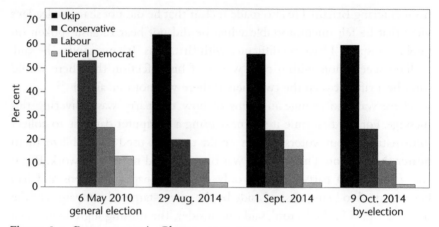

**Figure 8.3.** Party support in Clacton, 2010–2014

*Sources:* 2010 general election result, Survation and Lord Ashcroft polls, by-election result.

it was because they liked the party and its policies, compared to one-third who said it was because of Carswell, and one in ten who said it was a protest. In another poll, which asked people whether several factors had played a large or small role in their decision, four-fifths of those who were voting for Ukip said that 'having the best policies on the issues that they care about' had played a large role in their decision.[13] As polling day neared, it was clear that Carswell had connected.

Further north, meanwhile, Ukip was trying to make headway in a Labour heartland—the seat of Heywood and Middleton in Greater Manchester. The northern seat was not as ideal as Clacton. Labour was well entrenched. It had held the seat since the 1980s, had a majority of almost 6,000 votes, and had called a snap poll before the funeral of Jim Dobbin, which meant that the campaign would not even last one month.[14] Nonetheless, Ukip had still been pleasantly surprised by the reaction.

It was clear that we had a chance. On the first weekend we pulled up in a supermarket car park with three boxes of leaflets and started to hand them out. People were genuinely surprised that we were standing. They kept asking for more. They wanted the leaflets for their friends.

But Farage was trying to dampen expectations. Only a few weeks before, in Doncaster, he had briefed journalists that, while Ukip was beginning to advance in Labour areas, the prospect of capturing the seat was 'too big a mountain to climb in that short a space of time'. Initially, his view seemed to be vindicated when two polls put Ukip second, well behind Labour by nineteen points.[15]

Ukip's local organizers on the ground, however, held a different view. Paul Oakden was one who had objected to his leader's bleak prognosis. Pointing to Ukip's results at local elections in the recent past, he tried to persuade his party that its support was far stronger than the polls suggested—and that with more manpower he could even win the seat. 'In areas where we had done well in local elections we had strong and active people. But in other areas we only stood paper candidates who had not knocked on doors. So we did not know how we would do until we worked them.' When Oakden and his small team began to make their way through the constituency, they often encountered a positive reaction, fuelling their hopes for a surprise breakthrough.

'Ignore the Ashcroft poll!' Oakden had screamed down the phone, pleading with Ukip's organizers in Clacton to send him more resources. 'It does not reflect what we are seeing on the ground!' He was convinced that Ukip could cause a major upset, taking a Labour heartland and forcing the resignation of Miliband. It would transform the party. But his argument was falling on deaf ears. Most of the activists were heading to Clacton, wanting to say that they had played a role in the election of Ukip's first ever MP. 'The problem', said Paul Nuttall, the deputy leader who was working alongside Oakden, 'was that all of the resources and people who had ever run a by-election were sitting in an office in Clacton. Douglas was demanding every resource under the sun. We were given the scraps. The team came in, set up the office but then buggered off.'

Some traced the disparity between the two campaigns to a desire among senior officials to appease their new recruit. 'Douglas was at that point very influential,' said Oakden. 'So he got the resources. He was obsessed with being the first MP. Everything else was secondary.' Others, who had been brought in to help the national campaign, shared a similar view. 'Douglas was the new bright shiny thing, so nobody wanted to say no'. Others claimed that Carswell had been influenced by one particular day. With the polls suggesting that he held a forty-point lead, and that the battle was a done deal, only a few activists had come to help. 'He went ballistic,' said one. 'He was walking around with Jerusalem playing in the background muttering that a bird in the hand is worth two in the bush.' A few days later, Oakden, already depressed, reached new depths of despair. He heard that a convoy of enthusiastic activists from Ukip's northern branches had trundled straight past Heywood and Middleton, on their way south to help Carswell.

Oakden's irritation had been fuelled by his belief that he had a strong candidate. John Bickley was a businessman who had grown up locally, in a staunch Labour family. And, unlike other Ukip candidates, he knew how to campaign, having already finished second in a northern by-election earlier in the year.[16] Hoping to prove both the polls and Farage wrong, they began to mobilize a different kind of campaign from the one being run in Clacton. It was more abrasive, hard-hitting, and closer to Ukip's instinctive and tribal brand of politics. They focused heavily on immigration and the issue of child sexual exploitation, which Farage had urged his foot soldiers to target in Doncaster, and which, because of the seat's proximity to Rochdale, was generating a significant amount of concern. 'This is a prime example', said Farage, while opening Bickley's office on the high street, 'of the local authority failing to protect vulnerable residents because the people in power were more afraid of being seen as racist than of [not] taking action'.

From one door to the next, activists were pushing through literature that relentlessly targeted the issue and was presented under the title 'Ukip Understands Ordinary Working People'. On several evenings, amid a back-lash from their opponents who argued that they were pushing an openly racist agenda, the team debated whether or not they should give the issue prominence. 'Those debates were always about a simple question,' said Oakden. 'Is it right for us to talk about this? We decided that it was because it was clear people were very concerned about it and we felt that we were the best campaign to take it to Labour.' While Carswell was talking about the need to offer a more inclusive narrative, Oakden and his team were delivering an altogether different kind of message: 'Labour's betrayal is no more apparent than with the young, white, working-class girls of Rotherham and Rochdale, where, rather than upset immigrant communities, years of abuse were ignored and complaints swept under the carpet.'

Labour, meanwhile, was grappling with the question of how to respond. Having realized around the time of the European elections that dismissing Ukip as a racist party would not work, and even risked amplifying Labour's own perceived negatives, the party had turned its attention to the NHS. 'All of our research consistently found that attacking Farage on the basis that he wanted to privatize the NHS, and presenting him as the heir to Thatcher, was our strongest route to voters in Labour–Ukip battlegrounds,' said one of Labour's number-crunchers. 'Shouting he was racist didn't work.' But Heywood and Middleton was seeing the beginnings of a Ukip fightback. 'We have got to push back!' Bickley told his team. 'If Labour keep coming out with this stuff, we will get bogged down. But if we counter-claim, then who knows what could happen.'

Trying to push back, Ukip released a new billboard. Against a flat Labour Party balloon it asked voters: 'How many more times are they going to let you down?' The campaign team had then swamped the seat with a leaflet called 'Labour Lies', denying that Ukip would charge voters to see their GP, privatize the NHS, give tax breaks for the rich, and end maternity pay. Another leaflet listed reasons why, Ukip claimed, Labour had betrayed the working class—supporting immigration, failing to resolve child sexual exploitation because of political correctness, allowing American corporations to run parts of the health service, and letting 'Fat Cats' make billions out of Private Financial Initiative (PFI) contracts in the NHS.

Whether or not the attacks and counter-attacks made a difference is unclear, but what was certain was that, as in Clacton, policy issues were again at the heart of Ukip's appeal. Its support was not just protest against Labour, although this certainly contributed. When people were asked about their political loyalties, those who said they were voting for Labour over-whelmingly traced their support to tribal loyalty—they had always voted for them. But, among those leaving for Ukip, the most popular answer given was that they liked its policies. It was also clear that Ukip was continuing to draw much of its strength from the economically disaffected. When asked to think about their own situation, those who were supporting Farage and his party were the most likely of all, even more so than Labour voters, to say that they were not feeling the economic recovery.[17]

Despite the strident campaign, two weeks before polling day Oakden's claims seemed to be validated when it was reported that some in Labour feared that, after all, they could lose the seat. 'Middleton don't even like Rochdale,' quipped one Labour official. 'Why would they like Westminster?'[18] Labour was worried about the way in which, despite its lack of manpower, Ukip was managing to keep pace (see Figure 8.4). More than two-thirds of voters, or 68 per cent, had heard from Ukip, which was only one point below the percentage who had heard from Labour (the Tories were a dis-tant third on 29 per cent).[19] With the ground war so close, Oakden again called and asked for manpower. 'If we get people up here something could happen!' he shouted. 'Everybody just appeased Douglas. The people never came.' With few people canvassing, Oakden was forced to spread his activ-ists thinly across the seat and then, on the day of the election, have them stand outside the polling stations. 'Did we knock on doors or did we man

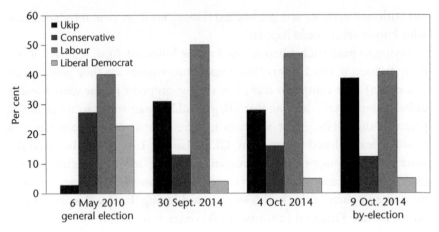

**Figure 8.4.** Party support in Heywood and Middleton, 2010–2014

*Sources*: 2010 general election result, Survation and Lord Ashcroft polls, by-election result.

the stations? That was my decision. I would have loved to have a serious get-out-the-vote operation. But in the end we just met voters at the polling stations, with a rosette and a smile.' With the result yet to come, the arguments over resources had thrown light on an internal rift. But they had also revealed how Ukip was struggling to fight on multiple fronts, raising doubts about whether it could compete with the main parties outside of a by-election and in the midst of a far more demanding general election campaign.

Ukip always knew that it had taken a risk in Rochester and Strood. Before Reckless had defected, the party's own internal polls had put their candidate only a few points ahead. They had always known that the by-election would be close. 'We always knew it would be nothing like Clacton,' recalled one insider. The problems stemmed from demography and politics. The seat in Kent was nowhere near as 'Ukip-friendly' as Clacton and was even less favourable than Heywood and Middleton. The number of voters who were pensioners or without qualifications was almost half the number in Carswell's seat. In terms of the types of voters that would decide Reckless's fate, the seat looked more like Newark, where Ukip had been crushed. And Reckless had struggled before, having failed to cross the line in this part of Kent on two previous occasions. It was clear that some local Conservatives were unwilling to play ball. After impressing Ukip with his campaign skills, Bruni-Lowe had been brought in to oversee the battle in Kent, and his initial assessment was far from positive. 'On the first weekend after Mark defected I didn't think he could win. The hostility was extraordinary. Local Conservatives had whipped themselves into a frenzy. They were literally chasing him around the seat.'

The Conservatives had decided to select their candidate through an open primary, sending ballots to 70,000 local voters and asking them to choose between two contenders. Ukip sought to dilute the impact of this and to cause confusion by running its own ballot, asking voters whether or not they would support Reckless. Some 8,000 people returned the ballots, providing Bruni-Lowe with another wave of data. 'The Tories were briefing the media constantly about what they were doing, which was idiotic, because we always knew what was about to happen.' In the end, and on a low turnout, Kelly Tolhurst was selected as the Conservative Party candidate—a councillor who did not strike many as a strong choice.[20] In interviews and at hustings Tolhurst often appeared abrasive and angry when discussing immigration, sparking fears that she might alienate moderate Tories.

Labour, meanwhile, selected the promising Naushabah Khan, although she received little support from the central party. Senior Labour officials made it known that they would not be investing heavily in the Tory-held seat, which was ranked 129th on their list of target seats, well outside the 106 that would receive the bulk of the effort. 'We were constrained financially,' noted one senior Labour insider.

The chance of a Labour win was slim. The only upside of fighting seriously was that we would keep quiet the people who said that we were not doing enough about Ukip. But you don't spend thousands of pounds on keeping people quiet. The only realistic win that was good for Labour was a Ukip win.

Angered by what they saw as 'defeatist briefings' and a capitulation, some Labour activists went public with their criticism, arguing that their party's timid stance in the face of the challenge from Ukip was undermining their efforts and creating problems for Labour in the future. 'Apparently there is a route map to British electoral victory that doesn't go through the Medway towns, Thurrock and Basildon, but through cloud cuckoo land,' complained one. 'We have just over six months left to work out if we actually still want to be the party that represents the hopes and aspirations of the British working classes or if we are prepared to give up that role to Ukip.'[21]

Ukip soon found momentum. Whereas Clacton had seen the beginnings of a professional approach to campaigning, the battle had not been competitive. But Rochester and Strood was much closer, which pushed Ukip to move to the next level of professionalism. Its effort was coordinated by the triumvirate of Reckless, Farage, and Bruni-Lowe, with the latter often talking between twenty and thirty times each day. The dynamics within Ukip were beginning to change. Farage and his campaigner were becoming close, pushing each other to work harder and bringing new innovations into the campaign. 'Right, Chris, what have we got?' Farage would say as he walked into the campaign office, sitting down and reading through numbers in the system. Farage felt that it was the first election in his entire career where his ideas about how to campaign could actually be implemented on the ground. As he walked around, he would often ignore Ukip's veteran organizers, whom some claimed that Farage saw as 'representing failure'.

In Rochester and Strood, Ukip canvassed the entire seat twice, collecting data about voters for its new computer system. The better quality of data meant that, for the first time, the party could deploy squeeze messages in a more targeted manner. Over the course of six weeks it distributed eighteen targeted mailings and around 100,000 pieces of literature. The targeted messaging was done on a house-by-house basis, with messages tailored around individuals rather than neighbourhoods. In some cases voters in the same households received different letters based on how they voted in 2010, whom they were supporting at the by-election, and the issues they had raised to canvassers. That Ukip was delivering a higher-quality ground game was reflected in the opinion polls. Towards the end of the campaign 84 per cent of voters said they had been contacted by the party, compared to 81 per cent who had been contacted by the Conservatives and 63 per cent by Labour.[22]

Ukip and its campaigners had not yet made a full transition to professionalism, however. The campaign was hampered by a lack of grass-roots experience, which became glaringly obvious to Bruni-Lowe, the campaigner-in-chief, when he met his foot soldiers after a day of canvassing. The activists had been sent into the streets with specific instructions—to ask people how they intended to vote and record the response using a simple coding scheme. Responses could then be used to map the seat according to whether people pledged their support (P), were against Ukip (A), or undecided (U). While the canvassing had generated around 15,000 pledges for Reckless, it had also exposed some of Ukip's major weaknesses. When Bruni-Lowe looked through some of the returned canvassing sheets, he noticed that they had been filled with the letter (L). 'Why is everybody in this street Labour?' he asked. 'That is impossible.' The activists looked at each other. 'They are not Labour,' came the reply.

'L means we leafleted them'. Bruni-Lowe put his head on his desk—the information was meaningless.

It was bizarre. Some even used their own cryptic codes like 0, 1, 2, or stars and symbols. They simply had no training in how to campaign. Even though some were elected councillors, they had never done proper grass-roots work. They often won their seats because of Ukip's name not their campaigning skills—because, to be frank, some of them had no skills.

Ukip, however, was becoming more responsive. As in Clacton, the party had initially focused on local issues—concerns about a hospital that had been put into special measures and an unpopular plan to build thousands of homes on a nearby peninsula. Farage had also suggested that they campaign to return City status to Rochester, a popular idea locally. But towards the end of the campaign, and as the race tightened, the strategy changed. Some activists had already been disgruntled with the local focus. 'Why am I delivering leaflets about traffic in Strood?' asked one. 'What about immigration?' Such concerns gathered pace when the Conservative candidate, Tolhurst, changed track, targeting immigration heavily and hinting that Cameron had been too soft on the issue.

There was certainly a receptive audience—evidence from the polls suggested that, whereas all voters in the seat were chiefly concerned about the NHS, those backing Reckless were more concerned about immigration.[23] Bruni-Lowe and Farage held an emergency meeting in a pub. 'Our data identified people from all sides who named immigration as their top concern, which we had not touched for weeks because of the local stuff. But now Tolhurst was targeting them, starting to nick our clothes.' Farage urged Reckless to change gear. But the candidate refused. 'Douglas said no,' replied Reckless, 'we need to do the wholly local stuff'. Farage was becoming increasingly frustrated with the Clacton MP—his absence at the Doncaster conference, his few visits to help in Kent, his reluctance to talk about immigration, and his criticism of Reckless's casual appearance, who, Carswell had allegedly suggested, did not dress like an MP-in-waiting. 'He just did not get it,' said one activist who was close to Reckless. 'There is probably nothing worse for someone on a working-class estate than to open their door and see a politician dressed in a suit and shiny shoes.'

Bruni-Lowe had reinforced the message. 'You have to establish the local space, of course you do. But there has to be something more.' Farage looked directly at Reckless. 'If you do not do immigration you will lose.'

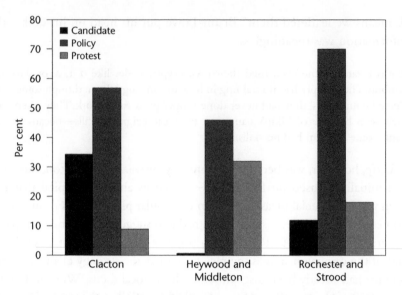

**Figure 8.5.** Motive for choosing Ukip in three parliamentary by-elections, 2014
*Source*: Survation.

The candidate eventually agreed, and a targeted letter was sent to 10,000 voters, outlining Ukip's opposition to free movement and desire for an Australian-based points system. The move reflected Farage's instincts, that, ultimately, Ukip should gamble on mobilizing its core support. It was a view—and a gamble—that would soon play a more central role.

Once again, policy rather than protest was key to making sense of Ukip's advance. As in the other by-elections, but even more so in Rochester and Strood, those who were endorsing the party identified policy as their main motive.[24] Whereas Reckless lacked the personal following of Carswell—and was not as dependent upon protest as the campaign in Heywood and Middleton—the unifying factor across all three campaigns is that it was concern about policy that fuelled Ukip supporters (see Figure 8.5). And in Kent 70 per cent of those who planned to vote for Reckless said that these identifiable policy concerns were their main motive.

Ukip also tried to exploit the fact that Cameron had personally aligned himself to the by-election. Ever since Birmingham, the Conservative Party leader had promised to lead from the front and throw the kitchen sink at finishing the revolt once and for all. 'Leading from the front helped Cameron inside the party', said one of his former advisers. 'But there was also an acknowledgement that we had nothing else to throw at driving down the

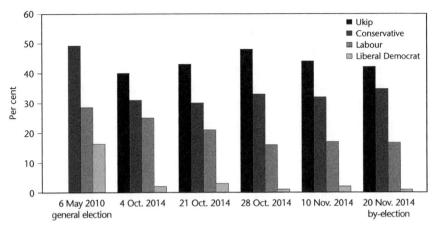

**Figure 8.6.** Party support in Rochester and Strood, 2010–2014

*Sources*: 2010 general election result, Survation, ComRes, and Lord Ashcroft polls, by-election result.

Ukip vote.' It was also not clear whether the Conservatives were mobilizing to the extent that they claimed. On one day during the campaign a journalist had stood at the local train station, watching MPs arrive and depart. While fifteen had passed through the station, ten had left within two hours. Others admitted that they had skipped the campaign altogether, citing back problems or confessing that they had gone to play golf.[25] And, while Cameron's determination had unsettled some in Ukip, Bruni-Lowe had seen his arrival as an opportunity. 'It made classifying Kelly Tolhurst as David Cameron's candidate so much easier,' he explained. 'The more Cameron came, the more I told voters to think back to the last time that a member of the Cabinet bothered to visit.' Cameron's visits also probably helped Reckless squeeze disillusioned Labour voters, who were now being bombarded regularly with Ukip literature that framed the contest as a once-in-a-lifetime opportunity to give Cameron a kicking. 'We just tied absolutely everything to Cameron.'

On the final day of the campaign Farage had planned to arrive in the seat at around three o'clock in the afternoon but because of his nerves he arrived at ten in the morning, stopping on the way to collect medicine for an ulcer that he associated with the stress of the by-election. He then spent time calling organizers and MEPs who had not turned up to help. 'You'd better get here,' warned their leader. Working with his campaigner, Farage then helped to mobilize the get-out-the-vote operation, the most professional in Ukip's history. Bruni-Lowe split the seat into four sections, collecting and analysing data that were coming in from the polling stations on iPads. The operation provided instant data about who was turning out and where, meaning that the party could redirect its 400 or so activists into areas where its supporters were not turning out in sufficient numbers. Farage himself kept knocking on doors until the polls closed. 'I don't think I will ever forget Nigel in those last hours,' recalled one activist. 'It was pitch black. He was completely alone, marching up and down the roads. He was obsessed with getting out the vote. He knew we had taken a major gamble.'

While each of the by-election results was significant for its own reasons, when seen as a whole they opened a window on Ukip's rise. In Clacton, Carswell polled almost 60 per cent of the vote and finished thirty-five points ahead of his Conservative rival. He had won the seat on a forty-four-point swing away from the Conservatives—one of the largest on record.[26] After a campaign that had divided some at the top of Ukip, the party finally had its first elected MP. But on the same day, and as Oakden had predicted, there was a much louder tremor further north.

In Heywood and Middleton Ukip polled almost 39 per cent, surging into second and finishing just two points behind Labour. The poorly equipped team watched their vote share jump by thirty-six points. Labour's majority was slashed, from more than 6,000 votes to only 617. The result rocked British politics, challenging those who had dismissed the claim that Ukip could rally strong support in Labour areas. Then, the party delivered another earthquake. In Rochester and Strood, Ukip took 42 per cent of the vote, 3,000 more than the Conservatives, who had given their all. It was an impressive win for Ukip, which, despite its continued weaknesses and the middle-of-the-road seat, had overcome the full weight of the Conservative Party machine.

The results set the stage for the general election. They had fuelled Ukip's confidence in its ability to overcome first-past-the-post and helped to push its support to new heights. The party's average poll rating would soon rise to over 16 per cent of the vote. 'Farage and his colleagues', concluded one team of number-crunchers who were analysing the polls, 'will certainly be among the nation's most confident politicians going into the Christmas break'.[27] Inside the party, meanwhile, the results had also entrenched Bruni-Lowe's position at the heart of the party. He would soon be rewarded with control over dozens of Ukip's target seats, responsible for orchestrating the ground game and fulfilling Farage's hopes of a breakthrough. The lessons

Table 8.1. Party support at the three by-elections, 2010–2014

| Party | Clacton | | Heywood and Middleton | | Rochester and Strood | |
|---|---|---|---|---|---|---|
| | Support 2014 (%) | Change 2010–14 | Support 2014 (%) | Change 2010–14 (%) | Support 2014 (%) | Change 2010–14 |
| Ukip | 59.7 | +59.7 | 38.7 | +36.1 | 42.1 | +42.1 |
| Conservative | 24.6 | −28.4 | 12.3 | −14.9 | 34.8 | −14.4 |
| Labour | 11.2 | −13.8 | 40.9 | +0.8 | 16.8 | −11.7 |
| Liberal Democrat | 1.3 | −11.6 | 5.1 | −17.6 | 0.9 | −15.4 |
| Other* | 0.8 | −6.9 | 3.1 | −4.3 | 0.1 | −4.4 |

* BNP, Tendring first, Independents in Clacton; BNP, Independents, Greens in Heywood and Middleton; England Democrats and Britain First in Rochester and Strood.

that had been learned would now be applied to the general election. The battles were over. The war was about to begin.

But the by-elections had also exposed weaknesses. Throughout the autumn, Ukip had struggled to fight against the main parties across multiple fronts and had continually suffered from a lack of firepower, inexperienced foot soldiers, and tensions over the message and strategy. One person who had noticed the problem was Raheem Kassam, who had recently joined the party as Nigel Farage's new senior adviser. Kassam had been brought in, essentially, to protect and promote Farage and would report only to the Ukip leader. Though only 28 years old, he was already a controversial figure in Westminster. After graduating from Westminster University, he had worked for the right-wing Henry Jackson Society before becoming editor of the UK division of Breitbart, an ultra-conservative media platform in the United States that is known for its aggressive strategy and sympathy for libertarian views. During the summer of 2014, before the by-elections, Kassam had travelled with Farage and Ukip's party secretary, Matthew Richardson, to the United States, helping them access US media. The activists had also met consultants to explore how the party might strengthen its campaigning with the use of new election technology. But as Kassam had watched the by-elections he had realized how much work there was to do. 'The whole team were still revelling in the European election victory,' he noted,

not quite understanding that the campaign was nothing like a general election. I think they thought that they could ride that wave into the general election. There were impediments to that which were supposedly good for the party, like the defections, but they drained the party. It was extraordinary to see how much time and effort they had to put in to get those two by-election victories.

Farage and his party had thrown everything that they had at the three by-elections, contests that voters often use to punish the governing parties and send a message to Westminster. The experience had left them exhausted. But soon, in only a few months, they would be fighting across dozens of battlefields in the general election and in a contest where voters were less inclined to abandon the main parties.

There was also tension in the ranks. Carswell, who would soon play a key role in the general election, was already attracting criticism from some in Ukip who felt that he had cost them a unique opportunity to score a truly historic breakthrough in the north. Others were questioning whether he shared their underlying philosophy. For his part, Carswell felt frustrated with what he saw as his new party's lack of professionalism and an instinctive reliance on toxic messages. Between thanking his constituents and criticizing the 'cosy cartel' in Westminster, Carswell used his victory speech in Clacton to offer his new colleagues some advice.

Humility when we win. Modesty when we're proved right. If we speak with passion, let it always be tempered by compassion. We must be a party for all Britain, and all Britons, first and second generation as much as any other. Our strength must lie in our breadth. If we stay true to that, there is nothing that we cannot achieve.

Farage, who had listened intently, had not been particularly impressed. 'Had it been a by-election in circa 1788, then it would have been exactly what I'd expect to hear. There was nothing wrong with it. It was just an entirely different approach to politics, a more cerebral approach.' Others who were close to Farage offered a less diplomatic view. 'Nigel was utterly pissed off at that speech. I was standing next to him.'

Aside from shedding light on these internal challenges, the results had also provided new evidence on Ukip's bases of support, once again challenging the argument that it was almost completely dependent on ex-Conservatives. Ukip's two victories were certainly accompanied by significant losses for the Conservatives, but Cameron's party was not the only one to lose support. In Clacton, Ukip's advance was joined by losses for all of the parties. The Conservatives had lost nearly thirty points on their 2010 vote share, but Ukip's advance was also accompanied by losses of at least ten points for

Labour and the Liberal Democrats, as well as losses for other minor parties. While we should not assume that all of these translated directly into Ukip gains, the survey data collected prior to the election indicated that Ukip was on track to pick up defectors from all three parties. Around half of those who had voted Conservative in 2010 told pollsters that they were planning to follow Carswell to Ukip, while, for Labour and the Liberal Democrats, it was closer to one-third. The campaign surveys are consistent with the final result, suggesting that Carswell's victory was helped by, but no means completely dependent upon, defections from his old party.

We see a similar picture in the other seats, except that the gap in the desertions to Ukip from the other parties is even smaller than in Clacton. In the other two battles, around 30 per cent of those who had voted for the Conservatives in 2010 said that they had planned to vote for Ukip, whereas Labour and the Liberal Democrats were each looking at defections from almost one in five of their supporters (see Figure 8.7). Moreover, the surveys conducted in both seats suggest that the Liberal Democrats were losing more defectors to Ukip than they were to Labour. Given that Nick Clegg and his party were widely expected to face significant losses at the general election, these results provide an interesting window into how defections from the

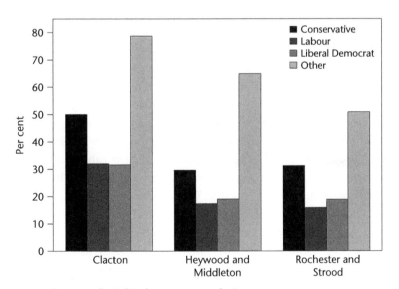

**Figure 8.7.** Support for Ukip by 2010 vote choice, 2014
*Source*: Survation.

former third party looked likely to fuel Ukip at the general election, a point that we shall return to in later chapters. But this was not the only collapse that had helped Ukip. In all three by-elections, the party had also picked up defectors from minor parties. While the surveys do not allow us to determine which other parties these voters supported in 2010, it is likely that Ukip benefited from the collapse of the far-right BNP and English Democrats, which in 2010 won between 4 and 7 per cent in the seats but were absent at the by-elections.[28]

The result in Heywood and Middleton had a particular impact on Labour. The shock breakthrough had strengthened the position of those advocating a more robust response. 'After that result', recalled Labour MP John Healey, 'a lot of MPs were running around like headless chickens thinking they were going to lose their seats to Ukip'. Labour's distant third place in Rochester and Strood also contributed to a feeling among some that the party was ducking the issue, and failing to take a stand. In the aftermath, Mark Reckless was even claiming that Ukip was now the true heir to a radical tradition in English politics—'the tradition that took power away from the elites and spread it amongst the people, the tradition of Levellers, Chartists and Suffragettes, the tradition that gave us appointment on merit, Gladstonian finance, universal suffrage, religious freedom, and racial tolerance'. The tradition that had once spoken up for the working class, said Reckless, had found a new home in Ukip. This time, Farage gave a different verdict. With tears in his eyes, he turned to one of his advisers. 'That is the best speech that I have heard. Phenomenal.' The night that followed would later be described by the Ukip leader as the greatest night of his entire career. 'The after-party was gate-crashed by the Monster Raving Loony Party. It was all *so* Ukip.'

To make matters worse for Labour, its efforts to re-engage with left-behind voters who had deserted for Ukip seemed to be further undermined when Emily Thornberry, Labour MP for Islington South and Finsbury and Shadow Attorney General, resigned from the shadow cabinet after appearing to sneer at the white working class—precisely the group that her party had been struggling to keep on side. While campaigning in Rochester and Strood, Thornberry had decided to tweet a picture of a house draped in St George's flags, with a white van parked outside. 'Image from Rochester,' read the tagline. The incident dominated Britain's political debate and appeared to reinforce everything that Farage had been telling Labour voters in public meetings up and down the country—that their party no longer cared about the working class, was not interested in Englishness, and could not speak authentically to their intense anxieties over national identity and belonging, and that a new generation of London-based middle-class Labour elites not only held a fundamentally different set of values but also felt distinctly uncomfortable around blue-collar Britain. 'Thornberry reinforced what we knew,' said one Labour insider, who pointed to the same divide that Farage was trying to mobilize.

There is a segment of the party that sees migration as a net positive—who like it, promote it, and defend it. That works in Islington. But it doesn't work in Rochdale, Grimsby, or Rotherham, where migration is seen as a sharp negative. Those two positions make sense, but they are irreconcilable, poles apart. And they are reflected in fundamental disagreements about immigration.

Meanwhile, on the centre-right, Ukip's victories sharpened those anxieties among Conservatives that had been on display in Birmingham. One week after the election of Reckless, Cameron delivered another major speech, this time on immigration. It followed yet another set of disappointing figures on net migration, which had risen to 260,000, a sharp rise on the previous year.[29] He set out a range of new promises that he would fulfil if he was still in power beyond May 2015—to clamp down on colleges and businesses that fail to prevent migrants from overstaying their visas, extend a 'deport first, appeal later' policy, instruct landlords to check the migration status of tenants, introduce a new fund for areas to help ease pressures, adopt a harder line on people traffickers, and restrict EU migrants from receiving state benefits for at least four years. It was, said one of his former advisers, 'one last push' to close down space for Ukip ahead of the general election, another attempt to provide Conservative defectors with answers. From here on, Cameron and his party would increasingly move away from a policy-based response to one that was based on tactics—to try and squeeze Ukip voters back into the mainstream fold, not through a positive offer but by pointing out problems with alternatives. 'After the speech', said the former adviser, 'they decided to rely on the tactical squeeze at the election, which was never likely to be enough'.

On a damp and cold morning in Westminster, gloomy-looking journalists, politicians, and tourists trudged along Whitehall, jostling for space on the wet pavements. There were few smiles on the streets and fewer rays of light in the sky. But there was one figure in the crowd who looked happy. Farage was standing at the entrance to parliament, surrounded by a handful of loyal followers. As the activists looked past the statue of Oliver Cromwell and up at the sand-coloured walls of the Palace of Westminster, they found the building both familiar and strange. Ukip had spent more than twenty years trying to secure a presence on the green benches inside, and yet most of its activists had never taken a step inside. A few minutes later they were in the building, walking briskly along the corridors and through Central Lobby— their purple rosettes and loud voices turning heads along the way. They had come to watch a moment of history. Douglas Carswell, their new MP, was about to be sworn in.

It was a special day for Farage. Some of the younger activists who were with him had not known the struggles that had preceded Ukip's rise. They had not known what it was like when, on a good day, the party polled 3 per cent. It was why some of the younger activists called the veterans 'three percenters'. But the wilderness years had profoundly shaped Farage, who, even now as he walked into the House of Commons, still felt like a complete outsider.

Farage had always assumed that he would have to watch the ceremony from the public gallery, squeezed between tourists who had little idea about what they were watching. Having to sit in the public gallery, behind a large protective screen, came with another irritation—MPs were not allowed to acknowledge the onlookers. But, when news of Farage's presence circulated around the corridors, a friend from across the divide, Conservative MP Philip Hollobone, who was often identified as a possible defector to Ukip, stepped forward. He ensured that the Ukip leader was given access to an adjoining gallery that was reserved for the friends and families of MPs. 'It was the civilized thing to do,' said Hollobone. Farage could now look directly over the chamber and down on the rows of politicians below. But among the sea of faces only two acknowledged him. William Hague, the former leader of the Conservative Party who had fought his own battles with the diehard Eurosceptics, met Farage with an icy stare. Then the government's Chief Whip Michael Gove caught Farage's eye and slowly tipped his head. It was taken as a sign of respect before the war that was about to commence.

Carswell was not the only MP being sworn in that day. The successful Labour candidate from Heywood and Middleton, which Ukip had almost captured—which would have forced a premature end to Ed Miliband's leadership—entered the chamber to a warm welcome. When Carswell followed, he was met with a completely different reaction. Flanked by two sponsors, the longest-serving MP or Father of the House, Sir Peter Tapsell, and Conservative MP Zac Goldsmith, he walked through a chamber that had fallen completely silent. 'That silence', he would claim afterwards, 'was fear. Not fear of me. Fear of the change that is to come.' When he reached the despatch box, Carswell made his oath of allegiance to the Crown and then, with his back to his old party, turned to the Speaker of the House. 'It's good to be back.' After the short ceremony was over, and with anxious MPs looking on, Carswell and Farage walked through the corridors and into the Commons Tea Room. 'Right', said Farage in a loud voice, 'let's order some fruit cake'.

# 9

# Targeting Territory

It was a typically chaotic afternoon in Ukip's headquarters on Brooks Mews. It was early January 2015, and the general election was only four months away. Most of the activists were huddled in the press office watching the latest instalment of Prime Minister's Questions. The office and adjoining rooms were a mess. They were littered with cardboard boxes, and the walls were covered with loose sheets of paper on which activists had scribbled their ideas for the campaign. They did not seem interested in keeping them a secret. The party's innermost thoughts about how to win support were instantly visible to anyone who walked in, including the numerous builders who were renovating the building.

Amid the chaos, toward the back of the offices, Chris Bruni-Lowe was sitting at his desk. He had now been handed the daunting task of having to organize Ukip's entire ground campaign, and it had come with some specific instructions. Farage was hoping to avoid the mistakes that had been made by his predecessors. When it came to fighting elections, past leaders of Ukip had often behaved like irresponsible military generals, throwing candidates over the top with no strategy or idea about where they might break through. The model was flawed, and Farage knew it. If Ukip was to stand a chance of winning seats, then it would need to follow a more professional approach, focusing on only a small number of areas where it already had support and where voters might be prepared to catapult the party into Westminster. 'What I do regard as being likely', he had said to journalists, 'is Ukip winning enough MPs next May in the House of Commons in Westminster to make a difference'. And, unlike in the past, it would try to accomplish this by 'targeting 20, 30 or 40 key seats at the general election'.[1]

Bruni-Lowe was now trying to turn the strategy into action. Behind him, pinned to the wall, was a large map of the country. It outlined every seat, from Orkney and Shetland in Scotland to St Ives in Cornwall. Thirty had been highlighted in bright pink. They were Ukip's target seats—the key battlegrounds where Farage and his party had decided to target their scarce resources in the hope of redrawing the political map. And they too were visible to anybody who walked in to the office. With only a few months until the election, the campaigner was trying to whittle down the list of thirty to a much shorter list of ten. He was trying to find the very best prospects. As his eyes flicked between the map on the wall and a fresh batch of internal polls on his desk, Bruni-Lowe was looking for seats that had the winning formula—where there was a history of support for Ukip, where the other parties looked vulnerable, and where his candidates had shown that they knew how to campaign. Once the seats had been found, they would be sent more support—money, literature, and visits from Farage. But as he worked he was interrupted by his phone. It was a candidate. And he sounded excited.

'Listen Chris, me and the guys went canvassing this morning, knocking on doors. *And you will not believe* the reaction on the doorstep. Everybody bloody loves us! We could win this seat!' Given the infighting that had started to emerge over Ukip's strategy for the election, it was just the kind of news that he needed to hear. 'So here is what I need to win,' continued the candidate. 'Fifteen of your best activists and fifty grand.' Bruni-Lowe, who had still not met many of the candidates, asked where he was standing. 'I am telling you, it is going to be a landslide! I'm in Brent Central!'

Bruni-Lowe put his head on his desk. Brent Central was a hopeless prospect. Even though the MP, Liberal Democrat Sarah Teather, was standing down, Ukip had little chance of replacing her. The seat in north-west London was younger and more educated than the party's usual stamping grounds. It also happened to be one of the most ethnically diverse seats in Britain. Only twelve seats had a higher number of people who described themselves as non-white. Ukip's dire prospects in this part of London, which had clearly not been noticed by its candidate, had been clear for a while. In 2010 the area had been considered such a lost cause that the party had not even bothered to stand a candidate. Four years later, at the European elections, it had finished in fourth place, with less than 10 per cent of the vote. It was no wonder then that the bookies now gave the party less than a 1 per cent chance of capturing the seat in 2015. 'When can you send the money?' asked the candidate. 'Hello?'

The conversation reflects one of the dilemmas that confronts every party ahead of an election—where to target its resources. It is especially pressing for smaller parties. With less money and manpower, they need to think very carefully about how to use their limited ammunition. It is also crucial under first-past-the-post, which rewards parties that get this right and punishes those that get it wrong. Bad decisions can ruin an entire campaign while good ones can greatly improve the chances of a breakthrough. 'He who knows when he can fight and when he cannot', said the famous military general Sun Tzu, 'will be victorious'.

The textbook example of what can happen when parties fail to build concentrated support came in 1983 when the Social Democratic Party (SDP), in alliance with the Liberals, set out on a campaign to replace the Labour Party, which had veered to the radical left. The new SDP–Liberal Alliance had talked excitedly about 'breaking the mould' of the two-party system. At the general election that year it delivered an impressive performance, attracting almost eight million votes or 25 per cent of the national vote. Labour had a fright. The new party finished only two points behind and with only 700,000 fewer votes. It was the best performance by a new third party since Ramsay MacDonald had led Labour into the general election of 1923. But when it came to distributing seats it was a different picture entirely. The Alliance, which had failed to cultivate the strongholds that are needed to finish first-past-the-post, won only twenty-three seats. More than 300 of its candidates finished second. Labour, which had the concentrated support, was handed 209 MPs.[2] For those who talked of redrawing the political map, it had been a harsh lesson.

It would not be until years later, when some from the Alliance had made their way into the Liberal Democrats, that they devoted more thought to targeting. Chris Rennard, who took control of campaigns, rejected the conventional view that where his party had won seats was simply down to luck. Rather than deploy their ammunition in a scattergun approach, he pushed the party to target territory more effectively—to focus only on seats where they had a history of support and the main parties looked vulnerable. It was called target-seat campaigning. Rennard even wrote a book, showing candidates how to identify issues, cultivate bastions of support, and put bar charts on their leaflets, framing the battle as a two-horse race and pushing back against a tendency among voters to see them as a wasted vote. 'Liberal Democrats winning here', read the leaflets.

Before long the strategy was on its way to becoming a science. The Liberal Democrats started to assess seats according to their number of party activists, locally elected councillors, votes at past elections, and the amount of literature that was being delivered. Only seats that collected these data received support. And it worked, at least for a while. In 1997 the Liberal Democrats won forty-six seats. It was their best result since 1929 and their largest number of new seats since 1906. As Rennard pointed out, most of the party's gains had come in areas where the party had already broken through onto the council.[3] Further advances followed as the party positioned itself as an alternative to Labour in the north and the Tories in the south. Within ten years the number of Liberal Democrat MPs had risen to sixty-two. It was the largest number since 1922. Unsurprisingly, some came to view the target strategy as more important than winning a large share of the national vote. Rennard, meanwhile, had become so confident that he offered activists a bet. If they followed his advice and failed to win, he would refund the price of his book.[4] It is rumoured that he never made a single refund.

In the early weeks of 2015, Bruni-Lowe was grappling with the same question that had faced Rennard twenty years earlier—where should Ukip target? Given the habit of leaking sensitive news, it was surprising that the party's list of seats had not already been made public. But this did not stop journalists speculating about where it was pinning its hopes. The party, many thought, would be targeting the two seats that it had won in the by-elections in Clacton, and Rochester and Strood, as well as other seats where the polls suggested it had strong support.

Around the time of the Ukip conference in Doncaster, *Sky News* claimed to have obtained a list of twelve seats that the party was planning to target and a wider hit list of twenty-five. Many were Conservative seats in southern England, including South Thanet, where Farage was standing, and the nearby Kent seats of North Thanet, and Sittingbourne and Sheppey. Others were the old mining area of Forest of Dean, the picturesque and affluent Aylesbury in Buckinghamshire, East Worthing and Shoreham on the Sussex coast, the struggling seaside seat of Great Yarmouth in Norfolk, Boston and Skegness in Lincolnshire, and the working-class seat of Thurrock in Essex. Ukip, it was claimed, was also about to turn its guns on the Liberal Democrat seats of Eastleigh and Portsmouth South, as well as the northern Labour seat of Great Grimsby.[5]

Two months later, the *Sunday Times* cited a leaked analysis of private polls as evidence for the claim that Ukip was 'on course to win up to 25 seats' and 'could even eclipse the Liberal Democrats'. After the by-elections it was also claimed that it had more than doubled its number of target seats from twelve to twenty-five. One anonymous insider was quoted as claiming that Ukip now expected to win at least five seats—Clacton, South Thanet, Thurrock, Boston and Skegness, and Great Yarmouth. Analyst Peter Kellner and academic Colin Rallings were also cited as suggesting that Ukip could win between ten and twelve seats. In the same month the *Daily Telegraph* claimed that the party was targeting sixteen seats. 'If Ukip were to win them all, the party would be the fourth largest party in the Commons, equal with the Democratic Unionists and larger than the SNP, Sinn Fein and Plaid Cymru.' Psephologist John Curtice, meanwhile, warned journalists that Ukip was likely to capture those kinds of numbers only if its support in the opinion polls breached the 20 per cent mark, a few points above its current 16 per cent rating.[6] But this did not stop interest from intensifying and others from talking about the party winning a decent number of seats.

Analysts at the *Guardian* suggested that Ukip could win 'at least' thirty seats, although the five seats of South Thanet, Boston and Skegness, Great Grimsby, Thurrock, and Clacton looked the most certain. The party was a 'good contender' in another ten, such as Great Yarmouth and Thanet North, and had 'a chance of winning' in another fifteen, including Heywood and Middleton and the Liberal Democrat coastal seats of Eastbourne in Sussex and St Austell and Newquay in Cornwall. Others claimed that Farage was secretly plotting to target Eurosceptic Conservatives in seats such as Amber Valley, Cleethorpes, Bury North, and Dudley South, who might be pressured into defecting like Carswell and Reckless. Based on only one poll, meanwhile, the *Mail on Sunday* concluded that public support for Ukip had soared to an all-time high of 25 per cent, 'enough for the party to take Parliament by storm'. Farage, said the newspaper, might soon have 128 MPs.[7]

There was also a debate within the main parties about Ukip's prospects. The centre-right Bow Group suggested that the party might soon capture twelve seats and urged Cameron to address concerns over the EU and immigration—where he had already set out a message.[8] Among left-wing circles, meanwhile, the Fabian Society released a report based on analysis by academic Robert Ford and analyst Ian Warren. They identified no less than thirty-six seats where Ukip was in a strong position to win, where a win was 'quite plausible' or 'possible'. Ford and Warren argued that the most likely Ukip gains included the Conservative seats of Clacton, South Thanet, Thurrock, Great Yarmouth, and Waveney, the Labour seats of Great Grimsby, Dudley North, Plymouth Moor View, Rother Valley, and Rotherham, and the Liberal Democrat seat of Eastleigh. Along with Labour officials they offered advice on how to quell the revolt. Labour, they argued, should focus on cost-of-living issues by offering a freeze on energy prices, raising the minimum wage, and capping rent increases. Other ideas that were put forward included introducing residency requirements for council house waiting lists, curbing welfare payments to families overseas, ring-fencing homes for local people, communicating a more inclusive message, and holding more conversations with voters.[9]

As the debate raged on, the truth was that Farage and his team had not yet decided where to direct their energy. How was the party deciding where to fight? And to what extent was it actually choosing seats that offered the best chances of a breakthrough?

Ukip had started to think about its seats in the shadow of the European election. The work of finding possible breakthrough areas was undertaken by John Harvey, a senior official, and Roger Bird, who had defected to Ukip after more than a decade with the Conservatives. Bird had risen through the ranks, becoming Chairman of the South East and then General Secretary. He had then spent the summer of 2014 writing a report on thirty seats that he thought should be targeted, using results at recent elections as a guide.

Bird saw himself as a keen psephologist, even if some saw his demeanour as rather odd. 'Bird saw everything as a chess game,' reflected one. 'He was the kind of person who probably timed when he went for a coffee in the office so that he would bump into the right person in the kitchen.' Some would also later claim that his assessments of seats had not always been based on objective criteria. 'Some seats were chosen based not on our chances but a desire to keep people happy,' said one official, who suggested that personal relationships often mattered more than the question of whether it was the right kind of territory for a breakthrough. Other senior activists talked of the difficulty of pursuing a target strategy when Ukip had been seriously fighting elections for only a few years. 'In creating target seats', said the Chairman, Steve Crowther, 'it was essentially a theoretical exercise. It is easy for the main parties to choose their targets, but we were going from a standing start and relying on our best guesses, and a lot of polling.'

The thirty target seats that were eventually selected are listed in Table 9.1, alongside our own assessment of how 'Ukip-friendly' they could be considered to be. The ranking of these seats is based on our analysis in Appendix B—which considers the types of voters who live in these seats, past support for Ukip, and whether or not they are politically vulnerable, all of which are analogous to criteria used by Chris Rennard in earlier years. Most of the

Table 9.1. Ukip's target seats, 2015

| Constituency | Region | Ukip favourability ranking | Incumbent | Majority (%) |
|---|---|---|---|---|
| *Top Targets* | | | | |
| Boston and Skegness | East Midlands | 4 | Conservative | 28.8* |
| Great Grimsby | Yorkshire | 13 | Labour | 2.2* |
| Hartlepool | North East | 33 | Labour | 14.4 |
| Rotherham | Yorkshire and Humber | 44 | Labour | 27.9 |
| Castle Point | East of England | 63 | Conservative | 16.9 |
| Dudley North | West Midlands | 96 | Labour | 1.7* |
| South Thanet | South East | 132 | Conservative | 16.6* |
| Heywood and Middleton | North West | 138 | Labour | 12.9 |
| Thurrock | East of England | 211 | Conservative | 0.2 |
| Rochester and Strood | South East | 256 | Conservative | 20.8 |
| *Other Targets* | | | | |
| Clacton | East of England | 2 | Conservative | 28.0 |
| Great Yarmouth | East of England | 15 | Conservative | 9.9 |
| Wentworth and Dearne | Yorkshire and Humber | 20 | Labour | 33.1 |
| Plymouth, Moor View | South West | 28 | Labour | 3.8 |
| North West Norfolk | East of England | 53 | Conservative | 31.0 |
| Cannock Chase | West Midlands | 56 | Conservative | 7.0* |
| St Austell and Newquay | South West | 61 | Liberal Democrat | 2.8 |
| Sittingbourne and Sheppey | South East | 69 | Conservative | 25.5 |

| | | | | |
|---|---|---|---|---|
| North Thanet | South East | 83 | Conservative | 31.2 |
| Camborne and Redruth | South West | 88 | Conservative | 0.2 |
| Torbay | South West | 90 | Liberal Democrat | 8.3 |
| Bognor Regis and Littlehampton | South East | 103 | Conservative | 27.9 |
| South Basildon and East Thurrock | East of England | 110 | Conservative | 12.9 |
| Dover | South East | 115 | Conservative | 10.5 |
| Wyre Forest | West Midlands | 112 | Conservative | 5.2 |
| North Devon | South West | 126 | Liberal Democrat | 11.3 |
| Delyn | Wales | 131 | Labour | 6.1 |
| Forest of Dean | South West | 151 | Conservative | 22.7 |
| Folkestone and Hythe | South East | 182 | Conservative | 19.2 |
| Basildon and Billericay | East of England | 221 | Conservative | 29.7 |
| Eastleigh | South East | 344 | Liberal Democrat | 7.2 |
| North West Cambridgeshire | East of England | 346 | Conservative | 28.6 |

★ Sitting MP retiring ahead of 2015 election.

*Source*: The source of the data on MPs' retirement is <http://parliamentarycandidates.org/data/mps-standing-down/ (accessed 5 April 2015).

seats that Ukip selected were held by the Conservatives and more than half were in its emerging strongholds in east and southern England. In all of them, Ukip had also won at least 30 per cent of the vote at the European elections.

Ukip made some good choices. Most of the thirty seats that were chosen also emerge in the top half of our list of the most friendly seats. Targeting seats such as Boston and Skegness, Great Grimsby, Clacton, and Great Yarmouth made sense, as they are filled with left-behind voters who tend to be receptive to Ukip. Other choices such as Castle Point, South Thanet, and Dudley North were also ranked in the top 150 seats in our list.

The party's choices also revealed how it was thinking about building for the long term. Ukip was planning to make a serious push in more northern Labour seats, such as Hartlepool, Rotherham, and Heywood and Middleton. Another seat on the list was Wentworth and Dearne, in south Yorkshire, also filled with white, poorly educated, working-class pensioners and among the twenty-five most Ukip-friendly seats in the country. But there were some hurdles, which reveal how Ukip was not always making the best choices. In Wentworth and Dearne the Labour MP John Healey had more than 50 per cent of the vote and a majority of almost 14,000. The party would have found more potential in the neighbouring seat of Don Valley. While this seat was slightly less favourable in terms of its demography, emerging at number 49 in our list of the most Ukip-friendly seats, the climate was more favourable. The local Labour MP Caroline Flint had only 38 per cent of the vote and a majority of less than 4,000.

It was a similar picture in Hartlepool, a seat that caught Farage's eye as a symbol of his anti-Labour strategy. Ukip had been impressed with its candidate, who worked in a local supermarket. It had also won the popular vote at the European elections. But the Labour MP had held the seat since 2001 and was unlikely to lose at a general election. Once again a more favourable prospect lay next door. Not only did the seat of Redcar have more receptive voters, but the Liberal Democrat MP was also standing down.

In other cases Ukip frequently made one of two mistakes. Either it was targeting seats that had a lot of voters who would probably have been receptive but that were not politically vulnerable, or it was targeting seats that were politically vulnerable but that did not have a lot of receptive voters. In a few cases the party made both errors, choosing seats that were neither vulnerable nor favourable.

One example was Rochester and Strood, which had political advantages for Ukip but lacked the ideal demography that was found in other seats. According to our analysis, this is 256th in the list of the most Ukip-friendly seats, which goes a long way to answering the question of why the by-election victory was much closer than Carswell's in Clacton. Even though both MPs had won similar support in 2010, Carswell had won his by-election with a majority of 12,000 while Reckless had gained a much slimmer majority of less than 3,000. Clearly, there were political reasons for choosing this seat, but it was also true that Ukip was now facing a much harder battle for re-election, which would divert its scarce resources from far more promising prospects.

Other seats had the opposite problem—they had receptive voters but were not politically vulnerable. In some, the incumbent MP was well entrenched, having won more than 45 per cent of the vote at the previous election or enjoying a majority of more than ten points. This was true in seats that would attract significant attention during the campaign, such as Castle Point in Essex, North West Norfolk, South Basildon and East Thurrock, the Kent seats of Sittingbourne and Sheppey, Thanet North, and Dover, Bognor Regis and Littlehampton in West Sussex, and the south-west seats of Torbay and North Devon. In many seats, like these, that had made it onto the list there were real obstacles that made a breakthrough in 2015 unlikely.

In 2010, for example, the Conservatives had won seats like North West Norfolk, Bognor Regis and Littlehampton, and Sittingbourne and Sheppey with more than 50 per cent of the vote—and were more than twenty-five points ahead of their nearest rival. This was true in North Thanet, an area that had been held by the Tories since the 1800s and Conservative MP Roger Gale since 1983. In North Devon, where Steve Crowther had decided to stand, the Liberal Democrats had over 45 per cent of the vote. Other seats in south England were also odd choices, being neither vulnerable not particularly receptive. One example was the working-class seat of Basildon and Billericay, which was ranked 221st in terms of its Ukip-friendliness. There were also other hurdles. The Conservative MP John Baron had 53 per cent of the vote and a majority of more than 12,000 votes.

Another bad choice was North West Cambridgeshire. This was the 346th most favourable seat. The sitting Conservative MP had 51 per cent of the vote and a majority of more than 16,000 votes. Ukip's organizers were even aware that this seat was unwinnable but had decided to reward a long-serving activist with target-seat status. Pete Reeve, a national organizer and the husband of Lisa Duffy, had spent years building up Ukip. 'It was on the list,' noted one insider, 'but we never thought we would win. It got love and attention because of Reeve.' Forest of Dean had also made the list for strange reasons. Some claimed that the seat had been included on the list of priority target seats in the hope that its candidate, the prominent Steve Stanbury, would help to lobby Ukip's treasurer for additional funds for the overall campaign. Either way, Ukip was not displaying the discipline that was required for a tightly focused target seat campaign.

One person who was not impressed with Bird's list of seats was David Soutter, who in July 2014 had been brought in as Head of Candidates and tasked with strengthening the campaign. Unlike others, Soutter had considerable experience, having worked on elections with Margaret Thatcher, John Major, Sir James Goldsmith, and Robert Kilroy-Silk. At the European elections in 2014, he had helped Ukip to finish first in his home area of Flintshire in north Wales. Shortly afterwards, he received a phone call from Brooks Mews. 'For God's sake,' said an agitated staffer, 'we need people who know what they are doing. Get down here!'

Soutter, who would soon be responsible for finding more than 500 candidates for the general election and ensuring that Ukip stood more than 9,000 others in local elections that were being held on the same day, was surprised by what he encountered in the headquarters of a party that had just won the European Parliament elections.

There were lots of people who saw Ukip as a hobby, a pressure group rather than a party. Very few had organized a party. They had opinions, strong opinions, and some were talented. But they did not know how to build. There were only eleven months until the general election when in reality I needed about two years to get things in shape.

Soutter had been particularly unimpressed with some of the candidates, and how they were being chosen. 'It was clear from the outset that there were already a number of candidates in place who left something to be desired, not in terms of commitment but in terms of ability to deliver a reasonable performance in the elections.' The process that had been used to select the candidates, he claimed, was 'deeply flawed' and unlikely to provide a pool of top calibre people.

A very senior assessor told me on my first visit to an assessment centre that his job was to help people through the process, not see if they were fit to be candidates. There was too much back patting and Buggins' turn about the whole process. All over the country, in particular in London, candidates who had not passed the assessment process had been adopted into seats, regardless of their abilities.

Patronage was playing a role: 'Candidates were allowed to stand or even stay as candidates because they were friends of senior officials and had what was seen as value despite being truly dreadful.'

But Soutter's criticisms did not end there. He was also critical about how the target seats had been chosen. 'Roger Bird had no election experience whatsoever. It was a dreadful list. But Roger was somebody who was right even when he was obviously wrong.' Soutter, who because of his role would quickly develop a firm grasp of the party's infrastructure, was worried about one problem in particular. 'Some of the key seats should simply never have been on the list. They often had crap candidates who were as useful as chocolate teapots, or they had no local branch. Some seats were literally a husband and wife effort. Others were one man and his dog and you would have been lucky if the dog turned up.'

While trying to ensure that some of the seats at least had competent candidates, Soutter encountered other, significant, problems. Shortly before the campaign commenced some activists had publicly criticized the party for allegedly imposing its preferred candidates in seats like Boston and Skegness, or the Labour-held seat of Great Grimsby. In the latter case, which was a promising prospect for the party, activists had taken issue with some offensive statements that had been made by Ukip's chosen candidate, Victoria Ayling. Others had voiced concerns relating to a lurid claim about her family.[10] Nonetheless, and despite these concerns about the lack of internal strength to support such an ambitious thirty-seat strategy, in September 2014 Ukip's National Executive Committee formally approved Bird's report.

The next month, October, saw the arrival of Douglas Carswell, who after defecting and then winning in Clacton had taken responsibility for organizing what would now be called the 'Key Seats Campaign'—the activity that would be happening across the thirty seats, as Ukip prepared for its moment of truth. Unlike Soutter, Carswell saw no major problems with the chosen territory. 'There was already a sensible list,' he explained, 'one or two that should have been on it and one or two that should not. But it was sensible. There was, however, a constant pressure to add to it, so we had to be firm and say no. There was a lot of that.' It was still not entirely clear why some of the seats had been chosen, however. Some insiders reiterated the view that several had been selected not because of objective criteria but rather because of patronage within the party and views about the local MP. 'Not all of the seats were based on demographics, results, or the chance of doing well,' said one. 'In reality some were chosen because of things that no other party would ever use as criteria like "I think this MP is shit".'

These debates would now continue within the Campaign Committee, a steering group comprised of Carswell, Crowther, and Soutter, the party's National Agent Paul Oakden, and veteran organizer Lisa Duffy. As part of the never-ending search for money, Ukip also made Paul Sykes, who had bankrolled the European election, Chairman of the Committee. 'We are very much on the path to Westminster,' said Sykes, while not confirming whether or not he would actually fund the campaign.[11] At the same time it was publicly confirmed that Bruni-Lowe had been given control of the thirty ground campaigns.

Carswell, however, was still anxious about Ukip's amateurism. When taking control of the key seats, he talked about reaching a new level of professionalism and finally moving away from the dismal campaigning that had been on display in battles like Newark. He had firm ideas about what he wanted, talking often about delivering targeted, professional, and tightly knit campaigns. But he was also overestimating his new party's ability. Ukip remained hampered by a severe lack of experience. Only a few people knew how to win a seat. This was also the first time that Ukip was taking a general election seriously, which meant that it had almost no reliable data on voters—data that other parties had gleaned from past campaigns. It was a major problem that put the party at an immediate disadvantage. Without information on who was planning to vote for whom and why, Ukip was unable to identify, target, and mobilize supporters.

'This was about scale,' said Carswell. 'If you need 40 per cent of the vote to win, you do not spend your time faffing about selling pieces of purple rock. It is a numbers game.' From one meeting to the next he talked again and again about the critical importance of gathering data, also urging the party to adopt a new computer system that would allow activists to record what was happening on the ground. 'Douglas had an energy and a passion about his target-seat campaign,' said one. 'It was amazingly planned to a micro level. It was all about getting over 15,000 pledges per target seat, using a carefully designed approach involving a rolling series of paid-for mass delivery of leaflets, plus postal surveys going out to 20,000 voters per target seat.' Carswell was importing much of this from his time in the Conservative Party.

But Ukip had never run this kind of campaign before. 'The big growing-up piece for us', said Crowther, 'is getting candidates to understand that if you can't do the get-out-the-vote at the end of the process then you cannot get into the mix. You have to have data. We were trying to catch up with data functions that the Liberal Democrats and others had been doing for generations.' Throughout October and November, Ukip's veteran activists looked on in bewilderment as the headquarters on Brooks Mews was taken over by telephone canvassers. The newcomers spent each day calling voters in the key seats, increasing the number of pledges—people who were promising to vote for Ukip, and to whom the candidates would return during the campaign. The operation had been funded by Arron Banks, the businessman and former Conservative donor.

Carswell had also proposed other changes, which would soon fuel the growing tension. As in Clacton, he wanted candidates in the key seats to anchor their campaigns in local issues and to present a softer and more inclusive image, avoiding the divisive tone and core-vote strategy that had been on display during the European elections. But some found him abrasive and dictatorial. 'Douglas was not good at team work,' recalled one. 'He treated Chris Bruni-Lowe more like a junior assistant than our campaign chief. He would issue a stream of micro instructions that he wanted done immediately, regardless of other work that we had.' Others talked of witnessing 'volcanic eruptions of anger', while even senior officials had started to refer to him openly as 'the Tory'. But, for his part, Carswell was willing to make enemies.

I think I should have been *more* abrasive and dictatorial. But you need to make compromises. One has to be forceful. I threw my weight around. If I have to scream and shout, then I will scream and shout. I felt I'd mortgaged the farm on this and I would do what it takes.

After Christmas, all the candidates and agents from the thirty seats assembled at a two-day conference in Stafford. Because of fears that the list of target seats might be leaked, candidates had not been allowed to wear name tags in case they could be traced to specific seats. They were then given several presentations. Bruni-Lowe first told them how he had defeated the Conservatives in Rochester and Strood. Then Ukip's new Director of Communications, Paul 'Gobby' Lambert, told them how they should deal

with his old employer. Before joining the party, Lambert had been a prominent producer in the BBC and was well known within Westminster. Paul
Oakden, who had overseen the battle in Heywood and Middleton, then
briefed the candidates on electoral law, while David Soutter told them what
to expect. 'From this point forward', he warned, 'all of you will be judged
constantly. The spotlight will be on you all.' Carswell then took over,
explaining how the campaign would be run and what he expected from the
candidates. It was an important moment. 'A lot of them had not fought seats
before,' he said. Carswell also felt concerned that the party had selected its
candidates only six months before the election. 'If you find out they are not
much good, then by that point it becomes difficult to do anything about it.'
It left only a very small amount of time to teach them the basics of how to
run a semi-professional campaign.

'It was hard to get them to conceptualize what twenty thousand votes
looked like,' Carswell said. 'Putting out street stalls are [sic] not enough.
Organizing meetings with existing supporters are [sic] not enough. We
talked again and again about canvassing.' In the past, Ukip had only ever
invested in what campaigners call 'set pieces'—events and action days that
were intended to generate publicity. But now activists were being told to
fight door-to-door, to collect and analyse data on voters meticulously, and
to undertake much of the battle away from the media glare. As he looked at
the candidates, Carswell said that he expected them to design and deliver at
least two personalized, locally focused leaflets that would be followed by
a mass survey exercise in each seat—again, designed to generate masses of
data. They should use the computer system, build up their number of
pledges, and then use the data to guide their canvassing sessions. But some
of the inexperienced candidates were clearly overwhelmed, and nervous.
One highlighted a problem that had already been noted by Soutter, and that
reflected a problem that was at the core of Ukip's campaign. 'I am in a target
seat but I don't even have a branch. How am I supposed to get thousands
of pledges?'

Carswell tried to calm nerves by explaining how each of the candidates
would be receiving around £30,000 in support. But this would not be
unconditional. Whether or not they would receive ongoing support would
be determined by the performance of candidates, including the quality of
their leaflets and the number of pledges that they had collected, as Rennard
and his Liberal Democrat team had done. 'Target seats were told they were
target seats but there would be a reconsideration about where the final push

would be in February,' said Crowther. 'This would be based not only on polls but on whether the candidate was equipped to go the whole way.' But not every candidate would make it through the process of natural selection. 'Some of them got huffy,' said Carswell. 'Some went away from that day and came back immediately with draft leaflets and proposals. But some of them, four months later, had still been unable to put together a basic leaflet.' In an attempt to steer clear of the problems that had repeatedly dogged its European campaign, the party had also warned both its candidates and its members away from using social media, in order 'to fill a notable hole in our code of discipline'. Supporters would now also be required to obtain written consent to use Ukip's logo.[12]

When the list of seats, which had been compiled before Bruni-Lowe's promotion, was finally handed to the campaign organizer, he was far from happy. 'The problem was that the seats had not been subject to much scrutiny as when they had been chosen we had been focused on the by-elections. Ideally, we would have spent two or three months looking at seats, polling them and getting a sense. But that was not the case.' Looking at the seats, where he was now responsible for overseeing the ground war, he identified one problem after another. 'These seats are completely unwinnable,' he said out loud. 'Why the fuck are we targeting Torbay? Why the fuck are we fighting in Delyn? Why the fuck are we doing North West Norfolk?'

Like Farage, Bruni-Lowe shared his belief that Ukip needed to dedicate its energy to only a handful of top prospects—seats that would be seen as a microcosm of its national vote. In this way, he hoped to win between four and five million votes nationwide while also maximizing the chance of a breakthrough in a few key areas. But it had also become clear that Ukip simply did not have enough money, manpower, and campaign experience to deliver such a broad assault. These constraints had become apparent during the by-elections, when the party had struggled to fight just two seats at the same time. Now, it was setting out to fight thirty—some of which were far from ideal battlegrounds.

The problem, not lost on insiders like Soutter, was compounded by the fact that some of the target seats were scattered far and wide, which made it difficult for Ukip to concentrate its older and inexperienced activists across thirty battlefields. 'We just didn't have the resources to fight over six hundred seats and then target the thirty,' he said. 'The strategy was all wrong. We didn't have the resources for it.' Instead, Soutter had wanted to run a cluster seat campaign, to focus Ukip's limited firepower on a smaller number of promising seats that were close to one another—allowing activists to spill over into other campaigns. 'The problem was that the other parties could clearly see where we were targeting,' he continued,

while our activists were spread thinly across the country, fighting in target seats that were often out on their own. I wanted to overcome that problem by focusing on clusters of seats in south Yorkshire, or the Lancashire mill towns, but Carswell and Bird were just southern Tories. They had no idea about our potential further north.

Nor was the problem lost on some who had been offered jobs with Ukip. 'A friend of mine was offered one of the jobs in communications,' said Raheem Kassam. 'He was told about the strategy, about the 600 seats and the 30 targets. He just turned it down. He had the foresight to see that the party was massively over-extending itself. It was threadbare.'

While the by-elections had helped to sustain momentum, they would increasingly be seen as a major distraction that had prevented the small and thinly resourced team from organizing more effective ground campaigns out in the constituencies—not least in South Thanet. During the winter, Bruni-Lowe had become anxious about the lack of work being undertaken in the Kent seat. The distraction of the by-elections had also meant that Ukip had struggled to spend what money it did have for the key seats before limits on what the parties were allowed to spend had been introduced towards the end of December. A good deal of this money had often already been spent on the key seats, some of which were poor prospects, had incompetent activists, and had almost no infrastructure on the ground. To make matters worse, at the meeting in Stafford, many candidates had been assured that they would receive ongoing support, which was about to cause new problems. Now, with the election only a few months away, little could be done to rectify the situation. By the time that Bruni-Lowe was sitting in his office, trying to find the top ten prospects, he faced a difficult conclusion— it was too late to overhaul the campaign.

'In March', he explained,

I tried to get the party to stop spending money on all these seats. I told them that some were simply not winnable, that we needed to be more ruthless and switch our resources to other seats where we had a chance. But the candidates had received certain promises and the party felt that it needed to honour those commitments. Because many of the initial seat selections were based on personal relationships this meant that when other promising seats emerged later on in the campaign, like Dagenham and Rainham, we could not take full advantage.

The campaigner also had a staggering workload. Though few people knew it, Ukip's central operation was wafer thin. No more than twenty staff ran the entire campaign, while there was rarely even half that number in Brooks Mews. And because so few had experience, this left the small number of competent activists spinning countless plates. 'There were hardly any of us there,' said Patrick O'Flynn, who in February would be brought back in as Campaign Director to try and strengthen the campaign.

There were one or two people, but most were not experienced and had not put a campaign together before. It was a ghost ship. It was overwhelming. Many times I would say, 'how the hell are we achieving this?' Maintaining a double figure poll rating felt miraculous. If the other parties knew how little we had. It was Rorke's drift every single day.

Whereas his counterparts in the main parties had dozens if not hundreds of campaigners who were on the payroll, Bruni-Lowe by contrast was often to be found in his bunker-room office alone. 'Chris had an activist working for him at one point, as in *one* activist, but she had little experience,' said Kassam. 'And I had a guy working under me who would turn up at eleven in the morning and leave at three in the afternoon.' When Bruni-Lowe's mobile phone could get a signal, it rang constantly, with candidates from across the country fielding questions about leaflets, polls, and prospects. Most evenings he would leave the office only to return home and answer emails into the early hours. He felt deeply anxious. He was seriously over-stretched. And he was exhausted.

The void that now seemed to be at the heart of Ukip's campaign was not helped by the fact that almost every senior official had decided to stand as a parliamentary candidate. Instead of coordinating the national effort, they were often out in the constituencies, fighting battles that they had no hope of winning. The Chairman Steve Crowther was standing in North Devon, his deputy Suzanne Evans was contesting the safe Conservative seat of Shrewsbury and Atcham, Steve Stanbury, a prominent activist in Brooks Mews, was in Forest of Dean, and Patrick O'Flynn, the actual Campaign Director, was standing as a candidate in Cambridge, one of the least friendly seats for Ukip in the entire country. Even junior activists who had helped to keep Brooks Mews ticking over, like the Young Independence Chairman Jack Duffin, had decamped to campaign against Boris Johnson in Uxbridge, taking other members of the youth wing with him. 'Why are you taking them to Uxbridge!' Kassam had shouted during a typically stressful day. 'They should be in South Thanet!'

Farage, meanwhile, would later acknowledge the problem, tracing the internal weakness to some of his own flaws as a leader.

I watched a documentary once about how a very successful cricket captain had man-managed his team, how he had used different techniques to get the most out of the different players. My failing as a leader is that I am too busy playing the game to man-manage. The whole of our high command were standing in key seats. We should have had separate functions.

Others agreed. 'Nothing would have pleased me more', said Kassam 'than to have all those people around a table in the morning thinking about the campaign, like they do in the main parties. But nobody wanted to do that.' Meanwhile Soutter, who was struggling to organize hundreds of Ukip candidates, observed the same problem.

You know the Godfather? Michael Corleone fell out with his consiglieri Tom Hagan because he needed a wartime adviser. Well, we were in wartime and needed a wartime chairman, who could take the party by the horns. But our chairman decided to stand in Devon. He was in the office two days a week during the election. It felt like the last days of Rome.

The lack of campaign strength became abundantly clear when Farage and Kassam flew off to Milan to visit Beppe Grillo's Five Star Movement. Whereas the Italians had a network of highly skilled and Internet-savvy campaigners, Ukip's campaign was increasingly falling on the shoulders of just one man. 'Chris Bruni-Lowe is brilliant,' reflected Carswell. 'He gets it. But we need twenty Chris Bruni-Lowes. We put him under enormous pressure. That is not a criticism of anybody but if we had selected candidates eighteen months earlier then we could have tried to incubate Chris's skills in others. But we didn't.' Others pointed to the same problems, echoing Soutter's earlier observation that Ukip did not have enough quality people for the chosen strategy. 'We needed an integrated campaign', said O'Flynn 'but we just did not have enough people of enough experience to optimize a campaign on that scale. If we had had a few more sensible bodies and people who could spread ideas in the media that would have helped enormously.' The fragility of the campaign became strikingly apparent at one meeting. 'We were talking about who would do what during the campaign,' said one insider who had sat around the table. 'It basically went like this. Target seats? Chris. Nigel's tour? Chris. Messaging? Chris. Strategy? Chris.'

Some of the candidates were generating further problems. Many were wildly optimistic and, like their colleague in Brent, were convinced that they were on course for victory. 'Many got what I call candidate's disease,' said Paul Nuttall, 'where they all thought they were going to win. Our expectation management wasn't good enough.' Typical of the interactions was one candidate who presented a single online poll as evidence for why she was about to win 60 per cent of the vote and should be given more money. 'It was probably the least scientific thing that I have ever seen,' sighed Bruni-Lowe. Meanwhile, when other candidates were handed internal polls, which showed them lagging well behind the other parties, they said that the data were wrong. 'It's a rogue poll. They're not sampling the right people.' Others noticed the same problem. 'There was no management of expectation. Everybody thought that everything was up for grabs.' And so did Ukip's voters. According to one poll by YouGov, more than half of them were expecting the party to win at least twenty-one MPs.

That expectations were beginning to spiral out of control was reflected in the reaction at one meeting of a Ukip regional organizer—a senior position. If the party did not win at least fifty seats, he said, then it would be a 'major failure' and 'people will need to be fired'. 'It is ridiculous,' said Bruni-Lowe. 'Many of them are not strong enough to be candidates, but they are drawing up the curtains for Downing Street. Nobody is being real with these people.'

The tension culminated at another heated meeting held after Bruni-Lowe had selected the top ten seats. 'They were the ones', said Crowther, 'where there was a strong grass-roots operation, where the demographics were right, the key seats campaign had been implemented on the ground, they had done good direct mails, they had gone out and got data, they had embraced everything that the key seat campaign was trying to do'. The seats included unsurprising choices such as South Thanet, Rochester and Strood, Thurrock, Castle Point, and Boston and Skegness. Others that continued to attract interest were dropped altogether. When internal polls suggested that Great Yarmouth could not be won, the party redeployed its local organizer to Boston and Skegness. Four Labour seats had also made the final list— Hartlepool, Great Grimsby, Heywood and Middleton, and Dudley North, all designed to symbolize Ukip's 2020 Strategy and its desire to push into the north. Bruni-Lowe, however, had remained reluctant to invest heavily in northern England. 'My view was that, however much we would spend in the north, we would get the same result. It was an election too early for us. We would finish second, possibly in more than one hundred seats, but we only gave an extra push in four.' This meant that in many northern Labour seats Ukip would essentially stand paper candidates, who received almost no support.

But when, at the meeting, some of the regional organizers were told that their seats had not been chosen, they were furious and refused to help those that had made it to the final stage. 'I am insulted that I am not a target seat,' said one. Soutter, who had spent decades working on campaigns, noticed how the problem was having a real effect on the ground. 'We told them, "Look you are not going to win in Bath or Uxbridge but if we work hard then we might win in Thurrock, South Thanet, or Great Grimsby. Please come and help." But they wouldn't.' The problem had been exacerbated by Ukip's decision to invest money in all the thirty seats, which removed any incentive for its foot soldiers to then redirect their energy into the top ten. 'Why should we give you our resources', said one candidate, 'when the party has already spent money on each seat?' Bruni-Lowe tried to explain why winning a handful of MPs in the most favourable seats was critical to the future of the party. But some of the organizers were not receptive and told the campaigner that he was on his own.

Nor was this situation helped by other events. Just as the campaign was getting underway, some felt that Douglas Carswell withdrew from the effort. 'He had a lot of stuff to share,' said Damian Wilson, a senior organizer, 'surveys, advance leaflets and such. Once all that was on stream he did make it clear that he had a seat to win and he would focus on that.' Others noted a similar break. 'He stopped coming to the meetings in February. He just didn't turn up any more.' Stanbury also observed how the MP, one of only a few with campaign experience, was redirecting his attention.

As time went on it became clear that Douglas's focus had shifted away from the target-seat campaign. He became insular and obsessed only with his campaign in Clacton. This was amazing and disappointing to see. He increasingly gave the impression that he had used his target-seat role to ensure that he got what he wanted from central resources for Clacton and that other seats were palpably less important'.

But others defended their new MP, noting how he had only ever promised to oversee the key seats until the start of the short campaign, at the end of March. 'Douglas designed the target-seat campaign,' said Crowther. 'Then he pushed it through and went off to get himself elected in Clacton. He was never the man to implement it in the seats.'

Either way, the fact remained that Ukip's central operation was left in an even weaker state, and an even heavier load was put onto the shoulders of only a few. The party had also lost Roger Bird, who some claimed had not always used objective criteria when selecting seats. He had been temporarily suspended amid a national media storm. One activist, Natasha Bolter, who had hoped to be selected as a candidate for a top seat, claimed that Bird had propositioned her in the snooker room of the Oxford and Cambridge Club, 'marking up' to ensure that she made it onto the approved list of candidates. He would later be cleared, although he left his position by mutual consent.[13]

Bruni-Lowe was under increasing pressure. He had been asked by Farage to assume responsibility for his campaign in South Thanet—a move that some, including Carswell, had opposed. By this time the campaigner had risen to the top of Ukip. He had made it into the leader's inner circle. 'Chris always had Nigel's ear,' said one official, 'and his relationship with Nigel grew and grew to the point where he became his number one political and strategy adviser'. Bruni-Lowe was now also sharing an office with Raheem Kassam, Farage's senior adviser. They were always together, sharing their ideas about the campaign and how the party needed to change if it was to grow. 'The reason that we got on so well', said Kassam, 'is that we could look each other in the eye and know we were not bullshitting each other'. Both were also fiercely loyal to Farage—whom they routinely called 'Boss Man'.

The advisers would continually defend their leader from any perceived criticism, although their proximity to Farage had started to alienate others. They were being supported by Steve Stanbury, who after Bird's departure had been recruited as the new Party Director. Stanbury, who had spent almost thirty years with the Conservative Party, and was now tasked with bringing more discipline to Brooks Mews, observed how the newfound influence of the young advisers had begun to generate unease. 'Chris was supported by everyone who was close to Nigel, who knew about the strategy,' reflected Stanbury. 'But of course there were huge jealousy issues from the others who resented his access to Nigel, his relative youth and recent joining of Ukip. The old guard resented the new control and strategy. But they were tactical implementers not campaign strategists.'

Carswell, meanwhile, had become concerned about Bruni-Lowe's proximity to Kassam, who, some claimed, was having a malign influence on Farage and the campaign. For some, the arrival of Kassam had been generating concern since the autumn—his links to libertarian right-wing groups in the United States and his involvement with the divisive Breitbart media group, which often ran toxic campaigns against immigration and established politicians, were seen as a symbol of his more aggressive style. 'Raheem was an utter disaster,' said Suzanne Evans. 'It was pure divide and rule politics.' Others pointed to a particular example of why some had found Kassam alienating from early on. 'Raheem [who controlled Farage's Twitter account] decided to have a Twitter war with comedian Frankie Boyle. This to me was nuts. If you have a war with Frankie Boyle, a professional comedian, you are going to lose. You are going to look like a twat. That was the kind of thing Nigel would not have done previously.' Patrick O'Flynn had also rounded on the influence of the adviser, though traced the disagreement as much to personality than to differences over ideology or political strategy. 'He comes from the very right-wing libertarian school of American thinking, but I don't think he tried to impose that on Nigel and the campaign. He recognized the context in which he was operating. But he was a very combative personality, he wanted self-glorification, name-checks for himself, which is not traditionally the way that you do the advisory role. He had an appalling relationship with the press office.'

Kassam knew that he was a polarizing figure, however. 'My problem is not that I start fights because, generally, I don't. My flaw is that when I am in a fight I don't know when to stop.' For his part, he would argue that his hands-on approach and thirst for political capital had alienated some in Ukip who lacked experience of front-line politics and had failed to push the party onto a more professional level. He was, he would claim, merely doing the job that he had been given to do.

Nigel didn't want me there as a soft touch. My job was to insulate, protect and promote Nigel as a person, as a brand, and as a party leader. People wanted Nigel to be their agony uncle, calling him with their personal problems. My job was to make sure that things like that did not happen any more.

Either way, such was the concern about Kassam's influence that, at one point, Carswell requested that Bruni-Lowe be given his own office, away from the adviser, or moved out of Brooks Mews altogether. 'He hated the fact that Chris and Raheem were working more and more together,' said Stanbury, who was now also working at the heart of the campaign. 'Douglas wanted control and Chris to answer to him only. This was never going to happen. Many times Douglas asked me as Party Director to move CBL away from Raheem or vice versa. I always refused, as we needed a positive dynamic of ideas and strategy.' One day, after his request was not granted, Carswell took matters into his own hands. 'Douglas just came into Brooks Mews,' recalled Kassam, 'picked up Chris's stuff, and put it in a different office. He treated him like a child, which just pushed him toward Nigel.'

Other problems were also quickly bubbling towards the surface. As the election neared, Farage and his advisers felt increasingly disillusioned with their press team, but especially Paul 'Gobby' Lambert, whom they had only recently hired as the new Director of Communications. Lambert, who had a reputation for straight-talking (hence 'Gobby'), had arrived at exactly the moment when the Roger Bird and Natasha Bolter scandal was plastered all over the media. 'For fuck's sake!' screamed Lambert, as he paced around Ukip's chaotic press office. 'It's my first fucking day!'

But, while Lambert was well regarded, and initially described by Farage as somebody who would 'fit Ukip like a glove', there were soon problems. Some in the party felt that he was out of his depth and unable to meet the demands of an anti-Westminster party. 'If you take people from the media and put them in a party press office,' reflected Steve Crowther, 'it is not always an easy transition. Paul had key strengths in terms of how to deal with broadcast media, but he did not have the time to make the transition from being the poacher into the gamekeeper.' Even some in the press team agreed that their new recruit had not remedied one of Ukip's weaknesses.

Nigel has this thing where he must have a star. And he did it with Gobby. But Paul was a bad hire. He is a producer, not a press officer. He was too nervous and lacking in confidence because he did not know what he was doing. The media room is fast moving so you need to know what you are doing.

Some complained how Lambert badged every piece of news as 'urgent' and that the press office had taken on a different mood, leading some to call it 'the depress office'.

Tensions between the communications and campaign wings would soon become a recurring theme of the election. When Bruni-Lowe suggested that Farage should use a northern Labour seat as a venue for a major speech,

Lambert disagreed, arguing that journalists would not leave London. 'They did not understand that we were running a core vote campaign. This was about us winning ten seats not pleasing the BBC or the Westminster lobby.' Some in the press team, meanwhile, were feeling increasingly annoyed at how key decisions were being made by the triumvirate of Farage, Bruni-Lowe, and Kassam, with little consultation.

Some drew a straight line from many of these problems to Ukip's history, which they argued had allowed amateurism and personal rivalries to flourish. Those at the very centre of the campaign, claimed some, had never had to work under the discipline and professionalism of the main parties. 'It was a not a job to them,' said Kassam.

It was a social club that they just happened to get paid to be in. The people who wanted success, *real* success, did not want that. Those people worked from seven in the morning until midnight, and then emailed when they got home. The others did not like that. It had not been done before. It was not so much amateurism as a wilful attempt not to be a professional party.

As the most important campaign in Ukip's history rapidly approached, and along with it a rare chance to achieve a truly historic breakthrough, the party looked increasingly like an amateur and thinly resourced rebel army that was about to be overwhelmed and outgunned by professional forces. While Farage and his party looked ahead to the day of reckoning, most of their high command had scattered, their head organizer was drowning in work, and some of their inexperienced foot soldiers were refusing to cooperate. 'If the other parties could really see how things were done, how little we had and the chaos,' said Stanbury, 'then they would not have believed it. They really wouldn't.' Ukip was in turmoil—and the fight had not yet even begun.

# 10

# Into Battle

Ukip was not the only party moving into campaign mode. As Britain headed into 2015, the other parties were also embarking on the so-called 'long campaign'. It would continue until the end of March, when parliament would be dissolved and the 'short campaign' would take over, taking the country through to polling day. According to the polls, the election was too close to call. While a few months earlier Labour had enjoyed a lead over the Conservatives that, on some days, had extended to nine points, its advantage had now disappeared.[1] Only two points separated the two main parties, which were hovering between 31 and 33 per cent of the vote. There was a consensus that neither would secure an overall majority. When one journalist opened the New Year by sitting down with the leading pollsters, not one of them predicted that Britain would soon have a majority government.[2]

Yet, despite the apparent closeness of the race, the Conservatives looked confident. Whether theirs was the look of the true believer, or of somebody who knew something about the race ahead that nobody else did, the party appeared convinced that its message of economic competence combined with David Cameron's lead over Miliband in the leadership ratings, which was now a striking twenty-five points, would pull them through.[3] It was not even close. The belief that now seemed to run deep among Conservatives was quiet but persistent—the people would soon come to their senses, even if the pollsters suggested that they had not.

Cameron began the year on the *Andrew Marr Show*, reiterating his 'competency versus chaos' narrative and relentlessly framing Miliband and Labour as the harbingers of financial ruin. But he also had a carrot for those who had left for Ukip. The promised referendum on Britain's continued EU membership might be brought forward. 'The referendum must take place before the end of 2017. If we could do that earlier, I would be

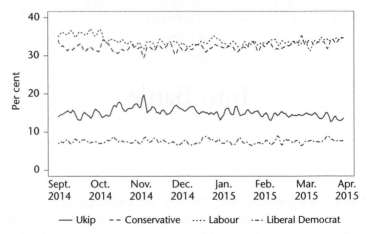

**Figure 10.1.** Party support in the opinion polls, September 2014 to April 2015
*Source*: UK Polling Report.

delighted.' It was one of his last rolls of the dice. At the start of the year, some had described Ukip as a deflating balloon, but this was far from accurate.[4] While numerous problems were undermining its campaign, from a lack of money to inexperience, Farage and his party were still averaging over 15 per cent in the polls. There had been no collapse (see Figure 10.1). Conscious of this fact, and ever since the big speech in Birmingham, those around the prime minister had now decided to downplay the issues that lay at the heart of Ukip's appeal. They would continue to provide answers when asked, but they would not go toe-to-toe with Farage. Pointing to how Cameron was avoiding immigration, some saw the shift as an admission that the centre-right had ultimately failed to defeat its rival in political debate, or had finally acknowledged that there was 'no point wrestling a pig in the mud: you both get dirty but the pig doesn't care'.[5]

Farage, meanwhile, had wanted to start the year quietly. As he sat in his office in January, a few days after being named 'Briton of the Year' by *The Times*, he felt a mixture of optimism and apprehension. 'I think that we are going to win eight to ten seats as we are, but if we get it right we might win thirty. And I think we will come second to Labour in 150 seats. If Miliband wins this thing, Ukip will be in a remarkable position long term.' But he was also concerned about his party's readiness. Like Bruni-Lowe, who was grappling to get the campaign into shape, Farage also felt overwhelmed and distracted. 'I am aware of where we need to go. But I worry about whether I will have the time to think and prepare myself to do the job properly to the level that is required. How I perform in the next eight weeks will be key to our position at the dissolution of parliament.'

That he felt anxious had become clear during the Christmas break. One night, while sleeping in the early hours, he had suddenly bolted upright with a realization. 'I've got to have a break,' he thought. Over the years he had become used to ignoring the various voices in his life that had urged him to slow down—the relatives and friends who had expressed concern about how he routinely burned the candle at both ends, the activists who felt anxious about how the fortunes of their party and Farage were intimately entwined, and the supporters who would write into Brooks Mews, urging party officials to 'tell Nigel to put down the cigarettes and alcohol for the sake of the country'. That events had taken their toll was reflected in the decision that Farage now made. Before yet another gruelling campaign, he would have a dry January. He would avoid alcohol for an entire month. He had not taken such a break for ten years.

Ukip was also planning a quiet start, although it would not last. At the start of the campaign the mood among insiders had been buoyed by news that the UK broadcasting regulator OfCom thought Ukip was likely to qualify for 'major party status'. The proposed change, based on election results and the polls, was not just symbolic. It would influence the regulation of election coverage, giving major parties at least two election broadcasts. But if Ukip was to capitalize on this, then it would need to have something to say—and its campaign was not getting off to the best of starts.

Some in the press office had wanted to launch the campaign at the same time as the main parties, anxious to sustain the publicity that had followed the by-elections. But, as was routine, those around Farage thought differently. They wanted to hold back. There was more political capital to be had, they argued, by watching the main parties 'slug it out' in a negative war of attrition, firing artillery at each other while Ukip lurked in the shadows. 'If we bide our time and wait for the opportunities, then we will come through the smoke on the battlefield with something that sounds completely different. That's our opportunity.' But the reality was that the decision to hold back owed more to constraints than to strategy.

The election was four months away, and Farage worried that his party did not have enough to say. 'We simply don't have enough for one speech every week,' he had told one of his advisers. The manifesto was not finished. It was still being drafted by Suzanne Evans, who, during long eighteen-hour days, was trying to craft a message that would simultaneously appeal to 'the working-class and to the

Tory heartlands' while also tackling some of Ukip's weaknesses. 'My feeling', said Evans, 'was that we needed to tackle the idea that we were a single-issue party and one-man band, that we didn't just bang on about immigration and the EU, to show that we were bigger than all that'. But it was not yet clear whether the party would focus on mobilizing its core voters, as in the European elections, and the last days in Rochester and Strood, or try to reach out beyond its core base, as Carswell and Evans had been advocating.

There was also another constraint. Some of the donors who had promised big injections of cash had gone quiet. 'Paul Sykes promised all sorts', said Soutter, 'but in the end he delivered nothing'. The lack of firepower, or even of a strategy for obtaining money, was a major problem. 'The fundraising strategy when I got there', said Kassam, 'well, there wasn't one. It just consisted of Nigel having some dinners. I tried to implement a Rand Paul-type online operation, which seemed to work well, but it was all a bit late.' With Sykes no longer bankrolling the campaign, the party became dependent on an even smaller list of donors, including Arron Banks and Richard Desmond. The latter owned the *Express* newspaper and was about to hand £1.3 million to Farage—to 'stand up for people who are struggling'.[6] But much of the money from the donors would not arrive until April, which restricted Ukip's ability to match the longer offensive that was being waged by the main parties. 'A lot of the money came really late on,' said one. 'We could use it, but it would have been more helpful if we'd had it earlier.'

The problem was compounded by the fact that, when they did throw money into the war chest, some of Ukip's inexperienced donors liked to invest in their own projects. Donations came with strings attached. Some wanted to invest only in particular regions of the country, while others wanted their money spent on unconventional initiatives. One afternoon, the campaign team listened quietly to one donor explain how he wanted his donation to fund giant advertisement balloons, or 'blimps', that would pass through the skies advertising Ukip. The idea never got off the ground. But there was a serious point. Rather than channel money into a central operation, which could support an overarching strategy, Ukip had parallel operations running at the same time, with little coordination. This further weakened the campaign. The constraints led the party to revert to its traditional campaign model—trying to deliver a shorter and loud campaign, like that run ahead of the European election in 2014. The campaign for the general election would not begin until February at the earliest. But the plan for a quiet start soon met a premature end.

Infighting had long been a defining feature of Ukip. Through much of December and January, Farage had been holed up in Brooks Mews and distracted by a problem. The fallout revolved around Neil Hamilton, a former Conservative MP who was now a senior Ukip official. In 1994, while a minister in John Major's government, Hamilton had been embroiled in a 'cash-for-questions' scandal, accused of taking cash-stuffed envelopes to ask questions in parliament. He was found guilty by the Parliamentary Standards Commissioner but had refused to resign from his seat in Tatton, one of the safest Conservative seats. In 1997 he lost the seat to Independent Martin Bell and would soon declare bankruptcy.[7] Five years later, Farage invited the Hamiltons to a restaurant to try and persuade them to stand for Ukip in the 2004 European elections. While they declined, they did agree to join the party. 'It was the least I could do after a four-bottle lunch,' Neil Hamilton would later joke. The former Conservative kept a low profile, declining other invitations to stand in elections. But by 2010, and with his finances restored, Hamilton set out on a quest for political redemption. He had soon won election to the party's National Executive Committee. His ambition, like Ukip's support, was on the rise. Hamilton was impressed with the party's appeal to Labour voters, which he witnessed on the campaign trail in the north. 'There I was, an old member of Thatcher's government, and I was mobbed by Labour voters. They liked me! I mean, they actually liked me!'

With the 2015 election on the horizon, he decided to pursue a return to the House of Commons. But he would need two things—a seat he could win and an endorsement from his new party. By this time, however, the fringe party that he had joined was a different beast. Success had underlined the need for credibility. Whereas Ukip had once welcomed Hamilton's parliamentary experience, it now worried that the tainted MP would undermine its claim to be a radical alternative. 'People like me', said one activist, 'did not get into politics to prop up corrupt old Tories'. Senior officials agreed and set out to thwart the comeback. 'I was told that whatever happened he should not be on the list,' said Soutter, who had been brought in to strengthen Ukip's candidates.

But Hamilton pushed on and was supported by Stuart Wheeler, a major donor. During the summer of 2014 he had put his name forward for Boston and Skegness—a top prospect. But when it became apparent that he might secure the nomination, insiders stepped in. 'I mean seriously,' asked one, 'do you want Brown Envelope Man representing Ukip in Westminster?' To block the move, some had commissioned a poll to test the effect of Hamilton on the party's prospects in the seat. The results were contested. Some claimed that they showed that, while Ukip could still win the seat, his presence would cost them around five points, although Hamilton maintains that he had a small positive effect and that the results were 'suppressed and never shown to the NEC, for whom it had been commissioned'.[8] Either way, Hamilton was overruled. He would later claim that Farage had warned that he would unleash a 'scorched-earth' policy to destroy the former Conservative if he did not withdraw. The promising seat was instead given to a local Ukip councillor, Robin Hunter-Clarke. He was only 22 years old.

Then, only weeks before the long campaign, Hamilton's attention turned to South Basildon and East Thurrock, in Essex, where Ukip's popular candidate had been deselected. Kerry Smith was a competent working-class organizer. He had already been elected as a county councillor and had led Ukip to success. In 2014, Smith's local branch had captured eleven of fifteen seats on Basildon council, forcing the Conservatives to lose control of the authority. But within months the central party had deselected him as the candidate, which angered the local branch. Officially, Ukip claimed that a 'big fish' was about to defect, and might want to stand in the seat. Speculation was fuelled when John Baron, Conservative MP for the nearby seat of Basildon and Billericay, gave a coded reply when asked whether it was him: 'You should never say never in politics.'[9] Baron never defected to Ukip, but there had been another reason for the deselection.

Ukip had been handed a recorded conversation in which Smith had made a series of offensive remarks, referring to 'f***cking disgusting old pooftahs', 'a Chinky', joking about 'shooting peasants', and suggesting that Farage was corrupt.[10] The recording had been delivered by activists who did not want Smith, whom they saw as a ticking time bomb, standing for parliament and threatening their prospects in nearby seats. 'You can get away with being a complete idiot locally', said one, 'but not when the entire media is on you'. In December, Hamilton, who had spotted an opportunity, moved in and applied for the nomination. He was put on the shortlist, alongside Ian Luder, a former Labour candidate and Lord Mayor of the City of London. His arrival triggered a bizarre chain of events. Despite knowledge of Smith's remarks, the party put the deselected organizer back on the list of candidates. He was seen as the lesser of two evils—the only way of stopping the tainted Conservative MP. As Hamilton was driving to the selection meeting, somebody then leaked details of his expense claims, trying to jog memories about old skeletons. 'The timing was deliberate', Hamilton would later claim, 'to make it impossible for me to respond before the selection. It was an example of Farage's ruthlessness and unscrupulousness.' He saw it as a 'dirty trick' and called on Ukip to take action against those peddling 'the black arts of selective briefing, misrepresentation and outright lies'.[11]

By this time, senior officials were beginning to sympathize, arguing that Hamilton should never have been given the chance to go for seats in the first place. 'To march someone up the hill and then make a fool of them on several occasions was just not on,' said Nuttall, the deputy leader. 'We should have just given him a seat like Camborne and Redruth. They just let him put his name forward time and time again and then publicly humiliated him.' Farage, meanwhile, felt that Hamilton was in denial about what had happened during the 1990s and was frustrated with the lingering factionalism. 'I can be very nice, but when people mess with me I do not put up with it.' Commentators joined in, urging Farage to 'ditch' Hamilton and claiming that the former MP stood 'for everything which is sleaziest and most morally disgusting about the old-fashioned right in British politics'.[12] 'In the end', said Farage, 'I had to step in and say "I'm sorry son it ain't going to happen"'. But even then the turmoil did not end.

After Hamilton had stepped aside and endorsed Smith, those in Ukip who had opposed the Essex organizer from the start then leaked the recording to the media, forcing him to stand down for a second time. The seat eventually went to Luder. Farage felt awful about the way that Smith, whom he saw as a 'rough diamond', had been treated. And he put his head above the parapet to say so. Some people, said Farage, are 'very snobbish in London about condemning people perhaps for the colloquial language they use'.[13] The entire drawn-out episode had been a major distraction, casting a shadow over the start of the campaign, fuelling tension, and once again highlighting Ukip's tendency to suffer from self-inflicted wounds.

Other distractions were less predictable. On the morning of Wednesday, 7 January, two violent Islamists, loyal to al-Qaeda and armed with assault rifles, burst into the Paris office of a satirical magazine, *Charlie Hebdo*, murdering eleven cartoonists and injuring around a dozen others. The terrorists then went on a rampage, murdering another six people and triggering a nationwide manhunt, much of which was followed live on television. They had targeted the magazine because it had published cartoons of the prophet Muhammad.

Unlike other radical right politicians in Europe, such as Geert Wilders in the Netherlands or Marine Le Pen in France, who had aggressively targeted anxieties over Islam, Farage had long been reluctant to address the issue head on. But in the aftermath of the attacks he became more confident, believing that the events would reignite a debate over multiculturalism that would benefit Ukip, helping its advance into northern Labour seats, like Rotherham, where concerns over the involvement of British Muslim men in child sexual exploitation remained a toxic issue.

Within hours of the attacks Farage deliberately put himself at the centre of a media storm. On the controversial Fox News channel in the United States he warned that the West was under threat from a 'fifth column living within our own countries', which, though 'mercifully small', was 'out to destroy our whole civilization and our way of life'. He talked of the West 'failing to stand up for Christian values', claimed that mosques were 'pushing a deeply unpleasant and anti-Christian heritage culture', criticized multiculturalism for failing to foster integration, and argued that Western states should more actively defend and promote its Judaeo-Christian heritage. 'We've got to start being a bit more assertive about who we are and what our values are...We come from countries with Christian culture and Christian constitutions and we've got to start standing up for that.' As was routine, Farage was projecting his own thoughts into the public debate after little, if any, consultation with others in his party. 'Nigel just did his normal thing,' said one press officer.

But not everybody in the party endorsed the fifth-column line. 'He was being told by almost everybody,' said Kassam, 'including me, to stop saying fifth column. He was just telling the truth, as he saw it, but we were not convinced that it was a good narrative.' Others were also strongly critical. One journalist claimed that the Ukip leader, who had long pushed back against accusations that his party was related to the far right, was 'entering that loopy, cranky, far-right Nick Griffin territory that grabs headlines but also unsettles the electorate'.[14] But Farage was unrepentant. In the days that followed he reiterated his view that Britain's traditional approach to managing multiculturalism was promoting segregation and a 'tick-box approach' to identity politics.[15] In the following weeks he also tried to draw further attention to his defence of Christian values by attempting to recruit George Hargreaves, the former leader of the Christian Party who had also campaigned against gay rights, into Ukip. 'Nigel thought that it was a good opportunity to make a Judeao-Christian point,' said one insider. But there had been strong opposition. Suzanne Evans made it clear that she would resign if Hargreaves was recruited. 'I was adamant that someone who held extreme views should not stand as a candidate for us.'

Two weeks after the attacks, on Saturday, 24 January, Ukip's start to the campaign was rocked by yet another event. One of its MEPs, Amjad Bashir, was defecting to the Conservative Party. Some in Ukip suspected that the defection had been orchestrated by a Conservative MEP, Daniel Hannan, who, they claimed, was trying to destabilize their party ahead of the election. With only a few hours until the news went public Farage turned to his advisers. 'You need to throw Bashir under a bus, *now*,' said one. Ukip announced that it was suspending Bashir and investigating 'serious issues'. The allegations focused on questions about Bashir's finances, his alleged interference with a candidate selection process, and links to a Pakistani terrorist group. Farage was working overtime to present one of his own MEPs as a poisoned chalice—and the mud was beginning to stick. A few hours later, Grant Schapps, Chairman of the Conservative Party, was quizzed on the *Daily Politics Show* about why his party had not investigated Bashir, who had already been photographed with Cameron. 'I think we can be pretty sure', quipped Nicholas Watt, the *Guardian's* chief political correspondent, 'that when Hillary Clinton launches her vetting procedure to find her vice-presidential candidate, she will not be going to the Conservative Party'.[16]

In Scotland, meanwhile, things now looked very bleak for Labour. Its support had been seriously eroded by the continued rise of the Scottish National Party. At the end of October, only one month after the SNP had lost the referendum on independence, two polls captivated political debate. They pointed to a remarkable shift of support. One, by Ipsos-MORI, put the insurgent party on 52 per cent of the vote, almost thirty points clear of Labour and with a thirty-two-point increase on its support in 2010. Such a shift would result in the SNP winning all but two seats north of the border. The other, by YouGov, suggested a less extreme outcome but still put the SNP on 43 per cent, a striking sixteen points ahead of Labour.

Two months later, after Nicola Sturgeon had replaced Salmond as the leader of the SNP, and Jim Murphy had taken control of Scottish Labour, YouGov went back to Scotland and found that, far from fading, the surge was advancing—the SNP's lead had widened to twenty points.[17] Its strength was then confirmed in early 2015, by new constituency polls, which suggested that there had been a twenty-five-point swing to the SNP in Labour seats and that one in three of Labour's 2010 voters had deserted to the insurgents.[18] Most SNP voters wanted to see a coalition between their own party and Labour, but the continued advance of their revolt was making this outcome look increasingly unlikely. The advance of the SNP in Scotland was leaving Labour with a mountain to climb in England.

There was no doubt that the surge was real. Evidence in the British Election Study, collected during the long campaign, revealed that not only had the SNP gained more supporters but that they were unlikely to leave. Those who had moved over to Sturgeon were more committed than supporters of every other party—almost 90 per cent were highly certain about their decision to vote for the SNP, which was almost ten points higher than for supporters of the other parties. Conversely, not only was Scottish Labour losing support, but only around three-quarters of Labour supporters felt highly certain about their commitment, leaving an eleven-point gap in the commitment of Labour and SNP voters.

There were also interesting overlaps in support for the SNP and Ukip. It was certainly true that the policy issues that were driving the two parties could not have been more different. While more than 80 per cent of Ukip voters voiced strong concerns about Europe and immigration, only one-third of SNP supporters felt the same way. Like voters in general, those who had flocked to Sturgeon prioritized the economy. But both parties were more likely than the others to draw their votes from the working class, from people with few qualifications, and from those who were unhappy with how Britain's democracy was working. And, while Ukip voters were less certain than SNP voters about their choice, they too were showing higher levels of commitment than many thought (see Figure 10.2). They were not lagging far behind the major parties.

Initially at least, Farage saw the events in Scotland as an opportunity. 'The very thought that Miliband cannot hope to govern without forty SNP MPs is very big for us in northern England,' he said, arguing that the Scottish insurgency would fuel feelings of Englishness among voters who felt under threat from Sturgeon and her tartan army. 'I think this is a huge weapon for us against Labour. Miliband denies Englishness at every given opportunity. He just doesn't get it. And the Emily Thornberry thing plays into that.' By pitching to working-class voters who identified with England, and exploiting Labour's fraying relationship with these voters, which had been symbolized by Thornberry's dismissive stance towards blue-collar

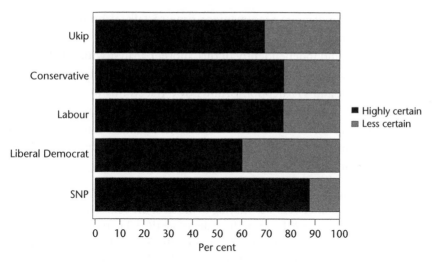

**Figure 10.2.** Certainty of vote choice by party, March 2015
*Source:* 2014–2017 British Election Study Internet Panel (Wave 4).

patriotism in Rochester and Strood, Farage hoped that the turn in Scotland would work to Ukip's advantage. But he and his party would soon think differently.

For now, however, that Labour was clearly feeling the pressure that had been brought by the events in Scotland and a static rating in the polls had become clear to Ukip. Greg Beales was Labour's Director of Strategy and Planning and a senior adviser to Ed Miliband. He also attended meetings for those in Labour who were tasked with winning the general election. In November 2014, he had met one of Ukip's press officers, Alex Phillips, while the two were involved in negotiations about forthcoming debates between the party leaders. Labour, the Liberal Democrats, and Ukip would soon write separate but identical letters to Cameron, arguing that the prime minister should take part in any debates. Beales and Phillips had met to discuss the detail. Shortly before the letter was sent, the Westminster blogger Guido Fawkes had accidentally observed one of their meetings. 'I'm not defecting,' quipped Miliband's adviser.[19]

But that was not the end of the story. In late February, the head of Ukip's election campaign, Bruni-Lowe, contacted Beales, saying that Phillips had told him that he [Beales] was 'interested in having a chat.' Beales responded promptly and a short text exchange ensued in which the two tried to arrange a convenient time to talk, although in the end the Labour strategist firmly denied that they ever did.

Meanwhile, and independently of this, another analyst within Labour was reaching out, sharing his views about Labour-held seats such as Thurrock, Great Grimsby, and Hartlepool. Bruni-Lowe traced this to anxiety within Labour about its prospects. 'They had no idea what they were doing and were trying to find a way to screw the Tories, to find a way of screeching over the line in just enough seats.' 'In seats like Thurrock,' said Bruni-Lowe, who was passing on details of each conversation to Farage,

they were telling me that they would rather have Ukip win, as it would help them get to the magic number. He was relaying to me all of the conversations that he was having with the Labour MPs, about how desperate the Ukip problem was, in areas where very little work had been done historically. We would never have done a deal, but it seemed that they just had such a bad idea of what was going on that they were reaching out.

But the Labour official was overestimating Ukip's capabilities. 'You cannot just turn their fire elsewhere,' Bruni-Lowe had said; 'they are not that kind of fighting machine'. The talks about possible deals in key seats would soon fizzle out, but behind the scenes, and right up until the election, Ukip's head of campaigns would continue to talk to some of those at the heart of the Labour camp.

Ukip, meanwhile, was also trying to decide on its message, and whether it should continue with the same core-vote strategy that had dominated its European campaign. It was a source of endless debate inside the party. From the outset, Farage had talked of anchoring the campaign in three issues that the electorate rated as the most important for Britain and that would dom-inate the election—the economy, immigration, and the National Health Service. 'There are three issues,' said Farage in January.

The NHS, which Labour is trying to own, the economy, which Conservatives are trying to own, and immigration is the issue that we own. There is also a fourth dimension, which is the political class being against us, so I do not see us being in a bad position. Our positive message on immigration can be better-handled and better run, but I think that immigration impacts on the other two as well. If we can get the health debate centred around, 'well of course there is a health crisis the population is going through the bloody roof', then that would be good.

But there was also a clear view among some insiders that Ukip needed to modify its appeal. One voice was Patrick O'Flynn, who, after the European elections, which saw the party branded as racist, had become anxious about the need to modify the offer.

We had two tracks in the European campaign. Track One was 'the EU interferes far too much in your life'. Track Two was 'we've got to get back control of our borders'. It was a double A-side single and it topped the charts. But do you remember when Wet Wet Wet had that song 'Love is All Around' and it was number one for 14 weeks? In the end *they* had to withdraw the single. Ukip was in a similar position. We had our two hits, but now we had to come back with an entire LP. Our audience expect those two tracks, but they also want ten other songs.

Some early ideas about how to widen the message had surfaced a few months after the European poll, when the activist put in charge of a policy review shared his thoughts. Though only 28 years old, Tim Aker had already been elected a Ukip MEP in south-east England and was also preparing to stand for the party in Thurrock—another top prospect. While claiming that Ukip was 'beyond left–right, authoritarian-libertarian', Aker outlined what he called a 'blue-collar platform'—an attempt to reach out to financially insecure Britons who felt culturally under threat. The party would abolish the top rate of tax of 45p, take low-income earners out of income tax, oppose the 'bedroom tax', restrict welfare benefits for migrants to those who had paid tax and national insurance for at least five years, enforce compulsory health insurance for migrants, reduce foreign aid, abolish the Climate Change Act, create a department for veterans, and restrict child benefit to two children.[20]

Ukip would later also modify its stance on health. There was no doubt that the NHS had become a more important feature on the political landscape—the percentage of voters who rated it as one of the most important issues facing Britain had increased from 22 per cent at the end of 2013 to 45 per cent at the start of the campaign.[21] Labour had also been using the issue to attack Ukip as a hard right libertarian party, which secretly wanted to privatize the NHS—an institution cherished by the white working-class pensioners whom Farage was trying to win over. Labour's claims appeared to be legitimized at the start of 2015 when Louise Bours, Ukip's health spokesperson, publicly rejected an earlier suggestion from Farage that the health service be funded through a private insurance-based system. Shortly after that, leaked documents from a Ukip NEC meeting two years earlier appeared to show the ruling body speaking positively about privatization. Then, a wave of publicity followed the release of a recording, which showed one of Ukip's most senior officials, Matthew Richardson, describing the NHS as a waste of money and comparing it to the 'Reichstag bunker of Nazi Germany'. Labour was quick to respond. 'A vote for Ukip', said Andy Burnham, Labour's Shadow Health Secretary, 'is a vote for the privatization of the NHS and for a full American healthcare system'.[22]

Such episodes fuelled a belief inside the party, one that John Bickley had voiced in Heywood and Middleton, that it needed to 'build a shield' to fend off such attacks. O'Flynn was anxious. 'Our earlier message on the NHS, that there was too much red tape, wasn't good enough. There was no resource offer. So we devised a plan to put £3 billion a year into the NHS to emphasize our policy of supporting it, and show up Labour's falsehoods.' Ukip now actively tried to push back, promising to direct new funds into front-line services. The shift prompted one newspaper to claim that the party had swapped a 'robustly conservative' position for 'social democratic populism', and that it now saw its future in stealing votes from Labour.[23]

But the reality was that few voters noticed the change. Ukip might have been trying to widen its offer—talking about investing in the NHS, putting more police on the streets, holding referendums, cutting council tax, ending foreign wars, and reducing foreign aid—but it was not cutting through. As shown in Figure 10.3, between the European elections and the long

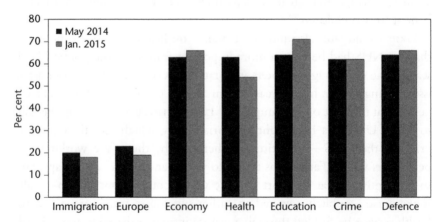

**Figure 10.3.** 'Don't Know Anything about Ukip's Policy in the Area'
Source: YouGov.

campaign there was little difference in levels of public awareness about where Ukip stood on a range of issues. Consistently, large majorities of the electorate said that they 'did not know anything' about what the party thought in a large number of areas.[24] Only on immigration and Europe did a large number of voters know what Ukip had to say, which reflected how, historically, the party had invested in little else. Though more people did become aware of what the party thought about the NHS, it is difficult to know whether this was because of Ukip's efforts or those of its opponents, who were trying to encourage a perception of the party as hell-bent on privatization. But, even so, more than half of those who were surveyed did not know anything about what the party thought.

While Ukip's initial plan had been to deliver three speeches on immigration, the NHS, and the economy, some, including Farage, had wanted to be more ambitious. Ukip, they argued, was now a major force. So, rather than have the party just outlining policies, they wanted to wrap its campaign in a wider narrative for voters—about where Ukip was from and what it believed. 'You know', Farage said,

we have come so far but it's almost as though we starting all over again. The level of misconception out there about what Ukip stands for is massive. We have to deconstruct that. It has to be optimistic and positive—positive visions about democracy and self-government, positive visions about our engagement with the Commonwealth, positive messages about increasing inequality in British society, and I think something unashamedly patriotic with a small 'p'. I think that there is a market waiting to listen to that and engage with that.

Farage had also talked about developing a more positive narrative around immigration. 'The Ukip message', he said in early 2015,

does need to be slightly more nuanced than it's been in the past. We are going into a general election when the others are going to fight each other with negativity, American-style politics. We absolutely must not do that. We have to be the people offering an optimistic vision of how things can be done differently. I really do believe that.

Farage elaborated on what this might mean for Ukip's core issue, even if some of his ideas would soon be discarded. 'Therefore, the immigration message is less about the "stop" sign and the white cliffs of Dover and moves on to the Australian points-based system.'

Rooting the campaign in a more optimistic narrative was also seen as an important way of pushing back against the claim that Ukip was a pessimistic, reactionary force. Insiders had talked about using the election to begin a journey that would continue through elections in Wales and London in

2016, a referendum on Britain's EU membership, and into the 2020 general election. The narrative would be rooted in a new slogan, which would underline the more inclusive and optimistic tone. After rejecting 'Building a Better Future with You', the party decided on 'Believe in Britain'. It had been suggested by O'Flynn, who had wanted something 'patriotic and positive'. 'Yes that's it,' said Farage. 'That's the campaign.' On some leaflets the slogan would be joined by 'Together we can', which Kassam had lifted from a Mother Theresa quotation.[25] The main 'Believe in Britain' message had been inspired by a line that Farage had used in the debates with Clegg, who had claimed that Britain would be less influential were it to leave the EU. 'To say we are not good enough...shows that you frankly don't believe in this country and don't believe in the ability of the people to govern themselves.' The new message, Farage said, was for Britain's neglected, hard-up voters and small business-owners.[26]

But there was some tension. On one side were those who generally wanted to shift the party away from its core issues and present a broader front—who at various points during the campaign included Carswell, Steve Crowther, the Director of Communications Paul Lambert, and Patrick O'Flynn. As the long campaign had got underway, Carswell had again set out his ideas publicly, stating on Twitter and in an article that he wanted Ukip's vision in 2015 to be 'optimistic, internationalist, inclusive'. Writing in the *Mail on Sunday*, the MP had elaborated on his belief in the free market and his view that, in a global world, 'a dislike of foreigners is not merely offensive, but absurd'. Rather than being a party that 'tolerates pejorative comments about people's heritage and background, Ukip had to show that it had a serious internationalist agenda'.[27] The article, which had not been signed off by anybody in the party, did not go down well among those who were closest to Farage. 'It was completely inconsistent,' said one. 'Nigel was talking about a fifth column while Douglas was talking about being internationally inclusive.' Others argued that the article marked an important moment.

I would say that it was a real turning point in their relationship. Nigel and Douglas are two very different people. They were cordial and polite but they were never going to be best friends. But at that point it looked as though Douglas had gone behind Nigel's back and set out his own course. And at that point we were having very fragile discussions about the campaign. We were way behind. That article set things on a different course.

One person who held similar views was Paul Nuttall, Farage's right hand man who had also become worried about Carswell's ideas. 'It could have been written by Cameron,' he said. 'Or Tony Blair.'

Unlike Carswell, Farage loyalists argued that immigration should remain front and centre and be used to mobilize Ukip's core supporters. They included Bruni-Lowe, Kassam, Matthew Richardson, and Steve Stanbury. 'We need to focus on what we are strong on!' shouted one during a heated meeting. Those around Farage were anxious that Carswell and others were leading what was supposed to be a radical insurgent into what one described as a 'vanilla' campaign. 'There is now a tension', said one adviser at the time, 'between what Carswell thinks and what everybody else thinks'. One journalist described the chasm as between academic free marketeers who saw the EU as a threat to trade and direct democracy, and those, like Farage, who were inclined towards a more tribal and nativist conception of politics.[28] It was an accurate description.

The debate played itself out in meetings on Brooks Mews that were typically attended by Carswell, Bruni-Lowe, Crowther, Soutter, and Lisa Duffy, with Kassam and Stanbury also feeding into conversations. Farage was rarely present during the early discussions. Ukip, as part of its earlier quest to obtain money from Paul Sykes, had once again recruited Family, the agency that had played a key role in the European campaign. In early February, and after talking to Carswell and others about what they wanted from the campaign, Family presented some initial ideas. It talked about a campaign that would appeal to 'those who are uneasy about the direction our country is taking'—people who are 'disaffected, pessimistic and feel that they have no influence or power' and 'that the traditional parties do not champion their causes'. Ukip should 'represent fairness and be inclusive', 'offer hope and reassurance', and not be 'the angry party or the doom-mongers'. It should be 'with you—the British voter'. Little attention was devoted to migration, defence, or foreign aid. It also talked about a forward-looking and 'surprising' campaign that had 'creative bite' but would specifically not be a 'shock and awe campaign'.

But others in the room had disagreed. 'This did not look like a Ukip campaign,' complained one. 'It looked like a campaign that [the radical left-wing party] Syriza would run in Greece.' As the activists looked up at the PowerPoint slides, listened to the ideas, and looked at the draft literature, some felt that the campaign was beginning to lose sight of 'who the enemy is'. They had been particularly appalled by one idea that had been proposed by those who were keen to push Ukip in a new direction. It was to have a billboard with 'Positive Immigration' in neon lights. 'I was sat listening to these ideas', reflected one, 'and just thought: what would the white van man say?' Others took a similar view.

'They wanted to reposition Ukip and reach out to liberal Tories. It would be fun to do intellectually and they thought it was clever, but we just looked at it and thought "this is insane".' Farage's response was also weighing on people's minds. 'There was just nothing there that we could go to Nigel with. There was nothing there on our wedge issues.'

After a long day listening to the presentations, a demoralized Bruni-Lowe went into his office. 'I'm not sure people have a clue about what the message should be.' Those who were closest to Farage felt that a campaign that talked about the positive effects of immigration, the price of energy, or that complained about Starbucks not paying tax, would not appeal to people in Ukip's target seats. 'They just kept saying they wanted the campaign to be surprising,' recalled Stanbury. 'You don't want a campaign to be surprising. You want it to be effective.' With little firepower and only three months left, they also worried that Ukip did not have sufficient time or resources to support an ambitious attempt to reach into new groups of voters whom, in a highly competitive election, they felt would most likely side with the main parties. 'We knew what the upper limit to our support was', said Kassam, 'and what our resources would allow us to do. Douglas and Patrick genuinely thought that if they started to talk about fluffy bunnies and quinoa salads then people might think "oh yeah, Ukip, not bad". But it was the same mistake that Cameron made when he went off to hug the huskies.' Stanbury, who was now an influential voice in the party, concurred. 'If you are running a key seat campaign, then you should have a core-vote campaign.' He had also become concerned about the amount of money that was being spent on messages that did not reflect the core thinking of the party. 'People kept telling us that the amounts they were charging was the industry standard. That may be true. But we rely on little old ladies sending us ten quid.' Such concerns were contributing to the dispute. Bruni-Lowe, meanwhile, was so anxious about the direction of the work that he insisted that Farage attend any future meetings about messaging.

Tension was escalating and time was running out. Advertisement space was already booked. 'We knew that we could not change agencies. All we could do was wrest back control of the campaign.' A few weeks later Family returned to Brooks Mews to present some revised ideas. This time, Farage was in the room. He sat quietly and listened to the discussion, which revolved around the question of how Ukip could surprise observers by targeting a wider range of issues and adopting a softer tone. 'We could all sense that Nigel was surprised and disappointed but he held himself back,' said one. After the presentation, Farage then left the room and summoned his closest advisers into his office. 'PPE bollocks,' he said. 'This is madness. What is going on?' Contrary to what he had just heard, Farage was clear in stating that he wanted to use the campaign to 'own the immigration debate'. Nobody dissented. 'Immigration, immigration, immigration and Nigel. That is what we thought,' said Stanbury. It was at this moment that Farage and his loyalists took ownership of the campaign, deciding there and then that the controversial issue would be placed at the heart of their campaign—that once again the party would focus heavily on mobilizing its core vote.

Farage believed that Ukip had a historic opportunity. By underling its opposition to immigration and presenting itself as the protector of national identity, the party could achieve something that it had never had before—ownership of a major issue. By pitching clearly and directly to the not insignificant number of Britons who shared concerns about immigration and its effects, and a deep anxiety about the direction of the country more generally, Ukip could emerge from the contest as the main vehicle for these voters, laying a stronger foundation for future campaigns.

But this was also a fundamentally different strategy from the approach that was being advocated by others. 'Carswell is desperate to reach beyond our base', said one, 'but at the cost of losing our core vote'. Others felt that the MP was approaching the campaign as he had the by-election in Clacton, where he had told voters that they were wrong to feel worried about immigration. 'He is trying to find the perfect Ukip voter,' complained another, 'but that voter does not exist'. Farage was keenly aware that the dynamic within his party was changing. But he also felt that his new rival had become disconnected from grass-roots opinion within Ukip. 'The more that they know about Carswell,' he said, 'the less Ukip activists will like him. He will find himself an isolated figure in time. It is not that he contradicts our message but he has a completely different priority in life. And he is a little bit preachy.' Sitting back in his chair, Farage paused. 'He sounds like Cameron actually.'

Farage might not have agreed with Carswell's views, but he accepted that his new recruit was a radical. 'You cannot control Douglas,' he had told his activists. 'He will say what he wants to say.' But a fundamental point had also crystallized in his mind. Ideologically, Carswell was not 'true Ukip'—and had probably never been to begin with. Farage illustrated the point by comparing his two MPs, during one interview in January 2015.

Reckless is true Ukip in his instincts on Europe and immigration. They are his core beliefs and values, with some bits on social mobility and pro-business chucked in. But Douglas is a completely different animal. He is a political and social reformer on a late Victorian dimension. To him, the EU is just one barrier to getting the kind of direct democracy à la Beppe Grillo and Five Star in Italy. Douglas is a Five Starrer. He is part of the upper middle-class, Daniel Hannan-intellectual-Eurosceptic camp that does not see immigration as an issue. They do not get it. They've never felt it. When constituents tell Douglas in the street that they are worried about immigration, he just says 'you don't understand'. And they *still* vote for him. It is a carefully cultivated image, him being the ordinary man. But it's bollocks.

The tension escalated at the end of February, when insiders discovered that Carswell was planning to deliver a major speech at a think tank, entitled 'Why Enoch Powell Was Wrong'. Powell, a Conservative and Eurosceptic MP, was best known for his 'Rivers of Blood' speech in 1968, which set out his opposition to immigration and compared it to 'like watching a nation busily engaged in heaping up its own funeral pyre'. He was a deeply controversial politician but respected by Farage, who had met Powell on several occasions. When the Ukip leader heard about the speech, he called Carswell into his office and demanded to see a draft. The growing disconnect between the two was reflected in the fact that the speech had originally been scheduled to be given only two days before Farage was due to launch Ukip's campaign. It was eventually postponed. Not long afterwards, in a late-night meeting, Farage was discussing the fallout with Bruni-Lowe. Midway through the discussion, the Ukip leader turned to his campaigner and said simply: 'Douglas has lost the room.'

A few weeks later, in March, Farage loyalists took back control of the campaign. One night, Bruni-Lowe, Kassam, Stanbury, and another official, Adam Richardson, stayed behind in Brooks Mews. They opened some wine, covered the walls with blank sheets of paper, and designed an entirely new billboard campaign. It was all about immigration and Farage. The change of direction would become known as the 'March Tilt', the moment when Farage's team wrested back control and imposed a hard-hitting core-vote strategy. 'We blue-skied thirty different ideas and posters,' said Kassam. 'We just said, "sorry guys, Chris is in charge of the campaign and I speak for Nigel". I think it was at this point that Douglas left. He saw that he had been completely pushed out of the campaign.'

Some of the ideas that the group had put forward would later be discarded. One billboard that sought to capitalize on public concern about the amount that Britain was spending on foreign aid compared a picture of a foreign dictator with struggling workers donating money. Another idea, which would be approved, was to update one of the billboards from the European campaign. Instead of just one escalator running out of the Channel to the top of the white cliffs of Dover, it featured three. 'We decided to put our fingers up at Westminster and critics inside the party.'. It signalled a more deliberately divisive tone that, only a few months beforehand, Farage had said he wanted to get away from.

They also reorganized the campaign more clearly around Farage, who had encouraged the change of direction. 'I was absolutely adamant', he would later say, 'that if we did not take back control and win the major issue of immigration then we would end up polling between 6 and 7 per cent'. Yet, while Farage approved, the shift also sharpened the divide between those in the campaign and those in the communication wings. Ukip's press officers felt that they were not being consulted and were forced to spend time 'fighting fires' rather than designing a proactive media strategy. Those in the campaign, meanwhile, felt that Ukip's press officers were 'not ruthless enough' and did not understand the basics of political strategy. 'They are so desperate to be insiders', complained one, 'that they want to act like the rest. But we are an insurgent movement not an established party.' When some in the press office had once again suggested that Farage should set out his stall in Westminster, Bruni-Lowe stepped in. 'What a statement it would be', the campaigner said at one meeting, 'for Nigel to say that this, a seat in the north, is the Britain that we represent. But all the press officers would talk about is how the other journalists wouldn't want to leave London.'

Infighting was not the only thing keeping Farage awake at night. Like Bruni-Lowe, he had become deeply anxious about his prospects in South Thanet. 'I sit here at the start of the year', he said, 'and I'm not looking forward to any of it. I don't think I am going to enjoy it like I did last year. The sheer time pressures on me are becoming almost impossible. And I understand that Thanet is going to be very, very difficult.' There were several reasons why he felt that the race would be harder than perhaps he had once thought. Since declaring his candidacy five months previously, and amid the distraction of the by-elections, Farage had barely visited the seat. It was a weakness that had already been identified by his rivals, like the Labour candidate Will Scobie. 'They had an opportunity to flood us after his selection in August but he spent two or three months not being in the seat. It was a massive tactical error. Whoever was running his campaign either didn't know what they were doing or they had made a major error.'

There was also another weakness—the Ukip branch in Thanet. It was far from ideal, as Farage knew. His ground operation would be in the hands of largely inexperienced pensioners who were led by Martyn Heale, an old member of the far right National Front who would attract negative publicity. The branch might have enjoyed some success at local elections, but it was about to feel the full weight of the Conservative Party machine. Farage's anxiety had been fuelled in January when comedian Al Murray announced that he would also be fighting the seat, representing the 'Free United Kingdom Party'. It was time, said the comedian, whose character is a working-class, straight-talking pub landlord, 'for a bloke waving a pint offering common-sense solutions'. Farage welcomed the news, joking that it introduced 'serious competition'. But his nerves were coming to the surface.[29]

One person who felt the pressure more than most was Bruni-Lowe, who had now been entrusted with the South Thanet campaign. 'I know the pressures are absolutely massive', he had said to Farage, 'but I will do everything in my power to get you elected'. But if he was to make up the lost ground and catapult his leader into parliament, then he would need a plan—and quickly. He decided to anchor the campaign in what Farage did best—public meetings. Over the coming weeks, hoping to compensate for the lack of work that had been done during the autumn, he quietly organized twenty meetings on a ward-by-ward basis, trying to fill community halls and pubs with as many undecided voters as possible. That those invited were not simply Ukip supporters was reflected in the fact that the party had only around 400 members in Thanet. Nor did the campaigner want the race to be turned into the Nigel Farage Show. He felt that the way to win was to hold meetings under the radar, to try and keep journalists away for as long as possible. Some meetings were even kept secret from Ukip's press officers. 'It is vital', he explained, 'that Nigel talks to as many undecided voters without media pressure'. The plan was that, by the end of the campaign, Farage would have talked personally to more than 3,000 voters, who would tell their friends and relatives. The meetings would be supported by action days, where hundreds of activists would descend on Thanet to canvass and collect data. But not everybody approved of the amount of time that Bruni-Lowe was spending in Kent. 'What are you doing in Thanet?' asked Carswell. 'You should be in Westminster helping the other candidates, not getting distracted by Nigel and Thanet.'

On a cold evening in February a few dozen people turned out for the first meeting in South Thanet. The village hall was dark and cold. Against a large poster that read 'Join the People's Army', Farage set out his stall. He often began by trying to neutralize local opposition. 'Whether you are here because you like me or loathe me, you are all welcome. This is a real public meeting.' He was joined by two candidates who were standing for Ukip in local elections that were to be held on the same day. Farage hoped that his party might also take control of Thanet District Council. The two candidates that evening traced their support for Ukip to the decline of the community, messy streets, the closure of the local Manston Airport, and a lack of local pride.

From one event to the next Farage had a specific offer. 'I won't promise that I can change the world,' he said. 'But I can give you a powerful voice. They will have to listen to me, which means they will listen to Thanet.' With his advisers looking on, he was to use the meetings like focus groups, testing the receptiveness of voters to ideas and lines that might be used later on, in the national campaign. It was in Thanet that Farage first tested the 'Believe in Britain' narrative, the idea of scrapping hospital car-parking charges, the proposal to adopt an Australian-based points system, and lines on health tourism that would soon attract national attention. He also used the events to try and raise funds for Ukip's far from impressive war chest. 'The best donations', he would say, while shaking a bucket, 'are the silent donations'. But behind closed doors, away from the jokes, he worried about the distractions in London and was nervous. 'Losing South Thanet is the biggest risk that we face. That is a big worry. I am trying to do something about it but I need more of Chris's time.'

Farage's anxieties had also made him hostile to the idea of repeating the national tour that had preceded the European elections. Bruni-Lowe was pushing for it to take place, wanting to draw attention to the other seats. But Farage was ruling it out, using a phrase that would frequently end discussions. 'Nope. Not doing it.' Opposition to the tour was also being encouraged by the veterans in Ukip who owed their position to Farage and worried about what a loss in South Thanet might mean. Some said openly that, even if Ukip won a handful of MPs, it would be a 'pyrrhic victory' unless Farage was among them. 'We want four MPs plus the boss,' said Matthew Richardson, an influential voice. With Carswell and Reckless already elected, the party knew that it would be difficult, if not impossible, for Farage to remain as leader if he failed to enter parliament. Such a loss would almost certainly trigger a messy fight for the leadership, and it was not clear who would win, or whether the victor would even be 'true Ukip'.

The growing anxiety fuelled suspicion about Carswell. Mutterings could be heard along the corridors on Brooks Mews that the new recruit was plotting a coup and was involved in a 'hijack strategy' with other prominent Eurosceptic Conservative politicians like Daniel Hannan.

On the morning of 12 February, Ukip arrived on a fading esplanade on Canvey Island in the Essex seat of Castle Point. It had come to launch its campaign. The venue was a screening room in a small movie theatre. Journalists and activists were seated awkwardly next to each other holding cartons of Ukip-branded popcorn. While the party's press team had never warmed to the idea of a launch outside London, Farage's advisers had wanted to start in the north. Canvey Island was the compromise. It was a symbol of Ukip's emerging Essex heartland and had a tradition of insurgent politicians.[30] Locally, the Canvey Island Independents held sixteen seats on the council and were a serious force. Now, they had pledged allegiance to Jamie Huntman, Ukip's blue-collar candidate and a self-made millionaire, who kicked off the event. 'I'm the working class deserted by Labour. I'm the small businessman let down by the Tories.'

Farage then arrived, with his 'Believe in Britain' speech, which had been hastily written by Kassam in the car as they had made their way back from Strasbourg. 'We had stopped at the Vimy Ridge,' said his adviser. 'Nigel walked around, telling me all about the terrain and battles in the past. It was moving to watch this man who is derided talking about men who had given their lives for British sovereignty. His world view has been shaped by him being a history buff. He looks at what Britain is going through as a civilizational and generational struggle. He doesn't think in election cycles.' A few hours later, Farage was standing on Canvey Island, setting out his pitch. 'There's a country beyond Westminster, crying out for attention, respect, and assistance at a time when politicians are trying to convince them that everything is absolutely fine.'

Less than two weeks after the launch, Ukip trundled on to Rochester and Strood for its second speech—this time on the NHS. It was designed to draw attention to Mark Reckless, whose campaign was focused heavily on a local hospital and who faced a tough battle to hold his seat in a contest where Ukip would be stretched. But the event was overshadowed. The week before the speech, more than one million people had tuned in to watch a Channel Four docu-drama on the 'first one hundred days' of a Ukip government. It portrayed Britain as being embroiled by riots, raids on illegal migrants, and rampant unemployment—using footage from events that had actually taken place under previous governments. But within days the party was hit by another and more significant documentary.

*Meet the Ukippers* aired the night before the speech in Rochester and Strood. It was focused on the South Thanet branch of Ukip and painted a grim picture of elderly inexperienced activists who held racist views. 'The only people I do have a problem with are negroes,' said one. 'And I don't know why. I don't know whether there is something in my psyche or whether it's karma from a previous life...But I really do have a problem with negroid features.' While some in Ukip had laughed off earlier shows, this one generated greater concern. 'Meet the Kippers has really fucked us in that seat,' said Bruni-Lowe, who already felt that he was facing an uphill struggle to turn Farage's campaign around. Others saw the show as a reflection of Ukip's amateurism, worrying about what lay ahead in the South Thanet race. 'I can still see the [documentary] film crew arriving at one of the events. They were just obviously doing a hit job,' said Kassam. 'But the South Thanet organizer, Martyn Heale, said "no, they are really nice. They have been interviewing me for hours." I just thought to myself, "Christ you amateur".'

Less than two weeks later, in the first week of March, Farage set out Ukip's offer on its central issue—immigration. The speech coincided with new figures that had put net migration at nearly 300,000. The party would ban unskilled migrants from working in Britain for five years, install an Australian-style points-based system, establish a watchdog to curb migration, increase border staff, have compulsory health insurance for migrants, and aim to return to 'normal' levels of migration, of between 20,000 and 50,000 migrant workers each year. 'Normal', said Farage, 'was from 1950 until the year 2000'. But he had also ruled out the idea of a cap, one week after Ukip's migration spokesperson, Steven Woolfe, said there should be a cap of 50,000 migrants each year. 'We absolutely messed up the immigration launch,' said Paul Nuttall. 'We couldn't get it right. First there was a cap and then there wasn't. Then spokespersons went on the radio, contradicting each other. That was our open goal and we shot the ball past the post.' Farage also attracted publicity after appearing to suggest that Ukip would scrap legislation against racial discrimination in the workplace. He would claim that he was talking about nationality rather than race.

To what extent was the core-vote strategy cutting through? There was no doubt that the party's decision to focus heavily on its core, anti-immigration and anti-EU message resonated strongly with a section of the electorate that felt intensely concerned about these issues. According to data from the British Election Study, during the long campaign people who felt concerned about Britain's EU membership *and* felt negative towards immigration were nearly three times more likely to plan on voting for Ukip than those who were not intensely opposed to immigration, and twelve times more likely than those who held neither of these views. Importantly, people who shared Ukip's two concerns were also more likely to be confident about their decision to support the party—three in four were highly certain that they would vote for Ukip.[31] If, therefore, Farage's goal was to maximize support among a core audience of committed voters who shared his angst over Europe and immigration, then he was succeeding. On the other hand, however, if his goal was to deliver a large number of seats and reach across British society more widely, then the evidence suggested that it might not be enough.

While Farage was connecting with core Ukip voters, this group represented only a small portion of the overall electorate. Just 13 per cent of the people who planned to vote were both Eurosceptic *and* strongly opposed to immigration. This meant that, while the controversial strategy was almost certainly playing a role in sustaining public support for the party within this group, which was something that Ukip had never managed to achieve before at a general election, the narrow focus of the campaign was unlikely to attract a large number of voters who did not feel as intensely concerned about immigration and Europe.

In fact, lots of voters who cared about Europe or immigration were not supporting Ukip. While more than half of the public expressed concern about Britain's relationship with the EU, fewer than one in five of these Eurosceptics planned to support Ukip. The largest share of these voters were going instead to the Conservatives. One reason why is that many of these people who felt concerned about Europe did not feel as intensely anxious about immigration. While Ukip had attracted some of those voters who were Eurosceptic but not massively opposed to immigration, these people tended to be less certain about their decision to vote for the party—'only' two-thirds were highly certain about their choice, which was notably lower than the proportion among Ukip's core voters.

This reinforced what Farage had come to realize—that Europe was not enough. But neither, it seems, was immigration on its own. Roughly one in five voters felt intensely anxious about migration, but Ukip was not overwhelmingly their first choice. Among these voters the Conservatives had a slight edge, although both Farage and Cameron were attracting around one-third of this group. In short, therefore, it was clear that, while Ukip needed its supporters to feel both strongly Eurosceptic *and* concerned over immigration, actually only a small proportion of the overall electorate—around one in eight—was motivated as intensely as the party about both of these areas.

Another way of looking at the strategy is to consider 'Ukip leaners'—people who had Ukip as their second preference and who comprised around one in six of the voters who were planning to vote for one of the other parties. These people did not tend to be as motivated by Ukip's core issues. They were strongly Eurosceptic. But far fewer, only around one-third, felt intensely negative about immigration. Fewer of these leaners were in line with Ukip on *both* of its core issues, which meant that they were unlikely to defect to the party in large numbers and were arguably more likely to be won back by the main parties. These leaners tended to be more educated, less dissatisfied with politics, and more likely to feel the economic recovery.

There was also a growing concern inside Ukip that the Conservative strategy of relentlessly framing the election as a binary choice between Cameron and Miliband was having an effect—that the outsiders would be squeezed. 'We always knew that we would get squeezed at some point,' said one. 'It was more a question of how badly we would be squeezed and how far would it go. We were obsessed with the squeeze, largely because we felt that we were getting completely shafted by the media in terms of the amount of coverage that we were receiving.'

Cameron and his party were now religiously framing the contest as a stark choice, between 'the chaos of a weak Ed Miliband with no economic plan being propped up by Sinn Fein and Alex Salmond...Or the stability and competence of David Cameron delivering our long-term economic plan.'[32] After already hinting that an EU referendum could be brought forward, the Conservatives now also ruled out another idea that might have encouraged some Ukip defectors to stay with Farage—that after the election there could be a deal between the two parties. It would never happen, said the Conservatives.

Bruni-Lowe's internal polls were also suggesting that the strategy was having an effect. In Conservative seats such as Thanet North, Sittingbourne and Sheppey, and Folkestone and Hythe, Ukip was still polling well, but its support was down a few points on where it had been previously. It seemed to be struggling, especially in seats where there was a Conservative incumbent who had name recognition.

As the short campaign approached, Lord Ashcroft returned to gauge the views of voters across several marginal seats. Some were in the south-west, where Ukip had been quietly optimistic—seats such as North Devon, North Cornwall, St Austell and Newquay, St Ives, Torbay, and Camborne and Redruth. Farage had visited several of these seats during a whistle-stop tour during the long campaign, where an enthusiastic reception had fuelled hopes. One voter told journalists that the Ukip leader been 'sent by god' to protect people from the European Union. 'I'm not the Messiah,' he replied. 'I'm a very naughty boy.' But, despite his efforts, support for the party appeared to be on the slide, falling by an average of five points. In many of the seats it was the Conservatives who seemed to be benefiting. In Camborne and Redruth Ukip was down twelve points while the Conservatives had gained eight. Here, as in St Austell and Newquay (the places where Ukip had worked hardest in the south-west), it was in third place.[33]

Something that was probably contributing to the decline was the way in which Ukip was failing to keep pace with the main parties on the ground. On the one hand, being contacted by Ukip had a meaningful effect on its support—people who were contacted by the party were three times more likely to say that they planned to vote for it than those who had not been contacted.[34] This was bigger than the effect that contact had on support for either of the two main parties, though it was not as large as the effect of contact on support for the Liberal Democrats. The problem was that Ukip's campaign was not reaching as far. When people were asked who had contacted them in the previous four weeks, only one in twenty had heard from Ukip, compared to a ratio of one in five for the two main parties. Even the Liberal Democrats had reached one in ten. Outside of its top prospects, and as some in the party had feared, Ukip simply did not have sufficient resources to mobilize a serious fight, and across multiple fronts. 'The problem', said Arron Banks, one of Ukip's major donors during the campaign, 'was that the party had grown so quickly it was trying to fight on every front so people were running their own campaigns. It was up to them to run a good

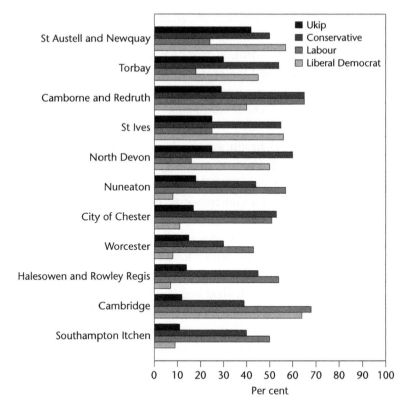

**Figure 10.4.** Party contact rates in eleven marginal seats
*Source*: Lord Ashcroft Polls.

campaign or a bad campaign. We should have trained a team of agents like the Conservatives do.' But there was no such support, and so Ukip was often heavily outgunned. In seats like Camborne and Redruth, for example, less than 30 per cent of voters had heard from the party, while almost 70 per cent had been contacted by the main parties. It was the same picture in many other places. The lack of manpower, money, and the overly ambitious number of target seats had spread the party thin and wide (see Figure 10.4).

Such problems were also prompting a change in the party's priorities. The initial list of thirty seats had already been trimmed to only ten. But with the election rapidly approaching, and Ukip feeling as though it was losing momentum, attention was increasingly shifting to only one seat, South Thanet—and it looked close. While a poll at the end of February, funded by a Ukip donor, suggested that Farage was at least ten points clear of his nearest rival, giving him a much-needed boost, another snapshot put him second, with only three points separating the Conservatives, Labour, and Ukip. There was all to play for. But, as the final stretch approached, Farage was beginning to feel low. One morning he rang Bruni-Lowe and said that he was struggling to get up for the campaign. 'He is clearly feeling the strain of having an entire campaign built around him,' said the campaigner.

Questions over Farage's health were underlined at Ukip's spring conference in Margate, which had been deliberately based in South Thanet to try and draw attention to his campaign. While some insiders were annoyed by Farage's decision to attend a conference in the United States only a day before Ukip's own event, he was also forced publicly to repudiate claims that he was unwell. 'It's said that I am seriously ill and that is why I have not been seen but... rumours of my demise have been greatly exaggerated.' Two months later, after further claims in the newspapers that he looked tired and unwell, Farage conceded that he had been in 'horrible' pain following the recurrence of a serious spinal injury, was receiving hospital treatment twice a week, and had been prescribed strong sleeping pills to help him during the campaign.[35] 'We would notice that he didn't look well', said Kassam, 'but we didn't realize just quite how reckless he was being, not taking his medication, not doing a set of exercises that he has to do every day, not going to physio. He just wasn't doing it.'

With the election now less than six weeks away, Ukip looked increasingly unlikely to fulfil its prediction of securing at least ten MPs. But it was not all bad news. In the polls, the party was holding fairly steady. Despite there being some evidence of a squeeze on the ground, many of those who had defected to Ukip seemed to be staying loyal—at least for now. Though some, as we will see, had started to drift back to the Conservatives, there had been no mass exodus. Cameron's gains were still relatively small compared to the number of voters that, overall, he had lost to Ukip since 2010. For Farage, despite the weaknesses and disputes within his party, and worries about his own health, he was managing to hold on to significant support. For this reason alone, and as the parties headed into the final stretch of the campaign, there was still much to play for.

# 11

# Ground Game

On the afternoon of Monday, 30 March 2015, Farage and his team arrived in Smith Square, in the heart of Westminster. There were only thirty-eight days until the election. It was the start of the short campaign— the final phase of the race. This meant that there were some new rules. The amount that the parties could spend in their seats was now further restricted, which meant that there was only so much that campaigners could do to change their ground game.[1] And something else was new. With its new-found status as a major party, Ukip hoped that it was about to benefit from increased publicity, which might help to sustain what felt to insiders like a very fragile position in the polls. As he stood in front of Europe House, once home to the legendary Conservative teams that had orchestrated a string of victories for Margaret Thatcher, Farage might have been wishing that he had the same quality of support. Looking ahead to a gruelling five weeks, he knew that his party was only just managing to keep its head above water. But Farage, the entertainer, needed to put on a brave face. 'What we have just passed through is the phoney war,' he declared. 'The real battle starts today.'

Ukip had already tried to establish a head start. In the days before the launch of the short campaign, and while speaking to Labour voters in South Thanet, Farage had made an announcement. 'Our modern political class', he said, with a St George's flag draped behind him, 'think it's shameful to be English'. The Ukip leader, who had talked often about his belief in the power of Englishness to propel his party forward, had then outlined his party's plan to make St George's day a public holiday. It was another attempt to highlight his core-vote strategy, to present Ukip as an alternative for patriotic and working-class Britons.

Now, in Smith Square, he was unveiling a new Ukip pledge card—a giant version of which had been plastered across a billboard van. The idea of the card had been suggested by Bruni-Lowe, who had wanted to keep Ukip's campaign message simple and focused squarely on core supporters. The card, inspired by one that had been used by Tony Blair and New Labour in 1997, would be sent to voters in the target seats along with a personalized letter from Farage. It highlighted five messages—'Say No' to the EU; control borders; invest an extra £3 billion into the NHS; cut foreign-aid spending; and take minimum wage-earners out of tax. But, as normal, there had been some last-minute problems. Suzanne Evans, who had been overseeing the manifesto, had initially not wanted the card to include overseas aid. 'It is a core policy!' Steve Stanbury had fumed. 'It does not matter what people in Tunbridge Wells think!' It had also been only in the final moments that somebody had realized that the party's founding policy of withdrawing Britain from the European Union was missing.

The other parties were also firing the starting gun on their campaigns. Earlier that day, David Cameron's car had swept through Westminster, down the Mall and into Buckingham Palace. After informing the Queen that parliament had been dissolved, he had returned to Downing Street to underline his own core message for voters—that this election was a stark choice between chaos or competence, turmoil or economic security. 'The next prime minister walking through that door will be me or Ed Miliband.' It was, claimed Cameron, a choice between a Conservative-led economy that was creating jobs, an improved health service, tax cuts, and security or 'the economic chaos of Ed Miliband's Britain'.

Meanwhile, in a different part of London, Ed Miliband and Labour were underway with a pitch for business. Miliband was talking about Britain's productivity gap and taking aim at Cameron's promise to hold a referendum on its continuing EU membership, which he dismissed as a 'clear and present danger' to the economy. Some in Labour felt confident. Over the weekend, newspapers had claimed that it was Miliband who had drawn 'first blood' in television interviews between the two main leaders and Jeremy Paxman. The other leaders had not been included, though Farage had turned up in the media spin room, anxious to remain as visible as possible.

In the opinion polls, the situation was actually not that different from the one that had met the parties at the beginning of the year. In the aftermath of the Paxman interviews, one poll had put Labour four points ahead, exciting journalists, who had developed a bad habit of reading too much into single snapshots, but within hours another had put the Conservatives four points ahead.[2] Neither of the main parties had established a decisive lead,

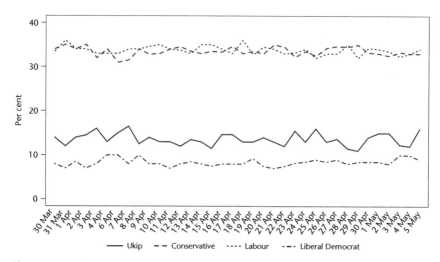

**Figure 11.1.** Average party support in national opinion polls, 30 March–5 May 2015
*Source*: UK Polling Report.

with each hovering around 34 per cent of the vote. Or so the pollsters were claiming. One party that had advanced, however, was the SNP, which was continuing to eat into Labour's support north of the border. It was reflected in a new batch of polls from Lord Ashcroft, which suggested that the insurgents were averaging 42 per cent of the vote, a striking increase of thirty points on their support in 2010. Labour was in trouble—and everybody in Scotland knew it.[3]

For Ukip, the picture was mixed. In the polls, there were good reasons for Farage to feel cautiously optimistic. Despite the internal problems, continual fears about a complete collapse of support had still not been realized. While at the start of the short campaign one national poll had put Ukip on 10 per cent, its lowest level since the poll had started in the spring of 2014, across all the different polling companies Ukip was retaining support.[4] It was averaging 14 per cent of the vote—a modest two-point drop from the autumn but an improvement on its ratings during the summer of 2014, following its earthquake at the European Parliament elections.

But there were also reasons for Farage to worry. Internally, Ukip was continuing to struggle. Its central operation remained wafer-thin, while the campaign was suffering from a lack of funding, inexperience, and infighting. And that was not all. Other problems that now faced Farage were more serious than the revelation that one of his candidates led a secret life as a porn star named Johnny Rockard, or that another was being questioned by police over allegations that he had tried to influence voters by giving them free sausage rolls.[5] While Ukip's national support seemed to be holding up, behind the headlines there was evidence that it was being squeezed on the ground. In Conservative-held seats, where Cameron was hoping that his relentless narrative of economic competence was cutting through, Ukip's support seemed to be ebbing away. Its average had fallen by six points, and it was the Conservatives who were benefiting.[6]

Against this backdrop, much of the first week of the short campaign focused on a seven-way television debate between leaders of the major parties and the SNP, the Greens, and Plaid Cymru. Farage and his team saw the debate as a major opportunity to boost their visibility and shore up their support. They felt anxious that their major party status did not seem to be generating the expected amounts of media attention, and that the startling rise of the SNP had effectively created a new third party. Farage had prepared for the debate by taking questions from his team, and then continuing to exchange ideas in a sauna with his advisers. Bruni-Lowe and Kassam were anxious that their leader look as fresh as possible and avoid the sweaty appearance that had become a talking point during his debates with Nick Clegg, in 2014.

These concerns had also occasionally fuelled a more general debate in Ukip about Farage's image. Some had wanted to cultivate an 'elder statesman' image for their leader, to bring an end to the continual pictures of him holding a pint of beer, wearing tweed blazers or yellow corduroy trousers. Others had talked of encouraging an image of Farage as a 'family man', perhaps by releasing photographs of the leader with his wife and children and pushing back against the stereotype of Ukip as a party that was filled with angry men. But those who were close to Farage knew that it would never happen—he would instantly rule out any suggestion of using his family for political purposes.

More than seven million people tuned into the debate and, as Farage had planned, one of the main talking points involved him. 'There are', he had said, while looking straight at the camera, 'seven thousand diagnoses in this country every year for people who are HIV positive, which is not a good place for any of them to be, I know. But sixty per cent of them are not British nationals. You can come into Britain from anywhere in the world, get diagnosed for HIV and get the retroviral drugs that cost up to £25,000 per year per patient.' It was not the first time that he had voiced the idea. During the by-election in Clacton he had made the same argument, and, as then, he was widely criticized. Leanne Wood, leader of Plaid Cymru, was the first to respond. 'I think you ought to be ashamed of yourself.' It was one of the few comments to be met with applause from the studio audience.

Further criticism would follow, but Farage and his advisers were delighted with the line. Ever since the 'March Tilt', when they had wrested back control of the campaign, those around the leader had actively supported any attempt to put immigration at the forefront, even if they had not always known what was coming. 'The HIV line just happened,' recalled his adviser, Raheem Kassam. 'We had briefly discussed the top line stuff about health tourism, immigration and the economy and within that conversation HIV came up. But there was no moment where we thought "let's do that". He just said it and we thought, "ok that's interesting".'

In the aftermath of the debate, Farage's strategy was described in one newspaper as 'shock and awe, or call it shock and awful'—it was the type of campaign that Carswell and others in the party had made a point of wanting to avoid. But Farage had enjoyed the intervention. It had been deliberate—to the point. 'Listen,' he had said to his team immediately after the debate, 'I am not trying to charm the nation. I am trying to turn out our core vote.' He would make the same point two months later, while reflecting on the campaign. 'I should have gone further than HIV. It was actually delivered in a gentle tone. It was not Donald Trump-style attack dog politics.'

Many viewers found Farage's argument distasteful, but it was also true that a large portion of the electorate endorsed the idea. After the debate, a sample of the population were asked whether or not they thought that people coming to live in Britain should be banned from receiving treatment on the NHS for five years (see Figure 11.2). Some 50 per cent thought that they should, and that Farage had been right to raise the issue. Among those who were voting for Ukip, the figure rocketed to 89 per cent—revealing how, on this issue, he was in touch with his core base.[7] Support was strongest among older and working-class Britons, while the young and middle class were the most likely to object. Pensioners were almost twice as likely as 18–24-year-olds to support a ban on the treatment of migrants with HIV.

There was also no doubt that many voters thought that Farage had, compared to the other leaders, performed strongly in the debate. In one poll he was second only to the SNP leader Nicola Sturgeon, who had impressed many with her solid performance (see Figure 11.3).[8] Farage had also struck a chord in his core areas. When voters were asked to think about the discussion about immigration, he had come top, thirty points ahead of his nearest rival. He was, however, noticeably less strong on other areas, such as the

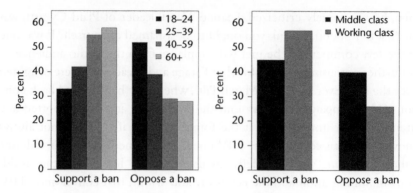

**Figure 11.2.** 'Would you support or oppose people coming to live in the UK being banned from receiving treatment on the NHS for a period of five years?'
*Source*: YouGov/*Sunday Times* Survey.

economy, health, and education, on which he lagged well behind other leaders. The message was clear—Farage was connecting but only in a few core areas and only with particular groups of voters.[9]

Yet, despite all of this, some in Ukip had started to feel concerned about the tone of the campaign. One was Gawain Towler, a long-serving activist. For many years he had been Farage's right-hand man, but during the

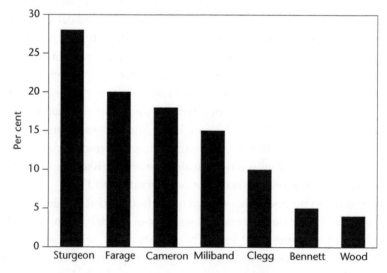

**Figure 11.3.** Best performance in leaders' debate, April 2015
*Source*: YouGov/*Times* Survey.

campaign he had felt increasingly isolated. Towler had been at the meeting ahead of the debate. 'I suggested that we mention tuberculosis. I was concerned that HIV would make it look like we were going after the weakest, that we were mean-hearted. It's not that it was false because it wasn't. Health tourism is a thing. But they said it was shock and awful. Well I don't want a campaign that is shock and awful.'

A couple of weeks later, in a debate between the leaders of the challenger parties, others had felt similarly anxious when Farage had decided openly to criticize the studio audience when discussing immigration. 'It is a remarkable audience even by the left-wing standards of the BBC, I mean this lot's pretty left-wing believe me.' It was yet another intervention that Farage had deliberately used to try and boost his visibility and reach out to Ukip's core supporters. But the provocation was making some in his party feel uncomfortable, as did Ukip's complaint to the police over comments that had been made about Farage on the comedy quiz show *Have I Got News for You*. One guest, journalist Camilla Long, who was not well liked within the party, suggested that he had barely visited South Thanet. While Kent Police said that it would not take action, the aggressive response from Farage and his team had alarmed some. Towler, who knew Farage well, rejected the idea that the campaign had seen a fundamental break from the past. But he had detected a shift.

I would not say Nigel changed, as there was nothing that he did that was not always there. It is not accurate to say that he was reinvented by Raheem [Kassam]. But we saw more of a side of Nigel that had not been given the same amount of licence in the past. He used to be aloof from the toxicity, floating above the bad side of Ukip. Everyone liked Nigel. The traditional interview would start with the journalist saying 'I wanted to hate him, but actually he is a nice bloke'. But what happened in this campaign, suddenly Nigel became as toxic as the party and that was a big change. Interviews no longer went like that. We lost that goodwill. He dipped into toxicity. It is a problem going forward.

Such concerns had arguably been fuelled by the decision, once again, to wage a presidential strategy. 'Nigel's face should be on everything!' Bruni-Lowe had shouted in one meeting. 'When you have a superstar you use that superstar!' Having been influenced by feedback from the target seats where his candidates had said that was a major asset, the campaigner wanted Farage to ask voters whether or not they agreed with the Ukip leader. Both Bruni-Lowe and Kassam wanted to build everything around him, including the election broadcast. In meetings, they had talked about trying to harness the freshness and optimism that had surrounded Tony Blair during the 1997 general election—at least among Ukip's core voters.

But their plans had been continually beset by internal problems. One example was Ukip's general election broadcast, which had been rushed after staff had failed to obtain permission slips from people who had contributed to an earlier version. The last-minute replacement simply featured Farage, sitting on a chair, alone, setting out his pitch. 'We're living in a country where if you're rich things are pretty good but if you're not rich life actually has been getting worse.' He looked tired and sounded unwell, which was not helped by the decision to use high definition. 'When I watched it,' said Kassam, 'I was forlorn and despondent. I think at that point I had somewhat given up. I just watched it. My heart sank. Somebody had commissioned music for it too. We never used it. It cost an arm and a leg but it made you want to kill yourself.'

And not everybody had shared the enthusiasm for the presidential strategy, including, some claimed, Douglas Carswell. 'He called me one afternoon', said David Soutter, 'and told me that he did not want anything with a picture of Nigel on it to enter Clacton. A few weeks later he called again to complain that one of our billboard vans in the neighbouring seat of Harwich had accidentally ventured into Clacton.'

Such anecdotes invited the question of whether, as some now seemed to be worrying, Farage was still the major asset that he had once been. There was no doubt that his leadership was central to explaining Ukip's support. Unlike the other parties, very few of the party's voters had been long-term loyalists. In 2015, only one in ten of those who were planning to vote for Ukip had supported it in 2010.[10] Without tribal supporters, who would vote for Ukip out of habit even if they were not particularly fond of its leader, the party had to rely more heavily on the here and now to attract support, almost all of which had been built around Farage. And he was a major asset. When we analyse the drivers of Ukip's support in 2015, we find that people who liked Nigel Farage were *sixteen* times more likely to say that they planned to vote for Ukip than those who were indifferent or disliked him.[11] In fact, how somebody felt about Farage had a stronger effect on Ukip's support than concerns about both the EU and immigration—revealing how important he was to explaining Ukip's appeal. Moreover, feelings about Farage were more important in predicting support for Ukip than feelings about Cameron were in predicting support for the Tories, Miliband for Labour, or Clegg for the Liberal Democrats.

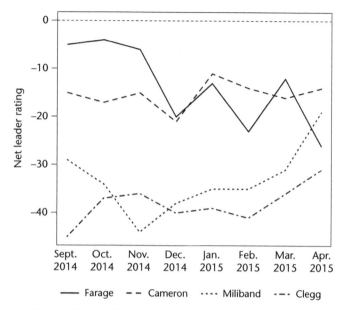

**Figure 11.4.** Net leader satisfaction ratings, September 2014–April 2015
*Source*: Ipsos-Mori.

Clearly, therefore, Ukip could not afford his image to suffer. But was this really happening? Was Farage becoming a liability during the campaign? One way of looking at this is to analyse data collected by Ipsos-MORI, which, since the 1970s, has asked *all voters* to rate their political leaders.[12] If we take the percentage of people who were 'satisfied' and subtract the percentage who were 'dissatisfied', then we are left with a 'net rating' for leaders. Numbers below zero mean that there were more people who were dissatisfied than satisfied. In Figure 11.4, we then track these ratings throughout the campaign, from the autumn of 2014 until the spring of 2015. It reveals how some had been right to voice concerns about Farage's broader image.

In September 2014, at the time of Ukip's conference in Doncaster, there had been no question that Farage was a major asset. He was the most popular political leader in Britain. Even though his overall ratings were negative, he was ten points ahead of Cameron, twenty-four points ahead of Miliband, and a striking forty points clear of Clegg. From these numbers, it is easy to see why Ukip's campaign team decided on a presidential strategy. However, amid the by-elections in October and November, which saw Farage and his party attract more publicity, his ratings took a hit. At the turn of the year, it was Cameron, not Farage, who was receiving the most favourable ratings from voters. The Ukip leader was second, enjoying a more positive rating than either Miliband or Clegg, but the electorate as a whole was noticeably less satisfied with Farage than they had been only a few months previously.[13]

While during the long campaign Farage had again briefly pulled ahead, in the short campaign, which saw his controversial interventions over HIV, his haranguing of the BBC audience, and his increased visibility more generally, his ratings fell to a new low. He was pushed into third place. By this time, and among the population more generally, the percentage of people who felt dissatisfied with Farage exceeded those who were satisfied by twenty-five points. Nor was it just Farage's image that had taken a hit. When Ipsos-MORI also probed the public image of the parties, they found that, compared to September 2014, fewer people now thought that Ukip understood the problems that were facing Britain, would keep its promises, would look after the interests of the people, had a good team of leaders, or was fit to govern. Around two-thirds continued to view Ukip as extreme and two-fifths saw it as divided.[14]

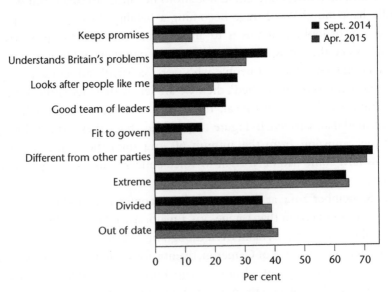

**Figure 11.5.** Ukip's image, September 2014–April 2015
*Source*: Ipsos-Mori.

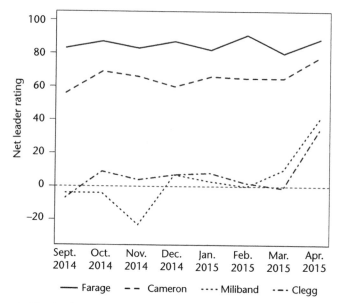

**Figure 11.6.** Net leader satisfaction ratings among supporters, September 2014–April 2015

Yet while there was evidence to suggest that, throughout the campaign, Farage had become less popular among the electorate as a whole, it was not the same picture among Ukip's voters. As shown in Figure 11.6, in the months leading up to the general election, his net satisfaction among Ukip supporters never fell below 80 per cent and was often closer to 90 per cent. Not only did Farage's ratings remain consistent; they were also noticeably higher than the other leaders' ratings among their supporters. Cameron, the next most popular leader, was on average nearly twenty points behind Farage. Though both Miliband and Clegg managed to improve their ratings heading into the short campaign, they still lagged far behind the other two leaders. During the autumn months Miliband's ratings were particularly poor. His net rating dropped below zero, meaning that even in his own camp more Labour supporters were dissatisfied than satisfied with his performance.

While the debates had sharpened concerns among some about the campaign, they had also thrown light on the continuing rise of the SNP and Nicola Sturgeon, who had performed solidly throughout. During the second debate, between the leaders of the challenger parties, Sturgeon had turned to Miliband and pledged her support. 'This election is about getting rid of the Tories. And Ed, whatever differences you have with me, surely they are as nothing to the differences that both of us have with the Tories.' Worried that Sturgeon's argument was validating Cameron's claims to voters that Labour and the SNP would soon be working together, threatening the economic recovery and the interests of English voters, Miliband tried to distance himself, ruling out a coalition with the Scottish insurgents. But Sturgeon pushed on. As the Labour leader stood, shaking his head, she appeared to confirm directly the fears of right-leaning voters in England. 'The reality is this,' said Sturgeon. 'If on May 8 there are more anti-Tory MPs in the House of Commons than there are Tory MPs, then if we work together we can lock David Cameron out of Downing Street so tell me tonight, is it the case that you would rather see David Cameron go back into Downing Street than work with the SNP? Surely that cannot be your position Ed.'

Farage was on the stage, watching the exchange closely. 'The whole dynamics of the campaign', he would later say, 'shifted after that'. No longer believing that the rise of the SNP was good for Ukip, both Farage and his party from hereon became increasingly anxious that events might push voters into the arms of Cameron. There was no doubt that Sturgeon's performance had helped to push her to the forefront of Britain's political debate. That her reach was widening beyond Scotland had been reflected in one poll, which suggested that one in ten voters would consider voting for the SNP if it ran candidates outside Scotland.[15] But her impact was about more than popularity. As Cameron had hoped, Sturgeon's performance was fuelling a perception among voters that the Scottish nationalists were now a credible contender for government. Before the short campaign, two in three people had thought that the SNP had some chance of being in the next government. But by the short campaign this had increased to three out of four. It played directly into Cameron's narrative and started to dominate the minds of those at the very top of Ukip, like its deputy leader, Paul Nuttall.

The SNP factor came about by accident not design. Cameron did not want to debate Farage and then invited Sturgeon on, letting the English see her in action. If she had been on that platform in the big debates, well, whether it was a stroke of genius or by accident it created a bogeyman. That was meant to be us but it turned out to be Sturgeon.

From this point on, Cameron and the Conservatives tweaked their 'squeeze' strategy and focused relentlessly on the perceived threat of an Ed

Miliband-led Labour government that was either in coalition with the SNP, or propped up by the insurgent party. The message was reflected on Conservative Party leaflets that were now bombarding voters in marginal seats—including ones that Ukip was targeting. 'The SNP would prop up Ed Miliband—meaning chaos for Britain.' 'SNP puts Miliband in Downing Street. Your vote can stop this.' 'Coalition of chaos. Spending up. More debt. Higher taxes. Jobs lost. Britain can't afford it, and you'll pay for it.' Cameron was also taking every moment of opportunity to underline the message. Typical of these interventions was an article that was published the day before postal vote forms were sent out. After reminding voters about his offer of a referendum on Britain's continued EU membership, and his long-term economic plan, Cameron said: 'And to anyone whose pen hovers over the Ukip box on their postal vote, let's be clear: a vote for Ukip works directly against the Conservative party and makes a Labour government more likely.' Cameron then asked voters to reflect on what a Labour government propped up by the SNP might mean—'the party that would bankrupt our country and the party that would break up our country'.[16]

The narrative was also being reinforced in the right-wing newspapers. Until this point, for example, the *Daily Telegraph* had given Farage a considerable amount of neutral and even positive coverage. The publication of his new book—*The Purple Revolution*—had been covered extensively in three consecutive front-page stories, which Ukip insiders saw as an important contribution to 'the brand'. But now, two weeks into the short campaign, the newspaper began urging its conservative readers to resist any temptation to support Farage and his party.

No matter how hard Ukip attempts to argue otherwise, or stir up anger in the hope that voters' judgement will be clouded...every vote cast for Ukip makes it more likely that next month, Mr Miliband and his party will take power, possibly in cahoots with the SNP. Britain cannot afford that.'

The *Sun* set out a similar message for its working-class readership. 'A week today', it claimed,

Britain could be plunged into the abyss. A fragile left-wing Labour minority, led by Ed Miliband and his union paymasters and supported by the wreckers of the Scottish National Party, could take power...You may still be considering Ukip. But every Ukip vote, especially in the South, brings a Labour/SNP nightmare closer by eroding Tory chances.[17]

Cameron, meanwhile, was issuing a more direct plea to Ukip defectors. Much like Margaret Thatcher had done in 1978, when trying to win back

voters who felt threatened by immigration and who might desert to the far
right National Front, Cameron publicly sympathized with disillusioned
Conservatives who felt frustrated with immigration and Britain's EU membership. He had, he said, heard them 'loud and clear'. He then proceeded to
underline the choice.

But this election is not a time to send a message or make a protest. This election
is about choosing the government of our country for the next five years, and
the choice could not be starker between a Conservative government led by me,
continuing with a plan that's working, and putting it all at risk.

Those who had defected to Ukip, he continued, should 'come with us,
come back home to us, rather than risk all of this good work being undone
by Labour'. The intervention angered Farage, who quickly fired back.
'Neither former Labour nor Conservative voters who have switched to
Ukip are going back. They've found a new, more authentic home, one in
which they don't get roundly abused by their hosts.'[18] But was he right? Was
Ukip retaining its support?

The British Election Study surveyed many of the same people at several points between the European Parliament elections in 2014 and the
general election in 2015. It provides a unique window through which we
can see how people's loyalties were changing over time. And it shows that
not only was Ukip experiencing defections but that it was Cameron
who had reaped the rewards. In the aftermath of the European elections,
Ukip had lost around one-quarter of its support (see Table 11.1). While
Cameron had gained more of these defectors than any of the other parties, the largest share was now on the fence—these people were undecided about how they would vote in 2015. Over the winter, Ukip had
then lost another third of its support. By the time that Britain got to the
long campaign, around one in three of the people who had planned to
vote for Ukip during the autumn had switched to one of the other parties. It was during this later period that the Conservatives began to win
over a more significant share of Ukip defectors, with Cameron collecting
more than half of those who had decided to leave Farage. In the final
months of the campaign, Farage and his party lost almost one-quarter of
their remaining support and, again, almost half of these voters headed to
Cameron and the Conservatives. So, by the short campaign, Ukip had
lost around half, or 48 per cent, of those who had supported it in the
spring of 2014.

Table 11.1. Ukip defections, May 2014–April 2015

| Defections | May 2014 to Autumn 2014 | Autumn 2014 to March 2015 | March 2015 to April 2015 | May 2014 to April 2015 |
|---|---|---|---|---|
| % of Ukip voters defecting | 25 | 32 | 22 | 48 |
| *Where were they going?* | | | | |
| Conservative | 28 | 55 | 48 | 52 |
| Labour | 22 | 15 | 21 | 23 |
| Other | 17 | 11 | 14 | 13 |
| Don't know | 33 | 19 | 17 | 12 |

*Note:* The figures in the first row represent the weighted percentage of Ukip supporters who indicated that they no longer planned to vote for Ukip when re-surveyed in the subsequent wave of the BES. The bottom four rows indicate the new vote choice of the defectors—the figures represent the weighted percentage of defectors that plan to vote for each party.

*Source*: 2014–2017 British Election Study Internet Panel (Waves 2–5).

This drift had been noticed by some inside the party, like Nuttall, who had been typically spending much of his time trying to rally voters at the grass roots.

I did notice when I was doing the public meetings that I was getting really big numbers in February and March but then the numbers fell off in late April. This could have been because people were getting tired of politics, or because some of our support was slipping away.

What had motivated some of Ukip's voters to jump ship? Part, but not all, of the story was about the party's message. Farage was tending to retain the loyalty of those who felt the most intensely concerned about Europe and immigration—his core issues. In fact, people who shared these concerns, and who were being aggressively targeted by Ukip's core-vote strategy, were nearly five times more likely to stay loyal than people who cared about neither of these two issues—so the strategy was indeed helping to keep people on board. Similarly, people who felt the most strongly dissatisfied with the way that British politics was working were twice as likely to stay loyal to the party as those who did not. If Ukip's relentless appeals to its core voters were designed to hold on to these groups, then it was clearly succeeding.

Farage's problem, however, was that, as polling day neared, he was more likely to lose votes from those who did *not* feel as intensely concerned about his core issues. People who shared neither of the party's core concerns were six times more likely to defect than those who sympathized with its central worries over immigration and the EU. As one might expect, the people who were the most likely to desert Ukip were often the least likely to see their concerns reflected back in its core-vote strategy.

But it was not only about issues. Farage himself was also part of the story. When the people who had supported Ukip at the time of the European elections were surveyed again shortly before the general election in 2015, one in three of them liked Farage less than before, while one-quarter liked him more. These different responses to Ukip's leader led people down very different paths. Those who liked him less were almost three times as likely as those whose feelings were unchanged to abandon Ukip. Those who liked Farage more, however, were three times as likely to have stayed loyal than those who liked him less. There was also some evidence that Cameron's strategy was having its intended effect. Individuals who said that they pre-ferred the idea of a Conservative government were five times more likely to defect away from Ukip.

So why, if people were leaving Ukip, was the party's broader support hold-ing steady? Well, this was not just a story about defections. Farage and his party had also picked up some new support during the campaign, and from the other parties. Shortly before the general election, one-fifth of those who were planning to vote for Ukip had, during the spring of 2014, planned to support a different party. While the arrival of these new supporters did not completely offset Ukip's losses, they did prevent it from experiencing the cataclysmic collapse of public support that Cameron was hoped for and Farage was fearing. Many of those who, since 2014, had been persuaded into Ukip's camp had previously been undecided, or were people who had planned to support the Conservatives. But, even though they were new Ukip supporters, they often shared the same outlook as the loyalists. They felt strongly concerned about Europe and immigration, were dissatisfied with how British politics was functioning, and liked Farage more than they had in the past. Far from having recruited a static army of voters, therefore, below the surface Ukip was witnessing significant churn in its electorate.

On Wednesday, 8 April, Farage was in Boston and Skegness. He was slumped in a chair. His feet were resting on a coffee table and he was struggling to stay awake. Sitting around him were Bruni-Lowe, one of the press officers, Alex Phillips, and Ukip's events manager, Lizzy Vaid. They were nearing the end of an intensive two-day tour of Ukip's target seats. With only a few weeks to go, Farage had been trying to generate publicity for his top-tier candidates, hoping to push some of them across the line. The schedule had been punishing. On the first day, Farage and his team had trundled through areas in the Midlands such as Cannock and Dudley, launching Ukip's defence policy and speaking to 400 people at a public meeting. He had given twenty-five media interviews throughout the day and at times had felt irritated that his press team did not seem to be filtering the slots. 'At one point I was sat with Sikh TV thinking "what am I doing"?'

On the second day, Farage had woken at six in the morning, headed to Grimsby docks for a photo opportunity, spoken at a public meeting in the town hall, done more interviews over lunch, unveiled a new billboard that focused on the plight of the fishing industry, met a group of disgruntled fishermen in Cleethorpes, and done yet more interviews. He had also reluctantly agreed to share a boat trip with television celebrity Joey Essex, who was making a documentary about young people and the general election. Some in Ukip had thought the entire episode pointless, noting how young people were not central to the core-vote strategy. Their irritation was then fuelled when Essex had kept Farage waiting. 'There is only one celebrity here!', fumed Bruni-Lowe, 'and it is definitely not Joey Essex!' When the boat that was being used for the show had finally arrived, it was not big enough for the press team or any of the other journalists. Farage subsequently found himself being left alone with Joey Essex and a television camera crew. 'Anything could be happening out there,' said a Ukip press officer, as they watched the boat drift out of the harbour.

Farage had then headed to a school in Boston and Skegness to speak to 400 people at another meeting. It was at meetings such as these that some veterans, who had been with Ukip from the start, had noticed a different Farage. 'There was a different tone, the way that he was getting angry with people, the way he was saying he would not talk to certain newspapers. And the security. There was now always distance between him and voters. There were always the goons around him.' There was no doubt that Farage, who was carrying much of the campaign, was feeling the burden of the campaign. After the meeting, he had immediately slumped into the nearest chair. He looked exhausted. And, in a few moments he would have to put on a smile and do it all over again, speaking to another 400 voters. There had been so much interest in the Lincolnshire seat that Ukip had organized two back-to-back meetings. 'Right,' Farage said, his voice about to go. 'What shall I say at this one?'

Away from the spotlight, Ukip was also continuing to grapple with an array of problems. Bruni-Lowe, who could often be found staring into his iPad, was receiving a constant stream of information from the key seats. It did not look good. The latest data suggested that the party was now also being squeezed in its target seats—not only in those where it was not trying. According to Ukip's internal polls its lead in top prospects, like Thurrock, was slipping away, even if public polls continued to put the party ahead.[19] 'It is squeaky bum time,' whispered one activist over Bruni-Lowe's shoulder.

Similar problems were surfacing in other seats, where a lack of experience and weak candidates were undermining Ukip's effort. 'Tell Nigel not to bother coming,' said one organizer in Cornwall. 'The activists down here don't know how to campaign. Nobody is knocking on doors. You've wasted £50,000.' David Soutter, who had long been complaining about the lack of preparation for the election, had noticed the same challenge. 'The problem for the party was that these under-performing candidates were in essence good people, very loyal to both the party and in most cases to Nigel Farage but totally useless as modern political campaigners. They were fighting a general election campaign for twenty years ago, not 2015.' The problem was not lost on Farage. It was, he would say, 'old Ukip'—a generation of followers who were fiercely loyal but did not know how to fight and win elections.

The problem had been apparent even in some of the seats that were at the very top of Ukip's target list. Boston and Skegness, where Farage had been speaking, had given the party its strongest vote at the European Parliament elections. Shortly after, a constituency poll had put Ukip on 46 per cent of the vote and a striking twenty points ahead of the incumbent Conservative Party. 'We were delighted,' said Ukip's candidate, Robin Hunter-Clarke, who, after Hamilton's failed push, had been selected to fight the seat. 'Why on earth did we need to waste time campaigning?! Well, that's what we thought at the time.' The complacency would not last. In the early weeks of 2015, Lord Ashcroft went back to the seat and found that Ukip was on 35 per cent, trailing the Conservatives by three points.[20] Bruni-Lowe's internal polls had spotted the same slump, which some traced to their inexperienced, young candidate. 'I mean, come on guys', complained one. 'We are supposed to be the People's Army but this guy still lives at home with his mum.'

Such was the concern about losing a top prospect that a crisis meeting had been held at Ukip's spring conference in Margate, less than ten weeks before polling day. Bruni-Lowe had pushed for radical action, even commissioning a poll to explore whether the people of Boston and Skegness might be more receptive to an older candidate. The results suggested that it would. Patrick O'Flynn and Paul Nuttall had shared the angst and there was talk of parachuting in an older candidate, such as Diane James or the MEP Margot Parker. But when it was put to Farage he vetoed the idea. It was not, he argued, and despite all of the manœuvrings that had been used to thwart Hamilton, the Ukip way. The candidate would stay in place.

There were other challenges. In its target seats, Ukip was generally managing to stay active. As the election neared, research by Lord Ashcroft revealed how the party was keeping pace with the main parties.[21] In South Thanet, for example, 89 per cent of those who were surveyed had been contacted by Ukip. This put the party more than ten points ahead of the Conservatives and almost twenty points ahead of Labour. While it had started to fall behind Labour in the top prospect of Great Grimsby, Ukip also had an edge in Rochester and Strood, and Castle Point, and was engaged in a close race with the main parties in Thurrock. But, even though polls suggested that Ukip was holding its own in some seats, they also delivered a powerful blow to the party's hopes.

The problem was that the contact was not yielding rewards. In spite of its efforts, Ukip's support in the polls was waning (see Figure 11.7). In Great Grimsby, for example, its support had fallen from around 34 per cent at the end of 2014 to 25 per cent. In a seat that was packed full of ideal voters, Ukip was now seventeen points behind Labour. More crushing were the figures from Rochester and Strood, where Reckless saw his support drop by nine points, putting him three behind the Tories. And, even though the party seemed to be on track to win in Thurrock, the race was becoming closer by the day—Ukip, the Tories, and Labour were all within five points of each other.[22] But it was the picture in South Thanet that was now really worrying Farage and his team.

Ever since Farage had declared his candidacy, South Thanet had always looked set to be one of the great battles of the election. The seat had attracted intense interest from pollsters. Even before the short campaign there had been no less than six separate polls from the seat.[23] Their results had been mixed. Three had put the Conservatives ahead, two had put Ukip in front,

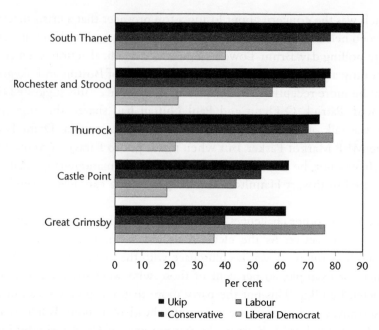

**Figure 11.7.** Party contact in five Ukip target seats, 2015
*Source*: Lord Ashcroft Polls.

and the oldest, in 2013, had Labour in first place. Across all polls the Conservatives, Labour, and Ukip had each averaged 30 per cent of the vote—it
was the classic three-way marginal that Farage, who was still hoping to run
through the middle, had always wanted.

Despite the closeness of the race, for much of this time, in the betting
markets, the Ukip leader had also been the favourite. At one point Farage
had an implied 69 per cent chance of victory. This had followed one poll
by Survation in February 2015, which had been funded by a Ukip donor.
It had put him eleven points clear of his nearest rival. But the poll had
been a mixed blessing for Ukip. Initially, it had fuelled hopes among
insiders, who pointed to the fact that it was the only poll to have been
conducted since they had started the grass-roots public meetings. But it
had also put Labour in second place, which galvanized its 24-year-old
candidate, Will Scobie. The indefatigable activist had already been elected
as a local councillor, and Mayor of Margate. Now, he believed that he had
a genuine chance and started to work hard to reconnect with the struggling, Labour voters whom Farage desperately needed to carry him over
the line. Ukip knew it could make inroads into Labour's support, but it

had never done so in the face of a candidate who looked as determined as Scobie.

'The kid is like Rocky,' complained one Ukip activist, as the party discussed the Labour challenge. 'He just won't go away. He is canvassing from first thing in the morning until late at night. He doesn't stop.' As the campaign rolled on, Scobie even wrote to Conservative and Liberal Democrat voters, urging them to lend him their vote. It was an appeal for tactical voters that did not go down well among the other candidates, including Craig MacKinlay, the Conservative Party candidate, who noted how South Thanet was not a Labour target and had attracted little support from the central party.[24] In fact Scobie himself had declined offers of support from the central Labour Party. 'I rebuffed a lot of attempts to help. My view was that, with Farage in the seat, it was an insurgency anti-establishment campaign. If we had all these shadow ministers coming down and looking like machine politics, it would have fuelled him on.' But he did receive some help. One Labour analyst compiled a report on around 10,000 households in South Thanet that were receptive to Ukip—and that Scobie should focus on. It drew attention to 'blue-collar strivers', voters who were attracted to Farage 'because of the lack of mainstream voice for their combination of social conservatism, working-class identity and economic ambition', as well as older households on the council estates where people felt 'resentful of New Labour for allowing large-scale immigration and for failing to respond to their anxieties and concerns'.[25] Scobie also attracted support from anti-fascists and a grass-roots 'stop Ukip' campaign, some of whose activists Ukip claimed were not playing by the democratic rules. On one day the party alleged that every one of its twenty-seven billboards in the seat had been vandalized.

Scobie, meanwhile, was deliberately trying to frame himself as the anti-Farage candidate, as the only person who could end the revolt by ensuring that its leader fulfilled a promise that had featured in a newly published book about his life—that he would resign as Ukip's leader if he failed to win. Once again, it was double or quits, only this time Farage had raised the stakes considerably.

It is frankly just not credible for me to continue to lead the party without a Westminster seat of my own. What credibility would Ukip have in the Commons if others had to enunciate party policy in Parliament and the party leader was only allowed in as a guest? Am I supposed to brief Ukip policy from the 'Westminster Arms'? No—if I fail to win South Thanet, it is curtains for me. I will have to step down.[26]

The Conservatives had instead anchored their campaign in the Kent seat in high-profile visits, direct mail shots to key voters, and tangible incentives. Towards the end of the long campaign, the Conservative Party announced that it would be undertaking a review of locally unpopular decisions involving Manston Airport, which locals wanted to see reopened. Around the same time, it was revealed that South Thanet was to benefit from £12 million government funding for high-speed rail improvements, triggering some to accuse the Conservatives of pork-barrel politics.[27] 'It just goes to show what Ukip can do by bringing attention to an area,' quipped Farage. Mackinlay, meanwhile, was welcoming a series of frontline Conservatives into the seat, who were spending much of their time in the rock solid Conservative areas of Broadstairs and Sandwich, where Farage felt that he was struggling. They included the Work and Pensions Secretary Iain Duncan Smith, Health Secretary Jeremy Hunt, Home Secretary Theresa May, and former Leader of the House William Hague. Two weeks before the election, the Mayor of London, Boris Johnson, arrived to promote Mackinlay's 'five-point plan' for the town. The next week, he was followed by Chancellor George Osborne, who used South Thanet to announce a new round of funding for coastal communities and give a 'heavy hint' that the nearby area of Ramsgate would be included.

The activism of Labour and the Conservatives contrasted with a growing unease inside Ukip about the amount of time that Farage was spending in the seat. 'He is everywhere *but* Thanet until the second week of April,' said Bruni-Lowe, who reluctantly talked about his leader's commitments in other parts of the country. The distraction of the by-elections, the lack of planning and grass-roots work, and the weak local Ukip branch that some had noticed earlier in the year, were now coming back to haunt the party. Farage was continually on the campaign trail, juggling his roles as party leader, chief spokesperson, and candidate. He was in London to launch the campaign, Dover to unveil a billboard on immigration, Manchester for the leaders' debates, and then on a tour of the country to draw attention to other target seats. The days when he actually spent quality time in South Thanet—talking to voters in ice cream parlours, coffee shops, meetings, or at a local beer festival—felt few and far between. The party tried to fill the gap by holding half-a-dozen 'action days' with activists, but there remained problems. 'We'd basically say on Monday morning, right let's have an action day this weekend,' said Kassam. 'But the invite would often not go out until Wednesday. And we were asking activists to come to an area of the country that was not very accessible, and ask them to stay over where there were not many hotels.' Farage would nonetheless enjoy the action days, even if he had noticed that Carswell did not attend any.

The Ukip leader's absence from the constituency campaign would perhaps have been more manageable had the local branch in South Thanet been more competent and active. But it was not. Aside from generating a wave of damaging publicity, after the *Meet the Ukippers* documentary, the branch was also suspiciously quiet. One afternoon, Bruni-Lowe sat down to explore data from canvassing sessions that all branches were inputting onto computer software. He realized instantly that there was a problem. Between the public meetings and Farage's high-profile visits, little was being done in South Thanet; this had also been noted by Scobie.

Their [Ukip] campaign came in waves. They would come in for three or four days, they'd have activists everywhere, have a big campaign day, swamp the area, we would be knocked for six. The output was way above anything that we could do. But then it would go quiet. They would allow us and the Tories to get back in to it.

More bad news followed. Just before the short campaign, another poll surfaced, which had been carried out before the debates. The snapshot by ComRes put the Conservatives on 31 per cent, Farage on 30, and Labour on 29. It was also suggested that Ukip had tried to prevent the poll's release, which had been funded by one of its donors. On the first weekend of April the results were splashed on the front page of the *Mail on Sunday*. 'Farage buries "loser" poll,' screamed the headline. Whereas Ukip had in the past used polls to try and demoralize opponents, it was now feeling the reverse effect. The article claimed that Farage's career was coming to an end. In the days that followed, he was forced to concede that he was 'a bit stretched' and issued a public request for support from his candidates. 'I know a lot of you are fighting your own campaigns locally but if you could spare just one or two days I'd really appreciate the support.'[28] He was no longer the favourite. In the betting markets his chances of winning had dropped to 53 per cent (see Figure 11.8).

It was around this time that Farage made a private confession. 'I think I might have left it too late,' he said to Bruni-Lowe. He liked to gamble, but

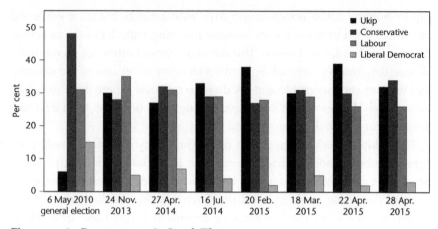

**Figure 11.8.** Party support in South Thanet, 2010–2015
*Sources*: 2010 general election result, and Survation, ComRes, and Lord Ashcroft Polls.

this time he had put his entire career on the table. While his instincts told him that he was beginning to fall behind, the wider campaign was continuing to demand his attention elsewhere. If he was to make it into Westminster, then something would have to change. 'There is no Plan B,' Farage had said to his advisers on one evening, staring into his glass of wine.

Trying to turn the tide, Bruni-Lowe and Kassam made a joint decision. 'Listen,' said the former to the latter, 'if you don't get down there we will lose the seat by 8,000 or 9,000 votes'. Kassam moved permanently to South Thanet, from where he could keep a close eye on the Ukip branch. Bruni-Lowe followed a few days later. He would take personal control of the final push while also trying to orchestrate the entire campaign from Kent. Everything else, including events that were designed to support Ukip's national effort, was now relegated down the list of priorities. It was now all about winning South Thanet. 'Chris was concerned about the numbers,' said one press officer.

There was a fixation about Thanet, a tension between wanting publicity and winning Thanet. We found a farmer to do a thing on agriculture. It was cancelled because it was not in Thanet. There was an opportunity for Nigel to open a factory. It was forty minutes from a meeting but it was stopped. Then we wanted to visit a friendly Asian doctor in London. It was a cancelled.

Those who were now becoming frantic about Farage's prospects saw many of these other activities as an unnecessary distraction. 'The press team are trying to get us to branch out to new people, to women and kids. It is ridiculous. Had it been a year ago then fine but to do it now would just seem totally and utterly contrived.'

The change of focus also meant that other Ukip candidates who wanted advice from their campaigner-in-chief—about literature, voters, and how to get out the vote on polling day—had to travel to Kent rather than London. 'It is lucky that nobody ever calls Ukip and wants to donate one million pounds,' said one, 'because there is never anybody in the office'. Bruni-Lowe's plan was to run the remaining campaign in South Thanet as if it were a by-election, using the same tactics that had delivered success in Clacton, and then Rochester and Strood. But it was clear that the battle that was now facing the team would be much harder. The last week of the campaign brought two new polls. One, by Survation, and which had been funded by a Ukip donor, put Farage nine points clear. But the other, by Lord Ashcroft, put him on 32 per cent, two points behind the Conservative Party candidate. Farage did not seem to be winning over a sufficient number of converts. And polling day was upon him.

Realizing that their destiny was now entwined with the outcome in Kent, senior Ukip officials now began to flood South Thanet. On one afternoon, everybody who was anybody in the party—Farage, Nuttall, the Richardson brothers, O'Flynn, Kassam, and everybody else who had been at the heart of the campaign—was sitting by the phones in Ukip's back-room office in Kent, frantically calling undecided voters. Anything that did not contribute directly to winning was sidelined. But, for Farage and his team, it was not clear whether or not the last-ditch effort would be enough. And now the day of reckoning had arrived.

# 12

# Counting the Votes

Nigel Farage and his team spent the last hours of the general election in South Thanet. It had become the epicentre of their entire campaign. Bruni-Lowe, like others in the party, had not been sleeping in the final days. He was preoccupied with the details of his get-out-the-vote operation, the last-ditch effort to get voters out of their homes and into the polling stations to vote for Farage. His plans were based on a specific calculation. During the course of the campaign, the Ukip leader had amassed around 16,000 pledges in the seat—people who had promised to vote for him. But it was not enough. Bruni-Lowe reckoned that he needed at least 18,000 to win—he was 2,000 short. This meant that, while the race would go to the wire, the campaigner knew that the odds were stacked against victory. Somehow, Ukip would need to make serious inroads into the 8,000 or so voters on its database who said that they had not yet decided whom to support. Two goals would dominate the last day—trying to ensure that Farage's pledges actually turned out to vote, and trying to convince as many of the undecided voters as possible to cast their ballot for Ukip. It was a daunting task.

The day of the election itself would be a day of two halves. In the morning, Farage and his team had allowed themselves to feel confident. As they had toured the seat, the initial reaction had seemed positive. Lots of their supporters had already voted. 'We're with you Nige!' shouted one as he left the polling station. 'All of the data that we were getting early on was that we were going to win by a mile,' said Bruni-Lowe. 'Our data suggested that ten thousand of our lot had voted by ten in the morning.' There were some unhelpful distractions, however. Amid the chaos, Paul Lambert, Ukip's Director of Communications, had suddenly turned up, having not spoken with Farage for weeks. He was now demanding to be at the declaration of the result, even threatening to resign if he was excluded. Bruni-Lowe escorted him outside. 'Listen!', said the irritated campaigner. 'I am trying to win this bloody thing! Piss off!' When he returned, he looked at the data that were coming in from the field. They were not as bad as he had feared. The quiet dread of defeat that he had felt leading up to polling day was making way for newfound optimism.

Now, Bruni-Lowe was trying to find any last-minute advantage that might push his leader over the line. He issued an order. During the campaign, Ukip's internal polls had suggested that a large number of Farage's pledges were people who had not voted before. The big question was whether they would turn out. To try and reduce the risk, the party had produced thousands of polling cards that showed voters the way to the nearest polling station. 'You could not have got more A to Z,' said one. The team began a mass telephone canvassing exercise, calling the pledges, reminding them to vote, and making sure that they knew where they were going. Then they turned their attention to the 8,000 undecided voters who would probably determine the outcome. Ukip had already targeted them with direct mail shots, highlighting local issues such as reviving a nearby airport, tackling corruption, and reforming Thanet District Council. But the party had not been the only ones reaching out. The Conservative Party had bombarded the same groups of voters with literature and telephone calls, warning them again and again about the likelihood of a Labour–SNP coalition. Now, it was not clear which way they would fall.

Farage, meanwhile, had been touring the polling stations with Raheem Kassam, trying to get a sense of how the ground war was concluding. But the confidence that they had felt earlier on in the day was making way for doubt. In the early afternoon, Kassam noticed half-a-dozen Conservative battle buses pulling into the seat. Then he saw long lines of voters forming in the Conservative-leaning areas of Broadstairs and Sandwich. Farage stayed quiet. 'I think he tried not to think about it,' said Kassam.

We went to every polling station and saw so many voters turning out. Nigel just kept saying 'I've never seen anything like it'. I couldn't work out whether that was a good thing or a bad thing. Was he thinking 'maybe this is all for me' or was he thinking 'this is all for them'?

The answer to that question was taking shape on Bruni-Lowe's computer. The campaigner had pinned his hopes on recruiting at least 35 per cent of the undecided voters. But the data told a very different story. Farage was attracting only around 15 per cent. It was not even half of what he needed. 'We were calling the undecideds relentlessly, but they kept telling us that they simply did not want Ed Miliband in Downing Street.' Worryingly for Bruni-Lowe, he was receiving the same message from Ukip's other target seats, like Thurrock, where activists reported that they were struggling, in particular among undecided voters. Until this point the campaigner had been sending his leader updates every hour. But now they stopped. 'When Chris goes quiet,' said Kassam, 'something is wrong'. Eventually, he called Farage. 'How is it looking?' said the hopeful candidate. 'Not good,' came the reply. 'We are not picking up enough undecided.' 'Oh really?' said Farage. He went quiet.

Within the hour Farage was back in the office, huddled around a computer with his advisers. They were staring at the numbers. 'I just don't think it is possible,' said Bruni-Lowe, leaning back in his chair as Farage stared blankly at the screen. Given that there was no way of knowing whether or not the data were accurate until the result was declared, the party could only continue to knock on doors. Farage himself stayed out on the campaign trail until ten o'clock at night, perhaps secretly hoping that the polls and his party's own data had been wrong all along and that a handful of votes might yet make all the difference. As he walked around the streets of South Thanet, he knew that the most important moment in his political career was upon him—and he did not like how it felt.

When the sun rose on the morning of Friday, 8 May, Britain's political map had changed—just not in the way that most people had expected. David Cameron and the Conservative Party had won an unexpected majority government. While they had increased their share of the national vote only by less than 1 per cent, they had almost 37 per cent, which was enough— and that was all that mattered. Cameron and his party had 330 seats in the House of Commons—their largest number since 1992.[1] They had lost eleven seats but they had gained thirty-five, capturing twenty-seven of these from their old partners in the Coalition government—the Liberal Democrats. This left Cameron and his party with a net increase of twenty-four seats and a majority of twelve. They would, at last, no longer be chained by a coalition. It was a result that Conservatives had been dreaming about for nearly twenty years—and one that almost every serious pollster and academic forecaster had failed to predict.[2]

This meant that it had been a disastrous night for Labour. Ed Miliband and his party, who had been widely tipped to return to power, but whose performance in the polls had remained so unconvincing, attracted only 30 per cent of the vote. It was Labour's third lowest share of the vote since it had first broken through in the 1920s. Only in 1983 and 2010 had the party received a lower percentage of the vote. Though Labour captured twenty-two seats, it had lost more than twice that number, with forty-eight slipping from its grasp. The number of Labour MPs slumped to 232, the third lowest since 1945. Only in 1983, under Michael Foot, and in 1987, under Neil Kinnock, had Labour been reduced to a smaller rump of MPs.[3] One of those who lost his seat, and whose defeat appeared to symbolize the public rejection of Labour, was Shadow Chancellor Ed Balls.

Popular explanations for Labour's defeat quickly and perhaps inevitably focused on events in Scotland, where Nicola Sturgeon and the SNP had delivered the political equivalent of a massacre. Their anti-austerity, anti-Westminster, and nationalist message had attracted 50 per cent of the vote in Scotland. At least there, if nowhere else, the pollsters had been right—the surge had been real. The number of SNP seats skyrocketed, from six to fifty-six, forty of which had been taken off Labour, which had only one seat left in Scotland.[4] It was an almost total wipe-out.

The seismic shift was nothing short of remarkable. The SNP's vote share had increased, on average, by thirty points.[5] Thirty-four of its candidates had won over more than 50 per cent of the vote. The Scottish nationalists were now the third largest party in the House of Commons. Several had replaced Labour's big beasts, including the leader of Scottish Labour, Jim Murphy, and former Shadow Foreign Secretary and head of Labour's election strategy, Douglas Alexander, who was felled by the SNP's 20-year-old Mhairi Black, one of the youngest MPs on record. The result cast a long shadow over Labour's prospects. As academic John Curtice pointed out, if the SNP was to retain 50 per cent of the vote at the next general election in 2020, to secure a majority Labour would somehow need to establish a thirteen-point lead over the Conservatives.[6] It was one hell of a challenge.

But Labour's defeat could not simply be explained by its annihilation in Scotland. Even if the party had not experienced a single loss north of the border, it would have still been left with only 272 seats, fifty-nine fewer than the Conservatives. Something had gone terribly wrong. Suddenly, the future of Labour, which only hours before the election had thought a return to power likely, looked incredibly grim.

In the weeks that followed, Labour's problems would be coldly dissected. A leaked memo from 2010 revealed how its own analysts had urged Miliband to adopt a new approach on 'very clear threshold issues'—immigration, benefits, and the deficit. Labour, they had argued, needed to think far more seriously about how to win back its lost working-class voters, who had voiced not only anxiety over competition from EU migrants for work, but cultural insecurity as well: 'This was partly about people adopting British culture when they come here and partly about standing up for British and in particular English traditions and English people.'[7] Miliband had tried to modify his party's approach on some of these issues, but it was now abundantly clear to all that he had failed to cut through—a point to which we shall return.

The groups that Labour had connected with were clearly identifiable. Whereas the Conservatives had successfully mobilized people who said that they had felt Britain's economic recovery, Labour had not made similar gains among the economically disaffected and left behind—people who were not feeling, and did not expect to feel, the financial turnaround. And while it had made some advances among young people, who were also less likely to turn out, Labour had suffered significant losses among older voters and pensioners, who had clearly not warmed to Miliband's proposed remedy for fixing the British economy. More generally it was clear that Labour had misread the national mood, failing to understand that most voters, including a large portion of its own supporters, had prioritized cutting the deficit over reducing the cost of living.[8] One person who accepted the reality was Miliband himself, who resigned. 'I'm so sorry to all those colleagues who lost their seats.'

A bad night for Labour was a catastrophic night for the Liberal Democrats. Nick Clegg and his party had watched in horror as a generation of hard work unravelled before their eyes. Neither veterans nor front-line politicians were saved: Charles Kennedy, Simon Hughes, Danny Alexander, Vince Cable, and Lynne Featherstone, among others, all lost their seats. With less than 8 per cent of the national vote, the liberals were left with their worst performance since 1970. The scale of their losses was reflected in their number of lost deposits. In 2010, the party had not lost a single deposit. But now it was humiliated, failing to reach 5 per cent in 341 seats—more than half the number that had been fought. More telling was that many Liberal Democrats had not even managed to finish in the top three. In 2010 they had done so in 602 seats. But that number had now plummeted to just 107. Parties that the Liberal Democrats had routinely beaten in the past were leaving them in the dust—they were now behind Ukip in 490 seats and behind the Greens in 140. More than forty years of hard work had seem-ingly vanished, in one night. Clegg followed Miliband, accepting his fate and resigning. The results, he said, had been 'immeasurably more crushing' than had been feared.

While it was a little better for the Greens, who did not have a long history of fighting elections, there was, in the end, little evidence of a surge. Their vote had increased by two points to almost 4 per cent, but almost four-fifths of their candidates failed to meet the 5 per cent threshold and so lost their deposits. They were successful only in their existing seat of Brighton Pavilion. Only four Greens finished in the top two—and even they were on average more than forty points behind the winners.[9]

Given these results, and the return of a single-party majority government, it might have been tempting to conclude that the fragmentation of British politics had come to an end. 'So much for the Great Fragmentation,' observed journalist John Rentoul. 'Two-party politics has turned to be more durable than fashionable opinion ever thought.'[10] In some respects this was true. Challengers such as the SNP and the Greens had attracted more votes, but the number of parties that had won votes at the national and constituency level was unchanged since 2010.[11] Meanwhile, the number of candidates who had won their seats with a majority of votes had actually increased, rising from around one in three in 2010 to one in two. But, below the surface, many of the problems that had come to be associated with first-past-the-post remained clearly visible. Almost fifteen million votes had been cast for can-didates who did not win. Half of those who had voted in the election saw a candidate whom they had not voted for win. Cameron's majority, mean-while, was less impressive than some would claim. Almost two out of every three voters had not cast their ballot for the Conservatives, and, given that the turnout was 66 per cent, Cameron's majority was based on support from just 25 per cent of the population. It was hardly a compelling mandate.

After numerous delays and some scattered sleep, Nigel Farage was finally on a stage in South Thanet—waiting to hear the people's judgement on his own campaign. He was flanked by the Labour candidate Will Scobie and the grinning comedian Al Murray. Farage had a fixed smile and a blank stare. He knew what was coming. It was the last place in the world that he wanted to be. In the end, it was announced that he had won more than 16,000 votes, or 32 per cent of the vote—exactly what Bruni-Lowe's data had suggested. It was not enough. He was in second place, behind the

Table 12.1. UK general election results, 2015

| Party | Votes | | | Seats | | |
|---|---|---|---|---|---|---|
| | No. | Share (%) | Change 2010–15 | No. | Change 2010–15 | Votes per seat |
| Conservative | 11,299,600 | 36.8 | +0.8 | 330 | +24 | 34,241 |
| Labour | 9,347,300 | 30.4 | +1.5 | 232 | −26 | 40,290 |
| Ukip | 3,881,100 | 12.6 | +9.5 | 1 | +1 | 3,881,100 |
| Liberal Democrat | 2,415,900 | 7.9 | −15.2 | 8 | −49 | 301,988 |
| SNP | 1,454,400 | 4.7 | +3.1 | 56 | +50 | 25,971 |
| Green | 1,157,600 | 3.8 | +2.8 | 1 | +0 | 1,157,600 |
| PC | 181,700 | 0.6 | +0.0 | 3 | +0 | 60,567 |
| Others | 959,900 | 3.1 | −2.5 | 19 | +0 | — |
| Turnout | | 66.2 | +1.1 | 650 | | |

*Note*: Figure for the Conservative Party number of seats does not include the Speaker.
*Source*: General Election 2015, House of Commons Library Briefing Paper, No. CBP7186.

Conservative Party candidate Craig MacKinlay, who had won almost 3,000 more votes, or 38 per cent of the vote. 'On a professional level,' said Farage, 'I express today a degree of disappointment. But on a personal level I feel an enormous weight has been lifted from my shoulders and I have never felt happier. Thank you.' Without waiting to listen to speeches by the other candidates, he left. For the seventh time in his career, he had failed to win election to the House of Commons.[12]

When the dust had settled, and the view became clear, Farage and his team surveyed the landscape. At first glance, what lay before them looked as depressing as the picture in South Thanet. Despite all the work—all the events, interviews, door-knocking, debates, arguments, and fund-raising—Ukip had won only one seat. And that seat was Clacton. Its only MP was the man whom many insiders had spent much of the campaign criticizing. As Farage's advisers watched the results roll in, Raheem Kassam had turned to Bruni-Lowe. 'It's only going to be Carswell, isn't it?' The two exhausted foot soldiers laughed, putting their heads in their hands. 'It was the worst-case scenario,' said Kassam. The result in Clacton had also contained a warning about what was to follow. Carswell had won, but his majority had been slashed by almost 9,000 votes. The commanding lead that had been established only a few months earlier had been whittled down to something that looked much less secure.[13] 'We were shocked by how close Clacton was,' reflected Bruni-Lowe. 'Once we saw that, we knew we were probably not going to win seats. The Tories did not target Clacton at all. They barely handed out a leaflet. When we saw that, we just knew. We were fucked.'

And so a night of disappointment ensued. From one seat to the next, a stream of bad news arrived. All but one of Ukip's candidates, many of whom had assumed that they were about to start new lives in Westminster, had failed to break through. And this was also true in the target seats—where the party had worked hardest. In Rochester and Strood, Ukip had lost its only other MP. The writing had been on the wall. Mark Reckless had won his by-election with a smaller majority than Carswell, which left him vulnerable to any swing back to the Conservatives. The changing tide had been noticed in a poll by Lord Ashcroft, which suggested that Reckless would probably lose by around seven points. Ukip had also polled the seat in the final week, but had not released the result. It too suggested a loss of seven points, Reckless had refused to believe the numbers. But, in the end, the outcome for the Conservative defector was even worse—he finished fourteen points behind.[14]

There was more bad news in Boston and Skegness—the Lincolnshire seat that had given Ukip its highest vote in the European elections. That victory was escaping the party had become clear during the final days. An internal poll, again not made public, had suggested that the Conservatives were ahead by seven points but once again the result was even worse.[15] Ukip was handed 34 per cent of the vote, an increase of twenty-four points on 2010 but ten points less than the Conservatives.

Then came Thurrock, where Ukip's candidate Tim Aker had enjoyed continued and strong support from the central party. Just three weeks before the election one poll had given Ukip a four-point lead. But only a few days before polling day an internal poll had put Aker third, trailing the Conservatives by five points and Labour by four.[16] It turned out to be accurate. While Aker was the closest of all Ukip candidates to winning his seat, he still finished in third place with 32 per cent, two points behind the Conservative incumbent, and less than one point behind Labour. In the closest three-way race in the election, fewer than 1,000 votes had separated the three candidates. It was a bitter blow for Bruni-Lowe, who had assumed for much of the campaign that the south Essex seat was guaranteed to go purple.

A few miles to the east, in working-class Castle Point, it was the same story. Initially, Jamie Huntman, who some had seen as a possible future leader, generated considerable excitement. Ukip had even chosen his seat for the launch of its entire campaign—around the time that one poll had suggested that only one point separated Ukip and the Conservatives. But as each month followed the last it had become clear that the seat could not be won. 'Huntman would never have won given the national trends,' explained Bruni-Lowe. 'But he also did not help himself. The branch did not go for the Labour vote in the seat and had not built up a database of pledges. We sent them boxes of pledge letters but they never delivered them. They just didn't have the resource'. An internal poll that had put Huntman second, and a striking eighteen points behind the Conservatives, also turned out to be accurate. Ukip was handed 31 per cent of the vote and finished second, twenty points behind the Conservatives.[17]

News was also arriving from Labour's northern heartlands, where Farage had hoped to entrench his party as the second force. In Heywood and Middleton, which had hosted the shock by-election result in the autumn of 2014, Ukip had entrenched its position but once again failed to beat Labour. John Bickley, who had urged a more assertive response to Labour, added

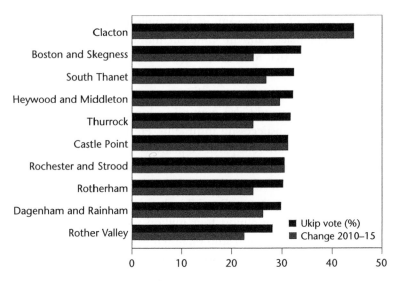

**Figure 12.1.** Ukip's top ten results, 2015

more than 4,000 votes to his by-election result. But amid higher turnout and increased support for the main parties he trailed by eleven points, rather than the two points that had given Labour a fright in the autumn. Ukip was second, but Labour's majority had increased eightfold.

The party had also failed to cross the line in the Labour and south Yorkshire seat of Rotherham. Few in the party had ever seriously thought that the seat could be won in 2015, but they had hoped that the race would be close. Since a by-election in 2012, the party had increased its share of the vote by eight points to reach 30 per cent. But Labour, which had held the seat since 1933, won more than 52 per cent and its largest number of votes since 1997. In the aftermath, some Ukip officials blamed the tone of their local campaign. 'The branch did not run a positive campaign. It was all about child exploitation and it was negative,' said one. But it was the same story from Great Grimsby to Great Yarmouth. Ukip's excitable talk about winning a handful of seats and redrawing the map had been replaced by something altogether different: almost no seats and almost no power (see Figure 12.1).

For Ukip, there was no doubt that the results were a bitter disappointment. For the first time in its history the party had attempted to play by the rules of first-past-the-post, running a targeted campaign and trying to use its limited firepower wisely. But, while the party had won over an impressive number of voters—almost four million—it had failed to win them in the right places and in sufficient number, as first-past-the-post requires. In the hours that followed, Farage would claim that his party had suffered from public fears over a Labour–SNP coalition, which had pushed voters into Cameron's arms. By pointing to the disproportionate nature of first-past-the-post, he would also continue a long tradition that has been upheld by numerous unsuccessful insurgents. He had a point. The system had not rewarded the different parties equally. The SNP had been the biggest winners, picking up one seat for every 26,000 votes that it had won. The Conservatives had won a seat for every 34,000 votes, while for Labour it was more than 40,000 votes. But Ukip had been the biggest loser—it had won only one seat for almost four million votes. As Sir David Butler, one of the founders of election studies, noted in the aftermath, it was 'the harshest treatment that our capricious electoral system has ever inflicted on a nationwide party'.[18]

But in the shadow of the election it was also true that Ukip could not be ignored. While it might have won only one seat, few commentators could dismiss the party—and for three main reasons, each of which shed light on the way that its revolt had impacted on the election and on British politics more widely.

The first reason was Ukip's wider performance. Some insiders had spent much of the night of the election holed up in the headquarters on Brooks Mews, watching the results roll in. Like others in the party, Gawain Towler, the long-serving press officer, had been particularly impressed with the results outside South Thanet.

It was a phenomenally good result but also incredibly disappointing. The numbers were superb. There were good numbers coming in from all over the place, but they were not enough. It was bittersweet. Then there was the realization that the Tories' strategy had delivered a major impact. The Labour–Ukip switchers had stayed with us but the Tories had not. That's what it felt like.

This was not entirely true, however. Based on data from the British Election Study, Ukip *had* lost a larger numbers of its Tory-switchers. But Towler was wrong to assume that former Labour voters were markedly more loyal. In reality, if there was any noticeable difference, then it was the Labour defectors to Ukip who were slightly more likely to have abandoned the party at the election. Ukip had lost 50 per cent of its Tory-switchers compared to 53 per cent of its Labour-switchers. So, former

Tories were not more inclined to defect—the party just had more of these switchers to lose.[19]

But in a way that was a side-point from the wider performance that Towler was pointing to. It was certainly impressive, even if it had failed to translate into seats. What was perhaps most remarkable was just how many votes Ukip had mobilized *despite* all the organizational constraints that we have encountered in this book—the party's lack of firepower, the infighting, the inexperience, the overly ambitious strategy, and the threadbare central office. Despite all of this, Ukip had still recruited more than 3.8 million voters, or almost one in eight of those who had turned out. It had won 2.7 million more votes than the Greens, 2.4 million more than the SNP, and 1.4 million more than Clegg and the Liberal Democrats. Ukip had emerged from the battle with only one seat, but at the same time it had delivered the most successful general election performance by an independent new party in English politics since the rise of Labour. To put the achievement in historical perspective, it had won almost one million more votes than the Liberals during their surge in 1964, twenty times as many as the far right National Front in the 1970s, and almost five times as many as the Referendum Party in 1997. According to its share of the national vote, Farage's party had also displaced the Liberal Democrats as the third most popular party. Its revolt had, ultimately, been stalled by first-past-the-post, but it had simultaneously displayed real electoral strength.

While the question of whether or not Ukip could survive remained, in electoral terms there was no question that it had put down stronger foundations. Up and down the country its candidates were more firmly entrenched. In 2010, more than four-fifths had failed to save their deposits, but now only around one in ten had failed to do so. In England and Wales, there was also no difference in Ukip's results in seats that it was fighting for the first time, compared to seats that it had fought before in 2010. It had averaged 14 per cent in both of these contexts, revealing how it had attracted a broader upsurge of support.[20] Interestingly, the party had even received respectable results in seats where its candidates had received almost no help. In places such as Rother Valley, West Bromwich West, and Mansfield, Ukip had won more than 25 per cent of the vote, despite making almost no investment in its campaigns. Similarly, in a large number of seats such as Doncaster Central, Don Valley, and Barnsley East, candidates who had been starved of support and forced to rely only on their regional organizer had won between 20 and 25 per cent of the vote.[21]

Table 12.2. Candidates and deposits lost in 2010 and 2015

| Party | 2015 | | | 2010 | | |
|---|---|---|---|---|---|---|
| | Candidates | Deposits lost | Deposits lost (%) | Candidates | Deposits lost | Deposits lost (%) |
| Conservative | 631 | 3 | 0.5 | 631 | 2 | 0.3 |
| Labour | 631 | 3 | 0.5 | 631 | 5 | 0.8 |
| Ukip | 614 | 73 | 11.9 | 558 | 459 | 82.3 |
| Liberal Democrat | 631 | 341 | 54.0 | 631 | 0 | 0.0 |
| SNP | 59 | 0 | 0.0 | 59 | 0 | 0.0 |
| Green | 568 | 439 | 77.3 | 335 | 328 | 97.9 |
| PC | 40 | 8 | 20.0 | 40 | 0 | 0.0 |

*Source:* General Election 2015, House of Commons Library Briefing Paper, No. CBP7186.

That the party had laid a stronger foundation was reflected in other statistics. In 2010, Ukip had breached the 10 per cent mark in only one seat, when Farage had stood against the Speaker of the House, John Bercow. But now the party had won at least 10 per cent of the vote in 450 seats, between 20 and 29 per cent in sixty-one of them, between 30 and 39 per cent in seven, and over 40 per cent in one (Clacton) (see Figure 12.2). Its target-seat strategy, which had spread Ukip thin and wide and fallen on the shoulders of just one activist, had failed to deliver seats. But it had helped to drive the party's vote. In three target seats Ukip's share of the vote had increased by more than thirty points, while in a further sixteen it had surged by more than twenty. Across the target seats as a whole, the party had averaged 24 per cent of the vote, ten points higher than its average across seats in England and Wales that had not been targeted. These differences were even more dramatic

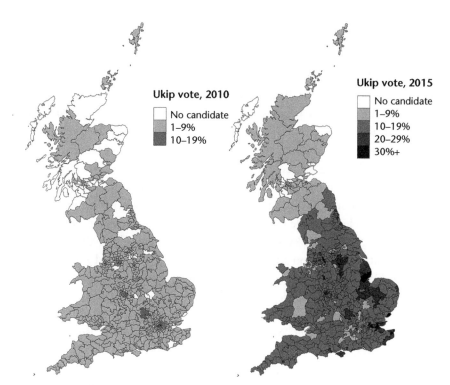

**Figure 12.2.** Ukip vote share by constituency in the 2010 and 2015 general elections

in its top targets, which had received more support. Here, Ukip had averaged 30 per cent compared to 21 per cent in seats that had been only targeted early on.

That Ukip's campaign had, despite all the problems, generated an impact was also reflected in other evidence from our analysis. Even after taking account of Ukip's past results and the demography of the seat, we find that seats that had made it onto the target list could be expected to give the party an extra eight points. This effect was smaller in seats that had not made it onto the final list, where only three points had been added. While the work had ultimately failed to win seats, it had left Ukip and its candidates in a stronger position. As Liberal Democrats will testify, it is easier for a party to appear as a credible alternative when it has a track record of winning serious support. If it was to take a page from the Liberal Democrats' playbook in 2020, Ukip would now be able to claim that it was in the 'two-horse race'.

This brings us to a second observation about Ukip's performance. Writing in the 1950s, Sir David Butler once remarked on how election campaigns can have less of an impact on the current contest than on the shape of the ones that follow.[22] Butler was referring to elections overall, but, as we have seen, the idea of planting seeds for future elections had been circulating within Ukip for months. Farage had long been talking publicly about using the general election as a springboard into future campaigns—as part of the so-called '2020 Strategy'. The party, he declared, would be 'the challenger in virtually every parliamentary seat from Birmingham up to Hadrian's Wall'.[23] Others in Ukip had shared the idea, discussing plans for how they could emerge as the main opposition in the north. The idea also attracted journalists, one of whom had cornered Bruni-Lowe as he watched the results roll in. After the release of the exit poll had temporarily stunned commentators and viewers, the first result of the night had arrived from the north-east Labour seat of Houghton and Sunderland South. Labour had easily won the seat, but Ukip was second, with more than 21 per cent of the vote. All those who had laughed at the idea that Farage's party could mobilize support in Labour areas went quiet. The journalist leant in. 'You are probably not going to win any seats,' he said. 'You've been fucked by the SNP. But your 2020 Strategy is on.'

While questions over Ukip's future remained, there was still clear evidence of its ability to emerge as a main opposition party. Back in 2010, it had finished second in one seat. Now, it was second in 120. If one goal of the

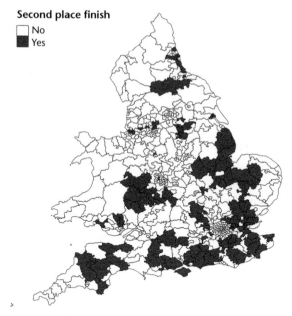

**Second place finish**
- ☐ No
- ■ Yes

**Figure 12.3.** Ukip's second place finishes, 2015

campaign had been to implant Ukip as a contender across a serious number of seats, then it had been accomplished.

The seats where Ukip was now second were an interesting mix. As shown in Figure 12.3, while six were in Wales, the vast majority were in England.[24] Seventy-six had been won by the Conservatives and forty-four had been won by Labour. Yet in terms of the voters in these seats, it was the Labour ones who tended to be more receptive to Ukip, being filled with 'left-behind' voters. Four-fifths of the Labour seats where Ukip was now second were among the most Ukip-friendly seats in the country in terms of voter profile, but only one-fifth of the Conservative seats where Ukip came second were as Ukip-friendly in terms of voter profile. While all the seats in the south where Ukip was now the runner-up were held by the Conservatives, in the north it was different. In the thirty-five northern seats where Ukip was second, all but one were held by Labour.[25] Farage's claim that his party could emerge as an opposition to Labour in its heartlands had been validated.

Ukip had often finished second where the former opposition party had slumped. Voters were more willing to desert to Ukip if the party that they had previously favoured was not in control of the seat. In most cases, Ukip filled a vacuum that had been left by the Liberal Democrats. In eighty-six of the seats where it had finished second, most of which were in the south, Ukip had replaced the traditional third party as the primary challenger. Where the party had displaced the Liberal Democrats, it averaged 17 per cent, increasing its support in 2010 by thirteen points—this was three points higher than its average support and growth across all seats.[26] That Ukip had made significant gains in tandem with the Liberal Democrats' collapse suggests that at least some of Clegg's voters now saw Farage's party as a viable alternative.

The British Election Study supports this picture. A little less than 10 per cent of those who said that they had voted for Clegg in 2010 defected to Ukip in 2015. This means that, when all was said and done, one-fifth of Ukip's support came from former Liberal Democrats. Meanwhile, in the twelve seats where Ukip had replaced Labour as the main opposition, the Liberal Democrats had continued to experience significant losses, but so too had Labour. Miliband's party had tended to make modest gains overall, but had lost an average of 3 per cent of the vote in seats where Ukip had replaced them as the opposition. Farage and his party had also supplanted the Tories as the second party in twenty-one seats, where the national victors lost, on average, 4 per cent of the vote. Defections from the Tories and Labour to Ukip were more likely in seats where these parties were not in control. Again, the defections that we see in the British Election Study support this story. Across all seats, 12 per cent of those who said that they had voted for the Tories in 2010 defected to Ukip in 2015. Labour and the Liberal Democrats had suffered fewer defections—just 5 per cent of those who had voted for Gordon Brown in 2010 defected to Ukip and 9 per cent of those who had supported Clegg in 2010 left the Liberal Democrats for Ukip. But all three parties had lost far more of their former supporters in seats where Ukip had replaced them as the main opposition. Cameron had lost 22 per cent of his former supporters to Ukip in seats where Ukip had replaced the Conservatives. And Labour had lost almost three times as many supporters to Ukip, 14 per cent, where Farage's party had bumped Labour from second place (see Table 12.3).

Even in seats where Ukip did not take second place, the party was making gains at the expense of the opposition. And further analysis suggests that these patterns played out in different ways in different parts of the country. Let us look at how Ukip performed in seats where the top two parties were Labour and the Conservatives, and then compare these seats in the north

Table 12.3. Party vote share change in seats where Ukip replaced the opposition, 2015

| Party | All seats | Ukip replaces Conservative | Ukip replaces Labour | Ukip replaces Liberal Democrat |
|---|---|---|---|---|
| Ukip | +10.0 | +20.2 | +21.4 | +17.3 |
| Conservative | +1.1 | −3.9 | −2.0 | +1.2 |
| Labour | +1.3 | +3.5 | −3.4 | +2.8 |
| Liberal Democrat | −15.3 | −12.8 | −12.0 | −17.7 |

Table 12.4. Ukip performance in Labour–Conservative battlegrounds

| Type of constituency | Ukip vote, 2015 (%) | Ukip change 2010–15 | Conservative change 2010–15 | Labour change 2010–15 |
|---|---|---|---|---|
| *North, Labour hold* | | | | |
| All | 17.8 | +14.8 | −2.0 | +3.5 |
| Marginal | 16.0 | +12.7 | −1.1 | +3.2 |
| Safe | 18.7 | +15.8 | −2.5 | +3.8 |
| *South, Conservative hold* | | | | |
| All | 17.9 | +14.0 | +1.4 | −1.0 |
| Marginal | 13.9 | +10.0 | +3.7 | +0.0 |
| Safe | 20.3 | +16.5 | +0.0 | −1.6 |

and the south (see Table 12.4). In the north, three in four of these seats were held by Labour. Across these northern Labour seats, Ukip averaged 18 per cent, increasing its vote by fifteen points. The Conservatives, meanwhile, saw their vote decline by 2 per cent, while Labour improved its position. This suggests that Ukip was reshuffling the opposition in the north, drawing support from voters who in the past may have supported another opposition party to Labour.

Ukip also tended to make stronger gains where Labour had a larger majority, averaging 19 per cent in these safe Labour seats compared to 16 per cent in more competitive or marginal seats.[27] But in more marginal seats Conservative losses were more modest, revealing how voters were less willing to defect to Ukip in seats where the race was close—and where Conservatives had a shot of capturing the seat from Labour. In contrast, voters appear to have been more willing to switch to Ukip in less competitive seats, meaning that the insurgent party was emerging as a more visible force in seats that were firmly in the hands of Labour.

The same pattern but in reverse can be seen in Labour–Conservative battlegrounds in southern England, in seats where the Conservatives are first and Labour is second. Across these seats Ukip averaged 18 per cent, fourteen points higher than in 2010. But, in these southern battlegrounds it is Labour that experienced losses, while the Conservatives tended to improve. Once again, Ukip performed better in safer seats. In more competitive or marginal seats, some of which Labour were trying to win, support for the Conservatives increased by almost four points, far higher than their average gains and one of the largest increases that we see across these battlegrounds. Ukip, meanwhile, averaged 14 per cent, lower than their average in England and Wales. But support for Labour had remained unchanged since 2010, emphasizing how the party had failed to advance in the critical marginal seats in southern England. Labour had made some of its biggest gains in northern seats that they already held while their support remained fairly static in more southern and more competitive seats. But in safer southern Conservative seats Labour had suffered significant losses—its support had dwindled by an average of two points, while Ukip had enjoyed more significant returns, with an average vote of more than 20 per cent.

This suggests that, as in the north, voters were far more willing to defect to Ukip in seats that were less competitive and where Conservatives were unlikely to be dislodged. That Ukip often prospered in less competitive environments was also observed by its campaigners, who often traced this to public anxiety over the Scottish nationalists. 'It is always tempting to say that something got in the way of our brilliant campaign but it did. The SNP.' Another organizer similarly noted:

In Tory-held marginal southern seats the SNP stuff really screwed us. But in the Labour-held seats, where we were not in contention and Tories did not operate the heavy targeting and squeezing strategy about the SNP–Labour threat, we did much better. We could push ourselves into second place. But in southern Conservative-held marginals the SNP narrative killed us. The direct mail shots were one thing. But the Conservatives were also using Scottish people to telephone swing voters. It was Braveheart shit and it fucked us.

So, even though Ukip was reshuffling the opposition, the second place finishes were not all good news for Ukip. In almost all these seats the party still had a mountain to climb. It had made its strongest gains in seats where it had had no chance of displacing the incumbent. And where Ukip came second it was on average more than thirty points behind the winner. On average, even in its top targets, the party had trailed the winning party by more than twelve points while in its next tier of targets it was behind by twenty-five. This was often true in Labour heartlands.

Consider Ed Miliband's seat of Doncaster North, where Ukip came second and saw its support surge to almost 23 per cent. Even then, the party was still almost 12,000 votes, or thirty points, behind Miliband. Another was Liverpool Walton, where Ukip was second but nearly 28,000 votes behind Labour. The same was true in southern seats such as Castle Point, where Ukip lagged twenty points behind the winner, or South West Norfolk, where it was 28 points behind. That the party was struggling to keep pace was reflected in the fact that there were only four seats where it finished within ten points of the winners—South Thanet, Hartlepool, and Boston and Skegness, where it was second, and Thurrock, where it was third.

Ukip's problem was compounded by the fact that it was more likely to suffer defections in marginal seats. Further analysis of the British Election Study indicates that, in marginal seats, Ukip lost 53 per cent of those voters who were planning to support the party in the spring of 2014. This was more than ten points higher than the rate of defections that Ukip suffered across safe seats—where the party lost just 42 per cent of those who were planning to support the party the year before. That being said, even though Ukip was often a long way behind, there was now some truth to its claim that it was the second force in a wide array of seats, even if obstacles lay ahead.

The third reason why the result was significant was because of the types of areas and voters that had given the party its strongest returns. Regionally, Ukip had polled best along the east coast, in Kent and Essex, further up the coast into Norfolk, Lincolnshire, and Yorkshire, and in the north-east, where it enjoyed its highest average support (of 17 per cent). In the latter region it had been in seats like Gateshead, which Farage had chosen as a symbol of his determination to target Labour, where people had turned to Ukip in significant numbers.[28] Overall, the party had won more than 20 per cent of the vote in more seats in the north than in seats in the south (see Figure 12.4). And these also tended to have particular types of voters.

Ukip had cemented its relationship with Britain's left-behind voters. Based on data in the British Election Study, we can see that, as had been the

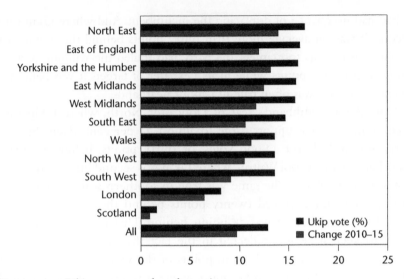

**Figure 12.4.** Ukip 2015 vote share by region
*Source*: General Election 2015. House of Commons Library Briefing Paper, No. CBP7186.

case during the European elections, the party continued to have a higher share of supporters than every other party who worked in more vulnerable routine and manual occupations. Only the SNP recruited more of its supporters from this group. Farage continued to have far more supporters who were older, white, and had few qualifications—as we would expect.[29] Our more complex analysis of Ukip's support in 2015 reveals that the demographic favourability of a seat was the most important predictor of how the party performed. Focusing purely on the demographic profile of a seat, our model tells us that Ukip's share of the vote in a highly favourable seat like Clacton is expected to be on average six points higher than its share in a highly unfavourable seat like Battersea, in London.[30] This matters, because it tells us that Ukip was putting down deeper roots in left-behind communities—where there are older, comparatively unskilled, and heavily white populations, which often grapple with entrenched deprivation, and where people are more likely to feel threatened by the dramatic cultural changes that are sweeping across Britain. While the party was not winning seats, it was increasingly positioning itself as a credible alternative for economically disaffected people who had few good reasons to feel optimistic about the future.

Another survey that was commissioned by Lord Ashcroft paints a similar picture, and throws light on the motives among those who voted for Ukip.[31]

It found that Ukip's supporters tended to be financially vulnerable and economically disaffected. While Labour had pitched itself as the main home for these voters, Ukip had clearly made inroads into voters who might otherwise have been open to the left. One in two of Ukip's voters said that he or she was not feeling the recovery.

That these supporters were not being driven simply by protest was reflected in the fact that they were likely to say that their vote had been motivated by policy. Four in five said that they had voted for Ukip because they trusted its motives and preferred its promises over those made by the other parties. And these policy concerns were overwhelmingly focused on immigration—by far their greatest concern. Almost nine in ten Ukip voters felt that controlling immigration was one of the three most important issues for Britain, more than twice the proportion among the full sample, while these voters were also more than twice as likely as any others to identify immigration as the top issue facing themselves and their family.

The overwhelming focus on immigration as a driver reinforces the idea that Ukip's continued success rests on the salience of this issue. It also suggests that, if the aim of the core-vote strategy was to mobilize Britons who felt chiefly anxious about immigration, then it was a success. Ukip might not have won seats, but it had cemented its bond with such voters.

In this respect, it is also interesting to note that the party had also clearly benefited from the collapse of the far right British National Party, which in earlier years had also sought to attract votes from these same social groups—but while offering a different message, and coming from a different ideological tradition. In 2015, Ukip performed much more strongly and made significant gains in areas where the BNP had previously been strong. Ukip averaged 19 per cent in seats where the far right had performed above average in 2010, an increase of sixteen points, but averaged only 13 per cent in seats where the far right had been weaker in 2010, growing by less than ten points. That Ukip made strong gains in areas where the BNP's decline had been more pronounced suggests that it benefited directly from the collapse of the old far right (see Figure 12.5).[32]

Given all this, what does the party's rise mean for the future? Because Ukip walked away with almost four million votes in an election where all the polls put the outcome on a knife's edge, it is difficult to imagine that the party's rise did not alter the fortunes of the two main parties, a pattern that could continue in 2020. But when we look at how Ukip's returns compared to the fortunes of the two main parties, we see that it was Labour's advance

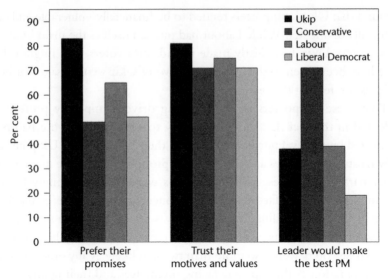

**Figure 12.5.** Motives for party support
*Source*: Lord Ashcroft, 'Post-Vote Day Poll, 7 May 2015'.

in England and Wales that was hindered in places where Ukip polled strongly. In seats where Ukip performed better, recruiting a higher than average level of support, Labour's share of the vote grew by only two points. However, in seats where Ukip was weaker, recruiting less than its average, Labour made far more significant gains, on average improving its share of the vote by five points.[33] Put differently, this means that Labour grew by an extra three points in seats where Ukip delivered a weak performance, a significant finding for a party that was trying to stage a comeback—and in which some still argued that the rise of Ukip had no real implication for the centre-left.

For the Conservatives, the difference in their gains in areas where Ukip was strong or weak was far more modest. Cameron's party grew by around two points in seats where Ukip were weak, and by one point where Ukip was stronger, leaving a one-point difference compared to Labour's three. Only in the north was the Conservative advance stalled more than Labour's by a stronger Ukip showing. In every other region it is the Labour advance that was stalled in seats where Ukip enjoyed stronger returns. For Ed Miliband and his party, who were trying to reverse their fortunes and return to power, their recovery was undermined by stagnant support in areas where Ukip was strong. Now, imagine that this pattern continues in 2020. We have

Table 12.5. Change in support for Labour and the Conservatives, 2010–2015

| Region | Highest Ukip | Lowest Ukip | Difference |
|---|---|---|---|
| *All (England/Wales)* | | | |
| Conservative | +0.8 | +1.9 | +1.1 |
| Labour | +1.9 | +5.0 | +3.1 |
| *South* | | | |
| Conservative | +1.7 | +3.0 | +1.3 |
| Labour | +0.8 | +3.6 | +2.8 |
| *North* | | | |
| Conservative | −0.6 | +1.3 | +1.9 |
| Labour | +4.0 | +5.6 | +1.6 |
| *Midlands* | | | |
| Conservative | +1.7 | +2.4 | +0.7 |
| Labour | +1.3 | +5.1 | +3.8 |
| *London* | | | |
| Conservative | −2.9 | +1.1 | +4.0 |
| Labour | +2.7 | +7.6 | +4.9 |
| *Wales* | | | |
| Conservative | +1.2 | +1.0 | +0.2 |
| Labour | +0.3 | +0.8 | +0.5 |

already heard academics argue that Labour will have a mountain to climb if the SNP retains its hold over Scotland. If Labour continues to face a war on two fronts—a battle from Scotland in the north and a challenge from Ukip in England and Wales—then this will make the mountain Labour has to climb to make its comeback that much higher (see Table 12.5).

In conclusion, Ukip might not have fulfilled its hopes of winning a handful of seats in 2015, but the party had nevertheless emerged as a more credible alternative to a large number of voters, who in some areas had propelled it to become the chief opposition. This was especially true among the economically disaffected left-behind voters who care far more intensely about immigration and cultural change. By cementing its relationship with these voters, and increasingly bearing down on the main parties, Ukip had entrenched itself as a serious force, at least in 2015. In the aftermath of one of the most unpredictable and exciting elections in British history, the party was now positioned as one that could look to the future with confidence, or so it seemed. But these advances were not immediately obvious to those who had given their all to trying to implant Ukip in the House of Commons.

Table 12.6. Ukip performance in target seats, 2015

| Target seats | Ukip vote (%) | Change 2010–15 (%) | Ukip rank | Difference Ukip vs winner |
|---|---|---|---|---|
| *Top target* | | | | |
| Boston and Skegness | 33.8 | +24.3 | 2 | −10.0 |
| South Thanet | 32.4 | +26.9 | 2 | −5.7 |
| Heywood and Middleton | 32.2 | +29.6 | 2 | −10.9 |
| Thurrock | 31.7 | +24.3 | 3 | −2.0 |
| Castle Point | 31.2 | +31.2 | 2 | −19.7 |
| Rochester and Strood | 30.5 | +30.5 | 2 | −13.6 |
| Rotherham | 30.2 | +24.3 | 2 | −22.3 |
| Hartlepool | 28.0 | +21.0 | 2 | −7.6 |
| Great Grimsby | 25.0 | +18.8 | 3 | −14.8 |
| Dudley North | 24.0 | +15.5 | 3 | −17.8 |
| **Average** | **29.9** | **+24.6** | | **−12.4** |
| *Other targets* | | | | |
| Clacton | 44.4 | +44.4 | 1 | — |
| South Basildon and East Thurrock | 26.5 | +20.6 | 2 | −16.9 |
| North Thanet | 25.7 | +19.2 | 2 | −23.3 |
| Wentworth and Dearne | 24.9 | +16.8 | 2 | −32.0 |
| Sittingbourne and Sheppey | 24.8 | +19.4 | 2 | −24.7 |
| Great Yarmouth | 23.1 | +18.3 | 3 | −19.8 |
| Folkestone and Hythe | 22.8 | +18.2 | 2 | −25.1 |
| Bognor Regis and Littlehampton | 21.7 | +15.2 | 2 | −29.6 |

| | | | | |
|---|---|---|---|---|
| Plymouth, Moor View | 21.5 | 3 | +13.8 | −16.1 |
| Dover | 20.3 | 3 | +16.8 | −23.0 |
| North West Cambridgeshire | 20.1 | 2 | +11.8 | −32.4 |
| Basildon and Billericay | 19.8 | 3 | +16.0 | −32.9 |
| Forest of Dean | 17.8 | 3 | +12.6 | −29.0 |
| North West Norfolk | 17.8 | 3 | +14.0 | −34.4 |
| Cannock Chase | 17.5 | 3 | +14.0 | −26.7 |
| St Austell and Newquay | 16.9 | 3 | +13.2 | −23.3 |
| Delyn | 16.4 | 3 | +14.6 | −24.1 |
| Wyre Forest | 16.1 | 3 | +13.2 | −29.2 |
| Eastleigh | 15.8 | 3 | +12.2 | −26.5 |
| Camborne and Redruth | 14.8 | 3 | +9.7 | −27.9 |
| North Devon | 14.8 | 3 | +7.6 | −25.4 |
| Torbay | 13.6 | 3 | +8.3 | −27.1 |
| Average | +20.8 | | +15.9 | −25.0 |

A few hours after the results had been declared, Chris Bruni-Lowe was sitting in Ukip's office in South Thanet. Around him were boxes of leaflets, telephone headsets, and posters that urged people to vote for Farage. Now, alone, his mind began to wander. He remembered walking around the House of Commons six months earlier and calling Farage. Standing in the Central Lobby, he had told his leader how much he wanted to get him into parliament and how awful it would be if they failed. 'I know,' Farage had replied. 'I know.' In the months that followed the campaigner had given everything that he had to the task—marshalling all that he knew about campaigns, and squeezing everything that he could out of his thinly resourced and chaotic party. Along the way, as the race had tightened, he had reoriented his entire campaign around South Thanet. But it had just not been enough. And he was now physically and emotionally drained. Sitting amid defeat, it seemed as though it had come to nothing. 'It felt like the end of a holiday romance. Everything that we had done was built around Nigel winning. Then you think, that's it.' The campaign had come to its end.

# 13

# Civil War

Shortly after the result in South Thanet had been declared, and in the pale light of morning, Chris Bruni-Lowe left the count to make a call. 'It's all over,' he said to one of his fellow activists. 'Nigel is about to resign.' He put down the phone. After another sleepless night and months of having given everything that he had, the campaigner was now staring defeat in the face. His dream of winning a handful of seats in Westminster, including one for Farage, and possibly even helping the party to hold the balance of power in a hung parliament, was over. Some had always argued that such a breakthrough would be extremely difficult—that the party was unlikely to establish itself as a permanent feature in the House of Commons, never mind redraw the map. Given Ukip's lack of firepower, experience, and unity, and Britain's formidable electoral system, the odds had always been stacked against it.

But on some nights, like those that had followed the earthquake at the European Parliament elections, the two defections, and the triumph over the Conservatives in Rochester and Strood, such a breakthrough had at least felt possible. Along the way, and despite its weaknesses, Bruni-Lowe had become convinced that Ukip could win more than three million votes, more than one hundred second places and a handful of new MPs. 'I just hoped that the votes would be condensed enough to win under first-past-the-post.' But, in the end, they were not. The party had fallen in the last stretch. On the map, there was now only one Ukip outpost, the seaside town of Clacton, where just seven months earlier a by-election victory had felt like the beginning of a major rebellion.

As defeat cast its shadow over the party, and after yet another failed attempt by a challenger to overcome the electoral system, Farage made good on his promise to resign. Some of those who were close to the Ukip leader would later claim that he had never fully invested in the idea of victory. 'I think that he always knew that it was fifty–fifty,' said Steve Stanbury, the party's director. 'He knew that it would be hard to close and he dealt with that internally, by himself. That way, emotionally, he had not put everything on red.' But such claims belied Farage's true nature. He was the ultimate gambler and always had been. Ever since he had wandered into his first Ukip meeting, he had built his entire political career by playing double or quits. Farage had surprised even himself with the frequency and size of his winnings and the inability of others to stall his rise. But this time, finally, and with the entire country looking on, he had lost—and lost big.

Politicians, it was once observed, are seldom at their best following election defeats.[1] Farage was no different. Surrounded by a handful of journalists and supporters, he marched off towards the local cliffs of Margate. The press conference that followed reflected some of Ukip's defining features—it was instinctive, chaotic, unpredictable, and emotional. As the reality of Farage's departure had surfaced, countless activists had urged him not to follow through. 'You've won four million votes, for God's sake!' screamed Soutter. 'You should see this as a victory!' Matthew Richardson, the party secretary, had also spent much of the preceding night trying to convince him not to follow through. 'You cannot leave us now!' In classic Ukip fashion there had been no plan for the eventuality of defeat. Farage had spent much of the campaign telling people that, if he lost, there was no Plan B. It had been true.

'People just had not planned for Nigel losing,' said Paul Nuttall, who as deputy leader was thinking about what the resignation might mean for him. 'I just don't think that he thought about it. I think it hit him very hard because of the amount that he had put in. It hit us all hard. On a personal level it must have been the lowest moment of his career. But not enough thought went into the question, what next?'

In fact, Nuttall had been far from impressed. Like others, he had found out about the resignation only a few minutes beforehand. He was furious. 'I should have been consulted as deputy leader. It made me look a fool. I have been Chairman and deputy leader. I was angry.' Others, like Arron Banks, who had invested hundreds of thousands of pounds in the campaign, demanded that Farage take the weekend to think it over, to wait until Monday, when a meeting of the National Executive Committee was due to take place in Brooks Mews. Some voiced their fear about a prediction that was routinely heard in conversations about Ukip—that without its charismatic leader the party could never survive. It had only ever known success under one man. Every other period in its history had been scarred by turmoil and failure.

But Farage would not listen. He was adamant. It was time to go. As he marched towards his new life, he looked like a lifelong prisoner who, finally, after years of being caged in a cell and staring at a would-be life through a small window, was nearing his moment of freedom. Perhaps he was thinking about what lay ahead, about recovering the weekends that he had lost with his children, the quiet moments with his wife, who had watched his hobby consume his life, and the lazy weekends playing golf, fishing, and talking to the other villagers in his local pub. In the coming hours, he would be contacted by commercial organizations with offers of money and a fresh start. 'I could see my future life coming together, as a presenter or commentator, and not just about politics.' The life that a big part of Farage had long craved was suddenly within reach—it was almost his. With seagulls circling overhead, and nothing but an empty horizon as his backdrop, he went after his new life. Farage, after Miliband and Clegg, became the third party leader to resign within twenty-four hours of the election:

I am a man of my word. I don't break my word. I shall be writing to Ukip's National Executive in a few minutes and say that I am standing down as leader. I shall recommend that *pro tem* they put in place as acting leader Suzanne Evans who has emerged from this campaign as a tower of strength.

Ukip would hold a leadership election in a few months. Its revolt was finally over. Or so it seemed.

Nuttall had been surprised when he heard Suzanne Evans's name. For ten years he had given his all to the party, and to Farage. He was widely seen as the heir-apparent. 'I would never have stood against Nigel in any leadership election. I mean, what is the point of putting a gun to your head and pulling the trigger?' But now his mentor had suddenly chosen Evans to become the interim leader, somebody who had been active in Ukip for only a couple of years. It had felt like a slap in the face. Like others in the party, Nuttall was not sure of her politics and feared that she might use the role to rally support ahead of a leadership election that was now on the horizon—perhaps by installing a new Chairman and replacing key players. This would jeopardize his own plans to succeed Farage. Nuttall also worried that Evans's southern Conservative background would alienate disillusioned voters in northern England, where Ukip was finally the second force in a significant number of Labour seats.

In the hours that followed, Nuttall called Matthew Richardson. 'If she is going to take over, then I want it in writing that she is not standing in the leadership election!' If she did not give this commitment, then Nuttall, who had spent years cultivating grass-roots support, warned that he would ensure that the NEC vetoed her appointment as Ukip's interim leader. 'I've known these people for years,' he said. 'I worked with them for years. People were calling me, saying I've got to stand up to Suzanne.' Nuttall then had a 'frank' conversation with Farage, who assured his deputy that Evans had been chosen only for geographical reasons. 'She was in London. Nigel guaranteed that he would support me at a leadership election later in the year.'

But, in the end, such assurances would not be needed. As Nuttall and others should have known, Farage was not quite done. The game was not yet over. Between his resignation and the NEC meeting, on the Sunday, the former leader joined David Soutter at celebrations in London to mark the seventieth anniversary of Victory in Europe (VE) day. It was everything that Farage loved about Britain—its history, military tradition, and patriotism. The streets of Westminster were filled with military personnel and veterans while in the skies above Spitfires, Hurricanes, and Lancasters flew past. He was soon swamped. 'Nigel was absolutely mobbed,' said Soutter.

I've done walkabouts with Thatcher but those were nothing like this. People were chanting, 'for he's a jolly good fellow', servicemen, policemen, ordinary people just coming up and telling him not to resign, to keep going. If tourists didn't know who our Prime Minister was, they would have assumed that it was Nigel.

Soutter began to detect a shift, wondering if the decision to stand down was as permanent as it had sounded. 'After a while, I started to see a spark.' Farage was certainly moved by the reaction, but it would not be as decisive as Soutter thought. 'It was very touching. Everybody was asking me not to go. It definitely affected my mood but it did not change my mind.' The real reasons were about to emerge—and they centred on something else entirely.

In the back of his mind, ever since the election, one thought had been quietly prodding Farage to reconsider his decision to stand down. The election of a Conservative majority government had put Britain on course for a referendum on the question of its continuing EU membership. It was the one thing that Farage had spent more than twenty years working for. All of the elections, the disputes, the interviews, the meetings, the *grind*: they had all been about this. And now, finally, the moment had arrived. 'The real clincher was this,' he explained. 'I'd spent all these years looking like the Patron Saint of Lost Causes but now we had finally got the referendum. I felt that to walk away now, when this great battle was upon us, was just not the right thing to do.' But, linked closely to this, was something else that had further convinced him of the need to stay—for just a little while longer.

'I could see and feel an undercurrent. The old Tory Eurosceptics were back, prancing around, telling the world that they were in charge.' Between the despair in South Thanet and the warm reception in Westminster, Farage had seen on television screens the same people who, more than twenty years before, had first led him to abandon mainstream conservatism—the 'gutless' politicians who had failed to stand up to John Major and oppose legislation that had pushed Britain into the arms of the EU. He felt like the striker who had been substituted, forced to sit on the bench for the remainder of the game. And it was hard to watch.

The change was also reflected within his own camp. It had been clear for some time that Farage had seen Douglas Carswell, Ukip's only MP, as part of the same problem—a member of the Tory elite who had never really grasped what Ukip believed or was trying to achieve. Few at the very top of the party had seen their more socially liberal, free-marketeer recruit who had talked about 'positive immigration' as 'true Ukip'. Farage had not felt truly threatened by Carswell, but it could be argued that he had encouraged his marginalization. But the defeat in South Thanet and the victory in Clacton had imposed a new reality. Farage would now have to watch from a distance as Carswell, or somebody who shared his vision, took control of everything that he had almost killed himself to create—and just at the moment when the greatest battle of all had arrived.

On the morning of Monday, 11 May, the day of the NEC meeting, the two men had talked on the phone. The conversation was brief and tense. 'Douglas was very keen that I was going,' said Farage, 'and that I would not be playing a role in the referendum debate'. Carswell would soon air similar views, arguing that politicians more generally should not front the referendum campaign.[2] For Farage, the prospect of having to watch Eurosceptic Tories take over the debate, people whom he felt did not understand public opinion or what it took to build a grass-roots movement, was too much to bear. Instinctively, he had also long rebelled against rejection. 'Some people clearly did not want me back,' he would later say. 'Two or three people in the upper echelons were trying to prevent me from coming back. They would sideline us in the referendum and give up on our core message.' As usual during these moments of decision he had fallen back on his instincts—which told him that he had to return. He would later present himself as the reluctant gambler who was returning for just one more hand. But it is a truism that gamblers relish the last hand as much as the first.

His decision was confirmed by the events that were about to unfold on Brooks Mews—or what the political warhorse David Soutter would later describe as 'the most bizarre day in my very long political life'. The old war room was still littered with debris from the campaign—the billboard designs on the walls, the boxes of Ukip-branded popcorn, and piles and piles of leaflets. As members of the high command arrived, they still looked battle-weary. And they were about to start a very long day. In the morning, the ruling body agreed that Bruni-Lowe would stay on with the party as its Campaign Director, taking charge of Ukip's referendum campaign and the next set of elections in London and Wales in 2016, where Ukip would try to learn from the mistakes of the 2015 campaign. They also confirmed that Matthew Richardson would stay as Party Secretary. Then Farage walked in.

'If you want me to go,' he said, looking around the table, 'then I will go'.

After a brief silence, Ukip's leading activists began to explain why they felt he should stay. Some had tears in their eyes. Nobody wanted him to leave. 'It was a free discussion,' said Steve Crowther, who chaired the meeting. 'But the feeling in the room was palpable. It was clear that the referendum campaign had already kicked off and clearly the one person who needed to lead us through that was Nigel.' The NEC was unanimous in wanting their old leader to return. At one moment, Soutter walked into the room and put a large pile of papers on the table. They were dozens of emails and letters that had been sent in by Ukip's candidates and members who, after watching their leader resign on television, were now urging him to change his mind. One was from Tim Aker, the candidate in Thurrock who had come the closest to joining Carswell on the green benches. 'I won 15,718 votes,' he said. 'I worked really hard. But I was only responsible for 718 of those votes. You were responsible for the other fifteen thousand.' As Farage listened, he looked around—into the eyes of veterans who had followed him for years, most of them in the political wilderness. 'It became apparent at that moment that coming back was the only option.'

Whether or not he would return immediately was still up for debate. Some, anxious about Farage's health, suggested that Crowther, the party's safe pair of hands, take over as interim leader until a leadership election in September, when Farage would stage a return. Evans, it was suggested, would be appeased by the offer of the chairmanship. Some claimed that she had already been sounded out about the idea and had initially agreed. Either way, the motion was voted on by the NEC and approved, though some would later say that the ruling body had been far from enthusiastic about Evans. 'At first, only a few hands were going up. It was clear that some people were not sure about it.' When the vote finally passed, a few officials left to find Evans, but she never returned. 'She never came in to the NEC. She'd obviously rejected it. Something happened between the start of the meeting and one hour later when she rejected the [offer of the] chairmanship. Something had gone on.' But what?

'I wanted time to think about it. My instinct was to say no because I did not know what the job entailed,' said Evans, who had already been serving the party as deputy chairman. 'I was not given any time to discuss it. And there were personal reasons why I did not accept.' Farage, meanwhile, had left for his office with Bruni-Lowe, Nuttall, Kassam, and Crowther. It was around this point that somebody claimed that, during the day, Evans had been called by Carswell, who had urged her not to accept the chairmanship and to hold out for the interim leadership. 'If the Tory Eurosceptics get Suzanne as leader,' said one of those present, 'they will tell Ukip when to engage and when not to engage during the referendum debate. If Farage is not leading us, we will not have any role in the debate.' Long-held suspicions that had bubbled below the surface of the campaign now flooded out into the open.

'There was an air of panic,' said Nuttall. 'It was after the shock of the result. Everybody was totally exhausted and the air was blue.' Matthew Richardson then stormed into the office. He had received an email from Carswell who was demanding control of the £650,000 of 'short money' that was now owed to Ukip every year until 2020—a reflection of its one seat and nearly four million votes.[3] In a party where a lack of resource had always been the Achilles Heel, it was a significant issue. Carswell was arguing that the party should accept only £350,000, that it should not be 'on the gravy train', and that he should oversee spending. This contrasted with the general view, which was to take the money and use it to raise the profile of the party and, some claimed, Carswell. 'We wanted to turn him into a Senator-type figure for our four million voters, establishing a policy unit and securing proper resource.' Whether or not that was true, what was clear was that, against the backdrop of the campaign, and the events earlier in the day, the email had fuelled suspicions. 'I've got a horrible feeling about all of this and where I think this is going,' said Farage, as he paced around his office, his followers looking on. 'I think we're being infiltrated.'

One of those in the room was Nuttall. 'He [Farage] definitely felt that we were being infiltrated and that the only way of batting it off was for him to come back. He made that quite explicit in the room'. Suddenly, in a party that had long entertained paranoia and anxiety about people's motives, mutterings about a 'hijack strategy' seemed to become the official view. 'It was like that scene in the film *Usual Suspects*', said one. 'Everything just came together. All of the pieces fell into place. It was clear that by sending the email Douglas was trying to raise the game.' Irrespective of their validity, these claims and suspicions were dominating the internal debate. Farage, now staring out of his window, was thinking about his next move. After listening to all of the talk about plots, infiltration, and how to keep Ukip at the heart of the referendum debate, he turned, smiled, and exclaimed what was usually reserved for evenings in the pub: 'Reload!' He would be coming back immediately.

In the following hours Bruni-Lowe and Richardson left to find Carswell. They needed to talk about the short money, and let him know that Farage was back. As they made their way through parliament, towards Central Lobby, they saw a journalist cornering Carswell, thrusting a mobile phone into his face. It was news of Farage's return. Carswell was not impressed. After finding a meeting room, he listened to the two advisers. Some would later claim that the MP was 'physically angry' about the refusal of Farage to leave and had threatened to leave Ukip unless he was given sole control of the short money. 'Well, you are going to have to walk,' said one.

Within days, Ukip had descended into civil war. To paraphrase one newspaper, the sudden eruption of infighting made the Tory split over the repeal of the Corn Laws and Labour's divisions over the Bennite insurgency of the early 1980s look tame.[4] This was perhaps an overstatement, given that only a handful of individuals were involved. But there was also no doubt that the dispute involved everybody who was anybody inside the party. Tension and animosity had only ever been thinly disguised. Disagreements over the message, strategy, defectors, and advisers had been well known for some time. But now people who had known each other for years, who had campaigned alongside one another, and had often been personally recruited by Farage wilfully engaged in a very public outbreak of infighting.

On the front page of *The Times*, one article claimed that Ukip's economics spokesman, Patrick O'Flynn, had described Farage as a 'snarling, thin-skinned, aggressive' man whose actions risked making Ukip look like a 'personality cult'. O'Flynn would later argue that he had been referring to the public perception of his leader rather than his own view. If he was genuinely worried about Farage's public image, then he had a point. While voters might not have seen the Ukip leader in quite these terms, they had, as we have seen, become less positive about him as the campaign had gone on. This was not the case for Ukip's own supporters, however—most of them adored Farage. He was a significant driver of their decision to vote for the party. Perhaps conscious of this disconnect, O'Flynn was now urging his leader to adopt a more consultative and consensual style of leadership, which he clearly saw as being blocked by 'aggressive' and 'inexperienced' aides who had introduced a 'Tea Party, ultra-aggressive American influence'.[5] A few days later, on the Andrew Marr Show, Suzanne Evans underscored the message. 'I think we've had some problems with some advisers around Nigel who very much kept him in their pocket. They were trying to take the party back to where it was several years ago.'

Evans also recycled arguments that had been made before the 'March Tilt', which had pushed Ukip's campaign in a different and more aggressive direction. The manifesto, she argued, had been 'very compassionate, very centre ground, very balanced', which is 'where he [Farage] wants to take the party and where the party needs to be going'. Evans talked about the need for Ukip to professionalize, diversify, be more inclusive, and reach out to women and minorities.

Nigel talked about the shy Kippers, who were not telling pollsters that they were Ukip voters. I think there is an issue there that we have to answer, why are these people shy? If our party brand is actually working at the moment, why don't our people want to sing and dance about it?

The disorganized rebellion, however, soon ran out of steam. As had so often happened in Ukip's past, Farage's opponents had underestimated his support within the upper echelons of the party. O'Flynn had soon resigned as economics spokesperson and issued a public apology. And, while it would be claimed that Raheem Kassam and Matthew Richardson had been thrown out as sacrificial lambs, the reality was quite different. Kassam's contract had been due to expire at the end of May, while Richardson had never left at all. Within two months, the party had started to use some of the short money for new support within parliament, while activists such as Crowther had started to point to far bigger challenges that were on the horizon.

We knew what we were doing and we knew where we were going. There was a certain amount of pent-up feeling that came out as a result of that situation but from the party's point of view that was it, it was done, it was resolved. There were a lot of tired people, there was a lot of post-election angst. We needed to calm down, take a deep breath, and look ahead to the referendum debate.

The national referendum, which Ukip had spent more than twenty years fighting for, was now on its way. It was finally here.

# 14

# Referendum

In September 2015, Ukip's faithful returned to the south Yorkshire town of Doncaster for their first major gathering since the general election. The mood contrasted sharply with the celebratory atmosphere that had been on display only one year before, when Mark Reckless had defected to join the rising party. This time around, quiet activists were huddled in the corners—disappointed by the past election and unsure of the future. Farage was still in charge, but the political landscape had fundamentally changed. Ukip's dream of overcoming the system and winning seats in the House of Commons remained just that. Despite all of the excitement, the energy, the predictions, the fighting, and the hope, they had, ultimately, failed. Now, the party's fall at the last hurdle risked fuelling its image as a busted flush—as a movement that had commenced a slow but inevitable journey to the graveyard of failed revolts. There were other challenges, too.

In the aftermath of the election it was not entirely clear how the return of the Liberal Democrats into opposition, under the new leadership of Tim Farron, would impact on Ukip. Since 2010, Farage and his party had always prospered amid an environment in which the traditional third party had been an insider member of government. But, while in the three months since the 2015 general election the Liberal Democrats were still averaging below 8 per cent of the vote, from hereon they too would be on the outside, using their stronger campaigning skills to pitch to political protesters and try to stage a comeback.

Others saw it differently, however. Ukip might have failed to capture new seats, but since the campaign the party had continued to average over 10 per cent. The pollsters, who were readying for an inquiry into what had gone wrong in their industry, had seemingly corrected the ratings of the other parties. The Conservatives were now riding high on 39 per cent, while Labour was struggling on 30 per cent, looking set to welcome the radical left-winger Jeremy Corbyn as its surprising new leader.[1] With Cameron back in power and Labour in disarray, some in Ukip felt cautiously optimistic. They thought that they could continue to draw strength from disillusioned social conservatives who had voted for the Conservatives with their head rather than with their heart—whose lingering and often intense anxieties over immigration, the EU, and the spread of liberal values might provide a source of ongoing support. Labour, meanwhile, looked unlikely to reconnect with its lost working-class voters, whose worries over migration were as much about cultural insecurity as competition over jobs, and some of whom had helped to entrench Ukip as a serious force in northern England 'Corbyn', said Farage, at his party's conference, 'is a gift for Ukip.'

Cameron's majority had also raised another, major opportunity. Ukip might not have gained any new seats, but the outcome of the election did present the party with a chance to remain relevant—and to move past the in-fighting. Cameron's promised referendum over Britain's continuing membership in the EU provided Ukip with a lifeboat into which the warring camps could climb, uniting activists behind the original goal that had first sparked their desire to enter politics—to pull Britain out of the EU. Insiders who only weeks before had been in open conflict now talked excitedly about creating 'an SNP effect in England', hoping to use the in-or-out vote, the surrounding debate, and all the publicity to bring a larger number of people into their camp. Even if Ukip was again defeated, by tapping once more into public anxieties over the free movement of EU migrants, perceived threats to national identity, and worries over a claimed lack of democracy within institutions in Brussels, some argued that the party could emerge with a stronger following. Or at least that was the plan.

But for the Eurosceptics like Ukip, or the 'Outers', the battle that was about to ensue against those who wanted to keep the country in the EU, or the 'Inners', looked set to be extremely difficult. There is no doubt that Britain has long been instinctively Eurosceptic. The last time that a referendum was held, in 1975, which asked people whether or not they wanted the country to stay in the European Community (the Common Market), a large majority opted to continue along this path. Overall, just over 67 per cent of people voted to stay. But, while many had seen that earlier result as a landslide, some pointed out that, while it was certainly unequivocal, it had also been unenthusiastic. 'Support for membership was wide but it did not run deep,' observed David Butler and Uwe Kitzinger, in the aftermath of that earlier referendum. It had been a vote for the status quo, for the existing state of affairs, rather than for a fundamentally new relationship with Europe. The outcome, they concluded, did not result 'in a girding of the loins for a great new European adventure'.[2]

This observation would hold true for much of the next forty years. Whether reflected in disputes inside Labour over its involvement with Europe in the 1970s, Margaret Thatcher's complaints over the size of Britain's contributions to the European budget in the 1980s, turmoil within the Conservative Party about Europe in the 1990s, or the rise of Ukip thereafter, Britain's relationship with the EU continued to be known chiefly for its doubt, scepticism, and awkwardness.

Not all of this was unique to Britain, of course. Across Europe, it has been observed how, since the 1990s, there has been a shift from what was known as a phase of 'permissive consensus', whereby citizens were willing to provide their governments with space to pursue a relationship with the EU, to a new era of 'constraining dissensus', whereby political leaders now face a much stronger streak of Eurosceptic opposition—and one that has arguably been hardened by the mismanagement of the post-2008 Eurozone crisis.[3] But this has been especially true in Britain, and remains so today.

It was clear, for example, in the spring of 2015, when the people went to the polls. Around three-fifths of the population tended towards a Eurosceptic position. Most people, when asked about their views towards EU membership, leaned closer to the idea that unification had gone too far, and that Britain should do more to protect its independence.[4] Of those who were not Eurosceptic, one-fifth were ambivalent—they neither wanted further integration, nor did they believe that it should be rolled back. This meant that, at the time of the 2015 general election, four in five people were sceptical or ambivalent about Britain's place in the EU. Most would probably have endorsed Winston Churchill's famous phrase from 1951, summing up the country's approach to Europe: 'We are with them, but not of them.'[5]

Yet, while many were Eurosceptic, when people were specifically asked about how they would *vote* in an in–out referendum, a different picture emerged. It was the Inners who had a strong lead. Three in five of those who would vote in a referendum said that they would vote to continue Britain's EU membership. And, even among those who felt anxious about this relationship, three in ten would vote to stay in. It was only among hardcore Eurosceptics, who expressed the most vehement opposition, that there was overwhelming support for leaving—among the most Eurosceptic people in Britain, nine out of ten would have voted to leave. The problem for Farage, Ukip, and the other Outers, is that, as of May 2015, these voters

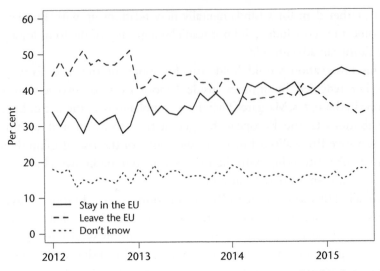

**Figure 14.1.** 'If there was a referendum on Britain's EU membership, how would you vote?'
*Source*: YouGov.

represented just one-quarter of the population. Lots of voters might not like the EU, but most of them, when you drill down, want to stay in.

It was not always this way, however. Between 2010 and 2013, when people were asked about their views towards the in-or-out vote, surveys suggested that clear and sometimes large majorities of the people would have opted to leave the EU. During the earlier years of the Coalition government, and as a global crisis rocked financial markets, the Outers had averaged a lead of eleven points in 2011, seventeen points in 2012, and almost eight points in 2013. On several occasions during this period they enjoyed a lead that stretched to twenty points.[6] So, the longer-term trends are more complex than some Inners suggest. It is certainly not the case that the country has consistently been in favour of cementing its arrangement with Europe. Nonetheless, the Inners have gradually closed the gap—and this, moreover, during a period that saw an ongoing economic crisis within the Eurozone, continued bail-outs for Greece, and deep-seated public concerns in Britain over immigration, which during the summer of 2015 were underscored by a major refugee crisis, following instability in the Middle East and North Africa, and a more specific challenge posed by illegal migrants trying to enter Britain through the port of Calais. But, despite all of this, by 2015 the Inners had established a lead of almost ten points. As support for Ukip was on the rise, so too was support for Britain's EU membership.

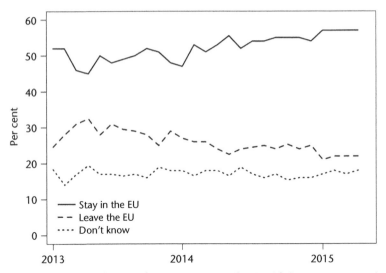

**Figure 14.2.** 'Imagine the British government under David Cameron renegotiated our relationship with Europe...how would you then vote in a referendum on the issue?'
*Source*: YouGov.

This brings us to a further problem for the Outers. If Cameron *were* successfully to renegotiate the terms of membership, victory would likely move even further away from the grasp of those who want out. This scenario is reflected in the response to one interesting question. When people are asked to imagine that Cameron has renegotiated Britain's EU membership, has reassured them that the country's interests are protected, and recommends that they vote to stay in, almost three-fifths of people would stay, while between one-fifth and a quarter would leave (see Figure 14.2).[7] In fact, when the question is asked this way, the Outers have *never* been ahead. While a large number of voters are certainly concerned about the current state of affairs, many prefer more modest change, rather than risk the dramatic change that is associated with leaving altogether.

There is also other evidence that the preference for modest change is not a new one. Since 1993, the British Social Attitudes surveys have sought to gauge what the public have thought over the longer term, by using a more nuanced question.[8] As shown in Figure 14.3, from 1996 onwards the largest segment of the population has favoured staying in the EU but reducing its powers. At that time, four out of ten respondents favoured the reduction of EU powers, while just one out of ten wanted to leave altogether. Even though support for leaving has increased over time, even at the height of these sentiments—in 2012 when three out of ten said that they wanted to

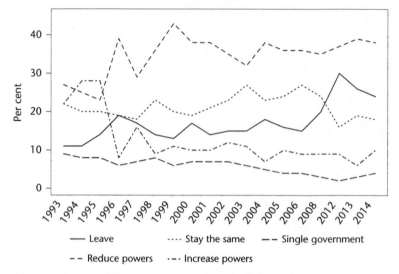

**Figure 14.3.** Britain's long-term policy regarding the European Union, 1993–2014
*Source*: British Social Attitudes Survey.

leave—there were still far more people who favoured staying, albeit in a reformed EU. And, when many of those who prefer to leave were given a choice, they actually preferred the idea of renegotiation. These figures obviously only reinforce our previous message—that, while large numbers of British voters are sceptical towards their EU membership, at the end of the day most do not want 'Brexit'.

The challenge facing the Eurosceptics in any referendum is borne out even more strongly if we drill down further into the opinions of the supporters of Britain's political parties. Ukip's supporters, as one might expect, are overwhelmingly hostile towards the EU. In such a referendum, more than nine out of every ten Ukip voters said they would opt to pull Britain out.[9] But, while the supporters of other parties expressed concern about the pace and scale of European integration, the percentages who are willing to leave altogether were significantly lower. Even among Conservatives, most of whom were Eurosceptic, less than one in two—45 per cent—said they would actually vote to leave. This figure drops to 27 per cent for the SNP, 26 per cent for Labour voters, 18 per cent for Liberal Democrats, and 15 per cent for the Greens (see Figure 14.4). To fuel their support, therefore, Outers would need to look to draw most of their support from those who voted for Farage or Cameron. But, if Cameron negotiates better terms and campaigns to stay in, advising his supporters to follow suit, then it is reasonable to assume that many Conservative voters, particularly those who prefer modest change over

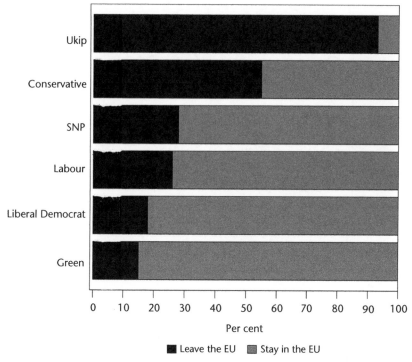

**Figure 14.4.** EU referendum vote choice by party support, May 2015
*Source*: 2014–2017 British Election Study Internet Panel (Wave 6).

the unknown upheavals of leaving, would follow his lead. And, given that such a large segment of the population favours reform of the EU over exit, it seems only logical to assume that many voters would probably vote to stay in, regardless of whether or not they had supported Cameron in 2015.

In addition to all of this, it is the Inners who have the easier argument to make. People often side with the status quo, as seen during the 2014 referendum in Scotland. Human beings are naturally averse to risk. Against the backdrop of Britain's young and fragile economic recovery, it is easy to see why millions of Britons might not want to take a leap into the unknown and leave one of the biggest single markets in the world. This gives the Inners a natural advantage, one that is underlined by a tendency among the Outers to be divided and their lack of a clear vision for what might replace Britain's EU membership. Those who want Britain to leave the EU often say contrasting things about their vision for a country outside the EU, from following the examples of Norway and Switzerland, to rebuilding bridges with the Commonwealth. This lack of clarity and a compelling vision is

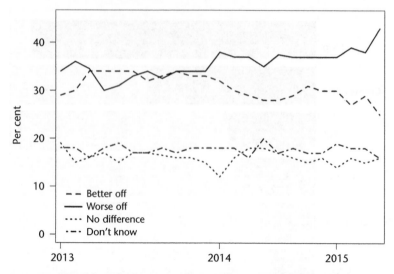

**Figure 14.5.** 'Would we be better or worse off economically if we left the EU?'
*Source*: YouGov.

unlikely to win over sceptical floating voters who do not have the time or inclination to contemplate several possible future scenarios—all of which are hypothetical.

This underlines a point that has been made by Andrew Gamble, one of the leading academics in the study of Britain's relationship with Europe—that the country's engagement with Brussels has often been seen as conditional, in the sense that 'identification with the EU seems not to be deep-seated and appears based on pragmatic calculations about costs and benefits, rather than any attachment to European ideals'.[10] The perceived economic costs and benefits of 'Brexit' that Gamble is referring to can be seen in Figure 14.5, which shows how, since the end of 2014, more voters have come to feel that leaving the EU would be bad for Britain's economy. By the spring of 2015 there was an eighteen-point gap between those who felt that the country would be worse off if it left the EU and those who thought it would be better off.[11] We see the same pattern when we look at attitudes towards how leaving the EU would affect jobs and employment, Britain's influence in the world, and people's personal situation.[12] In all cases, there has been a steady increase in the number of people who believe that leaving the EU would have negative consequences in all these areas. And, paradoxical as it might appear, the gap between those who see greater costs of departure and those who see greater benefits has steadily increased since Farage moved to the forefront of politics.

Indeed, Inners often like to point to how their rising support has coincided with the rise of Ukip. The last time that the Outers had enjoyed a lead, argue some, was before the party's rise. But, since then, and as Farage has fused Europe with the more controversial issue of immigration, the Outers have fallen behind—a trend that some refer to as the 'Farage Paradox'. As Sunder Katwala of the British Future think tank observed, 'the more that Ukip's media profile, poll rating and party membership has grown over the last two years, the more that support for the party's core mission—that Britain should leave the European Union—seems to have shrunk'. Indeed, evidence published by *British Future* in September 2015 suggested that most people, by a margin of almost three to one, felt that Farage and his party 'risked bringing prejudice into debates about immigration'. While this concern was rejected by most of those who were certain to vote to leave the EU, among those who were leaning toward Brexit, or who were open to changing their minds, majorities felt that the Ukip leader would toxify the debate.[13]

While, in 2015, the party won nearly four million votes, some Outers argue that Ukip, Farage, and its divisive strategy have made what was already a difficult mountain even harder to climb. Ukip has managed to alienate moderate Eurosceptics who might otherwise be open to their arguments, they claim. Moreover, some Outers worry that Farage, whose ratings took a hit during 2015, will allow Inners to turn the debate into a different question: do you agree with Nigel?

If people's feelings towards Farage do come into play during the debate, then the Outers will face another significant hurdle. While a majority of those who would vote to leave the EU say they like Farage to some degree, the same is not true of those who would vote to stay. Just one in six of those who support Britain staying in the EU said they liked Farage, while almost one-quarter disliked him strongly. Even more concerning for Outers is the view of those voters who are yet to make up their minds. Only one-quarter of undecided voters liked Farage, while a slightly larger proportion disliked him strongly. As Figure 14.6 shows, we see the same pattern when we look at how people feel about Ukip. In summary: if the referendum is framed as being all about Farage and Ukip, then the Outers will have a serious problem in recruiting people to their cause—or retaining them if they do.

So does this mean that Ukip is destined to disappear from British politics—that, if it fails to win the referendum, it will soon fall off the radar? One way to explore this and Ukip's potential future is to investigate what is driving these public attitudes towards the EU referendum vote—to shed light on the kinds of arguments that may galvanize this debate.

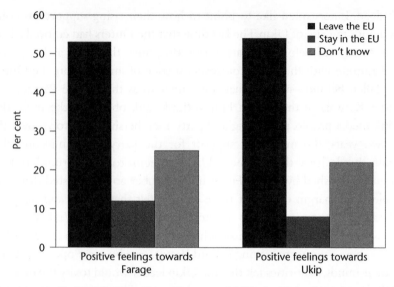

**Figure 14.6.** Positive feelings about Farage and Ukip by EU referendum vote choice, May 2015
Source: 2014–2017 British Election Study Internet Panel (Wave 6).

Across Europe, there is a large body of research that explores what shapes public opinion to European integration. The research is useful because it often tests approaches called 'economic' versus 'identity' arguments. The first contends that how people think about the EU is shaped mainly by whether or not they believe that membership brings instrumental benefits—that it is in their economic self-interest to be a member of the EU. If this is true, then we would expect to find that support for membership will be stronger among people who are in more financially secure and professional jobs, who have degrees, who are better able to adapt to increased competition, and who, like journalist Matthew Parris, enjoy travelling around the Continent, and identify with the idea of the 'European project'. But others argue that a more powerful driver of public attitudes is whether people feel attached to their national identity, are concerned about immigration, and worry that the EU and its further expansion threaten national culture, the sense of belonging, the overall integrity of the nation state, and established ways of life.

These identity-related factors obviously relate to a more diffuse set of concerns, but there is good evidence to suggest that they might be just as important, if not more so, than purely instrumental concerns about economic self-interest. After surveying public attitudes towards the EU, for instance, academic Lauren McLaren concludes that 'a general hostility towards other cultures' plays an important role in the formation of public attitudes, while other researchers have similarly revealed how intolerance towards other religions not only shapes a diffuse public scepticism but can trigger concerns over specific policies, like the enlargement of the EU to include predominantly Muslim countries like Turkey.[14] We might also add here a third layer of more specifically *political* concerns influencing public attitudes towards the referendum vote: namely, anxiety over a democratic deficit within the EU and a worry that decision-making in Brussels and Strasbourg often seems distant and unaccountable to ordinary people.

To explore the power of these different drivers in Britain, we can use some survey data from around the time of the 2015 general election. These suggest that there were significant differences between those who favoured staying in the EU and those who wanted to leave. Inners who wanted to stay in the EU were often quite young, worked in a relatively secure job, had a degree, and identified with left-wing progressive causes. Outers, however, looked rather different. They tended to be in their fifties or older, were less well educated, and were more likely to be employed in insecure, working-class occupations. They also tended to be more right-wing. Beyond obvious differences in their levels of Euroscepticism, these groups also thought very differently about immigration. While six out of ten Inners thought that immigration has been good for the economy, seven out of ten Outers thought that it has been bad. Four out of ten Outers thought that immigrants are a burden on Britain's welfare state, but only around one in ten Inners thinks the same. Most significantly, nearly three out of four Outers believed that immigration undermines Britain's culture, but only around one in four Inners held the same view. There were, however, only modest differences between Inners and Outers in terms of economic pessimism. In both cases, approximately three in ten believed that their personal economic situation or the general economic situation in the country had deteriorated over the previous twelve months.

But what about the undecided—those who are yet to make up their minds on the matter? In the polls, the Inners typically have around a six-point lead. But this is easily eclipsed by the 18 per cent of people who say that they do not know how they will vote. If a majority of these voters decide to support the 'In' campaign, then it could very well be a landslide in favour of staying in, but if a majority of them vote for Brexit, then the result could be closer than some think. And, if we look at the undecided voters more closely, then we find something interesting—they actually look more like the Outers than the Inners in a number of respects (see Table 14.1).

**Table 14.1.** Social background of EU Inners, Outers, and undecided voters, May 2015

| Characteristic | Stay | Leave | Don't know |
|---|---|---|---|
| *Social class* | | | |
| Higher managerial/professional | 21 | 14 | 14 |
| Lower managerial/professional | 35 | 28 | 29 |
| Intermediate occupations | 20 | 23 | 26 |
| Small employers/self-employed | 6 | 7 | 6 |
| Lower supervisory/technical | 6 | 9 | 6 |
| Semi-routine | 8 | 12 | 12 |
| Routine | 4 | 8 | 7 |
| *Education (Age left school)* | | | |
| 16 or younger | 24 | 48 | 36 |
| 17–18 | 22 | 24 | 28 |
| 19 or older, still in school | 54 | 29 | 37 |
| *Gender* | | | |
| Male | 53 | 50 | 34 |
| Female | 47 | 50 | 66 |
| *Age* | | | |
| 18–34 | 35 | 18 | 31 |
| 35–54 | 31 | 34 | 37 |
| 55+ | 33 | 48 | 31 |
| *Left–right ideology* | | | |
| Left | 41 | 14 | 23 |
| Centre | 39 | 37 | 41 |
| Right | 20 | 49 | 36 |
| *Euroscepticism* | | | |
| Unification 'gone too far' | 36 | 90 | 77 |
| Britain should protect its independence | 28 | 96 | 74 |
| Dissatisfaction with EU democracy | 65 | 94 | 84 |
| *Attitudes on immigration* | | | |
| Immigration bad for Britain's economy | 21 | 68 | 41 |
| Immigrants a burden on the welfare state | 11 | 45 | 26 |
| Immigration undermines Britain's culture | 28 | 73 | 47 |
| *Economic pessimism (retrospective)* | | | |
| Personal economic situation worse | 30 | 35 | 31 |
| General economic situation worse | 29 | 28 | 25 |

*Note*: Numbers in each column represent the weighted percentage of the Inners, Outers, and undecided individuals who belong to a given group.

*Source*: 2014–2017 British Election Study Internet Panel (Wave 6).

A significant portion did not go to university, were working class or self-employed, and were more likely than the Inners to be right-wing. They were also closer to the Outers when it came to immigration and their view of politics within the EU, being significantly more likely than Inners to hold negative feelings about immigration, and also being more likely to feel dissatisfied with how democracy is currently working within the EU. And while they might not have liked Farage, much will ultimately depend upon whether their distaste for the Ukip leader outweighs their dissatisfaction with the EU.

So, what do these differences tell us about the debate and the future of Ukip more generally? When we look at the drivers of support for leaving the EU more systematically, then we find some key messages for this debate. Aside from focusing on the risk-averse nature of voters, and pitching to the more financially secure, more highly educated, younger and pro-immigration voters, the Inners may be tempted to target public opposition to Farage himself. Individuals who disliked the leader of Ukip were, in our models, nearly six times more likely to say that they would vote to keep Britain in the EU than those who liked or were indifferent to him. The broader analysis above suggests that it is their battle to lose.

For the Outers, meanwhile, aside from trying to mobilize an older, less-well-educated, financially disaffected, and right-leaning electorate, our evidence suggests that they should target some other concerns. One is public anxiety over the perceived lack of democracy in the EU—people who were dissatisfied with the way that democracy is working in the EU were three times more likely to vote to leave than those who are not dissatisfied. Another is immigration. Those who felt that migrants are a burden on the welfare state and those who think that migrants have a negative effect on the economy were twice as likely to favour an exit, and those who think that migrants undermine Britain's culture were 1.5 times more likely to vote to leave. And Eurosceptics who express negative views on all three of these questions about immigration—who felt that migrants are bad for the economy, a burden on the welfare state, *and* undermine national culture—were sixteen times more likely to favour an exit. But, again, these individuals are in the minority—as of May 2015, just 12 per cent of the population was both Eurosceptic and intensely opposed to immigration.

It will be very difficult for Ukip and other Outers to win, but by targeting these anxieties Farage and his party may well emerge on the other side of the referendum debate enjoying a stronger relationship with those voters who feel anxious over identity-related issues. As we have seen in this book, throughout the European and general election campaigns, Ukip began to claim ownership over immigration and Europe—and it is likely that this process will be entrenched should the party focus heavily on mobilizing public concerns around the free movement of people and perceived threats to national identity. Many younger, university-educated, middle-class, and left-leaning voters would inevitably find the strategy alienating, confirming their existing dislike of Farage and Ukip. But, while it would not mean that the party would automatically survive and prosper over the longer term, a strategy that is built around public concerns over perceived threats to identity might well nevertheless succeed in entrenching Ukip as an alternative political home for a significant section of British society—an outlet for lingering worries over immigration, its effects on changing communities, and in an age when the ability of mainstream politicians to respond to these concerns has been greatly reduced.

# Appendix A: Ukip Election Results

Table A1. Ukip's 2009 and 2014 European election vote share by local authority

| Area | Region | 2014 vote (%) | 2009 vote (%) | Change (2009–14) |
|---|---|---|---|---|
| Aberdeen City | Scotland | 9.6 | 5.0 | +4.6 |
| Aberdeenshire | Scotland | 11.7 | 6.2 | +5.5 |
| Adur | South East | 36.3 | 25 | +11.3 |
| Allerdale | North West | 28.8 | 15.7 | +13.2 |
| Amber Valley | East Midlands | 32.2 | 14.2 | +18.0 |
| Angus | Scotland | 10.9 | 5.7 | +5.2 |
| Argyll and Bute | Scotland | 11.0 | 6.1 | +4.9 |
| Arun | South East | 42.6 | 26.3 | +16.3 |
| Ashfield | East Midlands | 37.4 | 15.6 | +21.8 |
| Ashford | South East | 38.9 | 19.8 | +19.1 |
| Aylesbury Vale | South East | 35.3 | 20.1 | +15.2 |
| Babergh | East of England | 3.05 | 23.8 | +11.2 |
| Barking and Dagenham | London | 28.1 | 14.8 | +13.3 |
| Barnet | London | 15.0 | 9.4 | +5.6 |
|  | Yorkshire and the Humber | 35.9 | 18.7 | +17.2 |
| Barrow-in-Furness | North West | 33.1 | 17.6 | +15.5 |
| Basildon | East of England | 44.8 | 22.9 | +21.9 |
| Basingstoke and Deane | South East | 29.7 | 17.7 | +12 |
| Bassetlaw | East Midlands | 33.2 | 17.0 | +16.2 |
| Bath and North East Somerset | South West | 24.8 | 16.7 | +8.1 |
| Bedford | East of England | 28.3 | 16.4 | +11.9 |
| Bexley | London | 37.6 | 20.7 | +16.9 |
| Birmingham | West Midlands | 22.5 | 15.2 | +7.3 |
| Blaby | East Midlands | 36.7 | 18.2 | +18.5 |
| Blackburn with Darwen | North West | 23.7 | 12.3 | +11.3 |
| Blackpool | North West | 33.9 | 18.4 | +15.4 |
| Blaenau Gwent | Wales | 30.2 | 14.6 | +15.6 |

(continued)

**Table A1.** Continued

| Area | Region | 2014 vote (%) | 2009 vote (%) | Change (2009–14) |
|---|---|---|---|---|
| Bolsover | East Midlands | 36.3 | 14.8 | +21.5 |
| Bolton | North West | 31.9 | 16.5 | +15.3 |
| Boston | East Midlands | 51.6 | 25.2 | +26.4 |
| Bournemouth | South West | 37.6 | 25.9 | +11.8 |
| Bracknell Forest | South East | 32.9 | 20.9 | +12.0 |
| Bradford | Yorkshire and the Humber | 24.8 | 14.9 | +9.9 |
| Braintree | East of England | 39.1 | 21.8 | +17.3 |
| Breckland | East of England | 42.2 | 24.8 | +17.4 |
| Brent | London | 8.7 | 5.5 | +3.2 |
| Brentwood | East of England | 37.5 | 21.2 | +16.2 |
| Bridgend | Wales | 28.7 | 12.6 | +16.1 |
| Brighton and Hove | South East | 18.7 | 12.1 | +6.7 |
| Bristol, City of | South West | 22.6 | 13.8 | +8.8 |
| Broadland | East of England | 36.6 | 22.1 | +14.5 |
| Bromley | London | 31.1 | 18.9 | +12.2 |
| Bromsgrove | West Midlands | 35.6 | 27.8 | +7.9 |
| Broxbourne | East of England | 41.4 | 21.4 | +19.9 |
| Broxtowe | East Midlands | 31.0 | 13.7 | +17.3 |
| Burnley | North West | 28.7 | 14.9 | +13.8 |
| Bury | North West | 27.6 | 15.3 | +12.3 |
| Caerphilly | Wales | 30.7 | 12.8 | +17.9 |
| Calderdale | Yorkshire and the Humber | 28.4 | 16.3 | +12.0 |
| Cambridge | East of England | 12.4 | 8.3 | +4.1 |
| Camden | London | 9.2 | 5.8 | +3.4 |
| Cannock Chase | West Midlands | 38.8 | 24.4 | +14.5 |
| Canterbury | South East | 34.4 | 18.6 | +15.8 |
| Cardiff | Wales | 22.7 | 11.1 | +11.6 |
| Carlisle | North West | 29.6 | 15.3 | +14.2 |
| Carmarthenshire | Wales | 24.7 | 10.8 | +13.9 |
| Castle Point | East of England | 47.8 | 28.2 | +19.6 |
| Central Bedfordshire | East of England | 36.8 | 18.9 | +17.9 |
| Ceredigion | Wales | 20.2 | 9.2 | +11.0 |
| Charnwood | East Midlands | 30.8 | 14.6 | +16.1 |
| Chelmsford | East of England | 36.8 | 20.8 | +16.0 |
| Cheltenham | South West | 24.9 | 16.3 | +8.6 |
| Cherwell | South East | 28.8 | 16.7 | +12.0 |
| Cheshire East | North West | 30.2 | 16.7 | +13.5 |
| Cheshire West and Chester | North West | 29.9 | 17.5 | +12.4 |
| Chesterfield | East Midlands | 30.4 | 14.4 | +16.1 |
| Chichester | South East | 32.4 | 20.7 | +11.7 |

| Chiltern | South East | 32.7 | 17.3 | +15.4 |
|---|---|---|---|---|
| Chorley | North West | 29.1 | 18.0 | +11.1 |
| Christchurch | South West | 40.7 | 29.7 | +11.0 |
| City of London | London | 13.8 | 8.8 | +5.0 |
| Clackmannanshire | Scotland | 10.0 | 3.6 | +6.4 |
| Colchester | East of England | 31.9 | 19.6 | +12.3 |
| Conwy | Wales | 30.2 | 13.0 | +17.2 |
| Copeland | North West | 29.2 | 14.9 | +14.3 |
| Corby | East Midlands | 35.0 | 16.1 | +18.9 |
| Cornwall | South West | 36.7 | 23.9 | +12.8 |
| Cotswold | South West | 26.4 | 17.2 | +9.2 |
| County Durham | North East | 30.7 | 16.1 | +14.6 |
| Coventry | West Midlands | 26.5 | 16.3 | +10.2 |
| Craven | Yorkshire and the Humber | 28.6 | 19.8 | +8.8 |
| Crawley | South East | 32.1 | 17.0 | +15.2 |
| Croydon | London | 20.0 | 13.5 | +6.5 |
| Dacorum | East of England | 30.7 | 16.1 | +14.6 |
| Darlington | North East | 28.1 | 14.7 | +13.4 |
| Dartford | South East | 35.0 | 18.9 | +16.1 |
| Daventry | East Midlands | 34.5 | 17.8 | +16.7 |
| Denbighshire | Wales | 27.0 | 14.6 | +12.4 |
| Derby | East Midlands | 29.8 | 14.2 | +15.7 |
| Derbyshire Dales | East Midlands | 27.9 | 14.5 | +13.4 |
| Doncaster | Yorkshire and the Humber | 35.1 | 16.0 | +19.0 |
| Dover | South East | 39.2 | 19.4 | +19.9 |
| Dudley | West Midlands | 38.4 | 27.5 | +10.9 |
| Dumfries and Galloway | Scotland | 13.5 | 3.8 | +9.7 |
| Dundee City | Scotland | 8.8 | 4.7 | +4.1 |
| Ealing | London | 11.2 | 8.0 | +3.2 |
| East Ayrshire | Scotland | 8.9 | 5.2 | +3.7 |
| East Cambridgeshire | East of England | 31.2 | 17.4 | +13.7 |
| East Devon | South West | 35.3 | 27.8 | +7.5 |
| East Dorset | South West | 38.4 | 26.8 | +11.6 |
| East Dunbartonshire | Scotland | 10.0 | 9.0 | +1.0 |
| East Hampshire | South East | 30.1 | 16.5 | +13.5 |
| East Hertfordshire | East of England | 31.6 | 19.9 | +11.7 |
| East Lindsey | East Midlands | 44.2 | 24.5 | +19.7 |
| East Lothian | Scotland | 9.9 | 4.2 | +5.7 |
| East Northamptonshire | East Midlands | 36.8 | 19.3 | +17.5 |
| East Renfrewshire | Scotland | 10.2 | 4.8 | +5.4 |
| East Riding of Yorkshire | Yorkshire and the Humber | 38.0 | 23.3 | +14.7 |

(continued)

**Table A1.** Continued

| Area | Region | 2014 vote (%) | 2009 vote (%) | Change (2009–14) |
|------|--------|---------------|---------------|-------------------|
| East Staffordshire | West Midlands | 33.9 | 19.2 | +14.8 |
| Eastbourne | South East | 36.4 | 20.8 | +15.6 |
| Eastleigh | South East | 35 | 21.3 | +13.7 |
| Eden | North West | 25.1 | 15.7 | +9.4 |
| Edinburgh, City of | Scotland | 7.8 | 4.8 | +3.0 |
| Eilean Siar | Scotland | 11.0 | 4.7 | +6.3 |
| Elmbridge | South East | 24.6 | 16.9 | +7.7 |
| Enfield | London | 18.5 | 12.2 | +6.3 |
| Epping Forest | East of England | 40.3 | 21.5 | +18.8 |
| Epsom and Ewell | South East | 32.0 | 21.0 | +11.0 |
| Erewash | East Midlands | 33.7 | 15.1 | +18.6 |
| Exeter | South West | 25.2 | 21.3 | +3.8 |
| Falkirk | Scotland | 12.8 | 5.0 | +7.8 |
| Fareham | South East | 34.0 | 21.3 | +12.7 |
| Fenland | East of England | 47.3 | 24.6 | +22.7 |
| Fife | Scotland | 10.4 | 5.7 | +4.7 |
| Flintshire | Wales | 32.7 | 16.8 | +15.9 |
| Forest Heath | East of England | 45.8 | 25.2 | +20.6 |
| Forest of Dean | South West | 35.2 | 21.8 | +13.5 |
| Fylde | North West | 33.2 | 20.7 | +12.5 |
| Gateshead | North East | 27.3 | 14.4 | +12.9 |
| Gedling | East Midlands | 34.2 | 16.6 | +17.6 |
| Glasgow City | Scotland | 9.8 | 5.7 | +4.1 |
| Gloucester | South West | 32.2 | 20.3 | +11.9 |
| Gosport | South East | 37.2 | 23.2 | +14.0 |
| Gravesham | South East | 41.5 | 19.8 | +21.7 |
| Great Yarmouth | East of England | 45.2 | 25.4 | +19.8 |
| Greenwich | London | 21 | 12.9 | +8.1 |
| Guildford | South East | 25.7 | 15.0 | +10.7 |
| Gwynedd | Wales | 19.8 | 9.6 | +10.2 |
| Hackney | London | 4.9 | 4.5 | +0.4 |
| Halton | North West | 28.4 | 17.8 | +10.6 |
| Hambleton | Yorkshire and the Humber | 29.3 | 16.3 | +13.0 |
| Hammersmith and Fulham | London | 12.3 | 7.2 | +5.1 |
| Harborough | East Midlands | 21.1 | 15.0 | +6.1 |
| Haringey | London | 7.1 | 4.4 | +2.7 |
| Harlow | East of England | 39.2 | 19.2 | +20.1 |
| Harrogate | Yorkshire and the Humber | 29.4 | 17.0 | +12.4 |
| Harrow | London | 14.0 | 9.4 | +4.6 |
| Hart | South East | 27.5 | 18.2 | +9.3 |

| | | | | |
|---|---|---|---|---|
| Hartlepool | North East | 39.0 | 25.3 | +13.7 |
| Hastings | South East | 30.6 | 19.5 | +11.1 |
| Havant | South East | 38.4 | 21.2 | +17.2 |
| Havering | London | 43.6 | 25.6 | +18.0 |
| Herefordshire, County of | West Midlands | 32.8 | 23.9 | +8.9 |
| Hertsmere | East of England | 29.0 | 16.6 | +12.4 |
| High Peak | East Midlands | 28.8 | 15.2 | +13.6 |
| Highland | Scotland | 12.0 | 6.6 | +5.4 |
| Hillingdon | London | 26.8 | 16.3 | +10.5 |
| Hinckley and Bosworth | East Midlands | 37.1 | 18.3 | +18.9 |
| Horsham | South East | 33.3 | 20.6 | +12.8 |
| Hounslow | London | 17.0 | 11.3 | +5.7 |
| Huntingdonshire | East of England | 36.7 | 22.4 | +14.4 |
| Hyndburn | North West | 34.6 | 17.7 | +16.8 |
| Inverclyde | Scotland | 9.3 | 4.9 | +4.4 |
| Ipswich | East of England | 31.1 | 17.0 | +14.1 |
| Isle of Anglesey | Wales | 27.6 | 12.4 | +15.2 |
| Isle of Wight | South East | 40.9 | 22.3 | +18.6 |
| Isles of Scilly | South West | 28.5 | 15.1 | +13.4 |
| Islington | London | 9.8 | 6.2 | +3.6 |
| Kensington and Chelsea | London | 14.7 | 8.4 | +6.3 |
| Kettering | East Midlands | 36.2 | 17.7 | +18.6 |
| King's Lynn and West Norfolk | East of England | 41.6 | 21.0 | +20.7 |
| Kingston upon Hull, City of | Yorkshire and the Humber | 35.8 | 21.4 | +14.3 |
| Kingston upon Thames | London | 19.4 | 11.5 | +7.9 |
| Kirklees | Yorkshire and the Humber | 26.9 | 15.9 | +11.0 |
| Knowsley | North West | 23.2 | 13.2 | +10.0 |
| Lambeth | London | 7.9 | 5.4 | +2.5 |
| Lancaster | North West | 26.6 | 16.4 | +10.3 |
| Leeds | Yorkshire and the Humber | 27.4 | 15.9 | +11.4 |
| Leicester | East Midlands | 18.2 | 8.7 | +9.5 |
| Lewes | South East | 32.5 | 18.9 | +13.6 |
| Lewisham | London | 12.3 | 8.9 | +3.4 |
| Lichfield | West Midlands | 35.5 | 22.5 | +13.0 |
| Lincoln | East Midlands | 30.1 | 16.2 | +13.9 |
| Liverpool | North West | 20.9 | 12.2 | +8.7 |
| Luton | East of England | 27.5 | 15.3 | +12.2 |
| Maidstone | South East | 37 | 19.8 | +17.2 |

(continued)

**Table A1.** Continued

| Area | Region | 2014 vote (%) | 2009 vote (%) | Change (2009–14) |
|---|---|---|---|---|
| Maldon | East of England | 41.1 | 23.8 | +17.3 |
| Malvern Hills | West Midlands | 31.4 | 22.3 | +9.2 |
| Manchester | North West | 15.9 | 8.9 | +7.0 |
| Mansfield | East Midlands | 40.1 | 20.8 | +19.2 |
| Medway | South East | 41.9 | 21.5 | +20.4 |
| Melton | East Midlands | 34 | 20.6 | +13.4 |
| Mendip | South West | 28.3 | 19.0 | +9.3 |
| Merthyr Tydfil | Wales | 33.8 | 12.5 | +21.3 |
| Merton | London | 16.0 | 9.8 | +6.2 |
| Mid Devon | South West | 32.5 | 23.2 | +9.3 |
| Mid Suffolk | East of England | 33.6 | 20.2 | +13.4 |
| Mid Sussex | South East | 31.9 | 17.5 | +14.4 |
| Middlesbrough | North East | 36.6 | 18.8 | +17.8 |
| Midlothian | Scotland | 10.7 | 4.8 | +5.9 |
| Milton Keynes | South East | 28.7 | 18.0 | +10.7 |
| Mole Valley | South East | 27.7 | 19.0 | +8.7 |
| Monmouthshire | Wales | 28.1 | 14.4 | +13.7 |
| Moray | Scotland | 13.6 | 8.0 | +5.6 |
| Neath Port Talbot | Wales | 26.4 | 10.8 | +15.6 |
| New Forest | South East | 37.3 | 22.8 | +14.5 |
| Newark and Sherwood | East Midlands | 32.4 | 15.5 | +17.0 |
| Newcastle upon Tyne | North East | 23.5 | 11.6 | +11.8 |
| Newcastle-under-Lyme | West Midlands | 35.2 | 25.6 | +9.6 |
| Newham | London | 8.3 | 5.7 | +2.6 |
| Newport | Wales | 32.6 | 14.5 | +18.1 |
| North Ayrshire | Scotland | 11.2 | 5.7 | +5.5 |
| North Devon | South West | 36.4 | 30.2 | +6.1 |
| North Dorset | South West | 35.6 | 22.3 | +13.3 |
| North East Derbyshire | East Midlands | 34.4 | 16.8 | +17.6 |
| North East Lincolnshire | Yorkshire and the Humber | 41.2 | 24.4 | +16.8 |
| North Hertfordshire | East of England | 26.7 | 15.6 | +11.0 |
| North Kesteven | East Midlands | 38.9 | 22.1 | +16.8 |
| North Lanarkshire | Scotland | 10.7 | 4.5 | +6.2 |
| North Lincolnshire | Yorkshire and the Humber | 36.2 | 21.4 | +14.8 |
| North Norfolk | East of England | 37.7 | 21.6 | +16.0 |
| North Somerset | South West | 32.9 | 21.9 | +11.0 |
| North Tyneside | North East | 26.3 | 13.2 | +13.1 |
| North Warwickshire | West Midlands | 39.3 | 23.7 | +15.6 |

| | | | | |
|---|---|---|---|---|
| North West Leicestershire | East Midlands | 35.0 | 16.3 | +18.7 |
| Northampton | East Midlands | 18.1 | 17.8 | +0.3 |
| Northumberland | North East | 27.4 | 14.8 | +12.6 |
| Norwich | East of England | 20.9 | 12.3 | +8.6 |
| Nottingham | East Midlands | 25.0 | 12.0 | +13.0 |
| Nuneaton and Bedworth | West Midlands | 32.8 | 19.9 | +12.9 |
| Oadby and Wigston | East Midlands | 30.4 | 16.5 | +13.9 |
| Oldham | North West | 29.1 | 15.8 | +13.3 |
| Orkney Islands | Scotland | 12.0 | 8.5 | +3.5 |
| Oxford | South East | 12.6 | 8.0 | +4.6 |
| Pembrokeshire | Wales | 28.1 | 12.6 | +15.5 |
| Pendle | North West | 26.3 | 14.5 | +11.8 |
| Perth and Kinross | Scotland | 10.1 | 6.1 | +4.0 |
| Peterborough | East of England | 33.5 | 20.2 | +13.3 |
| Plymouth | South West | 37 | 26.3 | +10.7 |
| Poole | South West | 38.5 | 24.8 | +13.7 |
| Portsmouth | South East | 34.2 | 19.1 | +15.1 |
| Powys | Wales | 27.7 | 16.1 | +11.6 |
| Preston | North West | 25.7 | 14.3 | +11.4 |
| Purbeck | South West | 34.0 | 24.0 | +9.9 |
| Reading | South East | 20.2 | 12.8 | +7.4 |
| Redbridge | London | 15.9 | 11.7 | +4.2 |
| Redcar and Cleveland | North East | 36.1 | 20.0 | +16.1 |
| Redditch | West Midlands | 36.2 | 25.1 | +11.1 |
| Reigate and Banstead | South East | 30.8 | 19.8 | +10.9 |
| Renfrewshire | Scotland | 10.4 | 4.4 | +6.0 |
| Rhondda Cynon Taf | Wales | 26.1 | 10.9 | +15.2 |
| Ribble Valley | North West | 33.5 | 19.1 | +14.4 |
| Richmond upon Thames | London | 15.5 | 9.1 | +6.4 |
| Richmondshire | Yorkshire and the Humber | 31.9 | 15.8 | +16.1 |
| Rochdale | North West | 30.0 | 16.2 | +13.8 |
| Rochford | East of England | 43.4 | 22.4 | +21.0 |
| Rossendale | North West | 31.5 | 16.8 | +14.7 |
| Rother | South East | 39.1 | 23.3 | +15.7 |
| Rotherham | Yorkshire and the Humber | 41.0 | 20.7 | +20.3 |
| Rugby | West Midlands | 29.3 | 20.1 | +9.1 |
| Runnymede | South East | 33.5 | 24.2 | +9.3 |
| Rushcliffe | East Midlands | 24.5 | 12.9 | +11.6 |
| Rushmoor | South East | 34.4 | 20.1 | +14.3 |
| Rutland | East Midlands | 31.2 | 18.4 | +12.8 |

(continued)

**Table A1.** Continued

| Area | Region | 2014 vote (%) | 2009 vote (%) | Change (2009–14) |
|------|--------|---------------|---------------|------------------|
| Ryedale | Yorkshire and the Humber | 29.3 | 17.2 | +12.1 |
| Salford | North West | 30.1 | 15.8 | +14.3 |
| Sandwell | West Midlands | 30.1 | 19.0 | +11.1 |
| Scarborough | Yorkshire and the Humber | 36.6 | 19.9 | +16.6 |
| Scottish Borders | Scotland | 12.4 | 7.4 | +5.0 |
| Sedgemoor | South West | 38 | 22.4 | +15.6 |
| Sefton | North West | 28.3 | 20.3 | +8.1 |
| Selby | Yorkshire and the Humber | 33.9 | 18.5 | +15.4 |
| Sevenoaks | South East | 36.9 | 18.6 | +18.3 |
| Sheffield | Yorkshire and the Humber | 27.7 | 14.4 | +13.3 |
| Shepway | South East | 43.3 | 22.7 | +20.6 |
| Shetland Islands | Scotland | 11.9 | 6.8 | +5.1 |
| Shropshire | West Midlands | 33.0 | 22.3 | +10.7 |
| Slough | South East | 20.0 | 15.0 | +5.0 |
| Solihull | West Midlands | 32.5 | 20.8 | +11.6 |
| South Ayrshire | Scotland | 10.3 | 5.7 | +4.6 |
| South Bucks | South East | 35.3 | 20.0 | +15.3 |
| South Cambridgeshire | East of England | 24.2 | 14.4 | +9.8 |
| South Derbyshire | East Midlands | 34.8 | 15.8 | +19.0 |
| South Gloucestershire | South West | 33.9 | 20.3 | +13.7 |
| South Hams | South West | 28.8 | 25.0 | +3.8 |
| South Holland | East Midlands | 48.5 | 24.1 | +24.4 |
| South Kesteven | East Midlands | 36.3 | 20.3 | +16.1 |
| South Lakeland | North West | 20.2 | 11.3 | +8.8 |
| South Lanarkshire | Scotland | 11.0 | 5.1 | +5.9 |
| South Norfolk | East of England | 31.9 | 18.7 | +13.2 |
| South Northamptonshire | East Midlands | 34.3 | 18.6 | +15.7 |
| South Oxfordshire | South East | 27.5 | 15.1 | +12.4 |
| South Ribble | North West | 34.6 | 18.0 | +16.5 |
| South Somerset | South West | 33.6 | 19.7 | +13.8 |
| South Staffordshire | West Midlands | 40.7 | 29.1 | +11.6 |
| South Tyneside | North East | 30.8 | 16.0 | +14.9 |
| Southampton | South East | 29.2 | 17.2 | +12.1 |
| Southend-on-Sea | East of England | 37.1 | 21.8 | +15.3 |
| Southwark | London | 11 | 6.8 | +4.2 |
| Spelthorne | South East | 40.1 | 25.4 | +14.7 |

| | | | | |
|---|---|---|---|---|
| St Albans | East of England | 21.4 | 13.2 | +8.3 |
| St Edmundsbury | East of England | 36.4 | 21.2 | +15.2 |
| St. Helens | North West | 25.7 | 14.9 | +10.8 |
| Stafford | West Midlands | 33.2 | 20.9 | +12.4 |
| Staffordshire Moorlands | West Midlands | 36.7 | 23.3 | +13.4 |
| Stevenage | East of England | 32.8 | 18.4 | +14.4 |
| Stirling | Scotland | 8.8 | 4.5 | +4.3 |
| Stockport | North West | 26.1 | 16.1 | +10.0 |
| Stockton-on-Tees | North East | 33.1 | 18.7 | +14.4 |
| Stoke-on-Trent | West Midlands | 39.7 | 22.1 | +17.6 |
| Stratford-on-Avon | West Midlands | 29.6 | 20 | +9.7 |
| Stroud | South West | 24.5 | 17.1 | +7.4 |
| Suffolk Coastal | East of England | 31.8 | 20.4 | +11.4 |
| Sunderland | North East | 30.0 | 14.0 | +16.0 |
| Surrey Heath | South East | 32.8 | 20.8 | +12.0 |
| Sutton | London | 27.1 | 16.9 | +10.2 |
| Swale | South East | 43.3 | 21.4 | +21.9 |
| Swansea | Wales | 28.2 | 12.3 | +15.9 |
| Swindon | South West | 30.7 | 22.9 | +7.8 |
| Tameside | North West | 31.7 | 16.5 | +15.2 |
| Tamworth | West Midlands | 34.7 | 25.1 | +9.7 |
| Tandridge | South East | 34.1 | 20.4 | +13.7 |
| Taunton Deane | South West | 31.5 | 19.9 | +11.6 |
| Teignbridge | South West | 46.7 | 25.7 | +21 |
| Telford and Wrekin | West Midlands | 36.2 | 25.3 | +10.8 |
| Tendring | East of England | 48.4 | 27.9 | +20.5 |
| Test Valley | South East | 32.8 | 18.0 | +14.8 |
| Tewkesbury | South West | 31.3 | 19.9 | +11.4 |
| Thanet | South East | 46.0 | 24.2 | +21.8 |
| Three Rivers | East of England | 29.3 | 15.6 | +13.7 |
| Thurrock | East of England | 45.9 | 21.7 | +24.2 |
| Tonbridge and Malling | South East | 35.9 | 19.2 | +16.7 |
| Torbay | South West | 43.2 | 34.4 | +8.8 |
| Torfaen | Wales | 28.2 | 11.4 | +16.8 |
| Torridge | South West | 40.3 | 31.1 | +9.2 |
| Tower Hamlets | London | 9.8 | 6.1 | +3.7 |
| Trafford | North West | 21.2 | 13.2 | +8.0 |
| Tunbridge Wells | South East | 30.1 | 18.1 | +11.9 |
| Uttlesford | East of England | 32.0 | 17.9 | +14.0 |
| Vale of Glamorgan | Wales | 32.5 | 18.8 | +13.7 |
| Wakefield | Yorkshire and the Humber | 36.0 | 18.8 | +17.3 |
| Walsall | West Midlands | 33.6 | 24.6 | +9.0 |
| Waltham Forest | London | 16.2 | 10.6 | +5.6 |

(continued)

**Table A1.** Continued

| Area | Region | 2014 vote (%) | 2009 vote (%) | Change (2009–14) |
|------|--------|---------------|---------------|------------------|
| Wandsworth | London | 10.9 | 6.5 | +4.4 |
| Warrington | North West | 29.5 | 15.6 | +13.9 |
| Warwick | West Midlands | 22.9 | 15.5 | +7.4 |
| Watford | East of England | 24.0 | 12.4 | +11.5 |
| Waveney | East of England | 36.9 | 24.2 | +12.7 |
| Waverley | South East | 26.4 | 15.4 | +11.0 |
| Wealden | South East | 37.4 | 22.6 | +14.8 |
| Wellingborough | East Midlands | 37.3 | 19.0 | +18.2 |
| Welwyn Hatfield | East of England | 29.8 | 15.1 | +14.8 |
| West Berkshire | South East | 29.0 | 14.5 | +14.5 |
| West Devon | South West | 34.1 | 25.6 | +8.5 |
| West Dorset | South West | 29.9 | 20.7 | +9.2 |
| West Dunbartonshire | Scotland | 10.5 | 4.6 | +5.9 |
| West Lancashire | North West | 29.7 | 20.5 | +9.2 |
| West Lindsey | East Midlands | 36.5 | 19.3 | +17.2 |
| West Lothian | Scotland | 11.9 | 5.1 | +6.8 |
| West Oxfordshire | South East | 25.2 | 16.6 | +8.6 |
| West Somerset | South West | 35.8 | 21.4 | +14.4 |
| Westminster | London | 13.6 | 7.8 | +5.8 |
| Weymouth and Portland | South West | 33.6 | 25.1 | +8.5 |
| Wigan | North West | 31.9 | 18.4 | +13.6 |
| Wiltshire | South West | 31.4 | 20.2 | +11.2 |
| Winchester | South East | 34.3 | 13.7 | +20.5 |
| Windsor and Maidenhead | South East | 28.2 | 17.0 | +11.2 |
| Wirral | North West | 26.2 | 16.9 | +9.3 |
| Woking | South East | 24.6 | 15.1 | +9.5 |
| Wokingham | South East | 25.2 | 17.5 | +7.7 |
| Wolverhampton | West Midlands | 31.3 | 20.2 | +11.1 |
| Worcester | West Midlands | 28.7 | 21.6 | +7.1 |
| Worthing | South East | 35.0 | 24.1 | +10.9 |
| Wrexham | Wales | 32.4 | 14.1 | +18.3 |
| Wychavon | West Midlands | 35.1 | 21.8 | +13.3 |
| Wycombe | South East | 30.2 | 18.4 | +11.8 |
| Wyre | North West | 35.4 | 20.2 | +15.2 |
| Wyre Forest | West Midlands | 36.6 | 27.3 | +9.3 |
| York | Yorkshire and the Humber | 23.9 | 13.7 | +10.2 |
| | Average: all areas | 29.1 | 16.9 | +12.2 |

*Source*: European Parliament Elections 2014 (June 2014), House of Commons Library Research Paper 14/32.

**Table A2.** Ukip's top 25 results at the 2014 European elections

| 2014 rank | 2009 rank | Area | Council control | 2014 vote (%) | 2009 vote (%) | Change (2009–14) |
|---|---|---|---|---|---|---|
| 1 | 25 | Boston | Conservative | 51.6 | 25.2 | +26.4 |
| 2 | 42 | South Holland | Conservative | 48.5 | 24.1 | +24.4 |
| 3 | 7 | Tendring | Conservative | 48.4 | 27.9 | +20.5 |
| 4 | 6 | Castle Point | Conservative | 47.8 | 28.2 | +19.6 |
| 5 | 33 | Fenland | Conservative | 47.3 | 24.6 | +22.7 |
| 6 | 16 | Teignbridge | Conservative | 46.7 | 25.7 | +21.0 |
| 7 | 38 | Thanet | NOC | 46.0 | 24.2 | +21.8 |
| 8 | 75 | Thurrock | Labour | 45.9 | 21.7 | +24.2 |
| 9 | 24 | Forest Heath | Conservative | 45.8 | 25.2 | +20.6 |
| 10 | 21 | Great Yarmouth | Labour | 45.2 | 25.4 | +19.8 |
| 11 | 55 | Basildon | Conservative | 44.8 | 22.9 | +21.9 |
| 12 | 35 | East Lindsey | NOC | 44.2 | 24.5 | +19.7 |
| 13 | 217 | Hillingdon | Conservative | 43.6 | 16.3 | +27.3 |
| 14 | 61 | Rochford | Conservative | 43.4 | 22.4 | +21.0 |
| 15 | 81 | Swale | Conservative | 43.3 | 21.4 | +21.9 |
| 16 | 57 | Shepway | Conservative | 43.3 | 22.7 | +20.6 |
| 17 | 1 | Torbay | Conservative | 43.2 | 34.4 | +8.8 |
| 18 | 13 | Arun | Conservative | 42.6 | 26.3 | +16.3 |
| 19 | 32 | Breckland | Conservative | 42.2 | 24.8 | +17.4 |
| 20 | 78 | Medway | Conservative | 41.9 | 21.5 | +20.4 |
| 21 | 92 | King's Lynn and West Norfolk | Conservative | 41.6 | 21.0 | +20.6 |
| 22 | 130 | Gravesham | Labour | 41.5 | 19.8 | +21.7 |
| 23 | 80 | Broxbourne | Conservative | 41.4 | 21.4 | +20.0 |
| 24 | 36 | North East Lincolnshire | Labour | 41.2 | 24.4 | +16.8 |
| 25 | 46 | Maldon | Conservative | 41.1 | 23.8 | +17.3 |
| | | Average: top 25 | | 44.5 | 24.0 | +20.5 |

*Note*: NOC = no overall control.

*Source*: European Parliament Elections 2014 (June 2014), House of Commons Library Research Paper 14/32.

**Table A3.** Ukip's strongest results at the 2014 European elections, Labour-controlled areas

| 2014 rank (Labour only) | 2009 rank (Labour only) | Area | 2014 vote (%) | 2009 vote (%) | Change (2009–14) |
|---|---|---|---|---|---|
| 1 | 2 | Thurrock | 45.9 | 21.7 | +24.2 |
| 2 | 4 | Great Yarmouth | 45.2 | 25.4 | +19.8 |
| 3 | 16 | Gravesham | 41.5 | 19.8 | +21.7 |
| 4 | 8 | North East Lincolnshire | 41.2 | 24.4 | +16.8 |
| 5 | 15 | Rotherham | 41.0 | 20.7 | +20.3 |
| 6 | 14 | Mansfield | 40.1 | 20.8 | +19.3 |
| 7 | 11 | Stoke-on-Trent | 39.7 | 22.1 | +17.6 |
| 8 | 10 | North Warwickshire | 39.3 | 23.7 | +15.6 |
| 9 | 17 | Harlow Council | 39.2 | 19.2 | +20.0 |
| 10 | 5 | Hartlepool | 39.0 | 25.3 | +13.7 |
| 11 | 9 | Cannock Chase | 38.8 | 24.4 | +14.4 |
| 12 | 1 | Dudley | 38.4 | 27.5 | +10.9 |
| 13 | 22 | Ashfield | 37.4 | 15.6 | +21.8 |
| 14 | 2 | Plymouth | 37.0 | 26.3 | +10.7 |
| 15 | — | Middlesbrough | 36.6 | — | — |
| 16 | 23 | Bolsover | 36.3 | 14.8 | +21.5 |
| 17 | 7 | Redditch | 36.2 | 25.1 | +11.1 |
| 18 | 6 | Telford and Wrekin | 36.2 | 25.3 | +10.9 |
| 19 | 18 | Wakefield | 36.0 | 18.8 | +17.2 |
| 20 | 19 | Barnsley | 35.9 | 18.7 | +17.2 |
| 21 | 13 | Kingston upon Hull | 35.8 | 21.4 | +14.4 |
| 22 | 3 | Newcastle-under-Lyme | 35.2 | 25.6 | +9.6 |
| 23 | 21 | Doncaster | 35.1 | 16.0 | +19.1 |
| 24 | 20 | Corby | 35.0 | 16.1 | +18.9 |
| 25 | 24 | Merthyr Tydfil | 34.8 | 12.5 | +22.3 |
| | Average: Labour top 25 | | 38.3 | 21.3 | +17.0 |

*Source*: European Parliament Elections 2014 (June 2014), House of Commons Library Research Paper 14/32.

## 2014 LOCAL ELECTIONS

**Table A4.** Ukip's 2014 local election vote share and seats by region

| Region | 2014 vote (%) | No. of seats |
|---|---|---|
| Yorkshire and Humber | 29.4 | 25 |
| East of England | 27.7 | 53 |
| West Midlands | 27.1 | 30 |
| East Midlands | 25.8 | 4 |
| North East | 24.6 | 2 |
| North West | 22.9 | 6 |
| South East | 22.2 | 26 |
| South West | 22.0 | 5 |
| London | 14.9 | 12 |
| All | 23.1 | 163 |

*Source*: Elections Centre, University of Plymouth.

**Table A5.** Ukip's 2014 local election vote share and seats by county

| Rank | County | 2014 vote (%) | No. of seats |
|---|---|---|---|
| 1 | Norfolk | 35.9 | 10 |
| 2 | Essex | 33.3 | 36 |
| 3 | South Yorkshire | 33.3 | 14 |
| 4 | Humberside | 32.8 | 8 |
| 5 | Staffordshire | 30.8 | 10 |
| 6 | Cleveland | 30.4 | 2 |
| 7 | Northants | 30.2 | 2 |
| 8 | West Sussex | 27.9 | 6 |
| 9 | Nottinghamshire | 27.1 | 0 |
| 10 | Devon | 27.0 | 3 |
| 11 | West Midlands | 26.8 | 13 |
| 12 | Cambridgeshire | 26.7 | 6 |
| 13 | Worcestershire | 26.4 | 7 |
| 14 | West Yorkshire | 25.7 | 3 |
| 15 | Kent | 25.6 | 4 |
| 16 | Cheshire | 25.2 | 0 |
| 17 | Dorset | 25.0 | 1 |
| 18 | Manchester | 24.7 | 4 |
| 19 | Derbyshire | 24.4 | 2 |
| 20 | Suffolk | 24.3 | 0 |
| 21 | Lancashire | 24.2 | 2 |
| 22 | Tyne and Wear | 24.0 | 0 |
| 23 | Warwickshire | 23.7 | 0 |
| 24 | Hampshire | 23.1 | 12 |
| 25 | East Sussex | 22.7 | 0 |

(continued)

**Table A5.** Continued

| Rank | County | 2014 vote (%) | No. of seats |
|------|--------|---------------|--------------|
| 26 | Wiltshire | 22.1 | 0 |
| 27 | Hertfordshire | 21.5 | I |
| 28 | Surrey | 21.3 | 2 |
| 29 | North Yorkshire | 20.2 | 0 |
| 30 | Bucks | 20.1 | I |
| 31 | Cumbria | 19.9 | 0 |
| 32 | Merseyside | 19.5 | 0 |
| 33 | Oxfordshire | 18.9 | 0 |
| 34 | Gloucestershire | 18.6 | 0 |
| 35 | Avon | 17.5 | I |
| 36 | Berkshire | 17.1 | I |
| 37 | London | 14.9 | 12 |
|  | Total |  | 163 |

*Source*: Elections Centre, University of Plymouth.

**Table A6.** Ukip's top 25 results in the 2014 local elections

| 2014 rank | Ward | Local authority | Region | 2014 vote (%) | Change (2010–14) |
|-----------|------|-----------------|--------|---------------|------------------|
| 1 | Ramsey | Huntingdonshire | East of England | 63.6 | +18.5 |
| 2 | Milnshaw | Hyndburn | North West | 54.3 | +54.3 |
| 3 | Wingfield | Rotherham | Yorkshire and the Humber | 53.2 | +47.0 |
| 4 | Rother Vale | Rotherham | Yorkshire and the Humber | 53.1 | +53.1 |
| 5 | Valley | Rotherham | Yorkshire and the Humber | 53.1 | +53.1 |
| 6 | Rawmarsh | Rotherham | Yorkshire and the Humber | 51.9 | +38.0 |
| 7 | Silverwood | Rotherham | Yorkshire and the Humber | 51.8 | +41.2 |
| 8 | Hellaby | Rotherham | Yorkshire and the Humber | 51.7 | +37.2 |
| 9 | Knutton and Silverdale | Newcastle-under-Lyme | West Midlands | 51.7 | +27.9 |
| 10 | Belhus | Thurrock | East of England | 51.6 | +51.6 |
| 11 | Holditch | Newcastle-under-Lyme | West Midlands | 50.6 | +24.5 |
| 12 | Keppel | Rotherham | Yorkshire and the Humber | 49.6 | +39.6 |
| 13 | Brinsworth and Catcliffe | Rotherham | Yorkshire and the Humber | 49.4 | +42.0 |
| 14 | Cedar Hall | Castle Point | East of England | 49.4 | +49.4 |

| 15 | Alvaston | Derby | East Midlands | 49.3 | +49.3 |
| 16 | Bradwell South and Hopton | Great Yarmouth | East of England | 49.7 | +49.7 |
| 17 | Humberston and New Waltham | North East Lincolnshire | Yorkshire and the Humber | 48.8 | +40.5 |
| 18 | Wickford Castledon | Basildon | East of England | 48.7 | +48.7 |
| 19 | Princes End | Sandwell | West Midlands | 48.6 | +48.6 |
| 20 | Grange (East of England) | Rochford | East of England | 47.7 | +47.7 |
| 21 | Honicknowle | Plymouth | South West | 47.3 | +35.4 |
| 22 | Aveley and Uplands | Thurrock | East of England | 47.2 | +32.7 |
| 23 | Kingshurst and Fordbridge | Solihull | West Midlands | 46.8 | +46.8 |
| 24 | Whitehouse | Rochford | East of England | 46.7 | +46.7 |
| 25 | West Heath | Rushmoor | South East | 46.6 | — |

*Source*: Elections Centre, University of Plymouth.

## 2015 GENERAL ELECTION

**Table A7.** Ukip's 2010 and 2015 general election vote share by parliamentary constituency

| Constituency | Region | 2015 vote (%) | 2010 vote (%) | Change (2010–15) |
|---|---|---|---|---|
| Aberavon | Wales | 15.8 | 1.6 | +14.2 |
| Aberconwy | Wales | 11.5 | 2.1 | +9.4 |
| Aberdeen North | Scotland | 0.0 | 0.0 | +0.0 |
| Aberdeen South | Scotland | 1.8 | 0.0 | +1.8 |
| Airdrie and Shotts | Scotland | 2.5 | 0.0 | +2.5 |
| Aldershot | South East | 17.9 | 4.5 | +13.4 |
| Aldridge-Brownhills | West Midlands | 19.6 | 0.0 | +19.6 |
| Altrincham and Sale West | North West | 8.0 | 3.2 | +4.8 |
| Alyn and Deeside | Wales | 17.6 | 2.5 | +15.1 |
| Amber Valley | East Midlands | 15.9 | 2.0 | +13.9 |
| Angus | Scotland | 3.0 | 1.5 | +1.5 |
| Arfon | Wales | 8.5 | 2.6 | +5.9 |
| Argyll and Bute | Scotland | 2.5 | 0.0 | +2.5 |
| Arundel and South Downs | South East | 14.4 | 5.7 | +8.7 |
| Ashfield | East Midlands | 21.4 | 1.9 | +19.5 |

(*continued*)

**Table A7.** Continued

| Constituency | Region | 2015 vote (%) | 2010 vote (%) | Change (2010–15) |
|---|---|---|---|---|
| Ashford | South East | 18.8 | 4.5 | +14.3 |
| Ashton-under-Lyne | North West | 21.8 | 4.4 | +17.4 |
| Aylesbury | South East | 19.7 | 6.8 | +12.9 |
| Ayr, Carrick and Cumnock | Scotland | 2.5 | 0.0 | +2.5 |
| Banbury | South East | 13.9 | 5.0 | +8.9 |
| Banff and Buchan | Scotland | 0.0 | 0.0 | +0.0 |
| Barking | London | 22.2 | 2.9 | +19.3 |
| Barnsley Central | Yorkshire and the Humber | 21.7 | 4.7 | +17.0 |
| Barnsley East | Yorkshire and the Humber | 23.5 | 4.5 | +19.0 |
| Barrow and Furness | North West | 11.7 | 1.9 | +9.8 |
| Basildon and Billericay | East of England | 19.8 | 3.8 | +16.0 |
| Basingstoke | South East | 15.6 | 4.1 | +11.5 |
| Bassetlaw | East Midlands | 16.0 | 3.6 | +12.4 |
| Bath | South West | 6.2 | 1.9 | +4.3 |
| Batley and Spen | Yorkshire and the Humber | 18.0 | 0.0 | +18.0 |
| Battersea | London | 3.1 | 1.0 | +2.1 |
| Beaconsfield | South East | 13.8 | 5.0 | +8.9 |
| Beckenham | London | 12.5 | 3.3 | +9.3 |
| Bedford | East of England | 9.6 | 2.5 | +7.1 |
| Bermondsey and Old Southwark | London | 6.3 | 0.0 | +6.3 |
| Berwickshire, Roxburgh and Selkirk | Scotland | 2.4 | 1.2 | +1.2 |
| Berwick-upon-Tweed | North East | 11.2 | 3.2 | +8.0 |
| Bethnal Green and Bow | London | 6.1 | 0.0 | +6.1 |
| Beverley and Holderness | Yorkshire and the Humber | 16.7 | 3.5 | +13.2 |
| Bexhill and Battle | South East | 18.4 | 0.0 | +18.4 |
| Bexleyheath and Crayford | London | 21.0 | 3.6 | +17.4 |
| Birkenhead | North West | 9.8 | 0.0 | +9.8 |
| Birmingham, Edgbaston | West Midlands | 10.1 | 1.8 | +8.3 |
| Birmingham, Erdington | West Midlands | 17.4 | 2.4 | +15.0 |
| Birmingham, Hall Green | West Midlands | 4.5 | 2.0 | +2.6 |
| Birmingham, Hodge Hill | West Midlands | 11.3 | 1.7 | +9.6 |
| Birmingham, Ladywood | West Midlands | 5.0 | 2.5 | +2.5 |
| Birmingham, Northfield | West Midlands | 16.7 | 3.3 | +13.4 |
| Birmingham, Perry Barr | West Midlands | 12.2 | 4.0 | +8.2 |

| Birmingham, Selly Oak | West Midlands | 12.7 | 2.4 | +10.3 |
| Birmingham, Yardley | West Midlands | 16.1 | 2.9 | +13.2 |
| Bishop Auckland | North East | 17.8 | 2.7 | +15.1 |
| Blackburn | North West | 14.3 | 2.1 | +12.2 |
| Blackley and Broughton | North West | 16.5 | 2.6 | +13.9 |
| Blackpool North and Cleveleys | North West | 14.8 | 4.1 | +10.7 |
| Blackpool South | North West | 17.3 | 3.8 | +13.5 |
| Blaenau Gwent | Wales | 17.9 | 1.5 | +16.4 |
| Blaydon | North East | 17.5 | 0.0 | +17.5 |
| Blyth Valley | North East | 22.3 | 4.3 | +18.0 |
| Bognor Regis and Littlehampton | South East | 21.7 | 6.5 | +15.2 |
| Bolsover | East Midlands | 21.0 | 3.9 | +17.1 |
| Bolton North East | North West | 18.8 | 4.2 | +14.6 |
| Bolton South East | North West | 23.6 | 4.0 | +19.7 |
| Bolton West | North West | 15.3 | 4.0 | +11.3 |
| Bootle | North West | 10.9 | 6.1 | +4.8 |
| Boston and Skegness | East Midlands | 33.8 | 9.5 | +24.3 |
| Bosworth | East Midlands | 17.4 | 2.0 | +15.4 |
| Bournemouth East | South West | 16.5 | 6.9 | +9.6 |
| Bournemouth West | South West | 18.5 | 7.2 | +11.3 |
| Bracknell | South East | 15.7 | 4.4 | +11.3 |
| Bradford East | Yorkshire and the Humber | 9.9 | 0.0 | +9.9 |
| Bradford South | Yorkshire and the Humber | 24.1 | 3.5 | +20.6 |
| Bradford West | Yorkshire and the Humber | 7.8 | 2.0 | +5.8 |
| Braintree | East of England | 18.8 | 5.0 | +13.8 |
| Brecon and Radnorshire | Wales | 8.3 | 2.3 | +6.0 |
| Brent Central | London | 3.9 | 0.0 | +3.9 |
| Brent North | London | 3.9 | 0.7 | +3.2 |
| Brentford and Isleworth | London | 5.6 | 1.6 | +4.0 |
| Brentwood and Ongar | East of England | 16.8 | 4.0 | +12.8 |
| Bridgend | Wales | 15.0 | 2.1 | +12.9 |
| Bridgwater and West Somerset | South West | 19.2 | 4.8 | +14.4 |
| Brigg and Goole | Yorkshire and the Humber | 15.5 | 4.0 | +11.5 |
| Brighton, Kemptown | South East | 9.8 | 3.2 | +6.6 |
| Brighton, Pavilion | South East | 5.0 | 1.8 | +3.2 |
| Bristol East | South West | 15.5 | 3.4 | +12.2 |
| Bristol North West | South West | 9.4 | 2.3 | +7.1 |
| Bristol South | South West | 16.5 | 2.6 | +13.9 |

(continued)

**Table A7.** Continued

| Constituency | Region | 2015 vote (%) | 2010 vote (%) | Change (2010–15) |
|---|---|---|---|---|
| Bristol West | South West | 3.0 | 1.2 | +1.8 |
| Broadland | East of England | 16.7 | 4.5 | +12.2 |
| Bromley and Chislehurst | London | 14.3 | 3.3 | +11.0 |
| Bromsgrove | West Midlands | 15.6 | 5.7 | +9.9 |
| Broxbourne | East of England | 19.7 | 4.1 | +15.6 |
| Broxtowe | East Midlands | 10.6 | 2.3 | +8.3 |
| Buckingham | South East | 21.7 | 17.4 | +4.3 |
| Burnley | North West | 17.3 | 2.2 | +15.1 |
| Burton | West Midlands | 17.5 | 2.9 | +14.6 |
| Bury North | North West | 12.4 | 2.9 | +9.6 |
| Bury South | North West | 13.3 | 2.1 | +11.2 |
| Bury St Edmunds | East of England | 14.7 | 5.1 | +9.6 |
| Caerphilly | Wales | 19.3 | 2.3 | +17.0 |
| Caithness, Sutherland and Easter Ross | Scotland | 2.9 | 0.0 | +2.9 |
| Calder Valley | Yorkshire and the Humber | 11.1 | 2.3 | +8.8 |
| Camberwell and Peckham | London | 4.7 | 0.0 | +4.7 |
| Camborne and Redruth | South West | 14.8 | 5.1 | +9.7 |
| Cambridge | East of England | 5.2 | 2.4 | +2.8 |
| Cannock Chase | West Midlands | 17.5 | 3.5 | +14.0 |
| Canterbury | South East | 13.6 | 3.9 | +9.7 |
| Cardiff Central | Wales | 6.5 | 2.1 | +4.4 |
| Cardiff North | Wales | 7.7 | 2.4 | +5.3 |
| Cardiff South and Penarth | Wales | 13.8 | 2.6 | +11.2 |
| Cardiff West | Wales | 11.2 | 2.7 | +8.5 |
| Carlisle | North West | 12.4 | 2.3 | +10.1 |
| Carmarthen East and Dinefwr | Wales | 11.1 | 3.4 | +7.7 |
| Carmarthen West and Pembrokeshire South | Wales | 11.6 | 2.8 | +8.8 |
| Carshalton and Wallington | London | 14.8 | 2.9 | +11.9 |
| Castle Point | East of England | 31.2 | 0.0 | +31.2 |
| Central Ayrshire | Scotland | 0.0 | 0.0 | +0.0 |
| Central Devon | South West | 13.2 | 5.3 | +7.9 |
| Central Suffolk and North Ipswich | East of England | 13.8 | 4.4 | +9.4 |
| Ceredigion | Wales | 10.2 | 2.6 | +7.7 |
| Charnwood | East Midlands | 15.9 | 3.4 | +12.5 |
| Chatham and Aylesford | South East | 19.9 | 3.0 | +16.9 |

| | | | | |
|---|---|---|---|---|
| Cheadle | North West | 8.3 | 2.7 | +5.6 |
| Chelmsford | East of England | 14.2 | 2.8 | +11.4 |
| Chelsea and Fulham | London | 5.1 | 1.2 | +3.9 |
| Cheltenham | South West | 7.1 | 2.3 | +4.8 |
| Chesham and Amersham | South East | 13.7 | 4.1 | +9.6 |
| Chesterfield | East Midlands | 16.5 | 3.1 | +13.4 |
| Chichester | South East | 14.9 | 6.8 | +8.1 |
| Chingford and Woodford Green | London | 12.9 | 2.6 | +10.3 |
| Chippenham | South West | 10.6 | 3.4 | +7.2 |
| Chipping Barnet | London | 7.8 | 2.9 | +5.0 |
| Chorley | North West | 13.5 | 4.1 | +9.4 |
| Christchurch | South West | 21.5 | 8.5 | +13.0 |
| Cities of London and Westminster | London | 5.2 | 1.8 | +3.4 |
| City of Chester | North West | 8.1 | 2.6 | +5.5 |
| City of Durham | North East | 11.4 | 1.9 | +9.6 |
| Clacton | East of England | 44.4 | 0.0 | +44.4 |
| Cleethorpes | Yorkshire and the Humber | 18.5 | 7.1 | +11.4 |
| Clwyd South | Wales | 15.6 | 2.4 | +13.2 |
| Clwyd West | Wales | 13.1 | 2.3 | +10.8 |
| Coatbridge, Chryston and Bellshill | Scotland | 2.1 | 0.0 | +2.1 |
| Colchester | East of England | 12.1 | 2.9 | +9.2 |
| Colne Valley | Yorkshire and the Humber | 10.1 | 2.1 | +8.0 |
| Congleton | North West | 13.6 | 4.2 | +9.4 |
| Copeland | North West | 15.5 | 2.3 | +13.2 |
| Corby | East Midlands | 13.7 | 0.0 | +13.7 |
| Coventry North East | West Midlands | 14.9 | 3.0 | +11.9 |
| Coventry North West | West Midlands | 15.7 | 2.8 | +12.9 |
| Coventry South | West Midlands | 13.1 | 3.9 | +9.3 |
| Crawley | South East | 14.4 | 2.9 | +11.5 |
| Crewe and Nantwich | North West | 14.5 | 2.8 | +11.7 |
| Croydon Central | London | 9.1 | 2.0 | +7.1 |
| Croydon North | London | 5.4 | 1.7 | +3.7 |
| Croydon South | London | 10.5 | 4.5 | +6.1 |
| Cumbernauld, Kilsyth and Kirkintilloch East | Scotland | 0.0 | 0.0 | +0.0 |
| Cynon Valley | Wales | 16.3 | 3.4 | +13.0 |
| Dagenham and Rainham | London | 29.8 | 3.6 | +26.3 |
| Darlington | North East | 13.1 | 2.8 | +10.3 |
| Dartford | South East | 19.9 | 3.7 | +16.2 |
| Daventry | East Midlands | 15.8 | 4.5 | +11.3 |

(continued)

**Table A7.** Continued

| Constituency | Region | 2015 vote (%) | 2010 vote (%) | Change (2010–15) |
|---|---|---|---|---|
| Delyn | Wales | 16.4 | 1.8 | +14.6 |
| Denton and Reddish | North West | 18.7 | 5.5 | +13.2 |
| Derby North | East Midlands | 14.6 | 1.8 | +12.8 |
| Derby South | East Midlands | 15.5 | 4.4 | +11.1 |
| Derbyshire Dales | East Midlands | 11.6 | 3.8 | +7.8 |
| Devizes | South West | 15.4 | 4.5 | +10.9 |
| Dewsbury | Yorkshire and the Humber | 12.4 | 0.0 | +12.4 |
| Don Valley | Yorkshire and the Humber | 23.5 | 4.4 | +19.1 |
| Doncaster Central | Yorkshire and the Humber | 24.1 | 3.4 | +20.7 |
| Doncaster North | Yorkshire and the Humber | 22.6 | 4.3 | +18.3 |
| Dover | South East | 20.3 | 3.5 | +16.8 |
| Dudley North | West Midlands | 24.0 | 8.5 | +15.5 |
| Dudley South | West Midlands | 18.9 | 8.2 | +10.7 |
| Dulwich and West Norwood | London | 3.1 | 1.5 | +1.6 |
| Dumfries and Galloway | Scotland | 2.3 | 1.3 | +1.0 |
| Dumfriesshire, Clydesdale and Tweeddale | Scotland | 2.8 | 1.4 | +1.4 |
| Dundee East | Scotland | 0.0 | 1.1 | −1.1 |
| Dundee West | Scotland | 0.0 | 0.0 | 0.0 |
| Dunfermline and West Fife | Scotland | 0.0 | 1.3 | −1.3 |
| Dwyfor Meirionnydd | Wales | 10.8 | 2.7 | +8.1 |
| Ealing Central and Acton | London | 3.8 | 1.6 | +2.2 |
| Ealing North | London | 8.1 | 1.4 | +6.7 |
| Ealing, Southall | London | 4.1 | 0.0 | +4.1 |
| Easington | North East | 18.7 | 4.7 | +14.0 |
| East Devon | South West | 12.6 | 8.2 | +4.4 |
| East Dunbartonshire | Scotland | 1.0 | 1.1 | −0.1 |
| East Ham | London | 5.0 | 0.0 | +5.0 |
| East Hampshire | South East | 12.0 | 2.9 | +9.1 |
| East Kilbride, Strathaven and Lesmahagow | Scotland | 2.0 | 0.0 | +2.0 |
| East Lothian | Scotland | 2.0 | 1.1 | +0.9 |
| East Renfrewshire | Scotland | 1.6 | 0.7 | +0.9 |
| East Surrey | South East | 17.0 | 6.9 | +10.1 |
| East Worthing and Shoreham | South East | 16.6 | 6.2 | +10.4 |

| East Yorkshire | Yorkshire and the Humber | 17.9 | 4.2 | +13.7 |
|---|---|---|---|---|
| Eastbourne | South East | 11.6 | 2.5 | +9.1 |
| Eastleigh | South East | 15.8 | 3.6 | +12.2 |
| Eddisbury | North West | 12.2 | 4.3 | +8.0 |
| Edinburgh East | Scotland | 1.9 | 0.0 | +1.9 |
| Edinburgh North and Leith | Scotland | 1.5 | 0.0 | +1.5 |
| Edinburgh South | Scotland | 1.2 | 0.0 | +1.2 |
| Edinburgh South West | Scotland | 2.1 | 0.0 | +2.1 |
| Edinburgh West | Scotland | 1.9 | 0.0 | +1.9 |
| Edmonton | London | 8.1 | 2.6 | +5.5 |
| Ellesmere Port and Neston | North West | 12.0 | 3.7 | +8.3 |
| Elmet and Rothwell | Yorkshire and the Humber | 11.1 | 2.9 | +8.2 |
| Eltham | London | 15.0 | 2.4 | +12.6 |
| Enfield North | London | 9.0 | 2.1 | +6.9 |
| Enfield, Southgate | London | 4.6 | 1.1 | +3.5 |
| Epping Forest | East of England | 18.3 | 4.0 | +14.3 |
| Epsom and Ewell | South East | 12.5 | 4.6 | +7.9 |
| Erewash | East Midlands | 16.1 | 1.8 | +14.3 |
| Erith and Thamesmead | London | 17.3 | 2.7 | +14.6 |
| Esher and Walton | South East | 9.7 | 3.3 | +6.4 |
| Exeter | South West | 9.4 | 3.7 | +5.7 |
| Falkirk | Scotland | 3.0 | 2.5 | +0.5 |
| Fareham | South East | 15.4 | 4.1 | +11.3 |
| Faversham and Mid Kent | South East | 18.0 | 3.7 | +14.3 |
| Feltham and Heston | London | 12.6 | 2.0 | +10.6 |
| Filton and Bradley Stoke | South West | 14.8 | 3.1 | +11.7 |
| Finchley and Golders Green | London | 3.4 | 1.7 | +1.7 |
| Folkestone and Hythe | South East | 22.8 | 4.6 | +18.2 |
| Forest of Dean | South West | 17.8 | 5.2 | +12.6 |
| Fylde | North West | 12.8 | 4.5 | +8.4 |
| Gainsborough | East Midlands | 15.7 | 4.2 | +11.5 |
| Garston and Halewood | North West | 9.2 | 3.6 | +5.6 |
| Gateshead | North East | 17.8 | 2.9 | +14.9 |
| Gedling | East Midlands | 14.4 | 3.0 | +11.4 |
| Gillingham and Rainham | South East | 19.5 | 3.2 | +16.3 |
| Glasgow Central | Scotland | 2.0 | 0.8 | +1.2 |
| Glasgow East | Scotland | 2.6 | 0.7 | +2.0 |
| Glasgow North | Scotland | 1.3 | 0.0 | +1.3 |
| Glasgow North East | Scotland | 0.0 | 0.0 | +0.0 |

(*continued*)

**Table A7.** Continued

| Constituency | Region | 2015 vote (%) | 2010 vote (%) | Change (2010–15) |
|---|---|---|---|---|
| Glasgow North West | Scotland | 0.0 | 0.0 | +0.0 |
| Glasgow South | Scotland | 0.0 | 0.0 | +0.0 |
| Glasgow South West | Scotland | 2.4 | 0.0 | +2.4 |
| Glenrothes | Scotland | 0.0 | 1.1 | −1.1 |
| Gloucester | South West | 14.3 | 3.6 | +10.7 |
| Gordon | Scotland | 2.0 | 0.0 | +2.0 |
| Gosport | South East | 19.4 | 3.2 | +16.2 |
| Gower | Wales | 11.2 | 1.6 | +9.6 |
| Grantham and Stamford | East Midlands | 17.5 | 3.0 | +14.5 |
| Gravesham | South East | 18.6 | 4.8 | +13.8 |
| Great Grimsby | Yorkshire and the Humber | 25.0 | 6.2 | +18.8 |
| Great Yarmouth | East of England | 23.1 | 4.8 | +18.3 |
| Greenwich and Woolwich | London | 8.3 | 0.0 | +8.3 |
| Guildford | South East | 8.8 | 1.8 | +7.0 |
| Hackney North and Stoke Newington | London | 2.2 | 0.0 | +2.2 |
| Hackney South and Shoreditch | London | 3.8 | 1.5 | +2.3 |
| Halesowen and Rowley Regis | West Midlands | 16.6 | 6.4 | +10.2 |
| Halifax | Yorkshire and the Humber | 12.8 | 1.5 | +11.3 |
| Haltemprice and Howden | Yorkshire and the Humber | 13.9 | 0.0 | +13.9 |
| Halton | North West | 14.1 | 3.0 | +11.1 |
| Hammersmith | London | 4.4 | 1.2 | +3.2 |
| Hampstead and Kilburn | London | 2.8 | 0.8 | +2.0 |
| Harborough | East Midlands | 14.4 | 2.7 | +11.7 |
| Harlow | East of England | 16.3 | 3.6 | +12.7 |
| Harrogate and Knaresborough | Yorkshire and the Humber | 10.6 | 2.0 | +8.6 |
| Harrow East | London | 4.8 | 1.9 | +2.9 |
| Harrow West | London | 4.4 | 2.1 | +2.3 |
| Hartlepool | North East | 28.0 | 7.0 | +21.0 |
| Harwich and North Essex | East of England | 17.5 | 5.2 | +12.3 |
| Hastings and Rye | South East | 13.3 | 2.8 | +10.5 |
| Havant | South East | 20.6 | 6.0 | +14.7 |
| Hayes and Harlington | London | 12.0 | 0.0 | +12.0 |
| Hazel Grove | North West | 12.2 | 5.1 | +7.1 |
| Hemel Hempstead | East of England | 14.6 | 2.5 | +12.1 |

| Hemsworth | Yorkshire and the Humber | 20.2 | 0.0 | +20.2 |
|---|---|---|---|---|
| Hendon | London | 5.2 | 2.1 | +3.1 |
| Henley | South East | 10.9 | 3.4 | +7.5 |
| Hereford and South Herefordshire | West Midlands | 16.8 | 3.4 | +13.4 |
| Hertford and Stortford | East of England | 13.4 | 3.1 | +10.3 |
| Hertsmere | East of England | 12.7 | 3.6 | +9.1 |
| Hexham | North East | 9.9 | 0.0 | +9.9 |
| Heywood and Middleton | North West | 32.2 | 2.6 | +29.6 |
| High Peak | East Midlands | 11.4 | 3.4 | +8.0 |
| Hitchin and Harpenden | East of England | 8.9 | 3.0 | +5.9 |
| Holborn and St Pancras | London | 5.0 | 1.1 | +3.9 |
| Hornchurch and Upminster | London | 25.3 | 5.3 | +20.0 |
| Hornsey and Wood Green | London | 2.2 | 0.0 | +2.2 |
| Horsham | South East | 14.0 | 5.1 | +8.9 |
| Houghton and Sunderland South | North East | 21.5 | 2.7 | +18.8 |
| Hove | South East | 6.3 | 2.4 | +3.9 |
| Huddersfield | Yorkshire and the Humber | 14.7 | 0.0 | +14.7 |
| Huntingdon | East of England | 16.9 | 6.0 | +10.9 |
| Hyndburn | North West | 21.3 | 3.5 | +17.8 |
| Ilford North | London | 8.9 | 1.9 | +7.1 |
| Ilford South | London | 5.2 | 2.2 | +3.0 |
| Inverclyde | Scotland | 1.6 | 1.2 | +0.5 |
| Inverness, Nairn, Badenoch and Strathspey | Scotland | 2.1 | 1.2 | +0.9 |
| Ipswich | East of England | 11.7 | 2.9 | +8.8 |
| Isle of Wight | South East | 21.2 | 3.5 | +17.7 |
| Islington North | London | 4.0 | 1.6 | +2.4 |
| Islington South and Finsbury | London | 7.6 | 1.6 | +6.0 |
| Islwyn | Wales | 19.6 | 2.7 | +16.9 |
| Jarrow | North East | 19.7 | 0.0 | +19.7 |
| Keighley | Yorkshire and the Humber | 11.5 | 3.1 | +8.4 |
| Kenilworth and Southam | West Midlands | 11.2 | 2.5 | +8.7 |
| Kensington | London | 4.5 | 2.2 | +2.4 |
| Kettering | East Midlands | 16.1 | 0.0 | +16.1 |

(*continued*)

**Table A7.** Continued

| Constituency | Region | 2015 vote (%) | 2010 vote (%) | Change (2010–15) |
|---|---|---|---|---|
| Kilmarnock and Loudoun | Scotland | 0.0 | 0.0 | +0.0 |
| Kingston and Surbiton | London | 7.3 | 2.5 | +4.8 |
| Kingston upon Hull East | Yorkshire and the Humber | 22.4 | 8.0 | +14.4 |
| Kingston upon Hull North | Yorkshire and the Humber | 16.3 | 4.1 | +12.2 |
| Kingston upon Hull West and Hessle | Yorkshire and the Humber | 19.9 | 5.4 | +14.5 |
| Kingswood | South West | 14.8 | 3.2 | +11.6 |
| Kirkcaldy and Cowdenbeath | Scotland | 2.3 | 1.7 | +0.6 |
| Knowsley | North West | 9.8 | 2.6 | +7.2 |
| Lanark and Hamilton East | Scotland | 2.6 | 1.3 | +1.3 |
| Lancaster and Fleetwood | North West | 9.7 | 2.4 | +7.3 |
| Leeds Central | Yorkshire and the Humber | 15.7 | 0.0 | +15.7 |
| Leeds East | Yorkshire and the Humber | 19.0 | 0.0 | +19.0 |
| Leeds North East | Yorkshire and the Humber | 7.7 | 1.8 | +5.9 |
| Leeds North West | Yorkshire and the Humber | 6.9 | 1.4 | +5.5 |
| Leeds West | Yorkshire and the Humber | 18.5 | 2.9 | +15.6 |
| Leicester East | East Midlands | 8.9 | 1.5 | +7.4 |
| Leicester South | East Midlands | 8.3 | 1.5 | +6.8 |
| Leicester West | East Midlands | 17.2 | 2.5 | +14.7 |
| Leigh | North West | 19.7 | 3.5 | +16.2 |
| Lewes | South East | 10.7 | 3.5 | +7.3 |
| Lewisham East | London | 9.1 | 1.9 | +7.3 |
| Lewisham West and Penge | London | 7.8 | 2.5 | +5.3 |
| Lewisham, Deptford | London | 4.2 | 0.0 | +4.2 |
| Leyton and Wanstead | London | 5.8 | 2.7 | +3.1 |
| Lichfield | West Midlands | 15.7 | 5.7 | +10.0 |
| Lincoln | East Midlands | 12.2 | 2.2 | +10.0 |
| Linlithgow and East Falkirk | Scotland | 2.7 | 0.0 | +2.7 |
| Liverpool, Riverside | North West | 5.7 | 1.7 | +4.0 |
| Liverpool, Walton | North West | 9.0 | 2.6 | +6.4 |
| Liverpool, Wavertree | North West | 8.2 | 2.4 | +5.9 |

| | | | | |
|---|---|---|---|---|
| Liverpool, West Derby | North West | 8.5 | 3.1 | +5.5 |
| Livingston | Scotland | 3.1 | 0.9 | +2.2 |
| Llanelli | Wales | 16.3 | 2.8 | +13.5 |
| Loughborough | East Midlands | 11.0 | 1.8 | +9.3 |
| Louth and Horncastle | East Midlands | 21.4 | 4.3 | +17.1 |
| Ludlow | West Midlands | 14.9 | 4.4 | +10.5 |
| Luton North | East of England | 12.5 | 3.6 | +8.9 |
| Luton South | East of England | 12.1 | 2.3 | +9.8 |
| Macclesfield | North West | 12.2 | 2.8 | +9.4 |
| Maidenhead | South East | 8.4 | 2.3 | +6.1 |
| Maidstone and The Weald | South East | 15.9 | 3.4 | +12.6 |
| Makerfield | North West | 22.4 | 0.0 | +22.4 |
| Maldon | East of England | 14.7 | 5.1 | +9.6 |
| Manchester Central | North West | 11.9 | 1.5 | +10.4 |
| Manchester, Gorton | North West | 8.2 | 0.0 | +8.2 |
| Manchester, Withington | North West | 4.3 | 1.6 | +2.8 |
| Mansfield | East Midlands | 25.1 | 6.2 | +18.9 |
| Meon Valley | South East | 14.8 | 2.9 | +11.9 |
| Meriden | West Midlands | 16.9 | 2.6 | +14.3 |
| Merthyr Tydfil and Rhymney | Wales | 18.7 | 2.7 | +16.0 |
| Mid Bedfordshire | East of England | 15.4 | 5.2 | +10.3 |
| Mid Derbyshire | East Midlands | 13.6 | 2.6 | +11.0 |
| Mid Dorset and North Poole | South West | 12.2 | 4.5 | +7.7 |
| Mid Norfolk | East of England | 19.0 | 5.5 | +13.5 |
| Mid Sussex | South East | 12.0 | 2.6 | +9.5 |
| Mid Worcestershire | West Midlands | 17.7 | 6.0 | +11.7 |
| Middlesbrough | North East | 18.7 | 3.7 | +15.0 |
| Middlesbrough South and East Cleveland | North East | 15.2 | 4.1 | +11.1 |
| Midlothian | Scotland | 2.4 | 0.9 | +1.5 |
| Milton Keynes North | South East | 11.9 | 3.3 | +8.6 |
| Milton Keynes South | South East | 13.2 | 3.8 | +9.5 |
| Mitcham and Morden | London | 9.5 | 2.0 | +7.5 |
| Mole Valley | South East | 11.2 | 5.1 | +6.1 |
| Monmouth | Wales | 10.4 | 2.4 | +8.0 |
| Montgomeryshire | Wales | 11.2 | 3.3 | +7.9 |
| Moray | Scotland | 3.9 | 2.7 | +1.3 |
| Morecambe and Lunesdale | North West | 12.4 | 4.2 | +8.2 |
| Morley and Outwood | Yorkshire and the Humber | 16.5 | 3.1 | +13.4 |
| Motherwell and Wishaw | Scotland | 2.7 | 0.0 | +2.7 |

(*continued*)

**Table A7.** Continued

| Constituency | Region | 2015 vote (%) | 2010 vote (%) | Change (2010–15) |
|---|---|---|---|---|
| Na h-Eileanan an Iar | Scotland | 0.0 | 0.0 | +0.0 |
| Neath | Wales | 16.4 | 2.2 | +14.2 |
| New Forest East | South East | 17.5 | 5.0 | +12.5 |
| New Forest West | South East | 16.5 | 5.9 | +10.7 |
| Newark | East Midlands | 12.0 | 3.8 | +8.2 |
| Newbury | South East | 10.8 | 2.5 | +8.3 |
| Newcastle upon Tyne Central | North East | 14.9 | 2.2 | +12.7 |
| Newcastle upon Tyne East | North East | 12.5 | 0.0 | +12.5 |
| Newcastle upon Tyne North | North East | 16.6 | 2.9 | +13.7 |
| Newcastle-under-Lyme | West Midlands | 16.9 | 8.1 | +8.8 |
| Newport East | Wales | 18.4 | 2.0 | +16.4 |
| Newport West | Wales | 15.2 | 2.9 | +12.3 |
| Newton Abbot | South West | 14.0 | 6.4 | +7.6 |
| Normanton, Pontefract and Castleford | Yorkshire and the Humber | 21.3 | 0.0 | +21.3 |
| North Ayrshire and Arran | Scotland | 2.4 | 0.0 | +2.4 |
| North Cornwall | South West | 12.7 | 4.9 | +7.8 |
| North Devon | South West | 14.8 | 7.3 | +7.6 |
| North Dorset | South West | 17.1 | 5.2 | +11.9 |
| North Durham | North East | 16.0 | 3.3 | +12.7 |
| North East Bedfordshire | East of England | 14.6 | 4.1 | +10.5 |
| North East Cambridgeshire | East of England | 22.5 | 5.7 | +16.8 |
| North East Derbyshire | East Midlands | 15.9 | 5.6 | +10.3 |
| North East Fife | Scotland | 0.0 | 2.6 | −2.6 |
| North East Hampshire | South East | 8.8 | 4.2 | +4.6 |
| North East Hertfordshire | East of England | 12.9 | 4.1 | +8.8 |
| North East Somerset | South West | 12.0 | 3.4 | +8.6 |
| North Herefordshire | West Midlands | 14.0 | 5.7 | +8.3 |
| North Norfolk | East of England | 16.9 | 5.4 | +11.5 |
| North Shropshire | West Midlands | 17.6 | 4.7 | +12.9 |
| North Somerset | South West | 13.0 | 3.9 | +9.1 |
| North Swindon | South West | 15.3 | 3.7 | +11.6 |
| North Thanet | South East | 25.7 | 6.5 | +19.2 |
| North Tyneside | North East | 16.3 | 2.8 | +13.5 |
| North Warwickshire | West Midlands | 17.4 | 2.8 | +14.6 |
| North West Cambridgeshire | East of England | 20.1 | 8.3 | +11.8 |

| North West Durham | North East | 17.0 | 2.9 | +14.1 |
|---|---|---|---|---|
| North West Hampshire | South East | 14.7 | 5.2 | +9.5 |
| North West Leicestershire | East Midlands | 16.9 | 2.2 | +14.7 |
| North West Norfolk | East of England | 17.8 | 3.9 | +14.0 |
| North Wiltshire | South West | 11.5 | 3.9 | +7.6 |
| Northampton North | East Midlands | 16.1 | 3.1 | +13.0 |
| Northampton South | East Midlands | 18.3 | 4.9 | +13.4 |
| Norwich North | East of England | 13.7 | 4.4 | +9.3 |
| Norwich South | East of England | 9.4 | 2.4 | +7.0 |
| Nottingham East | East Midlands | 9.9 | 3.4 | +6.5 |
| Nottingham North | East Midlands | 18.5 | 3.9 | +14.6 |
| Nottingham South | East Midlands | 11.3 | 2.4 | +8.9 |
| Nuneaton | West Midlands | 14.4 | 0.0 | +14.4 |
| Ochil and South Perthshire | Scotland | 2.3 | 1.4 | +0.9 |
| Ogmore | Wales | 15.4 | 2.3 | +13.2 |
| Old Bexley and Sidcup | London | 18.2 | 3.4 | +14.8 |
| Oldham East and Saddleworth | North West | 19.2 | 3.9 | +15.3 |
| Oldham West and Royton | North West | 20.6 | 3.2 | +17.4 |
| Orkney and Shetland | Scotland | 4.8 | 6.3 | −1.5 |
| Orpington | London | 16.7 | 2.8 | +13.9 |
| Oxford East | South East | 6.8 | 2.3 | +4.5 |
| Oxford West and Abingdon | South East | 6.9 | 2.7 | +4.2 |
| Paisley and Renfrewshire North | Scotland | 0.0 | 0.0 | +0.0 |
| Paisley and Renfrewshire South | Scotland | 0.0 | 0.0 | +0.0 |
| Pendle | North West | 12.2 | 3.3 | +8.9 |
| Penistone and Stocksbridge | Yorkshire and the Humber | 22.9 | 4.2 | +18.7 |
| Penrith and The Border | North West | 12.2 | 2.8 | +9.4 |
| Perth and North Perthshire | Scotland | 2.0 | 0.0 | +2.0 |
| Peterborough | East of England | 15.9 | 6.7 | +9.2 |
| Plymouth, Moor View | South West | 21.5 | 7.7 | +13.8 |
| Plymouth, Sutton and Devonport | South West | 14.0 | 6.5 | +7.5 |
| Pontypridd | Wales | 13.3 | 3.4 | +10.0 |
| Poole | South West | 16.8 | 5.3 | +11.5 |
| Poplar and Limehouse | London | 6.1 | 1.2 | +4.9 |
| Portsmouth North | South East | 19.1 | 4.1 | +15.0 |

(continued)

**Table A7.** Continued

| Constituency | Region | 2015 vote (%) | 2010 vote (%) | Change (2010–15) |
|---|---|---|---|---|
| Portsmouth South | South East | 13.4 | 2.1 | +11.3 |
| Preseli Pembrokeshire | Wales | 10.5 | 2.3 | +8.2 |
| Preston | North West | 15.4 | 4.5 | +10.9 |
| Pudsey | Yorkshire and the Humber | 9.2 | 2.5 | +6.7 |
| Putney | London | 4.6 | 1.1 | +3.5 |
| Rayleigh and Wickford | East of England | 22.3 | 4.2 | +18.1 |
| Reading East | South East | 7.2 | 2.2 | +5.0 |
| Reading West | South East | 10.0 | 3.2 | +6.8 |
| Redcar | North East | 18.4 | 4.5 | +13.9 |
| Redditch | West Midlands | 16.2 | 3.4 | +12.8 |
| Reigate | South East | 13.3 | 4.2 | +9.1 |
| Rhondda | Wales | 12.7 | 1.2 | +11.6 |
| Ribble Valley | North West | 15.8 | 6.7 | +9.1 |
| Richmond (Yorks) | Yorkshire and the Humber | 15.2 | 0.0 | +15.2 |
| Richmond Park | London | 4.2 | 1.1 | +3.1 |
| Rochdale | North West | 18.8 | 4.4 | +14.5 |
| Rochester and Strood | South East | 30.5 | 0.0 | +30.5 |
| Rochford and Southend East | East of England | 20.5 | 5.8 | +14.7 |
| Romford | London | 22.8 | 4.4 | +18.4 |
| Romsey and Southampton North | South East | 11.4 | 2.6 | +8.8 |
| Ross, Skye and Lochaber | Scotland | 1.9 | 1.9 | +0.0 |
| Rossendale and Darwen | North West | 14.0 | 3.4 | +10.6 |
| Rother Valley | Yorkshire and the Humber | 28.1 | 5.6 | +22.5 |
| Rotherham | Yorkshire and the Humber | 30.2 | 5.9 | +24.3 |
| Rugby | West Midlands | 14.0 | 0.9 | +13.1 |
| Ruislip, Northwood and Pinner | London | 10.9 | 2.7 | +8.2 |
| Runnymede and Weybridge | South East | 13.9 | 6.5 | +7.4 |
| Rushcliffe | East Midlands | 10.8 | 4.1 | +6.7 |
| Rutherglen and Hamilton West | Scotland | 2.3 | 1.4 | +0.9 |
| Rutland and Melton | East Midlands | 15.9 | 4.6 | +11.3 |
| Saffron Walden | East of England | 13.8 | 4.1 | +9.7 |
| Salford and Eccles | North West | 18.0 | 2.6 | +15.4 |
| Salisbury | South West | 12.1 | 2.9 | +9.2 |
| Scarborough and Whitby | Yorkshire and the Humber | 17.1 | 3.0 | +14.1 |

| | | | | |
|---|---|---|---|---|
| Scunthorpe | Yorkshire and the Humber | 17.1 | 4.6 | +12.6 |
| Sedgefield | North East | 16.6 | 3.7 | +12.9 |
| Sefton Central | North West | 10.0 | 4.2 | +5.8 |
| Selby and Ainsty | Yorkshire and the Humber | 14.0 | 3.2 | +10.8 |
| Sevenoaks | South East | 17.9 | 3.6 | +14.3 |
| Sheffield Central | Yorkshire and the Humber | 7.5 | 1.6 | +5.9 |
| Sheffield South East | Yorkshire and the Humber | 21.9 | 4.6 | +17.3 |
| Sheffield, Brightside and Hillsborough | Yorkshire and the Humber | 22.1 | 4.1 | +18.0 |
| Sheffield, Hallam | Yorkshire and the Humber | 6.4 | 2.3 | +4.1 |
| Sheffield, Heeley | Yorkshire and the Humber | 17.4 | 3.7 | +13.7 |
| Sherwood | East Midlands | 14.6 | 3.0 | +11.6 |
| Shipley | Yorkshire and the Humber | 8.9 | 0.0 | +8.9 |
| Shrewsbury and Atcham | West Midlands | 14.4 | 3.1 | +11.3 |
| Sittingbourne and Sheppey | South East | 24.8 | 5.4 | +19.4 |
| Skipton and Ripon | Yorkshire and the Humber | 14.0 | 3.5 | +10.5 |
| Sleaford and North Hykeham | East Midlands | 15.7 | 3.6 | +12.1 |
| Slough | South East | 13.0 | 3.2 | +9.8 |
| Solihull | West Midlands | 11.6 | 2.2 | +9.4 |
| Somerton and Frome | South West | 10.7 | 3.2 | +7.5 |
| South Basildon and East Thurrock | East of England | 26.5 | 5.9 | +20.6 |
| South Cambridgeshire | East of England | 9.8 | 3.2 | +6.6 |
| South Derbyshire | East Midlands | 17.7 | 2.4 | +15.3 |
| South Dorset | South West | 15.0 | 4.0 | +11.0 |
| South East Cambridgeshire | East of England | 11.1 | 3.7 | +7.4 |
| South East Cornwall | South West | 15.2 | 6.2 | +9.0 |
| South Holland and The Deepings | East Midlands | 21.8 | 6.5 | +15.3 |
| South Leicestershire | East Midlands | 17.4 | 3.6 | +13.8 |
| South Norfolk | East of England | 13.7 | 4.2 | +9.5 |
| South Northamptonshire | East Midlands | 13.5 | 4.0 | +9.5 |
| South Ribble | North West | 14.1 | 3.7 | +10.4 |

(*continued*)

**Table A7.** Continued

| Constituency | Region | 2015 vote (%) | 2010 vote (%) | Change (2010–15) |
|---|---|---|---|---|
| South Shields | North East | 22.0 | 0.0 | +22.0 |
| South Staffordshire | West Midlands | 16.7 | 5.5 | +11.2 |
| South Suffolk | East of England | 15.2 | 7.1 | +8.1 |
| South Swindon | South West | 12.0 | 4.3 | +7.7 |
| South Thanet | South East | 32.4 | 5.5 | +26.9 |
| South West Bedfordshire | East of England | 15.5 | 4.2 | +11.3 |
| South West Devon | South West | 14.5 | 6.2 | +8.3 |
| South West Hertfordshire | East of England | 11.5 | 2.6 | +8.9 |
| South West Norfolk | East of England | 23.3 | 6.2 | +17.1 |
| South West Surrey | South East | 9.9 | 2.6 | +7.3 |
| South West Wiltshire | South West | 17.5 | 5.5 | +12.0 |
| Southampton, Itchen | South East | 13.4 | 4.3 | +9.1 |
| Southampton, Test | South East | 12.8 | 3.9 | +8.9 |
| Southend West | East of England | 17.5 | 3.9 | +13.6 |
| Southport | North West | 16.8 | 5.1 | +11.7 |
| Spelthorne | South East | 20.9 | 8.5 | +12.4 |
| St Albans | East of England | 7.8 | 3.8 | +4.0 |
| St Austell and Newquay | South West | 16.9 | 3.7 | +13.2 |
| St Helens North | North West | 15.1 | 4.7 | +10.4 |
| St Helens South and Whiston | North West | 14.0 | 2.7 | +11.3 |
| St Ives | South West | 11.8 | 5.6 | +6.2 |
| Stafford | West Midlands | 12.9 | 3.4 | +9.5 |
| Staffordshire Moorlands | West Midlands | 14.6 | 8.2 | +6.4 |
| Stalybridge and Hyde | North West | 18.8 | 3.3 | +15.5 |
| Stevenage | East of England | 14.4 | 4.5 | +9.9 |
| Stirling | Scotland | 0.0 | 0.8 | −0.8 |
| Stockport | North West | 13.1 | 2.2 | +10.9 |
| Stockton North | North East | 19.2 | 3.9 | +15.3 |
| Stockton South | North East | 10.6 | 2.9 | +7.7 |
| Stoke-on-Trent Central | West Midlands | 22.7 | 4.3 | +18.4 |
| Stoke-on-Trent North | West Midlands | 24.7 | 6.2 | +18.5 |
| Stoke-on-Trent South | West Midlands | 21.2 | 3.4 | +17.8 |
| Stone | West Midlands | 16.2 | 5.3 | +11.0 |
| Stourbridge | West Midlands | 16.9 | 4.5 | +12.5 |
| Stratford-on-Avon | West Midlands | 13.2 | 3.7 | +9.6 |
| Streatham | London | 3.2 | 0.0 | +3.2 |
| Stretford and Urmston | North West | 10.9 | 3.4 | +7.5 |
| Stroud | South West | 8.0 | 2.2 | +5.8 |
| Suffolk Coastal | East of England | 15.6 | 5.8 | +9.9 |
| Sunderland Central | North East | 19.1 | 2.6 | +16.5 |
| Surrey Heath | South East | 14.3 | 6.3 | +8.0 |
| Sutton and Cheam | London | 10.7 | 2.0 | +8.7 |

| Sutton Coldfield | West Midlands | 14.7 | 3.1 | +11.6 |
| Swansea East | Wales | 17.2 | 2.6 | +14.6 |
| Swansea West | Wales | 13.5 | 2.0 | +11.5 |
| Tamworth | West Midlands | 18.5 | 4.9 | +13.6 |
| Tatton | North West | 10.8 | 0.0 | +10.8 |
| Taunton Deane | South West | 12.0 | 3.6 | +8.4 |
| Telford | West Midlands | 18.0 | 5.9 | +12.1 |
| Tewkesbury | South West | 12.9 | 4.1 | +8.8 |
| The Cotswolds | South West | 10.9 | 4.2 | +6.7 |
| The Wrekin | West Midlands | 16.8 | 4.5 | +12.3 |
| Thirsk and Malton | Yorkshire and the Humber | 14.9 | 6.6 | +14.9 |
| Thornbury and Yate | South West | 10.6 | 3.5 | +7.1 |
| Thurrock | East of England | 31.7 | 7.4 | +24.3 |
| Tiverton and Honiton | South West | 16.4 | 6.0 | +10.4 |
| Tonbridge and Malling | South East | 15.2 | 3.7 | +11.5 |
| Tooting | London | 2.9 | 1.2 | +1.7 |
| Torbay | South West | 13.6 | 5.3 | +8.3 |
| Torfaen | Wales | 19.0 | 2.3 | +16.7 |
| Torridge and West Devon | South West | 18.3 | 5.5 | +12.8 |
| Totnes | South West | 14.1 | 6.0 | +8.1 |
| Tottenham | London | 3.6 | 1.2 | +2.5 |
| Truro and Falmouth | South West | 11.6 | 3.9 | +7.7 |
| Tunbridge Wells | South East | 12.6 | 4.1 | +8.5 |
| Twickenham | London | 4.9 | 1.5 | +3.5 |
| Tynemouth | North East | 12.2 | 1.7 | +10.5 |
| Uxbridge and South Ruislip | London | 14.2 | 2.7 | +11.5 |
| Vale of Clwyd | Wales | 13.0 | 1.5 | +11.6 |
| Vale of Glamorgan | Wales | 10.7 | 3.1 | +7.6 |
| Vauxhall | London | 2.9 | 0.0 | +2.9 |
| Wakefield | Yorkshire and the Humber | 18.3 | 0.0 | +18.3 |
| Wallasey | North West | 11.7 | 2.9 | +8.8 |
| Walsall North | West Midlands | 22.0 | 4.8 | +17.2 |
| Walsall South | West Midlands | 15.6 | 8.4 | +7.2 |
| Walthamstow | London | 6.0 | 2.0 | +4.0 |
| Wansbeck | North East | 18.2 | 2.5 | +15.7 |
| Wantage | South East | 12.5 | 4.3 | +8.2 |
| Warley | West Midlands | 16.5 | 6.8 | +9.7 |
| Warrington North | North West | 17.1 | 0.0 | +17.1 |
| Warrington South | North West | 8.3 | 3.0 | +5.3 |
| Warwick and Leamington | West Midlands | 8.3 | 1.9 | +6.4 |

(*continued*)

**Table A7.** Continued

| Constituency | Region | 2015 vote (%) | 2010 vote (%) | Change (2010–15) |
|---|---|---|---|---|
| Washington and Sunderland West | North East | 19.6 | 3.4 | +16.2 |
| Watford | East of England | 9.8 | 2.2 | +7.6 |
| Waveney | East of England | 14.5 | 5.3 | +9.3 |
| Wealden | South East | 16.7 | 6.0 | +10.7 |
| Weaver Vale | North West | 9.7 | 2.3 | +7.4 |
| Wellingborough | East Midlands | 19.6 | 3.2 | +16.4 |
| Wells | South West | 9.9 | 3.1 | +6.8 |
| Welwyn Hatfield | East of England | 13.1 | 3.4 | +9.8 |
| Wentworth and Dearne | Yorkshire and the Humber | 24.9 | 8.1 | +16.8 |
| West Aberdeenshire and Kincardine | Scotland | 1.8 | 0.9 | +0.9 |
| West Bromwich East | West Midlands | 21.2 | 2.6 | +18.6 |
| West Bromwich West | West Midlands | 25.2 | 4.3 | +20.9 |
| West Dorset | South West | 12.5 | 3.8 | +8.7 |
| West Dunbartonshire | Scotland | 0.0 | 1.6 | −1.6 |
| West Ham | London | 7.5 | 1.6 | +5.9 |
| West Lancashire | North West | 12.2 | 3.7 | +8.5 |
| West Suffolk | East of England | 21.7 | 6.4 | +15.3 |
| West Worcestershire | West Midlands | 14.4 | 3.9 | +10.5 |
| Westminster North | London | 3.8 | 0.8 | +3.0 |
| Westmorland and Lonsdale | North West | 6.2 | 1.6 | +4.6 |
| Weston-Super-Mare | South West | 17.8 | 2.7 | +15.1 |
| Wigan | North West | 19.5 | 5.7 | +13.8 |
| Wimbledon | London | 5.1 | 1.9 | +3.2 |
| Winchester | South East | 7.5 | 2.0 | +5.5 |
| Windsor | South East | 10.0 | 3.3 | +6.8 |
| Wirral South | North West | 8.9 | 3.2 | +5.7 |
| Wirral West | North West | 6.6 | 2.3 | +4.3 |
| Witham | East of England | 16.0 | 6.5 | +9.5 |
| Witney | South East | 9.2 | 3.5 | +5.7 |
| Woking | South East | 11.3 | 3.8 | +7.5 |
| Wokingham | South East | 9.9 | 3.1 | +6.9 |
| Wolverhampton North East | West Midlands | 19.2 | 3.3 | +15.9 |
| Wolverhampton South East | West Midlands | 20.3 | 7.7 | +12.6 |
| Wolverhampton South West | West Midlands | 10.7 | 3.7 | +7.0 |
| Worcester | West Midlands | 12.8 | 2.8 | +10.0 |
| Workington | North West | 19.6 | 2.2 | +17.4 |

| | | | | |
|---|---|---|---|---|
| Worsley and Eccles South | North West | 18.3 | 4.9 | +13.4 |
| Worthing West | South East | 18.3 | 6.0 | +12.4 |
| Wrexham | Wales | 15.5 | 2.4 | +13.2 |
| Wycombe | South East | 10.1 | 4.4 | +5.7 |
| Wyre and Preston North | North West | 13.2 | 4.8 | +8.4 |
| Wyre Forest | West Midlands | 16.1 | 2.9 | +13.2 |
| Wythenshawe and Sale East | North West | 14.7 | 3.5 | +11.3 |
| Yeovil | South West | 13.4 | 4.1 | +9.3 |
| Ynys Môn | Wales | 14.7 | 3.5 | +11.2 |
| York Central | Yorkshire and the Humber | 10.1 | 2.4 | +7.7 |
| York Outer | Yorkshire and the Humber | 9.7 | 2.1 | +7.6 |
| Average: all constituencies | | 13.1 | 3.1 | +10.4 |
| Average: England and Wales | | 14.3 | 3.4 | +10.9 |

*Source*: 2015 British Election Study Constituency Results with Census and Candidate Data. Full results available at <www.britishelectionstudy.com> (accessed 15 June 2015).

**Table A8.** Ukip's top 25 results at the 2015 general election

| Rank | Constituency | 2010 party control | 2015 vote (%) | 2010 vote (%) | Change (2010–15) |
|---|---|---|---|---|---|
| 1 | Clacton | Conservative | 44.4 | 0.0 | +44.4 |
| 2 | Boston and Skegness | Conservative | 33.8 | 9.5 | +24.3 |
| 3 | South Thanet | Conservative | 32.4 | 5.5 | +26.9 |
| 4 | Heywood and Middleton | Labour | 32.2 | 2.6 | +29.6 |
| 5 | Thurrock | Conservative | 31.7 | 7.4 | +24.3 |
| 6 | Castle Point | Conservative | 31.2 | 0.0 | +31.2 |
| 7 | Rochester and Strood | Conservative | 30.5 | 0.0 | +30.5 |
| 8 | Rotherham | Labour | 30.2 | 5.9 | +24.3 |
| 9 | Dagenham and Rainham | Labour | 29.8 | 3.6 | +26.3 |
| 10 | Rother Valley | Labour | 28.1 | 5.6 | +22.5 |
| 11 | Hartlepool | Labour | 28 | 7.0 | +21.0 |
| 12 | South Basildon and East Thurrock | Conservative | 26.5 | 5.9 | +20.6 |
| 13 | North Thanet | Conservative | 25.7 | 6.5 | +19.2 |
| 14 | Hornchurch and Upminster | Conservative | 25.3 | 5.3 | +20.0 |
| 15 | West Bromwich West | Labour | 25.2 | 4.3 | +20.9 |

(*continued*)

**Table A8.** Continued

| Rank | Constituency | 2010 party control | 2015 vote (%) | 2010 vote (%) | Change (2010–15) |
|------|--------------|--------------------|---------------|---------------|-------------------|
| 16 | Mansfield | Labour | 25.1 | 6.2 | +18.9 |
| 17 | Great Grimsby | Labour | 25 | 6.2 | +18.8 |
| 18 | Wentworth and Dearne | Labour | 24.9 | 8.1 | +16.8 |
| 19 | Sittingbourne and Sheppey | Conservative | 24.8 | 5.4 | +19.4 |
| 20 | Stoke-on-Trent North | Labour | 24.7 | 6.2 | +18.5 |
| 21 | Bradford South | Labour | 24.1 | 3.5 | +20.6 |
| 22 | Doncaster Central | Labour | 24.1 | 3.4 | +20.7 |
| 23 | Dudley North | Labour | 24 | 8.5 | +15.5 |
| 24 | Bolton South East | Labour | 23.6 | 4.0 | +19.7 |
| 25 | Barnsley East | Labour | 23.5 | 4.5 | +19.0 |
| | Average: top 25 | | 28.0 | 5.0 | +23.0 |

*Source*: 2015 British Election Study Constituency Results with Census and Candidate Data. Full results available at <www.britishelectionstudy.com> (accessed 15 June 2015).

# Appendix B: Ukip Demographic Favourability

Our measure of Ukip favourability was created based on seven socio-demographic characteristics. All the data were taken from the 2011 census. We included four characteristics that have been shown in previous research to be associated with higher levels of Ukip support: the percentage of the population that does not have any formal education, the percentage that is employed in routine or manual occupations, the percentage above the age of 65 years, and the percentage that is white. We also included three characteristics that are generally associated with lower levels of support for Ukip: the percentage of the population that has advanced educational qualifications, the percentage that is employed in professional or administrative occupations, and the percentage that is between the ages of 18 and 29. When calculating this measure, we limited the analysis to England and Wales. Even though Ukip officially contested some elections in Scotland, the party found very little support and devoted few resources to winning votes in this region, a pattern that is unlikely to change in future contests.

To estimate the overall level of Ukip favourability, we used a technique called exploratory factor analysis, which analyses whether a number of variables group onto a single dimension. If so, we can use these variables to estimate a single measure of that underlying dimension. In our case, we used the seven socio-demographic characteristics to estimate one variable that captured an area's overall demographic favourability towards Ukip. Using multiple traits to estimate favourability allowed us to reduce the measurement error associated with any one of the traits and the underlying demographic favourability towards the party.

## UKIP FAVOURABILITY BY LOCAL AUTHORITY

For the Ukip favourability measure used in Chapter 4, all traits were measured at the level of the local authority. All seven categories had high loadings on a single dimension and the first factor explained 58 per cent of the variance in the seven traits. Each of the individual variables loaded on the underlying dimension

**Table B1.** Factor loadings for Ukip
demographic favourability by local authority

| Variable | Factor 1 |
|----------|----------|
| *Favourable Ukip traits* | +0.93 |
| Routine and manual (%) | |
| No formal qualifications (%) | +0.92 |
| White (%) | +0.45 |
| Aged 65+ (%) | +0.44 |
| | |
| *Unfavourable Ukip traits* | |
| Professional and administrative (%) | −0.87 |
| Advanced qualifications (%) | −0.95 |
| Aged 18–29 (%) | −0.29 |
| N | 348 |
| Eigenvalue | 3.82 |
| Variance explained | 0.64 |

*Note*: The eigenvalue of the first factor was 4.19.
*Source*: 2011 Census.

in the expected manner; the factor loadings for the four traits that are generally associated with greater support for Ukip had a positive sign, while the factor loadings for the three traits that are generally associated with lower Ukip support had a negative sign (Table B1). We used the predicted values from the first factor to estimate each area's overall favourability to Ukip. For ease of interpretation we rescaled the predicted values to fall between '0' and '1', where a value of '0' indicated that an area was highly unfavourable to Ukip and a value of '1' indicated that an area was highly favourable to the party. The Ukip favourability scores for all areas in England and Wales are presented in Table B2. Table B3 lists the top 25 areas that are most demographically favourable to Ukip, while Table B4 gives the top 25 areas that are most demographically *un*favourable to the party.

When we compared our measure of Ukip favourability with the party's share of the vote in the area at the European and local elections, we saw that our measure was a strong predictor of the party's performance. Figure B1 (a and b) displays support for Ukip on the vertical axis and the favourability score on the horizontal axis. The solid black line represents what social scientists call the line of 'best fit' (the regression line fitted to the data). As Figure B1 illustrates, there was a strong, positive correlation between the profile of an area and the performance of Ukip in 2014.[1] As areas became more favourable to Ukip, the party's vote share tended to increase. While we were unable to estimate our measure of demographic favourability at the ward level, we can compare Ukip's local results with the demographical favourability of the council area where

**Table B2.** Ukip demographic favourability by local authority

| Area | Ukip favourability score | Area | Ukip favourability score |
|---|---|---|---|
| Adur | 0.76 | Burnley | 0.86 |
| Allerdale | 0.85 | Bury | 0.69 |
| Amber Valley | 0.80 | Caerphilly | 0.88 |
| Arun | 0.79 | Calderdale | 0.72 |
| Ashfield | 0.93 | Cambridge | 0.34 |
| Ashford | 0.69 | Camden | 0.25 |
| Aylesbury Vale | 0.55 | Cannock Chase | 0.86 |
| Babergh | 0.72 | Canterbury | 0.64 |
| Barking and Dagenham | 0.75 | Cardiff | 0.56 |
| Barnet | 0.41 | Carlisle | 0.82 |
| Barnsley | 0.91 | Carmarthenshire | 0.81 |
| Barrow-in-Furness | 0.86 | Castle Point | 0.85 |
| Basildon | 0.77 | Central Bedfordshire | 0.62 |
| Basingstoke and Deane | 0.57 | Ceredigion | 0.66 |
| Bassetlaw | 0.85 | Charnwood | 0.65 |
| Bath and North East Somerset | 0.57 | Chelmsford | 0.59 |
| Bedford | 0.64 | Cheltenham | 0.53 |
| Bexley | 0.69 | Cherwell | 0.65 |
| Birmingham | 0.71 | Cheshire East | 0.61 |
| Blaby | 0.69 | Cheshire West and Chester | 0.66 |
| Blackburn with Darwen | 0.79 | Chesterfield | 0.83 |
| Blackpool | 0.91 | Chichester | 0.62 |
| Blaenau Gwent | 1.00 | Chiltern | 0.44 |
| Bolsover | 0.94 | Chorley | 0.67 |
| Bolton | 0.77 | Christchurch | 0.75 |
| Boston | 0.98 | City of London | 0.00 |
| Bournemouth | 0.66 | Colchester | 0.63 |
| Bracknell Forest | 0.53 | Conwy | 0.79 |
| Bradford | 0.74 | Copeland | 0.83 |
| Braintree | 0.72 | Corby | 0.94 |
| Breckland | 0.86 | Cornwall | 0.76 |
| Brent | 0.53 | Cotswold | 0.61 |
| Brentwood | 0.55 | County Durham | 0.83 |
| Bridgend | 0.82 | Coventry | 0.73 |
| Brighton and Hove | 0.47 | Craven | 0.65 |
| Bristol, City of | 0.58 | Crawley | 0.70 |
| Broadland | 0.75 | Croydon | 0.52 |
| Bromley | 0.51 | Dacorum | 0.57 |
| Bromsgrove | 0.61 | Darlington | 0.77 |
| Broxbourne | 0.75 | Dartford | 0.69 |
| Broxtowe | 0.68 | Daventry | 0.64 |
| | | Denbighshire | 0.79 |

(continued)

**Table B2.** Continued

| Area | Ukip favourability score | Area | Ukip favourability score |
|---|---|---|---|
| Derby | 0.73 | Harborough | 0.58 |
| Derbyshire Dales | 0.65 | Haringey | 0.43 |
| Doncaster | 0.90 | Harlow | 0.80 |
| Dover | 0.79 | Harrogate | 0.57 |
| Dudley | 0.84 | Harrow | 0.45 |
| Ealing | 0.46 | Hart | 0.45 |
| East Cambridgeshire | 0.64 | Hartlepool | 0.90 |
| East Devon | 0.71 | Hastings | 0.78 |
| East Dorset | 0.68 | Havant | 0.78 |
| East Hampshire | 0.56 | Havering | 0.74 |
| East Hertfordshire | 0.52 | Herefordshire, County of | 0.73 |
| East Lindsey | 0.93 | Hertsmere | 0.56 |
| East Northamptonshire | 0.72 | High Peak | 0.67 |
| East Riding of Yorkshire | 0.74 | Hillingdon | 0.58 |
| East Staffordshire | 0.78 | Hinckley and Bosworth | 0.74 |
| Eastbourne | 0.74 | Horsham | 0.55 |
| Eastleigh | 0.62 | Hounslow | 0.50 |
| Eden | 0.75 | Huntingdonshire | 0.63 |
| Elmbridge | 0.37 | Hyndburn | 0.84 |
| Enfield | 0.60 | Ipswich | 0.79 |
| Epping Forest | 0.64 | Isle of Anglesey | 0.77 |
| Epsom and Ewell | 0.47 | Isle of Wight | 0.81 |
| Erewash | 0.81 | Isles of Scilly | 0.65 |
| Exeter | 0.62 | Islington | 0.30 |
| Fareham | 0.60 | Kensington and Chelsea | 0.22 |
| Fenland | 0.94 | Kettering | 0.75 |
| Flintshire | 0.78 | King's Lynn and West Norfolk | 0.94 |
| Forest Heath | 0.78 | | |
| Forest of Dean | 0.78 | Kingston upon Hull, City of | 0.37 |
| Fylde | 0.65 | | |
| Gateshead | 0.82 | Kingston upon Thames | 0.85 |
| Gedling | 0.71 | Kirklees | 0.73 |
| Gloucester | 0.74 | Knowsley | 0.92 |
| Gosport | 0.75 | Lambeth | 0.31 |
| Gravesham | 0.77 | Lancaster | 0.69 |
| Great Yarmouth | 0.96 | Leeds | 0.65 |
| Greenwich | 0.54 | Leicester | 0.76 |
| Guildford | 0.43 | Lewes | 0.67 |
| Gwynedd | 0.74 | Lewisham | 0.45 |
| Hackney | 0.40 | Lichfield | 0.67 |
| Halton | 0.85 | Lincoln | 0.76 |
| Hambleton | 0.63 | Liverpool | 0.76 |
| Hammersmith and Fulham | 0.26 | Luton | 0.70 |
| | | Maidstone | 0.66 |

| | | | |
|---|---|---|---|
| Maldon | 0.71 | Portsmouth | 0.67 |
| Malvern Hills | 0.62 | Powys | 0.77 |
| Manchester | 0.61 | Preston | 0.70 |
| Mansfield | 0.91 | Purbeck | 0.73 |
| Medway | 0.76 | Reading | 0.50 |
| Melton | 0.71 | Redbridge | 0.48 |
| Mendip | 0.71 | Redcar and Cleveland | 0.88 |
| Merthyr Tydfil | 0.92 | Redditch | 0.78 |
| Merton | 0.40 | Reigate and Banstead | 0.50 |
| Mid Devon | 0.73 | Rhondda Cynon Taf | 0.87 |
| Mid Suffolk | 0.70 | Ribble Valley | 0.59 |
| Mid Sussex | 0.52 | Richmond upon Thames | 0.23 |
| Middlesbrough | 0.86 | Richmondshire | 0.63 |
| Milton Keynes | 0.60 | Rochdale | 0.81 |
| Mole Valley | 0.48 | Rochford | 0.72 |
| Monmouthshire | 0.64 | Rossendale | 0.72 |
| Neath Port Talbot | 0.90 | Rother | 0.74 |
| New Forest | 0.70 | Rotherham | 0.87 |
| Newark and Sherwood | 0.77 | Rugby | 0.67 |
| Newcastle upon Tyne | 0.66 | Runnymede | 0.55 |
| Newcastle-under-Lyme | 0.79 | Rushcliffe | 0.47 |
| Newham | 0.56 | Rushmoor | 0.63 |
| Newport | 0.77 | Rutland | 0.59 |
| North Devon | 0.80 | Ryedale | 0.76 |
| North Dorset | 0.70 | Salford | 0.76 |
| North East Derbyshire | 0.81 | Sandwell | 0.91 |
| North East Lincolnshire | 0.92 | Scarborough | 0.83 |
| North Hertfordshire | 0.54 | Sedgemoor | 0.82 |
| North Kesteven | 0.71 | Sefton | 0.76 |
| North Lincolnshire | 0.85 | Selby | 0.70 |
| North Norfolk | 0.85 | Sevenoaks | 0.57 |
| North Somerset | 0.67 | Sheffield | 0.69 |
| North Tyneside | 0.73 | Shepway | 0.77 |
| North Warwickshire | 0.83 | Shropshire | 0.71 |
| North West Leicestershire | 0.76 | Slough | 0.63 |
| Northampton | 0.71 | Solihull | 0.64 |
| Northumberland | 0.76 | South Bucks | 0.47 |
| Norwich | 0.68 | South Cambridgeshire | 0.46 |
| Nottingham | 0.72 | South Derbyshire | 0.70 |
| Nuneaton and Bedworth | 0.85 | South Gloucestershire | 0.65 |
| Oadby and Wigston | 0.68 | South Hams | 0.60 |
| Oldham | 0.82 | South Holland | 0.93 |
| Oxford | 0.40 | South Kesteven | 0.72 |
| Pembrokeshire | 0.80 | South Lakeland | 0.66 |
| Pendle | 0.82 | South Norfolk | 0.70 |
| Peterborough | 0.77 | South Northamptonshire | 0.58 |
| Plymouth | 0.76 | South Oxfordshire | 0.51 |
| Poole | 0.71 | South Ribble | 0.68 |

(continued)

**Table B2.** Continued

| Area | Ukip favourability score | Area | Ukip favourability score |
|---|---|---|---|
| South Somerset | 0.75 | Trafford | 0.55 |
| South Staffordshire | 0.71 | Tunbridge Wells | 0.54 |
| South Tyneside | 0.87 | Uttlesford | 0.55 |
| Southampton | 0.68 | Vale of Glamorgan | 0.64 |
| Southend–on–Sea | 0.72 | Wakefield | 0.89 |
| Southwark | 0.37 | Walsall | 0.88 |
| Spelthorne | 0.62 | Waltham Forest | 0.56 |
| St Albans | 0.35 | Wandsworth | 0.20 |
| St Edmundsbury | 0.73 | Warrington | 0.67 |
| St Helens | 0.84 | Warwick | 0.49 |
| Stafford | 0.64 | Watford | 0.53 |
| Staffordshire Moorlands | 0.79 | Waveney | 0.91 |
| Stevenage | 0.70 | Waverley | 0.46 |
| Stockport | 0.63 | Wealden | 0.64 |
| Stockton–on–Tees | 0.76 | Wellingborough | 0.80 |
| Stoke-on-Trent | 0.94 | Welwyn Hatfield | 0.56 |
| Stratford-on-Avon | 0.60 | West Berkshire | 0.56 |
| Stroud | 0.62 | West Devon | 0.68 |
| Suffolk Coastal | 0.68 | West Dorset | 0.68 |
| Sunderland | 0.88 | West Lancashire | 0.73 |
| Surrey Heath | 0.48 | West Lindsey | 0.74 |
| Sutton | 0.55 | West Oxfordshire | 0.58 |
| Swale | 0.81 | West Somerset | 0.82 |
| Swansea | 0.72 | Westminster | 0.25 |
| Swindon | 0.71 | Weymouth and Portland | 0.78 |
| Tameside | 0.84 | Wigan | 0.84 |
| Tamworth | 0.85 | Wiltshire | 0.63 |
| Tandridge | 0.52 | Winchester | 0.45 |
| Taunton Deane | 0.69 | Windsor and Maidenhead | 0.44 |
| Teignbridge | 0.71 | Wirral | 0.74 |
| Telford and Wrekin | 0.79 | Woking | 0.45 |
| Tendring | 0.94 | Wokingham | 0.40 |
| Test Valley | 0.61 | Wolverhampton | 0.84 |
| Tewkesbury | 0.64 | Worcester | 0.67 |
| Thanet | 0.84 | Worthing | 0.68 |
| Three Rivers | 0.51 | Wrexham | 0.81 |
| Thurrock | 0.80 | Wychavon | 0.68 |
| Tonbridge and Malling | 0.64 | Wycombe | 0.52 |
|  |  | Wyre | 0.78 |
| Torbay | 0.84 | Wyre Forest | 0.82 |
| Torfaen | 0.87 | York | 0.59 |
| Torridge | 0.84 |  |  |
| Tower Hamlets | 0.35 | *Source*: 2011 Census. |  |

**Table B3.** Top 25 most demographically favourable areas to Ukip

| Rank | Area | Region | Ukip favourability score | 2014 vote (%) |
|---|---|---|---|---|
| 1 | Blaenau Gwent | Wales | 1.00 | 30.2 |
| 2 | Boston | East Midlands | 0.98 | 51.6 |
| 3 | Great Yarmouth | East of England | 0.96 | 45.2 |
| 4 | Bolsover | East Midlands | 0.94 | 36.3 |
| 5 | King's Lynn and West Norfolk | East of England | 0.94 | 41.6 |
| 6 | Tendring | East of England | 0.94 | 48.4 |
| 7 | Stoke-on-Trent | West Midlands | 0.94 | 39.7 |
| 8 | Fenland | East of England | 0.94 | 47.3 |
| 9 | Corby | East Midlands | 0.94 | 35.0 |
| 10 | Ashfield | East Midlands | 0.93 | 37.4 |
| 11 | South Holland | East Midlands | 0.93 | 48.5 |
| 12 | East Lindsey | East Midlands | 0.93 | 44.2 |
| 13 | Merthyr Tydfil | Wales | 0.92 | 33.8 |
| 14 | Knowsley | North West | 0.92 | 23.2 |
| 15 | North East Lincolnshire | Yorkshire and the Humber | 0.92 | 41.2 |
| 16 | Sandwell | West Midlands | 0.91 | 30.1 |
| 17 | Waveney | East of England | 0.91 | 36.9 |
| 18 | Mansfield | East Midlands | 0.91 | 40.1 |
| 19 | Blackpool | North West | 0.91 | 33.9 |
| 20 | Barnsley | Yorkshire and the Humber | 0.91 | 35.9 |
| 21 | Doncaster | Yorkshire and the Humber | 0.90 | 35.1 |
| 22 | Neath Port Talbot | Wales | 0.90 | 26.4 |
| 23 | Hartlepool | North East | 0.90 | 39.0 |
| 24 | Wakefield | Yorkshire and the Humber | 0.89 | 36.0 |
| 25 | Walsall | West Midlands | 0.88 | 33.6 |
| | Average: top favourable | | 0.93 | 38.0 |

*Source*: European Parliament Elections 2014 (June 2014), House of Commons Library Research Paper 14/32; 2011 Census.

the ward was located. Once again, we see a positive trend in the data. Ukip performed most strongly in areas where the demography was more favourable to the party.[2]

## UKIP FAVOURABILITY BY PARLIAMENTARY CONSTITUENCY

To create the Ukip favourability measure referenced in Chapter 9, we used the same traits, but they were measured at the level of the parliament constituency. The first factor estimated using exploratory factor analysis explained 60 per cent

**Table B4.** Top 25 most demographically unfavourable areas to Ukip

| Rank | Area | Region | Ukip favourability score | 2014 vote (%) |
|---|---|---|---|---|
| 1 | City of London | London | 0.00 | 13.8 |
| 2 | Wandsworth | London | 0.20 | 10.9 |
| 3 | Kensington and Chelsea | London | 0.22 | 14.7 |
| 4 | Richmond upon Thames | London | 0.23 | 15.5 |
| 5 | Westminster | London | 0.25 | 13.6 |
| 6 | Camden | London | 0.25 | 9.2 |
| 7 | Hammersmith and Fulham | London | 0.26 | 12.3 |
| 8 | Islington | London | 0.30 | 9.8 |
| 9 | Lambeth | London | 0.31 | 7.9 |
| 10 | Cambridge | Eastern | 0.34 | 12.4 |
| 11 | St Albans | Eastern | 0.35 | 21.4 |
| 12 | Tower Hamlets | London | 0.35 | 9.8 |
| 13 | Elmbridge | South East | 0.37 | 24.6 |
| 14 | Kingston upon Hull, City of | Yorkshire and the Humber | 0.37 | 35.8 |
| 15 | Southwark | London | 0.37 | 11 |
| 16 | Oxford | South East | 0.40 | 12.6 |
| 17 | Hackney | London | 0.40 | 4.9 |
| 18 | Merton | London | 0.40 | 16 |
| 19 | Wokingham | South East | 0.40 | 25.2 |
| 20 | Barnet | London | 0.41 | 15 |
| 21 | Guildford | South East | 0.43 | 25.7 |
| 22 | Haringey | London | 0.43 | 7.1 |
| 23 | Chiltern | South East | 0.44 | 32.7 |
| 24 | Windsor and Maidenhead | South East | 0.44 | 28.2 |
| 25 | Hart | South East | 0.45 | 27.5 |
| | Average: top unfavourable | | 0.33 | 16.7 |

*Source*: European Parliament Elections 2014 (June 2014), House of Commons Library Research Paper 14/32; 2011 Census.

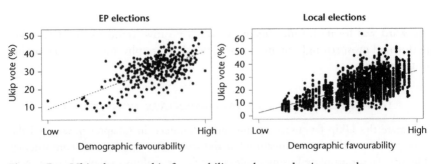

**Figure B1.** Ukip demographic favourability and 2014 elections results

**Table B5.** Factor loadings for Ukip demographic favourability by parliamentary constituency

| Variable | Factor 1 |
| --- | --- |
| *Favourable Ukip traits* | |
| Routine and manual (%) | +0.95 |
| No formal qualifications (%) | +0.91 |
| White (%) | +0.36 |
| Aged 65+ (%) | +0.35 |
| *Unfavourable Ukip traits* | |
| Professional and administrative (%) | −0.84 |
| Advanced qualifications (%) | −0.96 |
| Aged 18–30 (%) | −0.30 |
| N | 573 |
| Eigenvalue | 3.7 |
| Variance explained | 0.60 |

*Note*: The eigenvalue of the first factor was 3.70.
*Source*: 2011 Census.

of the variance in the seven traits. The factor loadings for the four traits that are generally associated with greater support for Ukip had a positive sign, while the factor loadings for the three traits that are generally associated with lower Ukip support had a negative sign (see Table B5). We used the predicted values from the first factor to measure a seat's overall favourability to Ukip and rescaled these values to fall between '0' (highly unfavourable) and '1' (highly favourable). Table B6 presents the Ukip demographic favourability scores for all local authorities in England and Wales. Table B7 contains the demographic favourability score for Ukip's 2015 target seats.

If we compare our measure of Ukip favourability with the party's share of the vote in the seat in the 2015 general election, we find that, once again, demographic favourability is a strong predictor of the party's performance. Figure B2 displays Ukip's 2015 vote share on the vertical axis and the favourability score on the horizontal axis. We see a strong, positive correlation between the demographic composition and Ukip's performance.[3] In seats that are more favourable to Ukip, the party received a higher share of the vote.

### IDENTIFYING GOOD PROSPECTS FOR UKIP IN 2015

In order to identify the seats that could have offered Ukip the best prospects in 2015, we started by using our Ukip favourability measure to identify the seats that

**Table B6.** Ukip demographic favourability by parliamentary constituency

| Name | Ukip favourability score | Name | Ukip favourability score |
|---|---|---|---|
| Aberavon | 0.94 | Birmingham, Perry Barr | 0.52 |
| Aberconwy | 0.77 | Birmingham, Selly Oak | 0.54 |
| Aldershot | 0.59 | Birmingham, Yardley | 0.74 |
| Aldridge-Brownhills | 0.80 | Bishop Auckland | 0.89 |
| Altrincham and Sale West | 0.44 | Blackburn | 0.67 |
| Alyn and Deeside | 0.80 | Blackley and Broughton | 0.70 |
| Amber Valley | 0.88 | Blackpool North and | 0.88 |
| Arfon | 0.67 | Cleveleys | |
| Arundel and South | 0.60 | Blackpool South | 0.93 |
| Downs | | Blaenau Gwent | 0.99 |
| Ashfield | 0.95 | Blaydon | 0.79 |
| Ashford | 0.70 | Blyth Valley | 0.84 |
| Ashton-under-Lyne | 0.84 | Bognor Regis and | 0.82 |
| Aylesbury | 0.54 | Littlehampton | |
| Banbury | 0.64 | Bolsover | 0.93 |
| Barking | 0.60 | Bolton North East | 0.72 |
| Barnsley Central | 0.90 | Bolton South East | 0.77 |
| Barnsley East | 0.95 | Bolton West | 0.67 |
| Barrow and Furness | 0.82 | Bootle | 0.90 |
| Basildon and Billericay | 0.73 | Boston and Skegness | 0.97 |
| Basingstoke | 0.57 | Bosworth | 0.75 |
| Bassetlaw | 0.86 | Bournemouth East | 0.62 |
| Bath | 0.43 | Bournemouth West | 0.66 |
| Batley and Spen | 0.72 | Bracknell | 0.53 |
| Battersea | 0.00 | Bradford East | 0.66 |
| Beaconsfield | 0.45 | Bradford South | 0.79 |
| Beckenham | 0.43 | Bradford West | 0.50 |
| Bedford | 0.60 | Braintree | 0.73 |
| Bermondsey and Old | 0.14 | Brecon and Radnorshire | 0.78 |
| Southwark | | Brent Central | 0.36 |
| Berwick-upon-Tweed | 0.79 | Brent North | 0.25 |
| Bethnal Green and Bow | 0.15 | Brentford and Isleworth | 0.23 |
| Beverley and Holderness | 0.73 | Brentwood and Ongar | 0.59 |
| Bexhill and Battle | 0.73 | Bridgend | 0.74 |
| Bexleyheath and Crayford | 0.69 | Bridgwater and West | 0.84 |
| Birkenhead | 0.84 | Somerset | |
| Birmingham, Edgbaston | 0.42 | Brigg and Goole | 0.85 |
| Birmingham, Erdington | 0.76 | Brighton, Kemptown | 0.63 |
| Birmingham, Hall Green | 0.39 | Brighton, Pavilion | 0.36 |
| Birmingham, Hodge Hill | 0.66 | Bristol East | 0.67 |
| Birmingham, Ladywood | 0.31 | Bristol North West | 0.57 |
| Birmingham, Northfield | 0.77 | Bristol South | 0.73 |

| | | | |
|---|---|---|---|
| Bristol West | 0.15 | Chipping Barnet | 0.36 |
| Broadland | 0.77 | Chorley | 0.68 |
| Bromley and Chislehurst | 0.48 | Christchurch | 0.75 |
| Bromsgrove | 0.62 | Cities of London and | 0.04 |
| Broxbourne | 0.73 | Westminster | |
| Broxtowe | 0.62 | City of Chester | 0.57 |
| Buckingham | 0.54 | City of Durham | 0.62 |
| Burnley | 0.81 | Clacton | 1.00 |
| Burton | 0.76 | Cleethorpes | 0.87 |
| Bury North | 0.66 | Clwyd South | 0.84 |
| Bury South | 0.67 | Clwyd West | 0.78 |
| Bury St Edmunds | 0.68 | Colchester | 0.58 |
| Caerphilly | 0.84 | Colne Valley | 0.62 |
| Calder Valley | 0.66 | Congleton | 0.65 |
| Camberwell and Peckham | 0.28 | Copeland | 0.82 |
| Camborne and Redruth | 0.83 | Corby | 0.81 |
| Cambridge | 0.28 | Coventry North East | 0.69 |
| Cannock Chase | 0.86 | Coventry North West | 0.67 |
| Canterbury | 0.54 | Coventry South | 0.51 |
| Cardiff Central | 0.35 | Crawley | 0.63 |
| Cardiff North | 0.46 | Crewe and Nantwich | 0.75 |
| Cardiff South and Penarth | 0.59 | Croydon Central | 0.43 |
| Cardiff West | 0.60 | Croydon North | 0.31 |
| Carlisle | 0.84 | Croydon South | 0.37 |
| Carmarthen East and | 0.81 | Cynon Valley | 0.93 |
| Dinefwr | | Dagenham and Rainham | 0.73 |
| Carmarthen West and | 0.81 | Darlington | 0.80 |
| Pembrokeshire South | | Dartford | 0.66 |
| Carshalton and Wallington | 0.55 | Daventry | 0.66 |
| Castle Point | 0.86 | Delyn | 0.80 |
| Central Devon | 0.71 | Denton and Reddish | 0.83 |
| Central Suffolk and North | 0.72 | Derby North | 0.62 |
| Ipswich | | Derby South | 0.70 |
| Ceredigion | 0.68 | Derbyshire Dales | 0.67 |
| Charnwood | 0.65 | Devizes | 0.59 |
| Chatham and Aylesford | 0.77 | Dewsbury | 0.68 |
| Cheadle | 0.49 | Don Valley | 0.88 |
| Chelmsford | 0.56 | Doncaster Central | 0.82 |
| Chelsea and Fulham | 0.09 | Doncaster North | 0.95 |
| Cheltenham | 0.51 | Dover | 0.81 |
| Chesham and Amersham | 0.44 | Dudley North | 0.83 |
| Chesterfield | 0.81 | Dudley South | 0.85 |
| Chichester | 0.62 | Dulwich and West | 0.18 |
| Chingford and Woodford | 0.48 | Norwood | |
| Green | | Dwyfor Meirionnydd | 0.83 |
| Chippenham | 0.65 | Ealing Central and Acton | 0.16 |

*(continued)*

**Table B6.** Continued

| Name | Ukip favourability score | Name | Ukip favourability score |
|---|---|---|---|
| Ealing North | 0.41 | Grantham and Stamford | 0.74 |
| Ealing, Southall | 0.30 | Gravesham | 0.71 |
| Easington | 0.96 | Great Grimsby | 0.95 |
| East Devon | 0.67 | Great Yarmouth | 0.94 |
| East Ham | 0.29 | Greenwich and Woolwich | 0.29 |
| East Hampshire | 0.58 | Guildford | 0.39 |
| East Surrey | 0.55 | Hackney North and Stoke Newington | 0.25 |
| East Worthing and Shoreham | 0.73 | Hackney South and Shoreditch | 0.21 |
| East Yorkshire and the Humber | 0.83 | Halesowen and Rowley Regis | 0.79 |
| Eastbourne | 0.72 | Halifax | 0.74 |
| Eastleigh | 0.65 | Haltemprice and Howden | 0.63 |
| Eddisbury | 0.69 | Halton | 0.86 |
| Edmonton | 0.53 | Hammersmith | 0.14 |
| Ellesmere Port and Neston | 0.77 | Hampstead and Kilburn | 0.08 |
| Elmet and Rothwell | 0.68 | Harborough | 0.59 |
| Eltham | 0.56 | Harlow | 0.75 |
| Enfield North | 0.55 | Harrogate and Knaresborough | 0.57 |
| Enfield, Southgate | 0.35 | | |
| Epping Forest | 0.61 | Harrow East | 0.30 |
| Epsom and Ewell | 0.46 | Harrow West | 0.20 |
| Erewash | 0.83 | Hartlepool | 0.90 |
| Erith and Thamesmead | 0.55 | Harwich and North Essex | 0.73 |
| Esher and Walton | 0.39 | Hastings and Rye | 0.78 |
| Exeter | 0.59 | Havant | 0.79 |
| Fareham | 0.61 | Hayes and Harlington | 0.48 |
| Faversham and Mid Kent | 0.70 | Hazel Grove | 0.68 |
| Feltham and Heston | 0.44 | Hemel Hempstead | 0.61 |
| Filton and Bradley Stoke | 0.56 | Hemsworth | 0.90 |
| Finchley and Golders Green | 0.23 | Hendon | 0.34 |
| Folkestone and Hythe | 0.76 | Henley | 0.51 |
| Forest of Dean | 0.79 | Hereford and South Herefordshire | 0.77 |
| Fylde | 0.65 | | |
| Gainsborough | 0.77 | Hertford and Stortford | 0.53 |
| Garston and Halewood | 0.80 | Hertsmere | 0.53 |
| Gateshead | 0.82 | Hexham | 0.61 |
| Gedling | 0.71 | Heywood and Middleton | 0.80 |
| Gillingham and Rainham | 0.72 | High Peak | 0.70 |
| Gloucester | 0.71 | Hitchin and Harpenden | 0.40 |
| Gosport | 0.73 | Holborn and St Pancras | 0.18 |
| Gower | 0.67 | | |

| | | | |
|---|---|---|---|
| Hornchurch and Upminster | 0.72 | Leyton and Wanstead | 0.28 |
| | | Lichfield | 0.67 |
| Hornsey and Wood Green | 0.18 | Lincoln | 0.71 |
| Horsham | 0.55 | Liverpool, Riverside | 0.43 |
| Houghton and Sunderland South | 0.92 | Liverpool, Walton | 0.95 |
| | | Liverpool, Wavertree | 0.63 |
| Hove | 0.46 | Liverpool, West Derby | 0.87 |
| Huddersfield | 0.62 | Llanelli | 0.86 |
| Huntingdon | 0.61 | Loughborough | 0.57 |
| Hyndburn | 0.79 | Louth and Horncastle | 0.89 |
| Ilford North | 0.38 | Ludlow | 0.75 |
| Ilford South | 0.23 | Luton North | 0.56 |
| Ipswich | 0.71 | Luton South | 0.53 |
| Isle of Wight | 0.81 | Macclesfield | 0.58 |
| Islington North | 0.17 | Maidenhead | 0.41 |
| Islington South and Finsbury | 0.16 | Maidstone and The Weald | 0.62 |
| | | Makerfield | 0.84 |
| Islwyn | 0.91 | Maldon | 0.70 |
| Jarrow | 0.85 | Manchester Central | 0.38 |
| Keighley | 0.66 | Manchester, Gorton | 0.43 |
| Kenilworth and Southam | 0.52 | Manchester, Withington | 0.23 |
| Kensington | 0.12 | Mansfield | 0.89 |
| Kettering | 0.73 | Meon Valley | 0.60 |
| Kingston and Surbiton | 0.34 | Meriden | 0.68 |
| Kingston upon Hull East | 0.97 | Merthyr Tydfil and Rhymney | 0.95 |
| Kingston upon Hull North | 0.79 | | |
| | | Mid Bedfordshire | 0.57 |
| Kingston upon Hull West and Hessle | 0.88 | Mid Derbyshire | 0.64 |
| | | Mid Dorset and North Poole | 0.69 |
| Kingswood | 0.73 | | |
| Knowsley | 0.96 | Mid Norfolk | 0.81 |
| Lancaster and Fleetwood | 0.65 | Mid Sussex | 0.53 |
| Leeds Central | 0.56 | Mid Worcestershire | 0.71 |
| Leeds East | 0.80 | Middlesbrough | 0.83 |
| Leeds North East | 0.33 | Middlesbrough South and East Cleveland | 0.82 |
| Leeds North West | 0.42 | | |
| Leeds West | 0.71 | Milton Keynes North | 0.51 |
| Leicester East | 0.55 | Milton Keynes South | 0.56 |
| Leicester South | 0.44 | Mitcham and Morden | 0.44 |
| Leicester West | 0.69 | Mole Valley | 0.50 |
| Leigh | 0.81 | Monmouth | 0.65 |
| Lewes | 0.66 | Montgomeryshire | 0.82 |
| Lewisham East | 0.36 | Morecambe and Lunesdale | 0.81 |
| Lewisham West and Penge | 0.34 | Morley and Outwood | 0.72 |
| Lewisham, Deptford | 0.21 | Neath | 0.87 |

*(continued)*

**Table B6.** Continued

| Name | Ukip favourability score | Name | Ukip favourability score |
|---|---|---|---|
| New Forest East | 0.71 | Northampton South | 0.66 |
| New Forest West | 0.71 | Norwich North | 0.80 |
| Newark | 0.70 | Norwich South | 0.56 |
| Newbury | 0.57 | Nottingham East | 0.49 |
| Newcastle upon Tyne Central | 0.61 | Nottingham North | 0.88 |
| | | Nottingham South | 0.45 |
| Newcastle upon Tyne East | 0.50 | Nuneaton | 0.80 |
| Newcastle upon Tyne North | 0.71 | Ogmore | 0.92 |
| | | Old Bexley and Sidcup | 0.64 |
| Newcastle-under-Lyme | 0.75 | Oldham East and Saddleworth | 0.71 |
| Newport East | 0.80 | | |
| Newport West | 0.69 | Oldham West and Royton | 0.75 |
| Newton Abbot | 0.76 | Orpington | 0.58 |
| Normanton, Pontefract and Castleford | 0.94 | Oxford East | 0.35 |
| | | Oxford West and Abingdon | 0.41 |
| North Cornwall | 0.84 | | |
| North Devon | 0.81 | Pendle | 0.74 |
| North Dorset | 0.70 | Penistone and Stocksbridge | 0.76 |
| North Durham | 0.85 | Penrith and The Border | 0.79 |
| North East Bedfordshire | 0.59 | Peterborough | 0.74 |
| North East Cambridgeshire | 0.90 | Plymouth, Moor View | 0.91 |
| | | Plymouth, Sutton and Devonport | 0.63 |
| North East Derbyshire | 0.80 | | |
| North East Hampshire | 0.44 | Pontypridd | 0.73 |
| North East Hertfordshire | 0.59 | Poole | 0.69 |
| North East Somerset | 0.69 | Poplar and Limehouse | 0.09 |
| North Herefordshire | 0.73 | Portsmouth North | 0.75 |
| North Norfolk | 0.85 | Portsmouth South | 0.51 |
| North Shropshire | 0.77 | Preseli Pembrokeshire | 0.81 |
| North Somerset | 0.58 | Preston | 0.68 |
| North Swindon | 0.71 | Pudsey | 0.57 |
| North Thanet | 0.84 | Putney | 0.14 |
| North Tyneside | 0.82 | Rayleigh and Wickford | 0.73 |
| North Warwickshire | 0.84 | Reading East | 0.32 |
| North West Cambridgeshire | 0.64 | Reading West | 0.57 |
| | | Redcar | 0.91 |
| North West Durham | 0.82 | Redditch | 0.75 |
| North West Hampshire | 0.64 | Reigate | 0.46 |
| North West Leicestershire | 0.77 | Rhondda | 1.00 |
| North West Norfolk | 0.87 | Ribble Valley | 0.67 |
| North Wiltshire | 0.60 | Richmond (Yorks) | 0.63 |
| Northampton North | 0.71 | Richmond Park | 0.17 |

| | | | |
|---|---|---|---|
| Rochdale | 0.71 | South Cambridgeshire | 0.45 |
| Rochester and Strood | 0.71 | South Derbyshire | 0.71 |
| Rochford and Southend East | 0.75 | South Dorset | 0.76 |
| | | South East Cambridgeshire | 0.56 |
| Romford | 0.67 | | |
| Romsey and Southampton North | 0.51 | South East Cornwall | 0.76 |
| | | South Holland and The Deepings | 0.89 |
| Rossendale and Darwen | 0.74 | | |
| Rother Valley | 0.81 | South Leicestershire | 0.67 |
| Rotherham | 0.88 | South Norfolk | 0.71 |
| Rugby | 0.67 | South Northamptonshire | 0.56 |
| Ruislip, Northwood and Pinner | 0.33 | South Ribble | 0.69 |
| | | South Shields | 0.87 |
| Runnymede and Weybridge | 0.47 | South Staffordshire | 0.71 |
| | | South Suffolk | 0.73 |
| Rushcliffe | 0.45 | South Swindon | 0.63 |
| Rutland and Melton | 0.65 | South Thanet | 0.80 |
| Saffron Walden | 0.59 | South West Bedfordshire | 0.67 |
| Salford and Eccles | 0.65 | South West Devon | 0.68 |
| Salisbury | 0.62 | South West Hertfordshire | 0.46 |
| Scarborough and Whitby | 0.83 | South West Norfolk | 0.86 |
| Scunthorpe | 0.88 | South West Surrey | 0.47 |
| Sedgefield | 0.85 | South West Wiltshire | 0.73 |
| Sefton Central | 0.66 | Southampton, Itchen | 0.69 |
| Selby and Ainsty | 0.70 | Southampton, Test | 0.57 |
| Sevenoaks | 0.58 | Southend West | 0.67 |
| Sheffield Central | 0.30 | Southport | 0.72 |
| Sheffield South East | 0.83 | Spelthorne | 0.59 |
| Sheffield, Brightside and Hillsborough | 0.82 | St Albans | 0.34 |
| | | St Austell and Newquay | 0.86 |
| Sheffield, Hallam | 0.37 | St Helens North | 0.84 |
| Sheffield, Heeley | 0.77 | St Helens South and Whiston | 0.84 |
| Sherwood | 0.83 | | |
| Shipley | 0.59 | St Ives | 0.78 |
| Shrewsbury and Atcham | 0.69 | Stafford | 0.64 |
| Sittingbourne and Sheppey | 0.85 | Staffordshire Moorlands | 0.80 |
| | | Stalybridge and Hyde | 0.79 |
| Skipton and Ripon | 0.66 | Stevenage | 0.64 |
| Sleaford and North Hykeham | 0.73 | Stockport | 0.67 |
| | | Stockton North | 0.86 |
| Slough | 0.43 | Stockton South | 0.66 |
| Solihull | 0.55 | Stoke-on-Trent Central | 0.82 |
| Somerton and Frome | 0.72 | Stoke-on-Trent North | 0.93 |
| South Basildon and East Thurrock | 0.82 | Stoke-on-Trent South | 0.91 |
| | | Stone | 0.68 |

(*continued*)

**Table B6.** Continued

| Name | Ukip favourability score | Name | Ukip favourability score |
|---|---|---|---|
| Stourbridge | 0.76 | Walthamstow | 0.37 |
| Stratford-on-Avon | 0.61 | Wansbeck | 0.82 |
| Streatham | 0.15 | Wantage | 0.55 |
| Stretford and Urmston | 0.63 | Warley | 0.66 |
| Stroud | 0.66 | Warrington North | 0.75 |
| Suffolk Coastal | 0.75 | Warrington South | 0.59 |
| Sunderland Central | 0.79 | Warwick and Leamington | 0.47 |
| Surrey Heath | 0.49 | Washington and | 0.91 |
| Sutton and Cheam | 0.46 | Sunderland West | |
| Sutton Coldfield | 0.49 | Watford | 0.46 |
| Swansea East | 0.88 | Waveney | 0.91 |
| Swansea West | 0.60 | Wealden | 0.63 |
| Tamworth | 0.80 | Weaver Vale | 0.71 |
| Tatton | 0.53 | Wellingborough | 0.77 |
| Taunton Deane | 0.70 | Wells | 0.76 |
| Telford | 0.82 | Welwyn Hatfield | 0.51 |
| Tewkesbury | 0.65 | Wentworth and Dearne | 0.93 |
| The Cotswolds | 0.63 | West Bromwich East | 0.78 |
| The Wrekin | 0.69 | West Bromwich West | 0.86 |
| Thirsk and Malton | 0.76 | West Dorset | 0.70 |
| Thornbury and Yate | 0.67 | West Ham | 0.31 |
| Thurrock | 0.73 | West Lancashire | 0.74 |
| Tiverton and Honiton | 0.79 | West Suffolk | 0.75 |
| Tonbridge and Malling | 0.61 | West Worcestershire | 0.65 |
| Tooting | 0.10 | Westminster North | 0.15 |
| Torbay | 0.83 | Westmorland and Lonsdale | 0.70 |
| Torfaen | 0.88 | Weston-Super-Mare | 0.76 |
| Torridge and West Devon | 0.80 | Wigan | 0.85 |
| Totnes | 0.75 | Wimbledon | 0.12 |
| Tottenham | 0.44 | Winchester | 0.45 |
| Truro and Falmouth | 0.66 | Windsor | 0.41 |
| Tunbridge Wells | 0.54 | Wirral South | 0.66 |
| Twickenham | 0.26 | Wirral West | 0.63 |
| Tynemouth | 0.65 | Witham | 0.71 |
| Uxbridge and South | 0.45 | Witney | 0.59 |
| Ruislip | | Woking | 0.41 |
| Vale of Clwyd | 0.84 | Wokingham | 0.37 |
| Vale of Glamorgan | 0.70 | Wolverhampton North | 0.83 |
| Vauxhall | 0.08 | East | |
| Wakefield | 0.79 | Wolverhampton South | 0.82 |
| Wallasey | 0.82 | East | |
| Walsall North | 0.94 | Wolverhampton South | 0.51 |
| Walsall South | 0.67 | West | |

| | | | |
|---|---|---|---|
| Worcester | 0.65 | Wythenshawe and Sale East | 0.69 |
| Workington | 0.88 | | |
| Worsley and Eccles South | 0.79 | Yeovil | 0.77 |
| Worthing West | 0.70 | Ynys Môn | 0.79 |
| Wrexham | 0.79 | York Central | 0.54 |
| Wycombe | 0.45 | York Outer | 0.61 |
| Wyre and Preston North | 0.60 | | |
| Wyre Forest | 0.81 | *Source*: 2011 Census. | |

**Table B7.** Demographic favourability of Ukip's 2015 target seats

| Name | Region | Ukip favourability score |
|---|---|---|
| Clacton | East of England | 1.00 |
| Boston and Skegness | East Midlands | 0.97 |
| Great Grimsby | Yorkshire | 0.95 |
| Great Yarmouth | East of England | 0.94 |
| Wentworth and Dearne | Yorkshire and the Humber | 0.93 |
| Plymouth, Moor View | South West | 0.91 |
| Hartlepool | North East | 0.90 |
| Rotherham | Yorkshire | 0.88 |
| North West Norfolk | East of England | 0.87 |
| Cannock Chase | West Midlands | 0.86 |
| St Austell and Newquay | South West | 0.86 |
| Castle Point | East of England | 0.86 |
| Sittingbourne and Sheppey | South East | 0.85 |
| North Thanet | South East | 0.84 |
| Camborne and Redruth | South West | 0.83 |
| Torbay | South West | 0.83 |
| Dudley North | West Midlands | 0.83 |
| Bognor Regis and Littlehampton | South East | 0.82 |
| South Basildon and East Thurrock | East of England | 0.82 |
| Dover | South East | 0.81 |
| Wyre Forest | West Midlands | 0.81 |
| North Devon | South West | 0.81 |
| Delyn | Wales | 0.80 |
| South Thanet | South East | 0.80 |
| Heywood and Middleton | North West | 0.80 |
| Forest of Dean | South West | 0.79 |
| Folkestone and Hythe | South East | 0.76 |
| Thurrock | East of England | 0.73 |
| Basildon and Billericay | East of England | 0.73 |
| Rochester and Strood | South East | 0.71 |
| Eastleigh | South East | 0.65 |
| North West Cambridgeshire | East of England | 0.64 |

*Source*: 2011 Census.

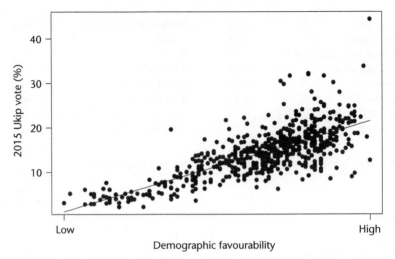

**Figure B2.** Ukip demographic favourability and 2015 support by parliamentary constituency

were demographically favourable to the party. Figure B3 presents the favourability scores for all seats in England and Wales. The more favourable a seat, the darker its shade. After we had filtered out all the seats that were not highly favourable—those in the top quartile of all seats—we were left with a long list of 142 seats that had lots of struggling, white, and older voters who lack qualifications. This left clusters on the east coast, in the East Midlands, South West, Yorkshire, Cumbria, and Wales. If we look only at the types of voters who reside in them, and not anything else, the five most favourable seats were the Labour seat of Rhonda in south Wales, Douglas Carswell's seat of Clacton, Blaenau Gwent, another Labour seat in south Wales, the Conservative seat of Boston and Skegness, and the Labour seat of Kingston upon Hull East, in Yorkshire. Many other seats in the top fifty were in Ukip's eastern heartlands and included some of the usual suspects—the old mining Labour seat of Ashfield in Nottinghamshire, the former fishing stronghold of Great Grimsby, the fading coastal seat of Great Yarmouth, the Conservative marginal seat of Waveney in Suffolk, the more northern Labour fiefdom of Hartlepool in County Durham, controlled by Labour since 1964, the safe Conservative and rural seat of North East Cambridgeshire, and Louth and Horncastle, another safe, rural, and coastal Conservative seat in Lincolnshire, held by the Tories since 1924. Of the 142 seats, 63 per cent were held by Labour and 31 per cent were held by Tories.

These seats contrasted sharply with those at the bottom of the list. Most were in London. Farage's appeal would probably have fallen flat in these typically urban, more financially secure, and diverse seats that have higher numbers of graduates and people working in more secure jobs and who come from quite different ethnic backgrounds. Battersea was the least favourable of all, an inner-city Conservative seat in south London that includes an eclectic mix of affluent neighbourhoods and pockets of high deprivation. It was followed by the landmark-filled Cities of London and Westminster, the seat of Vauxhall, which is across the river from Westminster, the leafy north London Labour seat of Hampstead and Kilburn, located next to Brent Central, where the candidate was convinced of victory, and Poplar and Limehouse, an area of London that has long been held by Labour and encompasses the affluence of Canary Wharf and the diversity in Tower Hamlets. Only eight of the fifty least favourable areas were located outside London. That being said, there were a few London seats that were considerably more favourable to Ukip—Dagenham and Rainham and Hornchurch and Upminister. Though neither has sufficiently large numbers of Ukip-friendly groups to be deemed highly favourable, both of the seats were outliers in London—nearly one in three individuals being working class or without qualifications. In the rest of London it is less than one in four. They are also less diverse than the typical London seat.

The map in Figure B3 offers interesting insights, but, even though some seats looked receptive, they were unlikely to see Ukip breakthrough. Consider seats in northern England like Easington in County Durham. This looked like a good prospect, but Easington was one of Labour's safest seats, having been represented since the 1920s by some of the most influential figures in the history of left-wing politics, such as Sidney Webb, Ramsay MacDonald, and the fireband Manny

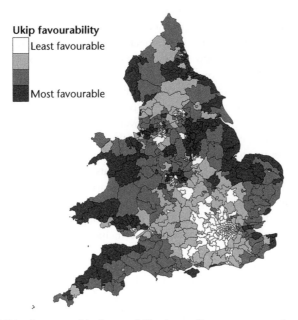

**Figure B3.** Ukip demographic favourability by parliamentary constituency

Shinwell. That Ukip would struggle was clear at the European elections, when it finished second with 28 per cent and eleven points behind Labour. Other seats that are filled with similar voters but were unlikely to see a breakthrough include Knowsley, where Labour often wins more than 70 per cent of the vote, and Liverpool Walton, which Labour has held since 1964. Despite their struggling areas, at the European elections Ukip had finished more than thirty points behind Labour.

This is why the favourable seats were put through a second stage of filtering, based on their support for Ukip at the 2014 European elections.[4] If the party struggled at these elections, then it was unlikely to perform strongly at a general election. Removing seats where Ukip failed to win more than 30 per cent of the vote reduces our list to sixty-seven seats, which have receptive voters *and* a history of giving Ukip strong support. While Clacton, Boston and Skegness, and Kingston-upon-Hull East remained in the top five, the Welsh seats of Rhonnda and Blaenau Gwent dropped out, and were replaced by the south Yorkshire Labour seats and old mining areas of Barnsley East and Doncaster North. One-quarter of the seats that made it through the second stage were in Eastern, South Eastern or South Western England, while almost half were in the Midlands, or Yorkshire. We also began to see more balance in the political control. Labour controlled 55 per cent of the remaining seats, the Tories 40 per cent. But, even if seats were filled with voters who find Ukip appealing, and had already given strong support, we also needed to consider whether they were vulnerable to a political challenge in a general election.

Consider Ed Miliband's seat of Doncaster North. The voters in this northern seat were ideal for Ukip, which was reflected in the fact that more than one in three of them voted for Ukip at the European elections, allowing the party to finish ahead of Labour by one point. But at general elections this seat has been electing Labour for generations. In 2010 Miliband won a majority of over 10,000 votes. Or think about Barnsley East. Ukip took 36 per cent at the European elections, but Labour had had a majority of over 11,000 votes. To find seats that are vulnerable we removed those where the sitting MP received more than 45 per cent of the vote in 2010 or held more than a 10 per cent lead over the second-placed candidate. This leaves us with marginal seats where the vote was split across two or even three candidates, giving insurgent parties a better chance of running through the middle. Seats are also more vulnerable if the MP had decided to stand down ahead of the general election in 2015, as this removed benefits associated with incumbency. For obvious reasons, we include Clacton and Rochester and Strood as politically favourable.

This reduced our list from sixty-seven to twenty-six seats, shown in Table B8. These were the best prospects for a breakthrough because they had the winning combination of receptive voters, strong support, and a political opening. Clacton stayed at number one. Next was Boston and Skegness, where Ukip had polled its

**Table B8.** Ukip's top prospects in 2015

| Rank | Constituency | Incumbent | Majority (%) |
|------|-------------|-----------|--------------|
| 1 | Clacton | Conservative | 28.0 |
| 2 | Boston & Skegness★ | Conservative | 28.8 |
| 3 | Ashfield | Labour | 0.4 |
| 4 | Great Grimsby | Labour | 2.2 |
| 5 | Great Yarmouth | Conservative | 9.9 |
| 6 | Stoke-on-Trent North★ | Labour | 20.5 |
| 7 | Redcar★ | Lib Dem | 12.4 |
| 8 | Plymouth, Moor View | Labour | 3.8 |
| 9 | Waveney | Conservative | 1.5 |
| 10 | Louth and Horncastle★ | Conservative | 27.5 |
| 11 | Scunthorpe | Labour | 6.9 |
| 12 | Blackpool North and Cleveleys | Conservative | 5.3 |
| 13 | Don Valley | Labour | 8.3 |
| 14 | Cleethorpes | Conservative | 9.6 |
| 15 | Cannock Chase★ | Conservative | 7.0 |
| 16 | St Austell and Newquay | Lib Dem | 2.8 |
| 17 | Dudley South★ | Conservative | 10.1 |
| 18 | North Warwickshire★ | Conservative | 0.1 |
| 19 | Camborne and Redruth | Conservative | 0.2 |
| 20 | Sherwood | Conservative | 0.4 |
| 21 | Dudley North | Labour | 1.7 |
| 22 | Telford | Labour | 2.4 |
| 23 | Middlesbrough South and East Cleveland | Labour | 3.6 |
| 24 | Corby | Conservative | 3.5 |
| 25 | South Thanet★ | Conservative | 16.6 |
| 26 | Nuneaton | Conservative | 4.6 |

★ Sitting MP stood down in 2015.

*Sources*: 2015 BES Constituency Results with Census and Candidate Data. Full results available at <www.britishelectionstudy.com> (accessed 15 June 2015); Parliamentary Candidates UK: <http://parliamentarycandidates.org/data/mps-standing-down/> (accessed 15 June 2015).

highest vote at the European election and the Conservative MP had decided to stand down. Third on the list was the former mining area of Ashfield in Nottinghamshire, which after 2010 was also the twelfth most marginal seat when Labour's Gloria De Piero won with a lead of only 192 votes. Ranked fourth is Great Grimsby, on the south bank of the Humber Estuary in north-east Lincolnshire. While the seat had been held by Labour since 1945—and by one MP, Austin Mitchell, since 1977—Mitchell returned to parliament in 2010 with a majority of only 714 votes. At the European elections Ukip won over 40 per cent in the area, finishing eighteen points ahead of Labour. It also won a handful of seats on the council. Then, one year before the general election, Mitchell announced that he would stand down, which seemed to clear the path for Ukip. Great Yarmouth, where Ukip won 45 per cent in the 2014 elections, rounds out the top five seats. In 2010, Conservative MP, Brandon Lewis, won 43 per cent of the vote, 4,000 votes more than Labour candidate Tony Wright.

Beyond these top prospects, the other seats included a cluster of northern Labour seats and marginal Conservative seats in Eastern England. While 58 per cent of them were held by the Tories, 34 per cent were held by Labour, and the remainder were held by Liberal Democrats. But this also paints a misleading picture. If we trace back the political power in these seats, then many that had elected Conservatives in 2010 had not been held by the party over the long term. Only four of the fifteen Conservative seats had been won by Tories in 2005. Twelve were previously held by Labour, like Great Yarmouth, Waveney, and Dudley South. By contrast, all nine of the seats that Labour had won in 2010 had also been won by Labour in 2005. In other words, while the Tories potentially stood to lose seats that they had only recently won from Labour, Ukip's rise also looked set to hamper Labour's attempt to regain seats that it had only recently lost to the Tories. In nine of these seats the MP was standing down ahead of the election, including Laura Sandys in South Thanet and Sir Peter Tapsell in Louth and Horncastle, while in seats where the MP was not standing down the median margin of victory was less than 5 per cent, underlining how these seats were highly competitive.

# Appendix C: Using the British Election Study to Explain Support for Ukip in 2014 and 2015

Throughout the book we have relied on data from the 2014–2017 British Election Study (BES) to help us explain why some people chose to support Ukip—while others did not—in the year and a half preceding the 2015 general election. The 2014–2017 BES was a collaborative effort between academics at the University of Manchester, the University of Oxford, and the University of Nottingham. Details on the study, as well as all the data, can be found on the study's website <www.britishelectionstudy.com>.

The 2014–2017 BES was an Internet panel survey conducted by YouGov. Internet panels are more cost effective than traditional face-to-face or telephone surveys, as they allow for a larger sample of respondents to be collected in a short period of time. The fact that Internet surveys rely on voluntary participation from those with access to the Internet has led many scholars to question the representativeness of the Internet-based surveys. Internet access tends to be lower among disadvantaged groups in society, thus the resulting pool of participants differs from the general population in important ways, and these differences may impact on our ability to study the political behaviour of the British public. That being said, YouGov takes extra care to recruit respondents from diverse backgrounds in order to ensure that views expressed reflect those of the general public. In addition, YouGov employs sophisticated weights based on census data, newspaper readership, and political identification to ensure that the data approximate to a representative sample.

Despite the potential drawbacks associated with Internet panels, the 2014–17 BES survey was ideal for our purposes for three reasons. First, BES respondents were asked a wide range of questions capturing their attitudes towards political parties and their leaders, their opinions on a variety of issues, their previous political engagements, and their perceptions of the political process. Taken together, these questions offer rich potential for scholars looking to understand the diverse motivations for Ukip support. Second, the 2014–2017 BES was a panel study that tracks the same people over time. Those who participated in the surveys were asked a series of questions about their political backgrounds, behaviour, and attitudes at key points in the electoral calendar. Therefore, the data gave us a picture of why more than four million people turned out for Ukip in the 2014 European elections, and helped us understand the motivations underlying loyalty to (and defection from) the party in the run-up to the 2015 general election. Finally, the survey contained a very large sample of self-identified Ukip supporters; more than 6,000 respondents reported that they had voted for Ukip in the European elections when surveyed in the second wave and more than 3,000 respondents said they had voted for the party in the 2015 general election when interviewed in the sixth wave of the survey. Having such a large sample of Ukip supporters aided our endeavour immensely. It allowed us to explore the roots of the party's appeal in a systematic way that would otherwise have been impossible were we to rely on just one survey or a few polls, which tend to contain very few supporters of smaller or newer parties.

The analyses presented in this book relied on the first six waves of the 2014–2017 BES study. Table C1 provides the Internet dates and sample size of the six waves.

Table C1. Summary 2014–17 British Election Study Internet Panel waves

| Wave | Interview period | Total respondents |
|------|------------------|-------------------|
| 1 | February 2014–March 2014 | 30,590 |
| 2 | May 2014–June 2014 | 30,219 |
| 3 | September 2014–October 2014 | 27,839 |
| 4 | March 2015 | 31,328 |
| 5 | March 2015–May 2015 | 30,725 |
| 6 | May 2015 | 30,027 |

*Source*: British Election Study <www.britishelectionstudy.com/>.

MEASUREMENT

In this section we present the question wording and the measurement of the key variables used in the analyses presented throughout the book. All the variables in our models are dichotomous—an individual either belongs to the given group or does not. This provided the more accessible interpretations of the effect sizes that are presented in the text.

**Age:** 'What is your age?'

**Class:** The measure of class is based on the National Statistics socio-economic classification (NS–SEC).

**Democracy in the EU:** 'On the whole, how satisfied or dissatisfied are you with the way that democracy works in the European Union.' Respondents who were 'very dissatisfied' or 'a little dissatisfied' were coded as having eurosceptic views.

**Economic evaluations (retrospective):** 'Now, a few questions about economic conditions. How does the financial situation of your household now compare with what it was 12 months ago? How do you think the general economic situation in this country has changed over the last 12 months?' Respondents who indicated that they believed the economic situation had 'got a lot worse' or 'got a little worse' were coded as having pessimistic retrospective economic evaluations.

**Economic evaluations (prospective):** 'How do you think the general economic situation in this country and the financial situation of your household will change over the next 12 months?' Respondents who indicated that they believed the economic situation had 'got a lot worse' or 'got a little worse' were coded as having pessimistic prospective economic evaluations.

**Education:** 'At what age did you finish full-time education?' We combine the categories for those who left school at 15 or younger and those who left school at 16. On the upper end of the scale, we also combined those who left school at 19, those who left at 20 or above, and those who are still enrolled in school.

**Ethnicity:** 'To which of these groups do you consider you belong?' Respondents are coded according to whether they selected 'White British' or 'Any other white background', and whether they selected any other group.

**European election vote choice:** 'Which party did you vote for in the European Elections?'

**Euroscepticism:** We used two variables to capture a respondent's attitudes towards Europe. The first question read: 'Some say European unification should be pushed further. Others say it has already gone too far. What is your opinion?' The second question read: 'Some people feel that Britain should do all it can to unite fully with the European Union. Other people feel that Britain should do all it can to protect its independence from the European Union. Where would you place yourself on this scale?' In both cases respondents were asked to self-place on a 10-point scale. Respondents who placed at five are taken as being neutral. Any respondent who indicated that he or she leans towards a eurosceptic position was coded as '1', while those who favour Europe or are neutral were coded as '0'. In the multivariate analyses we combined the two variables to create one measure of euroscepticism, as each scale was asked to only half of the respondents. This variable was coded '1' if a respondent gave a eurosceptic answer with regards to the question asked, and '0' otherwise.

**EU referendum vote choice:** 'If there was a referendum on Britain's membership of the European Union, how do you think you would vote?'

**Feelings about parties and party leaders:** 'How much do you like or dislike each of the following party/party leaders?' Respondents were asked to place each party and leader on a 10-point scale, where higher numbers indicate a more positive evaluation. Those respondents who placed the party/leader from '0' though '4' were coded as disliking the party/leader, those placed at '5' were coded as being indifferent, and those who placed the party/leader from '6' through '10' were coded as liking the party/leader.

**Gender:** 'Are you male or female?'

**General election vote choice:** 'If there were a UK General Election tomorrow, which party would you vote for?'

**General election vote choice certainty:** 'You said that you would be most likely to vote for [insert party] in a general election. How certain are you that you would vote for this party?' Respondents who self-placed at '6' or '7' on the 7-pt scale (higher numbers indicate greater certainty) were coded as being highly certain about their vote choice.

**Immigration:** Respondents' views on immigration were captured using three variables. The first question read: 'Do you think immigration is good or bad for Britain's economy?' The second question stated: 'And do you think that immigration undermines or enriches Britain's cultural life?' Both questions were measured on a 7-pt scale where lower numbers correspond to more negative views. Any respondent who selected '1', '2', or '3' was coded as having negative views on immigration. The third question read: 'How much do you agree or disagree with the following statement? Immigrants are a burden on the welfare state'. Those who answered 'strongly agree' were coded as having negative views on immigration. We also created an additional variable that captured whether respondents were *intensely* opposed to immigration. This was coded '1' if the respondent expressed negative views on immigration on all three questions and '0' otherwise.

**Left–right ideology:** 'In politics people sometimes talk of left and right. Where would you place yourself on the following scale?' Those respondents who self-placed from '0' though '4' were coded as left-wing, those who self-placed at '5' were coded as centrist, and those who self-placed from '6' through '10' were coded as right-wing.

**Left–right values:** We used two sets of questions to capture left–right values. The first set asked: 'How much do you agree or disagree with the following statements? Government should redistribute income from the better off to those who are less well off; Big business takes advantage of ordinary people; Ordinary working people do not get their fair share of the nation's wealth; There is one law for the rich and one for the poor; Management will always try to get the better of employees if it gets the chance.' Respondents who indicated that they 'strongly agree' or 'agree' with the given statement were coded as having more left-wing views. The second set of question stated: 'Do you think that each of these has gone too far or not far enough? Cuts to public spending in general/NHS spending/private companies running public services'. Those who said that cuts to public spending, the NHS, and privatization had gone 'too far' or 'much too far' were coded as having more left-wing views.

**Most important issue:** 'As far as you're concerned, what is the single most important issue facing the country at the present time?'

**No chance at coalition (SNP):** 'Which of these parties do you think has no real chance of being part of the next UK government (either forming a government by itself or as part of a coalition)?' Respondents who did *not* select the SNP were coded as believing that the SNP could play a role in the next government.

Party contact: 'Have any of the political parties contacted you during the past four weeks?' If the respondent gave an affirmative answer, a follow-up question was asked: 'Please indicate all the political parties that have contacted you during the past four weeks.' For all of the party contact variables, respondents are coded '1' if they were contacted by that party, and '0' if they were not contacted by the party.

Past general election vote choice: 'Thinking back to the General Election in May [2005/2010], do you remember which party you voted for then—or perhaps you didn't vote?'

Political dissatisfaction: Our first measure of disengagement was based on the extent to which respondents replied 'agree' or 'strongly agree' with the statement 'Politicians don't care what people like me think'. Trust in MPs is measured using a 7-pt scale, where higher numbers indicated more trust in an MP. We combine categories on the lower end of the scale, such that those who gave selected '1', '2', and '3' are coded as having little or no trust in MPs. Respondents who were coded as being dissatisfied with democracy included those who said that they are 'very dissatisfied' or 'a little dissatisfied' with the way that democracy works in the UK as a whole. In the multivariate analyses, we also used one composite measure of political dissatisfaction that was coded '1' if the respondent expressed all three of the following sentiments: they do not believe that politicians listen to ordinary people, they have little or no trust MPs, or they are 'very dissatisfied' or 'a little dissatisfied' with the way that democracy works in the UK. We also looked at whether respondents 'agree' or 'strongly agree' with the statement: 'It takes too much time and effort to be active in politics and public affairs.'.

Preferred election outcome: 'Please rank these election outcomes from your most preferred outcome to least preferred outcome: Conservative- led coalition, Labour led coalition, Conservative Majority, Labour Majority, Other government.' Those who ranked 'Conservative led coalition' and 'Conservative majority' as their top two choices were said to prefer a Conservative outcome, while those who ranked 'Labour led coalition' and 'Labour majority' as their top two choices were said to prefer a Labour outcome.

Propensity to vote: 'How likely is it that you would ever vote for each of the following parties?' We used this variable to determine a respondent's first and second preference across all parties.

Social protection: 'Please say whether you think these things have gone too far or have not gone far enough in Britain. Attempts to give equal opportunities to ethnic minorities/gays and lesbians.' Respondents were coded as having socially conservative views if they indicated that projects for the group had 'gone too far' and 'gone much too far'.

Ukip loyalists/defectors: In Chapter 5, Ukip loyalists are those respondents who reported that they voted for the party in the 2014 European elections and said that they would vote for the party again in a general election. Ukip defectors are those who voted for the party in the 2014 European Elections, but said they would vote for another party in a general election. In Chapter 11, loyalists are those who indicated that they planned to support Ukip when they were interviewed in Wave 2 and Wave 5. Defectors are those who said they planned to vote for Ukip when they were interviewed in Wave 2, but said they were no longer supporting the party when they were reinterviewed in Wave 5.

## METHODOLOGY

In the following sections, we present the analyses of BES data that inform our discussion throughout the book. In all models the data were weighted in accordance with recommendations made by the BES team. While the dependent variable of the models varies, in all cases, the outcome was a dichotomous variable—for example, someone either voted for Ukip or did not. Therefore, all our analyses were estimated using logistic regression. In each table the estimates are presented as 'odd ratios'—that is, they show the odds that a respondent with a certain trait would engage in the outcome of interest compared to a similar respondent who differs on that key trait. For example, when we model support for Ukip in the 2014 European elections, the estimates that relate to gender show the odds that a man would support Ukip, compared to a woman—the reference group. Figures greater than one indicate that men are more likely to support Ukip than women, while figures less than one indicate that men are less likely than women to vote for the party. The larger the odd ratio, the stronger the effect of that trait has on the respondent's vote choice. Where the reference group is not obvious, we have provided this information in parentheses; however, for all the survey response variables the reference group includes those who did not express or agree with the given sentiment.

## CHAPTER 5 FARAGE'S FOLLOWERS

**Table C2.** Models of Ukip support in the 2014 European elections

| Variable | Full model | Reduced model |
| --- | --- | --- |
| Social class (ref.: higher managerial/ professional) | | |
| Lower managerial/professional | 1.14 | 1.12 |
| Intermediate occupations | 1.07 | 1.08 |
| Small employers/self-employed | 1.27 | 1.17 |
| Lower supervisory/technical | 1.21 | 1.22 |
| Semi-routine | 1.05 | 1.04 |
| Routine | 1.40* | 1.46* |
| Education (ref.: left school after 18) | | |
| 16 or younger | 1.49** | 1.68** |
| 17–18 | 1.33** | 1.38** |
| Gender (ref.: female) | | |
| Male | 1.33** | 1.32** |
| Age (ref.: 18–24 years) | | |
| 25–34 | 2.06 | 2.22* |
| 35–44 | 2.43* | 2.65* |
| 45–54 | 2.67* | 2.94** |
| 55–64 | 2.96** | 3.19** |
| 65+ | 2.55* | 2.73** |
| Ethnicity (ref.: non-white) | | |
| White | 1.47* | 1.44* |
| Euroscepticism | 3.40** | |
| Immigrants a burden on welfare state | 1.60** | |
| Immigration bad for the economy | 1.78** | |
| Immigration undermines Britain's cultural life | 1.86** | |
| Composite issue variables (ref.: not eurosceptic or anti-immigration) | | |
| Eurosceptic only | | 4.91** |
| Anti-immigration only | | 4.44** |
| Anti-immigration and eurosceptic | | 10.61** |
| Left–right ideology (ref.: left) | | |
| Centre | 2.38** | 2.62** |
| Right | 3.52** | 3.59** |
| Social protection 'gone too far' | | |
| Ethnic minorities | 1.55** | 1.94** |
| Gays and lesbians | 1.12 | 1.19* |
| Women | 1.15 | 1.14 |
| Dissatisfaction with politics | | |
| Politicians don't care | 1.74** | |
| Little/no trust in MPs | 1.86** | |
| Dissatisfied with democracy | 1.50** | |
| High dissatisfaction | | 2.79** |

(continued)

**Table C2.** Continued

| Variable | Full model | Reduced model |
|---|---|---|
| Economic pessimism | | |
|   Household financial situation worse | 1.12 | 1.22* |
|   General economic situation worse | 0.89 | 0.98 |
| Party contact | | |
|   Ukip | 1.90** | 1.90** |
|   Conservative | 0.79* | 0.75** |
|   Labour | 0.72** | 0.73** |
|   Liberal Democrat | 0.85 | 0.81* |
| Constant | 0.00** | 0.00** |
| F-statistic | 48.93 | 51.38 |
| N | 10,942 | 10,942 |

*Notes:* \* p<0.05, \*\* p<0.01. The dependent variable was coded '1' if the respondent supported Ukip in the 2014 European elections and '0' if he voted for any other party. The first model included all of the key traits we discuss in Chapter 5. We then estimated a reduced model, which provides the figures referenced in Chapter 5.

*Source*: 2014–2017 British Election Study Internet Panel (Wave 2).

**Table C3.** Models of party support in the 2014 European elections

| Variable | Ukip | Conservative | Labour | Liberal Democrat | Non-voters |
|---|---|---|---|---|---|
| Social class (ref.: higher managerial/ professional) | | | | | |
|   Lower managerial/ professional | 1.14 | 0.99 | 1.09 | 0.89 | 0.99 |
|   Intermediate occupations | 1.07 | 0.84 | 1.70** | 0.66* | 1.11 |
|   Small employers/ self-employed | 1.27 | 0.81 | 0.94 | 0.99 | 1.27 |
|   Lower supervisory/ technical | 1.21 | 0.76 | 1.90** | 0.46* | 1.06 |
|   Semi-routine | 1.05 | 0.86 | 1.65** | 0.70 | 1.00 |
|   Routine | 1.40* | 0.79 | 1.07 | 0.93 | 1.14 |
| Education (ref.: left school after 18) | | | | | |
|   16 or younger | 1.49** | 0.91 | 1.62** | 0.47** | 1.19* |
|   17–18 | 1.33** | 1.03 | 1.21 | 0.73* | 1.18* |
| Gender (ref.: female) | | | | | |
|   Male | 1.33** | 0.75** | 1.10 | 1.28* | 0.85** |
| Age (ref.: 18–24 years) | | | | | |
|   25–34 | 2.06 | 1.38 | 0.53 | 1.47 | 0.70 |
|   35–44 | 2.43* | 1.14 | 0.54 | 1.59 | 0.59** |

| | | | | | |
|---|---|---|---|---|---|
| 45–54 | 2.67* | 0.97 | 0.52 | 1.80 | 0.39** |
| 55–64 | 2.96** | 0.96 | 0.41** | 2.46* | 0.37** |
| 65+ | 2.55* | 1.11 | 0.45* | 2.58* | 0.27** |
| Ethnicity (ref.: non-white) | | | | | |
| White | 1.47* | 1.09 | 0.40** | 1.26 | 0.88 |
| Euroscepticism | 3.40** | 1.18 | 0.61** | 0.36** | 0.87* |
| Immigrants a burden on welfare state | 1.60** | 0.78* | 0.91 | 0.30** | 0.78** |
| Immigration bad for the economy | 1.78** | 0.74** | 1.00 | 0.65* | 1.34** |
| Immigration undermines Britain's cultural life | 1.86** | 1.02 | 0.78* | 0.44** | 0.96 |
| Left–right ideology (ref.: left) | | | | | |
| Centre | 2.38** | 9.73** | 0.27** | 2.50** | 1.69** |
| Right | 3.52** | 24.58** | 0.08** | 0.79 | 1.15 |
| Social protection 'gone too far' | | | | | |
| Ethnic minorities | 1.55** | 0.89 | 0.78* | 0.93 | 1.11 |
| Gays and lesbians | 1.12 | 1.07 | 0.75** | 0.80 | 0.87 |
| Women | 1.15 | 0.99 | 1.04 | 1.23 | 0.84 |
| Dissatisfaction with politics | | | | | |
| Politicians don't care | 1.74** | 0.49** | 1.37** | 0.85 | 1.10 |
| Little/no trust in MPs | 1.86** | 0.56** | 0.53** | 0.79 | 1.31** |
| Dissatisfied with democracy | 1.50** | 0.48** | 0.78** | 0.97 | 0.91 |
| Economic pessimism (retrospective) | | | | | |
| Household financial situation worse | 1.12 | 0.80** | 1.33** | 0.98 | 0.84** |
| General economic situation worse | 0.89 | 0.35** | 2.07** | 0.50** | 0.85* |
| Party contact | | | | | |
| Ukip | 1.90** | 0.66** | 0.70** | 0.89 | 0.71** |
| Conservative | 0.79* | 1.93** | 0.76* | 0.67* | 0.73** |
| Labour | 0.72** | 0.72** | 2.80** | 0.40** | 0.69** |
| Liberal Democrat | 0.85 | 0.79* | 0.47** | 5.08** | 0.83 |
| Constant | 0.00** | 0.79* | 4.14** | 0.18** | 0.78 |
| F-statistic | 48.93 | 31.48 | 42.29 | 17.60 | 14.31 |
| N | 10,942 | 10,942 | 10,942 | 10,942 | 13,612 |

Notes: * p<0.05, ** p<0.01. The dependent variable is coded '1' if the respondent voted for the given party or abstained from voting, and '0' otherwise.

Source: 2014–2017 British Election Study Internet Panel (Wave 2).

**Table C4.** Models of Ukip loyalty, Ukip support only

| Variable | Full model | Reduced model |
|---|---|---|
| Social class (ref.: higher managerial/ professional) | | |
|    Lower managerial/professional | 0.96 | 0.94 |
|    Intermediate occupations | 0.73* | 0.72* |
|    Small employers/self-employed | 1.01 | 0.94 |
|    Lower supervisory/technical | 1.25 | 1.22 |
|    Semi-routine | 0.98 | 0.94 |
|    Routine | 1.26 | 1.26 |
| Education (ref.: left school after 18) | | |
|    16 or younger | 1.08 | 1.11 |
|    17–18 | 0.91 | 0.93 |
| Gender (ref.: female) | | |
|    Male | 0.94 | 0.92 |
| Age (ref.: 18–24 years) | | |
|    25–34 | 1.17 | 1.35 |
|    35–44 | 0.96 | 1.08 |
|    45–54 | 0.74 | 0.83 |
|    55–64 | 0.60 | 0.66 |
|    65+ | 0.76 | 0.82 |
| Ethnicity (ref.: non-white) | | |
|    White | 0.40** | 0.43** |
| Euroscepticism | 0.96 | |
| Immigrants a burden on welfare state | 1.70** | |
| Immigration bad for the economy | 1.71** | |
| Immigration undermines Britain's cultural life | 0.92 | |
| Composite issue variables (ref.: not eurosceptic or anti-immigration) | | |
|    Eurosceptic only | | 1.00 |
|    Anti-immigration only | | 1.92* |
|    Anti-immigration and eurosceptic | | 1.97** |
| Left–right ideology (ref.: left) | | |
|    Centre | 2.14** | 2.31** |
|    Right | 1.77** | 1.77** |
| Social protection 'gone too far' | | |
|    Ethnic minorities | 0.96 | 1.04 |
|    Gays and lesbians | 0.95 | 0.95 |
|    Women | 1.04 | 1.04 |
| Dissatisfaction with politics | | |
|    Politicians don't care | 1.27* | |
|    Little/no trust in MPs | 1.79** | |
|    Dissatisfied with democracy | 2.03** | |
|    High dissatisfaction | | 2.57** |
| Economic pessimism (retrospective) | | |
|    Household financial situation worse | 1.43** | 1.50** |
|    General economic situation worse | 1.55** | 1.62** |

| Party contact | | |
|---|---|---|
| Ukip | 1.37* | 1.45* |
| Conservative | 0.83 | 0.79 |
| Labour | 0.78 | 0.78 |
| Liberal Democrat | 1.00 | 1.01 |
| Constant | 0.40 | 0.74 |
| F-statistic | 10.07 | 10.24 |
| N | 3,760 | 3,760 |

*Notes*: * p<0.05, ** p<0.01. The dependent variable is coded '1' if the respondent said that he would also vote for the party in the general election and '0' if he indicated that he would defect from the party in the general election. The reduced model provided the figures referenced in Chapter 5.

*Source*: 2014–2017 British Election Study Internet Panel (Wave 2).

CHAPTER 10 INTO BATTLE

**Table C5.** Models of Ukip support during the long campaign

| Variable | Full model | Reduced model |
|---|---|---|
| Social class (ref.: higher managerial/ professional) | | |
| Lower managerial/professional | 0.93 | 0.95 |
| Intermediate occupations | 0.99 | 1.04 |
| Small employers/self-employed | 1.31 | 1.24 |
| Lower supervisory/technical | 1.20 | 1.29 |
| Semi-routine | 1.01 | 1.03 |
| Routine | 0.72 | 0.79 |
| Education (ref.: left school after 18) | | |
| 16 or younger | 1.34** | 1.48** |
| 17–18 | 1.23* | 1.31** |
| Gender (ref.: female) | | |
| Male | 1.45** | 1.45** |
| Age (ref.: 18–24 years) | | |
| 25–34 | 0.53 | 0.55 |
| 35–44 | 0.49 | 0.54 |
| 45–54 | 0.85 | 0.92 |
| 55–64 | 0.76 | 0.83 |
| 65+ | 0.71 | 0.76 |
| Ethnicity (ref.: non-white) | | |
| White | 1.35 | 1.44* |
| Euroscepticism | 3.04** | |
| Immigrants a burden on welfare state | 1.66** | |
| Immigration bad for the economy | 2.14** | |
| Immigration undermines Britain's cultural life | 1.89** | |
| Composite issue variables (ref.: not eurosceptic or anti-immigration) | | |

(*continued*)

**Table C5.** Continued

| Variable | Full model | Reduced model |
|---|---|---|
| Eurosceptic only | | 4.73** |
| Anti-immigration only | | 5.35** |
| Anti-immigration and eurosceptic | | 12.22** |
| Left–right ideology (ref.: left) | | |
|   Centre | 2.70** | 2.91** |
|   Right | 2.73** | 2.64** |
| Social protection 'gone too far' | | |
|   Ethnic minorities | 1.38** | 1.73** |
|   Gays and lesbians | 1.06 | 1.14 |
|   Women | 1.02 | 1.04 |
| Dissatisfaction with politics | | |
|   Politicians don't care | 2.12** | |
|   Little/no trust in MPs | 2.40** | |
|   Dissatisfied with democracy | 1.90** | |
|   High dissatisfaction | | 3.51** |
| Economic pessimism (retrospective) | | |
|   Household financial situation worse | 1.13 | 1.25* |
|   General economic in country worse | 1.1 | 1.24* |
| Party contact | | |
|   Ukip | 3.58** | 3.43** |
|   Conservative | 0.77** | 0.70** |
|   Labour | 0.72** | 0.70** |
|   Liberal Democrat | 0.72* | 0.73* |
| Constant | 0.00** | 0.00** |
| F-statistic | 46.66 | 44.96 |
| N | 13,248 | 13,248 |

*Notes:* * $p<0.05$, ** $p<0.01$. The dependent variable is coded '1' if the respondent indicated that he planned to vote for Ukip in the general election and '0' if he planned to vote for any other party. The reduced model provides the figures referenced in Chapter 10.

*Source:* 2014–2017 British Election Study Internet Panel (Wave 4).

**Table C6.** Models of party support during the long campaign

| Variable | Ukip | Conservative | Labour | Liberal Democrat |
|---|---|---|---|---|
| Social class (ref.: higher managerial/professional) | | | | |
|   Lower managerial/professional | 0.93 | 0.83* | 1.13 | 1.06 |
|   Intermediate occupations | 0.99 | 0.76* | 1.41** | 1.01 |
|   Small employers/self-employed | 1.31 | 1.00 | 0.71* | 1.27 |
|   Lower supervisory/technical | 1.20 | 0.71* | 1.25 | 0.60 |
|   Semi-routine | 1.01 | 0.75* | 1.33* | 1.10 |
|   Routine | 0.72 | 0.79 | 1.31 | 0.84 |

| | | | | |
|---|---|---|---|---|
| Education (ref.: left school after 18) | | | | |
| 16 or younger | 1.34** | 0.81* | 2.02** | 0.38** |
| 17–18 | 1.23* | 1.03 | 1.10 | 0.77* |
| Gender (ref.: female) | | | | |
| Male | 1.45** | 0.75** | 0.98 | 1.09 |
| Age (ref.: 18–24 years) | | | | |
| 25–34 | 0.53 | 1.07 | 0.87 | 1.73 |
| 35–44 | 0.49 | 1.05 | 0.84 | 2.67 |
| 45–54 | 0.85 | 0.70 | 0.85 | 3.16* |
| 55–64 | 0.76 | 0.95 | 0.69 | 3.91* |
| 65+ | 0.71 | 1.05 | 0.66 | 4.26** |
| Ethnicity (ref.: non-white) | | | | |
| White | 1.35 | 1.53 | 0.48** | 1.25 |
| Euroscepticism | 3.04** | 1.78** | 0.72** | 0.54** |
| Immigrants a burden on welfare state | 1.66** | 0.84* | 0.97 | 0.42** |
| Immigration bad for the economy | 2.14** | 0.83* | 0.93 | 0.64** |
| Immigration undermines Britain's cultural life | 1.89** | 1.17 | 0.94 | 0.67** |
| Left–right ideology (ref.: left) | | | | |
| Centre | 2.70** | 10.35** | 0.24** | 2.47** |
| Right | 2.73** | 38.80** | 0.06** | 0.74* |
| Social protection 'gone too far' | | | | |
| Ethnic minorities | 1.38** | 1.03 | 0.87 | 0.84 |
| Gays and lesbians | 1.06 | 1.12 | 1.02 | 0.78 |
| Women | 1.02 | 1.09 | 0.79* | 1.05 |
| Dissatisfaction with politics | | | | |
| Politicians don't care | 2.12** | 0.45** | 1.39** | 1.25* |
| Little/no trust in MPs | 2.40** | 0.61** | 0.60** | 0.87 |
| Dissatisfied with democracy | 1.90** | 0.52** | 0.59** | 1.02 |
| Economic pessimism (retrospective) | | | | |
| Household financial situation worse | 1.13 | 0.66** | 1.45** | 0.95 |
| General economic situation worse | 1.10 | 0.21** | 2.18** | 0.55** |
| Party contact | | | | |
| Ukip | 3.58** | 0.60** | 0.71** | 0.85 |
| Conservative | 0.77** | 2.25** | 0.71** | 0.72* |
| Labour | 0.72** | 0.70** | 2.01** | 0.48** |
| Liberal Democrat | 0.72* | 0.49** | 0.51** | 6.28** |
| Constant | 0.00** | 0.11** | 3.55** | 6.28** |
| F-statistic | 46.66 | 65.79 | 67.16 | 19.00 |
| N | 13,248 | 13,248 | 13,248 | 13,248 |

Notes: * $p < 0.05$, ** $p < 0.01$. The dependent variable is coded '1' if respondent voted for the given party and '0' otherwise.

Source: 2014–2017 British Election Study Internet Panel (Wave 4).

## CHAPTER 11 GROUND GAME

Table C7. Models of party support during the short campaign

| Variable | Ukip | Conservative | Labour | Liberal Democrat |
|---|---|---|---|---|
| Social class (ref.: higher managerial/professional) | | | | |
| Lower managerial/ professional | 1.06 | 0.82 | 0.94 | 1.14 |
| Intermediate occupations | 0.98 | 0.79 | 1.38* | 1.00 |
| Small employers/ self-employed | 1.06 | 0.91 | 0.71 | 1.31 |
| Lower supervisory/technical | 1.27 | 0.85 | 1.17 | 0.82 |
| Semi-routine | 1.00 | 1.05 | 0.93 | 0.99 |
| Routine | 0.79 | 0.84 | 1.17 | 0.66 |
| Education (ref.: left school after 18) | | | | |
| 16 or younger | 1.23 | 0.94 | 1.75** | 0.51** |
| 17–18 | 1.01 | 1.15 | 1.20 | 0.72* |
| Gender (ref.: female) | | | | |
| Male | 1.33** | 0.76** | 0.89 | 1.05 |
| Age (ref.: 18–24 years) | | | | |
| 25–34 | 0.43 | 0.61 | 0.97 | 3.33* |
| 35–44 | 0.49 | 0.63 | 0.8 | 3.92** |
| 45–54 | 0.90 | 0.44* | 0.70 | 5.25** |
| 55–64 | 0.74 | 0.52 | 0.57 | 5.83** |
| 65+ | 0.57 | 0.58 | 0.52* | 7.40** |
| Ethnicity (ref.: non-white) | | | | |
| White | 0.92 | 1.00 | 0.64 | 1.21 |
| Euroscepticism | 2.05** | 1.47** | 0.9 | 0.78 |
| Immigrants a burden on welfare state | 1.34** | 0.91 | 0.86 | 0.64* |
| Immigration bad for the economy | 2.06** | 0.84 | 1.03 | 0.70* |
| Immigration undermines Britain's cultural life | 1.37* | 1.36** | 0.94 | 0.88 |
| Left–right ideology (ref.: left) | | | | |
| Centre | 2.13** | 3.77** | 0.60** | 1.62** |
| Right | 1.76** | 10.64** | 0.26** | 0.48** |
| Social protection 'gone too far' | | | | |
| Ethnic minorities | 1.25 | 1.01 | 1.03 | 0.83 |
| Gays and lesbians | 0.88 | 1.15 | 1.05 | 0.97 |
| Women | 0.97 | 0.83 | 1.21 | 1.28 |

| | | | | |
|---|---|---|---|---|
| Dissatisfaction with politics | | | | |
| Politicians don't care | 1.88** | 0.56** | 1.20 | 1.60** |
| Little/no trust in MPs | 1.73** | 0.97 | 0.64** | 0.96 |
| Dissatisfied with democracy | 1.75** | 0.60** | 0.51** | 0.98 |
| Economic pessimism (retrospective) | | | | |
| Household financial situation worse | 1.27* | 0.63** | 1.40** | 0.93 |
| General economic situation worse | 1.03 | 0.48** | 1.19 | 0.86 |
| Positive leader evaluations (ref.: indifferent/dislike leader) | | | | |
| Farage | 15.97** | 0.39** | 0.52** | 0.57** |
| Cameron | 0.26** | 11.46** | 0.21** | 0.47** |
| Miliband | 0.26** | 0.18** | 14.98** | 0.38** |
| Clegg | 0.75* | 0.59** | 0.38** | 13.74** |
| Party contact | | | | |
| Ukip | 3.33** | 0.66* | 0.81 | 0.71 |
| Conservative | 0.61** | 1.82** | 0.99 | 0.75 |
| Labour | 0.75* | 0.75* | 1.74** | 0.61** |
| Liberal Democrat | 0.71 | 0.43** | 0.31** | 6.94** |
| Constant | 0.00** | 0.27** | 1.50 | 0.01** |
| F-statistic | 40.73 | 64.74 | 61.94 | 26.44 |
| N | 12,346 | 12,346 | 12,346 | 12,346 |

Notes: * $p<0.05$, ** $p<0.01$. The dependent variable is coded '1' if respondent voted for the given party and '0' otherwise. Wave 5 contained a more limited range of questions, so some variables were measured in Wave 4 of the survey.

Source: 2014–2017 British Election Study Internet Panel (Waves 4–5).

**Table C8.** Models of Ukip loyalty during the short campaign, 2014 Ukip supporters only

| Variable | Full model | Reduced model |
|---|---|---|
| Social class (ref.: higher managerial/professional) | | |
| Lower managerial/professional | 1.05 | 1.03 |
| Intermediate occupations | 0.93 | 0.92 |
| Small employers/self-employed | 1.16 | 1.06 |
| Lower supervisory/technical | 0.77 | 0.77 |
| Semi-routine | 1.35 | 1.27 |
| Routine | 0.96 | 0.93 |
| Education (ref.: left school after 18) | | |
| 16 or younger | 1.20 | 1.24 |
| 17–18 | 1.34 | 1.40 |

(continued)

**Table C8.** Continued

| Variable | Full model | Reduced model |
|---|---|---|
| Gender (ref.: female) | | |
|   Male | 2.07★★ | 2.06★★ |
| Age (ref.: 18–24 years) | | |
|   25–34 | 0.32 | 0.28 |
|   35–44 | 0.59 | 0.53 |
|   45–54 | 0.81 | 0.66 |
|   55–64 | 0.75 | 0.59 |
|   65+ | 0.43 | 0.34 |
| Ethnicity (ref.: non-white) | | |
|   White | 2.60★ | 2.53★ |
| Euroscepticism | 2.05★ | |
| Immigrants a burden on welfare state | 1.41 | |
| Immigration bad for the economy | 1.14 | |
| Immigration undermines Britain's cultural life | 1.34 | |
| Composite issue variables (ref.: not eurosceptic or anti-immigration) | | |
|   Eurosceptic only | | 3.58★★ |
|   Anti-immigration only | | 4.15★ |
|   Anti-immigration and eurosceptic | | 4.73★★ |
| Left–right ideology (ref.: left) | | |
|   Centre | 1.28 | 1.31 |
|   Right | 1.57 | 1.56 |
| Social protection 'gone too far' | | |
|   Ethnic minorities | 1.05 | 1.12 |
|   Gays and lesbians | 0.69★ | 0.68★ |
|   Women | 1.51 | 1.48 |
| Dissatisfaction with politics | | |
|   Politicians don't care | 1.55★ | |
|   Little/no trust in MPs | 1.17 | |
|   Dissatisfied with democracy | 1.82★★ | |
|   High dissatisfaction | | 2.25★★ |
| Economic pessimism (retrospective) | | |
|   Household financial situation worse | 1.39 | 1.40 |
|   General economic situation worse | 0.76 | 0.74 |
| Change in feelings about Ukip | | |
|   Like more than May 2014 | 2.94★★ | 3.02★★ |
|   Like same as May 2014 | 2.61★★ | 2.68★★ |
| Preferred election result | | |
|   Conservative result | 0.17★★ | 0.17★★ |
|   Labour result | 0.14★★ | 0.14★★ |
| Party contact | | |
|   Ukip | 2.11★ | 2.09★★ |

| | | |
|---|---|---|
| Conservative | 0.75 | 0.74 |
| Labour | 1.11 | 1.07 |
| Liberal Democrat | 0.93 | 0.94 |
| Constant | 0.07** | 0.12* |
| $F$-statistic | 6.12 | 6.59 |
| $N$ | 1,734 | 1,734 |

Notes: * $p<0.05$, ** $p<0.01$. The dependent variable is coded '1' if the respondent also planned to vote for Ukip when interviewed during the short campaign and '0' if he said he was now planning to vote for another party. The reduced model provides the figures referenced in Chapter 11.

*Source*: 2014–2017 British Election Study Internet Panel (Waves 2, 4, and 5).


## CHAPTER 12 COUNTING THE VOTES

**Table C9.** Social background of party supporters in the 2015 general election (%)

| Variable | Ukip | Conservative | Labour | Liberal Democrat | SNP | Green |
|---|---|---|---|---|---|---|
| Social class | | | | | | |
|   Higher managerial/professional | 13 | 20 | 14 | 23 | 14 | 23 |
|   Lower managerial/professional | 28 | 33 | 30 | 35 | 31 | 34 |
|   Intermediate occupations | 21 | 22 | 24 | 19 | 20 | 21 |
|   Small employers/self-employed | 9 | 7 | 5 | 7 | 5 | 6 |
|   Lower supervisory/technical | 10 | 7 | 8 | 4 | 9 | 4 |
|   Semi-routine | 12 | 7 | 12 | 9 | 12 | 9 |
|   Routine | 8 | 4 | 7 | 2 | 10 | 4 |
| Education (age left school) | | | | | | |
|   16 or younger | 52 | 34 | 36 | 22 | 35 | 12 |
|   17–18 | 22 | 25 | 21 | 19 | 19 | 18 |
|   19 or older, still in school | 26 | 42 | 43 | 60 | 45 | 70 |
| Gender | | | | | | |
|   Male | 54 | 51 | 53 | 49 | 49 | 54 |
|   Female | 46 | 49 | 47 | 51 | 51 | 46 |
| Age | | | | | | |
|   18–34 | 17 | 24 | 19 | 30 | 27 | 49 |
|   35–54 | 34 | 31 | 35 | 31 | 39 | 30 |
|   55+ | 49 | 44 | 35 | 39 | 33 | 19 |

(*continued*)

**Table C9.** Continued

| Variable | Ukip | Conservative | Labour | Liberal Democrat | SNP | Green |
|---|---|---|---|---|---|---|
| Ethnicity | | | | | | |
| White | 96 | 95 | 89 | 95 | 96 | 92 |
| Non-white | 4 | 5 | 11 | 5 | 4 | 8 |

*Notes*: Numbers in each column represent the weighted percentage of each party's 2015 voters who belong to a given group.

*Source*: 2014–2017 British Election Study Internet Panel (Wave 6).

CHAPTER 14 REFERENDUM

**Table C10.** Models of support for leaving the EU

| Variable | Full model | Reduced model |
|---|---|---|
| Social class (ref.: higher managerial/professional) | | |
| Lower managerial/professional | 0.96 | 0.98 |
| Intermediate occupations | 1.88* | 1.86* |
| Small employers/self-employed | 1.57 | 1.58 |
| Lower supervisory/technical | 1.87 | 1.98* |
| Semi-routine | 1.16 | 1.17 |
| Routine | 1.81 | 1.63 |
| Education (ref.: left school after 18) | | |
| 16 or younger | 2.14** | 2.58** |
| 17–18 | 1.57* | 1.80** |
| Gender (ref.: female) | | |
| Male | 0.63** | 0.62** |
| Age (ref.: 18–24 years) | | |
| 25–34 | 0.60 | 0.64 |
| 35–44 | 0.74 | 0.81 |
| 45–54 | 0.74 | 0.77 |
| 55–64 | 0.60 | 0.62 |
| 65+ | 0.54 | 0.55 |
| Ethnicity (ref.: non-white) | | |
| White | 0.27 | 0.3 |
| Euroscepticism | 4.23** | |
| Dissatisfied with EU democracy | 2.90** | 3.20** |
| Immigrants a burden on welfare state | 2.01** | |
| Immigration bad for the economy | 2.46** | |
| Immigration undermines Britain's cultural life | 1.50** | |
| Composite issue variables (ref.: not eurosceptic or anti-immigration) | | |
| Eurosceptic only | | 5.03** |
| Anti-immigration only | | 5.61** |
| Anti-immigration and eurosceptic | | 15.92** |

| | | |
|---|---|---|
| Left–right ideology (ref.: left) | | |
| Centre | 1.88* | 2.18** |
| Right | 1.82** | 2.04** |
| Economic pessimism (retrospective) | | |
| Household financial situation worse | 1.51 | 1.53 |
| General economic situation worse | 1.06 | 1.06 |
| Feelings about Ukip | | |
| Like Farage | 4.62** | 5.51** |
| Constant | 0.09* | 0.09* |
| F-statistic | 17.70 | 17.88 |
| N | 2,936 | 2,936 |

*Notes:* * p<0.05, ** p<0.01. The dependent variable is coded '1' if the respondent indicated that he would vote to leave the EU in a referendum and '0' if he said he would vote to stay. The reduced model provides the figures referenced in Chapter 13.

*Source:* 2014–2017 British Election Study Internet Panel (Wave 6).

# Appendix D: Explaining Ukip Performance in 2015

During the long campaign Lord Ashcroft conducted a second round of polls in eleven marginal seats that he had previously surveyed between June and October of 2014. A comparison of the results provides insight into how Ukip's support had evolved in the months leading up to the 2015 election. Table D1 presents change in the polling figures for Ukip, the Conservatives, Labour, and Liberal Democrats between the two rounds of surveys. Full results for both sets of polls can be found at <www.lordashcroftpolls.com/>.

In April 2015, he revisited ten more marginal seats that he had polled during the summer and autumn of 2014. Table D2 presents the change in support for all four parties between the two periods.

**Table D1.** Change in polling figures, summer/autumn 2014 to March 2015

| Constituency | Ukip | Con. | Lab. | Lib. Dem. |
|---|---|---|---|---|
| Camborne and Redruth | −12 | +8 | +0 | −1 |
| Halesowen and Rowley Regis | −9 | +3 | +4 | +2 |
| North Devon | −7 | +8 | −1 | +0 |
| St Ives | −7 | +4 | −1 | +4 |
| Chester | −5 | −2 | +8 | +0 |
| Nuneaton | −5 | −2 | 0 | +1 |
| St Austell and Newquay | −5 | +5 | −3 | 0 |
| Cambridge | −4 | −2 | −2 | +8 |
| Torbay | −4 | +3 | −4 | +4 |
| Worcester | −4 | +6 | −2 | −1 |
| Southampton Itchen | −2 | −3 | +5 | −3 |

*Source*: Lord Ashcroft Polls.

**Table D2.** Change in polling figures, summer/autumn 2014 to April 2015

| Constituency | Ukip | Con. | Lab. | Lib. Dem |
|---|---|---|---|---|
| Stockton South | −10 | +4 | +6 | −1 |
| Blackpool North and Cleveleys | −9 | +7 | +5 | −2 |
| Kingswood | −8 | +8 | +1 | −1 |
| Pendle | −7 | +5 | +4 | −3 |
| Pudsey | −7 | +4 | +4 | −4 |
| Gloucester | −6 | +6 | +3 | −3 |
| Morecambe and Lunesdale | −6 | +2 | +5 | −1 |
| Harrow East | −4 | −1 | +6 | 0 |
| Hove | −6 | +3 | +6 | −1 |
| Loughborough | 0 | +5 | −1 | −2 |

*Source*: Lord Ashcroft Polls.

## YOUGOV'S POST-ELECTION SURVEY

Between 6 and 18 May, YouGov polled 100,000 British adults to see how they had voted in the 2015 General Election. Table D3 summarizes the results of the survey with respect to socio-demographics. The figures represent the weighted percentage of each group that voted for the given party.

**Table D3.** Breakdown of 2015 party support by group (%)

| Variable | Con. | Lab. | Ukip | Lib. Dem. | SNP | Green |
|---|---|---|---|---|---|---|
| All | 38 | 31 | 13 | 8 | 5 | 4 |
| Social Grade | | | | | | |
| AB (middle class) | 44 | 28 | 9 | 10 | 4 | 4 |
| C1 (lower middle class) | 38 | 30 | 11 | 9 | 5 | 5 |
| C2 (skilled working class) | 36 | 31 | 17 | 6 | 5 | 3 |
| DE (working class, non-working) | 29 | 37 | 18 | 6 | 5 | 3 |
| Highest Qualification | | | | | | |
| GCSE or lower | 38 | 30 | 20 | 5 | 3 | 2 |
| A Level | 37 | 31 | 11 | 8 | 6 | 5 |
| University | 35 | 34 | 6 | 11 | 5 | 6 |
| Age | | | | | | |
| 18–29 | 32 | 36 | 9 | 9 | 5 | 7 |
| 30–39 | 36 | 34 | 10 | 8 | 5 | 5 |
| 40–49 | 33 | 33 | 14 | 7 | 5 | 4 |
| 50–59 | 36 | 32 | 16 | 7 | 5 | 3 |
| 60+ | 45 | 25 | 16 | 7 | 3 | 2 |
| Gender | | | | | | |
| Male | 37 | 28 | 15 | 8 | 5 | 4 |
| Female | 38 | 33 | 12 | 8 | 4 | 4 |

*Source*: YouGov/Prospect Survey.

## MULTIVARIATE ANALYSIS OF UKIP'S 2015 VOTE SHARE

Throughout the book we have emphasized the social distinctiveness of Ukip's support. Our analysis of the party's support in the 2014 European elections indicated that Ukip's supporters tend to be older and white, and that they tend to be employed in more vulnerable routine or manual occupations and have fewer educational qualifications. Our analysis of Ukip's political geography supported these conclusions, showing that areas with large concentrations of these Ukip's friendly groups tended to give the party its strongest results in both the European and local elections in 2014. That being said, we have also demonstrated that, for the first time, the party was determined to run a targeted campaign, focusing on building pockets of support large enough to overcome Britain's first-past-the-post system. But now that votes have been counted, how can we explain Ukip's performance in 2015? How important was political geography to the party's success? And, perhaps more importantly, how effective was the party campaign?

In order to explore Ukip's performance in 2015 in a more systematic fashion, we once again return to multivariate techniques, where we modelled the party's 2015 vote share in England and Wales as a function of a number of key predictors. In addition to the overall demographic favourability of the seat, we included two dichotomous variables that captured whether a seat was identified as one of Ukip's top targets or whether it was one of the party's original targets that did not make the final list—the non-top target seats. Because past performance often predicts future success, we also included the party's performance in the corresponding area in the 2014 European elections.[5] Finally, we also took into account the strength of the BNP in 2010, as our preliminary analyses suggested that Ukip was the likely beneficiary of the BNP's demise.[6] We used a technique called path analysis, which was ideal for our purposes because it allowed us to account for the fact that some predictors may have both direct and indirect effects. In our case, the demographic favourability of the area may have influenced Ukip's performance directly or it could have had an indirect effect by shaping the party's performance in the area in the 2014 elections. The logic here is simple. Seats with large numbers of Ukip-friendly groups may have given the party more support because individuals from these groups were more likely to support the party in 2015. However, demographics could have also shaped Ukip's support indirectly by helping the party to build more momentum following the 2014 elections. Figure D1 presents a simplified diagram of our full model. For clarity of presentation, we have omitted the error terms associated with the variables for the party's 2014 and 2015 vote share.

Table D4 presents the unstandardized estimates of the effects of our key variables on Ukip's vote share in 2015. The results of our analysis of the party's vote share indicated that demography was the strongest predictor of Ukip's electoral performance. The total effect of demographic favourability—which takes into account both the direct and the indirect effect via 2014 performance—is 17 points.[7] This means that, even if the party spent no extra resources on a seat, we would have expected a highly favourable seat like Clacton to have received a vote share that was 17 points higher than the one that the party could be expected to receive in an unfavourable seat such as Battersea based on the characteristics of the population alone. After demographics, the most influential predictor of Ukip's vote share in 2015 was whether a seat was chosen as one of the party's top target seats. Such seats would be expected to receive an extra 9.4 points on their vote share. However, the effect of being a Ukip target seat that did not make it to the final list was more modest. Here the difference in vote share was just 2.4 points. Finally, we found that Ukip performed better in areas where the BNP had been stronger in 2010. The BNP averaged 3.9 per cent of the vote in seats where it ran candidates in 2010. Ukip's vote share in these seats was 2.5 points higher than seats that the BNP did not contest in 2010.

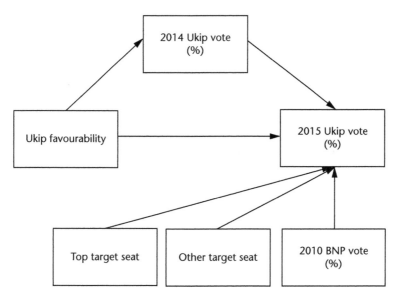

**Figure D1.** Path model of Ukip's 2015 vote share

**Table D4.** Explaining Ukip vote share in 2015

| Outcome → 2015 vote | |
| --- | --- |
| Demographic favourability | 11.03** |
| Top target | 9.35** |
| Other target | 2.34** |
| 2010 BNP Vote | 0.63** |
| 2014 EP Vote | 0.21** |
| Constant | −0.67 |
| *Outcome → 2014 EP Vote* | |
| Demographic favourability | 25.95** |
| Constant | 12.47** |
| N | 573 |

*Notes*: * p<0.05, ** p<0.01. Entries are unstandardized estimates. Error variances omitted for clarity.

*Sources*: 2011 Census; European Parliament Elections 2014 (June 2014), House of Commons Library Research Paper 14/32; 2015 British Election Study Constituency Results with Census and Candidate Data.

# Notes

## PREFACE

1. Ivor Crewe and Anthony King, *SDP: The Birth, Life and Death of the Social Democratic Party* (Oxford: Oxford University Press, 1995).
2. David Butler, *The British General Election of 1951* (London: Macmillan, 1952), 2.
3. The academic literature on campaigns and their effects is vast, including studies in the United States and Britain. See, in particular, the work of Ron Johnston, Charles Pattie, David Cutts, and Ed Fieldhouse, as well Paul Whiteley. For example, R. Johnston and C. Pattie, 'The Impact of Party Spending on Party Constituency Campaigns at Recent British General Elections', *Party Politics*, 1 (1995), 261–74; D. Denver, G. Hands, J. Fisher, and I. MacAllister, 'Constituency Campaigning in Britain 1992–2001: Centralisation and Modernisation', *Party Politics*, 9 (2003), 541–59; P. Seyd and P. Whiteley, *New Labour's Grass Roots: The Transformation of Party Membership* (London: Palgrave, 2002); P. Whiteley, P. Seyd, and A. Billinghurst, *Third Force Politics: Liberal Democrats at the Grassroots* (Oxford: Oxford University Press, 2006); D. Denver and G. Hands, *Modern Constituency Electioneering: Local Campaigning in the 1992 General Election*, (London: Frank Cass, 1997).
4. Hunter S. Thompson, *Fear and Loathing on the Campaign Trail* (London: Harper Perennial, 1973).
5. Robert Ford and Matthew J. Goodwin, *Revolt on the Right: Explaining Support for the Radical Right in Britain* (Abingdon: Routledge, 2014).

## CHAPTER 1. GATESHEAD

1. Steve Boggan, 'Come to Lovely Gateshead—if You Can Get Past Immigration', *Guardian*, 23 January 2007.
2. J. B. Priestley, *English Journey* (London: Heinemann, 1934).
3. The exceptions were when Gateshead went Liberal in 1923, and then National Liberal in 1931. When in 1981 the incumbent Labour MP in Gateshead West defected to the Social Democratic Party (SDP), Labour subsequently held the seat. Gateshead Council had been Labour controlled since becoming a Metropolitan Borough in 1974. Before that it was the County Borough of Gateshead, with Central Gateshead being held by Labour since the 1920s. Source: Gateshead Council Archives.

4. For a more detailed history of the UK Independence Party, see Robert Ford and Matthew J. Goodwin, *Revolt on the Right: Explaining Support for the Radical Right in Britain* (Abingdon: Routledge, 2014), chs 1 and 2.

5. Matthew D'Ancona, 'The Tories' Immigration Headache is of David Cameron's Making', *Guardian*, 26 February 2015.

6. Ukip did have one seat in the House of Commons for a few months in 2008, but only because the Conservative MP Bob Spink temporarily defected. Spink was never elected under the Ukip banner.

7. Ukip took control of Ramsey Town Council in Cambridgeshire in 2011, which had the same legal status as a parish council.

8. Helen Pidd, 'South Shields Byelection: Ukip Become "The Party of Opposition"', *Guardian*, 3 May 2013.

9. Lucy Fisher, 'Ukip Aiming to Steal Votes from Labour in the North', *Observer*, 9 February 2014.

10. In June 2005 19% of voters selected Europe as one of the most important issues facing Britain, making the issue only the fifth most important. Data obtained from the Ipsos-MORI issues tracker <http://www.ipsos-mori.com> (accessed 14 March 2015).

## CHAPTER 2. THE CHANGING LANDSCAPE

1. David Butler and Donald Stokes, *Political Change in Britain*, 2nd edn (London: Macmillan, 1974), 74.

2. David Denver, *Elections and Voters in Britain*, 2nd edn (Basingstoke: Macmillan, 2007).

3. Turnout recovered somewhat in 2005 and 2010; it nonetheless remains far lower than the pre-1997 period.

4. See the Electoral Reform Society, 'Safe Seats' <http://www.electoral-reform. org.uk/safe-seats> (accessed 19 August 2015).

5. Robert Ford and Matthew J. Goodwin, *Revolt on the Right: Explaining Support for the Radical Right in Britain* (Abingdon: Routledge, 2014), ch. 3, 'Origins: A Long Time Coming'.

6. Denver, *Elections and Voters in Britain*, 63.

7. Russell J. Dalton, 'Cognitive Mobilization and Partisan Dealignment in Advanced Industrial Democracies', *Journal of Politics*, 46 (1984), 264–8.

8. For example, after Michael Foot had challenged Margaret Thatcher in 1983, 84% of those surveyed in the British Election Study said they saw 'great differences' between the Labour and Conservative parties. But by the time Tony Blair took on John Major in 1997, this figure had dropped to just 28%.

9. Michael A. Ashcroft, *Smell the Coffee: A Wake-Up Call for the Conservative Party* (n.p., 2005). There is also a large academic literature on partisan and class dealignment. For some examples, see Ivor Crewe, Bo Sarlvik, and James E. Alt, 'Partisan Dealignment in Britain, 1964–1974', *British Journal of Political Science*, 7

(1977), 129–90; Bo Sarlvik and Ivor Crewe, *Decade of Dealignment: The Conservative Victory of 1970 and Electoral Trends in the 1970s* (Cambridge: Cambridge University Press, 1983); Harold D. Clarke, Marianne C. Stewart, and Paul Whiteley, 'Tory Trends: Party Identification and the Dynamics of Conservative Support since 1992', *British Journal of Political Science*, 26 (1997), 299–318; Harold D. Clarke, Marianne C. Stewart, and Paul Whiteley, 'New Models for New Labour: The Political Economy of Labour Party Support, January 1992–April 1997', *American Political Science Review*, 92 (1998), 559–7; Harold D. Clarke, David Sanders, Marianne C. Stewart, and Paul Whiteley, *Political Choice in Britain* (Oxford: Oxford University Press, 2004).

10. Ivor Crewe, 'The Electorate: Partisan Dealignment Ten Years on', in H. Berrington (ed.), *Change in British Politics* (London: Frank Cass, 1984), 183–215.

11. Neil O'Brien and Anthony Wells, *Northern Lights: Public Policy and the Geography of Political Attitudes* (London: Policy Exchange, 2012). On the Farage quotation, see Matt Chorley, 'Ukip Is Now the "Second Party of the North": Farage Declare Victory as Panicked Tories Hire New Guru who Warns Northern Voters Feel Ignored', *Mail Online*, 30 November 2012.

12. Andrew Russell and Edward Fieldhouse, *Neither Left nor Right: The Liberal Democrats and the Electorate* (Manchester: Manchester University Press, 2005).

13. Another way of looking at how Britain's system was fragmenting is to explore the number of parties winning votes. It would be wrong simply to count the number of parties that won votes in an election. If we did so, the Conservatives would have just as much weight as the Monster Raving Loonies. While both parties win votes, we know that one party wins far more than the other. This is why academics look at the 'effective number of parties'—a figure that takes into account both the number of parties that win votes and the size of those parties. When we do this, we find that, since the 1950s, the number of parties that have won a meaningful share of the vote has been steadily rising. When Anthony Eden and the Conservatives won the 1955 General Election, the effective number of parties that won votes was two, meaning that generally two parties had attracted significant support. But fifty-five years later, when Cameron and Clegg were forging their Coalition agreement, this number had climbed above three, meaning that more than three parties were winning seats nationally. This might not sound like a big difference, but it matters. While the battles to win seats have continued to be largely ones between only two parties, it is often no longer the same two parties that fight these elections on a national scale. This is why the average number of parties contesting seats tends to be lower than the average number of parties at the national level. Moreover, the difference between the number of parties at the national and local level has grown over time. This tells us that the landscape is more fragmented, with new challengers winning an ever larger share of the vote. See Markku Laakso and Rein Taagepera, '"Effective" Number of Parties: A Measure with Application to West Europe,' *Comparative Political Studies* 12/1 (1979): 3–27.

14. As Vernon Bogdanor also noted, not one MP since 1997 has secured the votes of a majority of the electorate in his or her constituency. In 1997, only fourteen MPs had such a majority, while in 1951 the number was 214. On this statistic and the discussion more generally, see the excellent report by Vernon Bogdanor, *The Crisis of the Constitution: The General Election and the Future of the United Kingdom* (London: The Constitution Society, 2015).

15. Across the four elections that spanned the 1979–92 period, the Conservative Party's share of the vote never fell below 41%. The exception was October 1974, when the Conservative Party polled just under 36% of the vote.

16. Tim Montgomerie, 'The Centre Ground Is not Broad Enough for Victory', *Independent*, 2 October 2006.

17. The deficit in 2009–10 was 10.2% of GDP. The Office for Budget Responsibility has data from 1948.

18. Cited by Jon Cruddas at Blue Labour Conference, University of Kent, 25 June 2015. See also James Morris, *Feeling Blue: Why Labour Lost and how it Can Win Again* (London: Greenberg Quinlan Rosner Research Report, 2015).

19. These points are based on data compiled by YouGov on public attitudes towards government cuts.

20. In 2014 38% of voters told YouGov that the government should stick to the current strategy, compared to 30% who thought it should change strategy, and 32% who said neither/not sure. Meanwhile, 38% thought that the government's policies had helped the economy, compared to 28% who thought they had made the economy worse and 24% who thought they had not made much difference (the remainder did not know). In 2014 an average of 34% of respondents thought that the economy was 'in a bad way, but signs of recovery', compared to an average of 29% who thought that the 'economy has stopped getting worse but no signs of recovery' and an average of 14% who thought it was improving and on the way to recovery, while only 16% thought the economy was still getting worse (the remainder said they did not know). Meanwhile, in the YouGov Economy tracker, in 2014, 39% of people thought that the economy would have been doing worse had Labour won the 2010 general election, compared to 29% who thought it would be 'much the same' and 19% who thought it would be 'doing better'. The same question has been asked each year since 2011 and similar percentages have been reported. Meanwhile, in 2014 Cameron and Osborne were trusted by an average of 38% to Miliband and Balls on 26%.

21. These are average levels of support for Labour in the opinion polls during the month before elections to the European Parliament. Data obtained from UK Polling Report <http://ukpollingreport.co.uk/> (accessed 25 June 2015). Beckett took over as interim leader following the sudden death of John Smith.

22. Based on the average poll ratings in April and May 1973. At the general election itself Harold Wilson and Labour would actually poll just over 37% of the vote and be forced to establish a minority government until a new election took

place in October, which gave Labour a majority of only three seats. In May 1978 Thatcher and the Conservatives averaged almost 44%, two points behind Labour. But this soon turned into a lead of four points by the following August, and almost twelve points by the following March. Thatcher would win the 1979 general election with almost 44% of the vote and a seven-point lead.

23. In terms of who would make the best prime minister, Miliband on average was behind Cameron by fifteen points in 2010, thirteen in 2011, fourteen across 2012 and 2013, and then sixteen in 2014. Based on the YouGov Leaders Perception tracker, which tracks public reactions to the various leaders over time, between September 2010 and 2011 (change in parentheses), 6% of people saw Miliband as strong (−6), 4% saw him being good in a crisis (+1), 8% saw him as decisive (−3), 5% saw him as a natural leader (−4), and only 6% saw him as charismatic (−3).

24. Calculated using the Ipsos-MORI party leadership ratings data. The question reads: 'Are you satisfied or dissatisfied with the way … is doing his/her job as Prime Minister/Leader of the Opposition/Leader of the Liberal Democrats?' In terms of overall net satisfaction with the leaders, and among all respondents, in 2010 Miliband had a rating of 9.6%, followed by −9.1 in 2011, −13.6 in 2012, −20.3 in 2013, and −29 in 2014. For Cameron it was 6.6 in 2010, −9.8 in 2011, −18.6 in 2012, −21 in 2103, and −16.9 in 2014. Between 2010 and 2014 Miliband's net satisfaction ratings among his own supporters were 44% in 2010, 22% in 2011, 17% in 2012, 11% in 2013, and just 6% in 2014. Cameron's were 85% in 2010, 65% in 2011, 52% in 2012 and 2013, and 61% in 2014. Cameron was 41 points ahead of Miliband in 2010, 43 points ahead in 2011, 35 points ahead in 2012, 41 points ahead in 2013, and 55 points ahead in 2014. See <https://www.ipsos-mori.com/researchpublications/researcharchive/2908/Satisfaction-with-leaders-amongst-party-supporters.aspx> (accessed 10 August 2015).

25. Ross Kaniuk, 'Nigel Farage Launches Stinging Attack on Rivals Calling Cameron, Clegg and Miliband Useless', *Daily Star*, 9 October 2014.

26. George Eaton, 'What Merkel Told Cameron about Coalitions' *New Statesman*, Staggers, blog, 23 January 2013.

27. On support for the Greens, see Sarah Birch (2009) 'Real Progress: Prospects for Green Party Support in Britain', *Parliamentary Affairs*, 62/1 (2009), 53–71. Also Sarah Birch 'The Traditional Parties Should Be on their Guard for a Green Surge', British Politics and Policy blog, London School of Economics <http://blogs.lse.ac.uk/politicsandpolicy/the-traditional-parties-should-be-on-their-guard-for-a-green-surge/> (accessed 29 July 2015).

28. First Minister Alex Salmond's address to Scottish National Party conference, October 2012.

29. Data taken from 'What Scotland Thinks' blog <http://whatscotlandthinks.org/questions/how-would-you-be-likely-to-vote-in-a-uk-general-election#table> (accessed 29 July 2015).

30. Vernon Bogdanor, 'Time to Ditch "First-Past-the-Post"', *Prospect Magazine* (February 2015), 56.

31. One reason for the faulty estimates was that some in government were working on the assumption that very few or no EU member states would impose temporary restrictions on the employment rights of EU citizens, when in fact large numbers of them did. On the estimates, see, e.g., C. Dustmann, M. Casanova, M. Fertig, I. Preston, and C. M. Schmidt, *The Impact of EU Enlargement on Migration Flows* (London: Home Office (Report 25/03), 2003). We have obtained these net migration figures from the revised calculations available on the Office for National Statistics website.

32. Between 2010 and 2015 the government introduced various policies to try and curb non-EU migration, also requiring people who want to bring a non-EU partner into the country to earn a minimum annual income, and imposing greater scrutiny of colleges that want to sponsor international students. For more on the Coalition government policy and immigration, see, e.g., Jonathan Portes (2015) 'The Coalition Government's Record on Immigration', National Institute of Economic and Social Research blog, 2015 <http://niesr.ac.uk/blog/coalition-government%E2%80%99s-record-immigration#.VakZyhNVhHw> (accessed 27 July 2015).

33. On this point, see Lauren McLaren, 'Immigration and Perceptions of the Political System in Britain', *Political Quarterly*, 84/1 (2013), 90–100.

34. For clarity of presentation, the figures have been lowess-smoothed.

35. These historic figures are taken from the Ipsos-MORI data on 'Best Party on Key Issues' <http://www.ipsos-mori.com> (accessed 19 August 2015).

36. In December 2014 YouGov asked a sample of the population: 'Who do you think is most to blame for targets to cut immigration being missed?' 25% said 'the actions of the current coalition government', 18% said 'the legacy of the last Labour government', 29% said 'both equally', 18% said 'neither—it is the result of factors beyond the control of either', and 9% did not know. YouGov and Times Redbox. Provided to the authors by YouGov.

## CHAPTER 3. EARTHQUAKE

1. Ukip was averaging 17%. These figures are the average for both parties, from 1 January 2014 until 19 February 2014, the day before Clegg issued his challenge to Farage.

2. The YouGov poll on the first debate ran on 26 March. Respondents were asked: 'Leaving aside your own party preference, who do you think performed best overall in tonight's debate?' Full results from the poll are available online: <http://yougov.co.uk> (20 September 2014). It is also worth noting that, while only one in three of those who wanted to remain in the EU saw Farage as the winner, almost nine in ten who wanted to withdraw put him ahead.

3. There were two opinion polls after the second debate. A Guardian and ICM poll suggested that 69% of respondents thought that Farage had won compared to 31% who thought Clegg. A YouGov poll (and which we report in Figure 3.1) suggested that these figures were 68% (Farage) and 27% (Clegg). Full results from the YouGov poll are available online: <http://yougov.co.uk> (accessed 22 September 2014).

4. As Colin Rallings and Michael Thrasher note, a record of 7.23 million postal votes were issued (15.6% of the eligible electorate), although in the end just less than five million would be returned. This compares with 15.3% at the 2010 general election and 13.9% at the European Parliament elections in 2009. Most local authorities sought to deliver postal voting ballot papers some two weeks to ten days before polling day, but in about fifty cases identified by Rallings and Thrasher the documentation was sent up to three weeks in advance of the election. For further information, see Colin Rallings and Michael Thrasher, *European Parliament Elections May 2014* (Plymouth University: Elections Centre, 2014).

5. Data obtained from the Electoral Commission.

6. Paul Sykes, 'No More Surrendering to EU Bureaucrats', *Daily Telegraph*, 21 April 2014.

7. Patrick O'Flynn became a registered supporter of Ukip in 2012, converting to a full member in early 2013. The *Daily Express* adopted its 'Better Off Out' position in November 2010. 'Get Britain out of Europe', *Daily Express*, 25 November 2010; Nigel Farage, 'Why We Could All Be Better Off out of this Chaos', *Daily Express*, 29 November 2010.

8. In March 2014 the *Observer* newspaper carried extensive quotation by Neil Hamilton, hinting at his dissatisfaction with Paul Sykes's delay in donating money and suggesting that Sykes was dissuading others from making donations. 'Ukip Conference Ends in Feud as Millionaire Donor Paul Sykes Is Accused of Delay in Paying up', *Observer*, 1 March 2014; see also 'Ukip Demotes Neil Hamilton as Party Fears over Sleaze Grow', *Observer*, 19 April 2014.

9. In July 2013 the vans were driven around the London boroughs of Barking and Dagenham, Redbridge, Barnet, Brent, Ealing, and Hounslow for around one week, although they attracted considerable media publicity. In early August 2013 YouGov asked voters whether they supported or opposed the scheme. Overall, 55% of the sample said that they strongly supported or tended to support the scheme, while 86% of Ukip voters did so. YouGov Survey Results, 11–12 August 2013 <http://yougov.co.uk> (accessed 18 July 2015).

10. These data are from the May 2015 estimates, based on the International Passenger Survey, for the year ending September 2014 <http://www.ons.gov.uk/ons/rel/migration1/migration-statistics-quarterly-report/may-2015/sty-eu2.html> (accessed 17 July2015).

11. In the Ipsos-MORI Issues Index, in May 2014 some 34% of voters ranked 'race relations/immigration/immigrants' as one of the most important issues facing

Britain, behind only the economy on 36%. Thereafter, and as we discuss in Chapter 3, immigration emerged as the most important issue for voters. Ipsos-MORI Issues Index. Available online: http://www.ipsos-mori.com (accessed 5 August 2014).

12. Laura Pitel, 'I Feel Awkward in Towns where No One Talks English, Farage Tells Party', *The Times*, 1 March 2014.

13. UKIP European manifesto, 2014; UKIP election leaflets <http://www.electionleaflets.org/> (accessed 12 May 2014).

14. 'Ukip's Nigel Farage Promises Political "Earthquake"', *BBC News*, 22 April 2014.

15. Mike Gapes, 'Why I Say Ukip Posters Are Racist', *New Statesman*, Staggers, blog <http://www.newstatesman.com/politics/2014/04/why-i-say-ukip-posters-are-racist> (accessed 31 October 2014). 'Ukip Poster Campaign "Divisive, Offensive and Ignorant", Says Tory MP Nicholas Soames', *Huffington Post UK* <http://www.huffingtonpost.co.uk/2014/04/22/ukip-poster-nicholas-soames-_n_5190388.html> (accessed 31 October 2014).

16. The exception was responses to the suggestion that the campaign was 'offensive and ignorant', to which 58% of 18–24 year olds agreed and 51% of people in London agreed. In response to other questions that probed the extent of opposition to the posters, and views of the billboards as racist, even among these 'Ukip-resistant groups' support did not extend above 50%.

17. On 12 March 2014 a poll by ComRes/*Independent on Sunday* put Ukip first (30%), Labour second (28%), and the Conservatives third (21%). On 28 March another poll by ComRes/*People* had Ukip and Labour joint first on 30%, with the Conservatives trailing on 22%. While Ukip peaked on 38%, another poll by YouGov on 15 May also gave Ukip an eleven-point lead over Labour but had Ukip on 35% (with Labour on 24%).

18. 'Ukip Spokesman Led Gang behind Karachi Kidnapping', *The Times*, 5 February 2014; 'Ex-Tory Stands for UKIP', *The Times*, 8 February 2014; 'Ukip Suspends Councillor who Claimed Floods Were Caused by Gay Marriage', *Guardian*, 19 January 2014; 'Orthodox Candidate Refuses to Shake Hands with Women', *The Times*, 17 February 2014; 'Ukip Set to Drop £25,000 Benefit Cheat', *The Times*, 25 February 2014; 'Let Shops Refuse Gays', *The Times*, 6 March 2014; 'Ukip Expels Builder and Decorator who Ranted about Race on Twitter', *The Times*, 25 April 2014; 'Ban Islam, Urges Ukip Candidate', *The Times*, 30 April 2014.

19. 'Beyond the Fringe', *The Times*, 10 March 2014.

20. 'Don't Laugh at Ukip—it's a Serious Force', *The Times*, 11 March 2014; also 'Ukip Facing an Inquiry into Misuse of Funds', *The Times*, 8 March 2014; 'Farage Accused of Affair with Ukip Aide', *The Times*, March 2014; 'The Truth about Ukip is Slowly Emerging', *The Times*, 15 April 2014.

21. 'Wrong Kind of People Are in Ukip, Farage Says', *The Times*, 28 January 2014.

22. On 19–20 May 2014 YouGov asked voters: 'Generally speaking do you think news media coverage of the following political parties has been biased in their

favour, biased against them, or basically fair and balanced? Overall 47% of voters thought the media were biased against Ukip, compared to 17% who thought it was biased against Labour, 23% against Liberal Democrats, and 14% against the Conservatives. One in five voters thought coverage of Ukip was fair and balanced.

23. 'European Elections: Tories Leap ahead of Ukip', *Daily Telegraph*, 17 May 2014. This was an ICM poll of 2,033 adults on 14–15 May 2014.

24. This is sometimes also known as 'sincere' versus 'insincere' voting. See Karlheinz Reif and Hermann Schmitt, 'Nine Second Order National Elections: A Conceptual Framework for the Analysis of European Election Results', *European Journal of Political Research*, 8 (1980), 3–44; Cees van der Eijk and Mark Franklin, *Choosing Europe? The European Electorate and National Politics in the Face of Union* (Ann Arbor: University of Michigan Press, 1996); Colin Rallings and Michael Thrasher (2003) 'Explaining Split Ticket Voting in the 1979 and 1997 General and Local Elections in England', *Political Studies* 51/3 (2003), 558–72; Michael Marsh, 'Testing the Second-Order Election Model after Four European Elections', *British Journal of Political Science*, 4 (1998), 591–607.

25. John Curtice, 'Messages from the Voters: The 2014 Local and European Elections', *Juncture*, 21/1 (2014), 77–81.

26. Combined support for the three main parties was 88.8% in 1994, 76.5% in 1999, 64.2% in 2004, 57.3% in 2009, and 56.2% in 2014. Colin Rallings and Michael Thrasher, *British Electoral Facts 1832–2012* (London: Biteback, 2012); House of Commons Research Paper, 'European Parliamentary Elections 2014' (Paper 14/32, June 2104).

27. As Curtice noted before the European elections, Labour had an average poll rating of 37%, which was enough to give it a lead over the Tories of 5–6 points. But this was well below the position of post-war opposition parties. The exception was in the spring of 1972, when Labour was only six points or so ahead, although at the following general election in February 1974 the party failed to secure an overall majority. John Curtice, 'Labour's Mid-Term Melancholy: Why Poll Position Isn't Everything', *Juncture*, 20/20 (2013), 155–8.

28. Nicholas Watt, Patrick Wintour, and Rowena Mason, 'Lib Dems Call for Clegg's Resignation in Wake of Dismal Election Result', *Guardian*, 26 May 2014.

### CHAPTER 4. LEFT-BEHIND BRITAIN

1. Ukip won the popular vote in Yorkshire and Humber (31.1%), the East Midlands (32.9%), the West Midlands (31.5%), the East (34.5%), the South East (32.1%) and the South West (32.3%). For a detailed study of the election results, see Oliver Hawkins, Vaughne Miller, and Jeremy Hardacre (2014) *European Elections 2014: Research Paper 14/32* (House of Commons Library Research Paper, 2014).

2. John Harris, 'Why Ukip's Little England Is Full of Eastern Promise', *Guardian*, 24 March 2014.

3. These were Torbay, Torridge, and North Devon. By 'areas' we refer here to local-authority areas.

4. The three exceptions were Teignbridge in Devon (where Ukip polled 47%), Hillingdon in London (44%), and Torbay in Devon (43%).

5. In this respect it is worth noting that Ukip's average support in its best areas was often growing faster than its average across the country, providing further evidence that it was beginning to build strong bastions of support. In areas where the party attracted more than 40% of the vote, it had often increased its support by more than 80%, which was fourteen points higher than its average growth across the country. These localized pockets of strength would be key if Ukip was to break through at a general election under first-past-the-post.

6. Ukip finished first in 88 of the 159 council areas controlled by the Conservative Party prior to the 2014 European Parliament elections. For example, in the East Midlands Ukip finished ahead of the Tories in fifteen of twenty-two Conservative councils. In Eastern England it had done so in twenty-two of thirty-two council areas. In the South East it was ahead in twenty-four of forty-nine, and in the South West it was ahead in eight of eleven.

7. The letter was organized by the Conservative grass-roots organization. A similar letter from business leaders, including Conservative donors, had been sent to the *Daily Telegraph* in the same week. Georgina Graham, 'Conservative Grassroots Tell Cameron he must Spell out EU Reform Plan to Defeat Ukip', *Daily Telegraph*, 30 May 2014.

8. George Parker, 'Ukip Surge Brings Four-Party Politics to Britain', *Financial Times*, 3 May 2013. The nine constituencies were Boston and Skegness in Lincolnshire, the coastal seat of Great Yarmouth in Norfolk, Bognor Regis and Littlehampton and also East Worthing and Shoreham on the south coast in West Sussex, Forest of Dean in Gloucestershire, Aylesbury in Buckinghamshire, and Camborne and Redruth in Cornwall.

9. The four seats where Ukip was second (based on responses to constituency voting intention) were Camborne and Redruth (where Ukip on the constituency voting intention Ukip was second on 26%), Newton Abbot (20%), Truro and Falmouth (22%), and St Austell and Newquay (25%). The Lord Ashcroft snapshots across seventeen marginal seats and released in June 2014 put Ukip on 14%. For further information, see Lord Ashcroft, 'The Conservative–Lib Dem Battleground', Lord Ashcroft Polls, 19 June 2014 <http://lordashcroftpolls. com/2014/06/conservative-lib-dem-battleground/> (accessed 26 April 2015).

10. In the Lord Ashcroft polls, released in July 2014, Ukip was first in South Thanet on 33% (constituency voting intention), ahead of the incumbent Conservatives and Labour by four points. Ukip was also first in Thurrock on 36%, ahead of Labour by six points and the incumbent Conservatives by eight points. In Great Yarmouth Ukip was on 31%, two points behind the incumbent Conservatives but three points ahead of Labour. Lord Ashcroft, 'Con–Lab Battleground: Swing from Tories Drops as UKIP Pick up Labour Votes <http://lordashcroftpolls.

com/2014/07/con-lab-battleground-swing-tories-drops-ukip-pick-labour-votes/> (accessed 26 April 2015). Paul Goodman, 'Ukip Hasn't Gone Away', Conservative Home, 23 July 2014 <http://www.conservativehome.com/thetorydiary/2014/07/ukip-hasnt-gone-away.html> (accessed 28 April 2015).

11. Lord Ashcroft, 'Con–Lab Battleground'.).

12. The research was undertaken by Ipsos-MORI and featured in the 'Ed Miliband' chapter in Fabian Society, *The Labour Leadership: How Important Is it that The Party Has a Distinctive Ideology?* (London: Fabian Society, 2010).

13. Simon Walters, 'Stupidity of Cameron's Priorities: Gay Marriage, Foreign Aid and Wind Farms: No Wonder Tory Voters Feel Closer to me', *Mail on Sunday*, 4 May 2013.

14. 'UKIP Can Beat Labour in North East, Says Leader', *Journal*, 20 August 2012.

15. In the North West Ukip won the popular vote across nine councils including four run by Labour, and in Yorkshire and the Humber it won the vote in six of nine Labour councils. In the North East Ukip won the popular vote in Darlington, Hartlepool, Middlesbrough, Redcar, and Cleveland, and Stockton-on-Tees. In the North West the party won the popular vote in Blackpool, Carlisle, Cheshire West, Hyndburn, Lancaster, Rossendale, South Ribble, Stockport, and Wyre. In Yorkshire and the Humber Ukip won the popular vote in Calderdale, Doncaster, East Riding of Yorkshire, Kingston-upon-Hull, North East Lincolnshire, North Lincolnshire, Rotherham, Scarborough, Selby, Wakefield, and York. The challenge to Labour could be seen elsewhere. In the Midlands Farage and his party had won the vote in more than half of the Labour-run councils, while in Eastern England it won the vote in five of seven. In Wales, Ukip won the highest share of the vote in Conwy, Denbighshire, Flintshire, Powys, the Vale of Glamorgan, and Wrexham.

16. Ukip recruited more than 35% in eighteen Labour-run areas—including parts of the Midlands such as Stoke-on-Trent, Cannock Chase, Dudley, the old coal-mining area of Ashfield, and the Labour stronghold of Hartlepool in the North East, scoring strongly in other industrial areas such as Barnsley, Bolsover, Corby, Kingston-upon-Hull, and Wakefield. We compile Ukip's strongest results in Labour-held areas in Appendix A—and in almost half of them its support since 2009 had almost doubled. It is worth noting that only four of the top twenty-five Conservative areas for Ukip saw the party's support increase by at least 100%—namely, Boston, South Holland, Hillingdon, and Swale.

17. Tim Shipman and Jack Grimston, 'Labour Star: We're Losing Core Voters', *Sunday Times*, 8 June 2014.

18. Rowena Mason and Aisha Gani, 'Half of Labour Candidates in Marginal Seats are Westminster Insiders', *Guardian*, 17 June 2014.

19. This is not to say that the party was not advancing into new territory. More than half of its twenty-five strongest results came in local wards that the party had not previously fought.

20. Simon Heffer, 'For Essex Man, the Only Way Is Ukip, Says Simon Heffer', *Daily Mail*, 24 May 2014.

21. As Fisher argued, based on the projected national share of the vote for each of the parties, based on their performance in the local elections, all three of the main parties were down on their support in 2012. But Labour had dropped more than either the Conservatives or the Liberal Democrats (Labour −9, Conservative −6, and Liberal Democrats −2). This suggested that Labour was the biggest loser and that Ukip had substantially hurt Labour at the elections. Certainly, noted Fisher, it is impossible to count for the rise of Ukip by Conservative losses alone. Steve Fisher, 'Local Elections 2013: UKIP Hurt Labour at Least as much as the Tories Compared with Last Year', *Elections etc.*, 9 May 2013 <http://electionsetc.blogspot.co.uk/2013/05/local-elections-2013-ukip-hurt-labour.html> (accessed 24 April 2015).

22. For each party we include only wards that were contested in 2010 and 2014.

23. We refer to Clacton and its predecessor seat of Harwich. Labour won Harwich in 1997 and 2001. The Conservatives won the seat at every other election since 1970. Before then the seat was controlled by National Liberals.

24. Mark Duell, 'Welcome to Misery-by-Sea: Dilapidated Homes, Boarded-up Shops and Rubbish-Strewn Streets', *Mail Online*, 4 April 2013 <http://www.dailymail.co.uk/news/article-2303489/East-Jaywick-Life-seaside-deprived-village-England.html> (accessed 3 December 2014). The Indices of Deprivation in 2010 identified Jaywick as the single most deprived 'Lower Super Output Area' in all of England. On Clacton as among the three most deprived seaside destinations, see Phil Humby, (2013). *A Profile of Deprivation in Larger English Seaside Destinations, 2007 and 2010* (Office for National Statistics, 2013) <www.ons.gov.uk> (accessed 13 March 2015).

25. Matthew Parris, 'Tories should Turn their Backs on Clacton', *The Times*, 6 September 2014.

26. In 2013 the right-wing Centre for Social Justice warned that England's seaside towns were becoming 'dumping grounds' for the vulnerable and set out ideas to reverse their fortunes, talking about additional infrastructure, increased localism, renewed investment, and a reformed welfare system that incentivized people to return to work. Centre for Social Justice (2013) *Turning the Tide* (London: Centre for Social Justice, 2013). The full thirty-eight seats are Bexhill and Battle, Bognor Regis and Littlehampton, Boston and Skegness, Brighton Kemptown, Brighton Pavilion, Canterbury, Castle Point, Chichester, Clacton, Cleethorpes, Dover, Eastbourne, Folkestone and Hythe, Great Grimsby, Great Yarmouth, Harwich and Essex North, Hastings and Rye, Havant, Hove, Lewes, Louth and Horncastle, Maldon, Norfolk North, Norfolk North West, Portsmouth South, Rochester and Strood, Rochford and Southend East, Sittingbourne and Sheppey, South Holland and The Deepings, Southend West, Suffolk Coastal, Suffolk South, Thanet North, Thanet South, Waveney, Witham, Worthing East and Shoreham, and Worthing West. Ian Warren, 'The East Coast: I Can See Parris from here!' *Election Data*, blog (since removed). Contact the authors for copy.

27. Data on socio-demographic characteristics of the local authorities comes from the 2011 census. We have not included local areas in Scotland, as the party finds little favour north of the border. Note, however, that the overall patterns and our substantive conclusions remain unchanged if Scotland is included in the analysis.

28. A detailed discussion of the measure can be found in the Appendix B.

29. This refers to the worst results once we have excluded Scotland. On Lambeth, see 'Lambeth: The State of the Borough', Report (Lambeth Council, 2012); The Office for National Statistics, 2011 Census Data <http://www.ons.gov.uk/ons/rel/census/2011-census-analysis/local-area-analysis-of-qualifications-across-england-and-wales/info-highest-qualifications.html> (accessed 3 May 2015). Also data from Hull City Council (2012) <http://www.hullcc.gov.uk/portal/page?_pageid=293,722103&_dad=portal&_schema=PORTAL> (accessed 3 May 2015).

30. Jonathan Freedland, 'London is Ukip's Worst Nightmare', *Guardian*, 23 May 2014; Eric Kaufman, 'The Myth of London Exceptionalism: London not as Invulnerable to UKIP as Commonly Reported', *Demos Quarterly*, 5 (2014–15). White British-born individuals are also less likely to move into diverse areas, such as those found in London. See Eric Kaufmann and Gareth Harris, '"White Flight" or Positive Contact? Local Diversity and Attitudes to Immigration in Britain', *Comparative Political Studies*, 13 May 2015, 0010414015581684.

## CHAPTER 5. FARAGE'S FOLLOWERS

1. Profiler can be accessed at <https://yougov.co.uk/find-solutions/profiles/> (accessed 23 July 2015).

2. A full description of our research methods can be found in the Appendix C. Suffice to say here that we are drawing on the second wave of the 2014–2017 British Election Study panel survey, in which respondents were interviewed during the month after the European elections.

3. Robert Ford and Matthew J. Goodwin, *Revolt on the Right: Explaining Public Support for the Radical Right in Britain* (Abingdon: Routledge, 2014).

4. The 'other' category includes those who voted for the SNP in 2010 (less than 1% of Ukip voters), the Plaid Cymru (less than 1%), the BNP (2%), Ukip (7%), and those who voted for any other party (less than 1%).

5. A similar point, using the same data, is made by Geoffrey Evans and Jon Mellon, 'Working Class Votes and Conservative Losses: Solving the UKIP Puzzle', *Parliamentary Affairs* (2015), advanced access.

6. Quotations in Evans and Mellon, 'Working Class Votes and Conservative Losses'. See also Geoffrey Evans (1999) 'Europe: A New Electoral Cleavage?', in G. Evans and P. Norris (eds), *Critical Elections: British Parties and Voters in Long-Term Perspective* (London: Sage, 1999), 207–22; G. Evans and K. Chzhen, 'Explaining Voters' Defection from Labour over the 2005–2010 Electoral Cycle: Leaders, Economics, and the Rising Importance of Immigration', *Political Studies*, 61 (2013), 3–22; G. Evans, 'The Working Class and New Labour: A

Parting of the Ways?, in R. Jowell, J. Curtice, A. Park, K. Thomson, C. Bromley, L. Jarvis, and N. Stratford (eds), *British Social Attitudes, the 17th Report: Focusing on Diversity* (London: Sage, 2000), 51–69; T. Bale, 'Putting it Right? The Labour Party's Big Shift on Immigration since 2010', *Political Quarterly*, 85/3 (2014), 296–303.

7. See Evans, 'Europe: A New Electoral Cleavage?'; Ford and Goodwin, *Revolt on the Right*, 109–38, and also pp. 174–75. See also the debate in the academic journal *Parliamentary Affairs*. Evans and Mellon (2015) 'Working Class Votes and Conservative Losses'.

8. Extracts taken from Ed Miliband's speech announcing his intention to stand for leadership. See 'Ed Miliband Announces his Intention to Stand for Leadership— Full Speech', Labour List, 15 May 2010 <http://labourlist.org/2010/05/ed-miliband-announces-his-intention-to-stand-for-leadership-full-speech/> (accessed 25 May 2015).

9. On the influential study, see P. M. Sniderman, L. Hagendoorn, and M. Prior, 'Predisposing Factors and Situational Triggers: Exclusionary Reactions to Immigrant Minorities', *American Political Science Review*, 98 (2004), 35–49. For some recent examples, see Marijn Van Klingeren, Hajo Boomgaarden, and Claes H. De Vreese, 'Going Soft or Staying Soft: Have Identity Factors Become More Important than Economic Rationale when Explaining Euroscepticism?' *Journal of European Integration*, 35/6 (2013), 689–704; and Jens Hainmueller and Daniel J. Hopkins, 'Public Attitudes toward Immigration', *Annual Review of Political Science*, 17 (2014) 225–49.

10. E. Kaufmann, E. (2014) 'Rochester and UKIP: We Shouldn't Leap to the Conclusion that this By-Election Is a Bellwether for 2015', LSE General Election Blog (2014) <http://blogs.lse.ac.uk/generalelection/rochester-and-ukip-we-shouldnt-leap-to-the-conclusion-that-this-by-election-is-a-bell-wether-for-2015/> (accessed 24 February 2015); see also R. Ford and M. J. Goodwin, 'Angry White Men: Individual and Contextual Predictors of Support for the British National Party', *Political Studies*, 58 (2010), 1–25.

11. For interested readers, these analyses can be found in the Appendix C.

12. Dan Hodges, 'The Great Ukip Panic Is under Way, and Labour Is Running from the Imaginary Threat', *Daily Telegraph*, blog, 23 May 23 2014 <http://blogs.telegraph.co.uk/news/danhodges/100272795/the-great-ukip-panic-is-under-way-and-labour-is-running-from-the-imaginary-threat/> (accessed 23 May 2014); John Rentoul, 'Nigel Farage has Bottled his By-Election Chance, and Ukip Is Over', *Independent*, 30 April 2014 <http://www.independent.co.uk/voices/comment/nigel-farage-has-bottled-his-byelection-chance-and-ukip-is-over-9308526.html> (accessed 23 May 2015); Georgia Graham, 'Conservative Voters Defecting to Ukip "Like Grooms Looking for Stag Night Fun"', *Daily Telegraph*, 7 May 2014 <http://www.telegraph.co.uk/news/politics/david-cameron/10812756/Conservative-voters-defecting-to-Ukip-like-grooms-looking-for-stag-night-fun.html> (accessed 23 May 2014). On earlier quotations, see

Jack Blanchard, 'UKIP's "Political Earthquake" Petering out with a Whimper according to By-Election Poll', *Mirror*, 2 June 2014 <http://www.mirror.co.uk/news/uk-news/ukips-political-earthquake-petering-out-3638091 (accessed 23 May 2015); Steven Swinford, 'Sir John Major: Ukip is "Very Intolerant" and Will not Last', *Daily Telegraph*, 30 May 2015 <http://www.telegraph.co.uk/news/politics/ukip/10864377/Sir-John-Major-Ukip-is-very-intolerant-and-will-not-last.html> (accessed 23 May 2015).

13. Tim Wigmore, 'Farage's Gamble Pays off—But Where Do Ukip Go Next?' *New Statesman*, blog, 26 May 2014 <http://www.newstatesman.com/politics/2014/05/farages-gamble-pays-where-do-ukip-go-next> (accessed May 23 2015).

14. Of the British Election Study post-election respondents, 28% said that they had voted for Ukip in the European election and 53% of those voters said they planned to stay loyal in a general election. Assuming there was no change to the party's support, the calculations for national vote in a general election would be 0.28*0.53=0.15 or 15%. Of course, this is only a very rough estimate, as there are many other factors that would alter the translation of votes to seats, including (but not limited to) the shift from a proportional electoral system to first-past-the-post, and the strategic calculations that come into play, particularly in marginal seats.

## CHAPTER 6. SUSTAINING MOMENTUM

1. At the European Parliament elections Ukip polled 32.4% across the Newark and Sherwood District Council area, finishing in first place but only ahead of the Conservatives by 1%. The party polled significantly more strongly in other areas of the East Midlands, notably Boston (51.6%), South Holland (48.5%), and Mansfield (48.5%). The exception was the 1997 general election, when the voters of Newark elected the Labour candidate Fiona Jones. Between 1950 and the general election in October 1974 the seat was held by Labour.

2. The exceptions during this early period came in the parliamentary by-elections in Wigan in September 1999, when Ukip finished fourth with 5.2%, in Hartlepool in September 2004 when the party finished third with 10.2%, in Bromley and Chislehurst in June 2006 when Nigel Farage finished third with 8.1%, and in Norwich North in July 2009 when Ukip finished fourth with 11.8%. Ukip polled less than 1% of the vote at by-elections in Wirral South in February 1997, Uxbridge in July 1997, Hamilton South in September 1999, Tottenham in June 2000, Brent East in September 2003, Livingston in September 2005, Dunfermline and West Fife in February 2006, Ealing Southall in July 2007, and Glenrothes in November 2008. For a more detailed discussion of these earlier years, see also Robert Ford and Matthew J. Goodwin, *Revolt on the Right: Explaining Support for the Radical Right in Britain* (Abingdon: Routledge, 2014), 20–106.

3. On these points, see also Robert Ford and Matthew Goodwin, 'Different Class? UKIP's Social Base and Political Impact: A Reply to Evans and Mellon', *Parliamentary Affairs* (2015) <http://pa.oxfordjournals.org/content/early/2015/04/16/pa.gsv013. abstract> (accessed 2 June 2015). Neil O'Brien and Anthony Wells, *Northern Lights: Public Policy and the Geography of Political Attitudes* (London, Policy Exchange, 2012); also Ron Johnston and Charles Pattie, 'The British General Election of 2010: A Three-Party Contest—or Three Two-Party Contests?', *Geographical Journal*, 177 (2011), 17–26.

4. The exceptions were Corby, which was held by the Conservatives after 2010, and Eastleigh, which was held by the Liberal Democrats.

5. Bagehot, 'The Relief of Newark', *The Economist*, 6 June 2014 <http://www. economist.com/blogs/blighty/2014/06/big-election> (accessed 24 March 2015).

6. For a selection of this coverage, see Christopher Hope, 'Ukip MEP who Said Homosexuality Was "Abnormal" Is Party's Candidate in Newark By-Election', *Daily Telegraph*, 6 May 2014; Rowena Mason, 'Nigel Farage Defends Ukip By-Election Candidate over Anti-Gay Remarks', *Guardian*, 11 May 2014.

7. Anoosh Chakelian, 'Meet Ukip's Seal-Hating, Gay-Baiting, Victim-Blaming Newark Candidate, Roger Helmer', *New Statesman*, Staggers Blog, 6 May 2014; Matt Chorley, 'Ukip Accused of "Hypocrisy" for Hiring EU Migrants to Deliver Leaflets in Election Campaign against Immigration', *Daily Mail*, 7 May 2014.

8. Lord Ashcroft, Newark By-Election Poll, 2 June 2014 <http://lordashcroftpolls. com/> (accessed 17 October 2015). The Conservative Party spent £96,000 on the campaign compared to Ukip's £84,000. 'Conservatives Spent £96,191 during Newark By-Election', *Newark Advertiser*, 14 July 2014.

9. John Rentoul, 'Nigel Farage has Bottled his By-Election Chance, and Ukip Is Over', *Independent*, 30 April 2014; Dan Hodges, 'Newark By-Election: Can we Drop this Ludicrous Fiction that Ukip Is a Real Political Force?', *Daily Telegraph*, blog, 6 June 2014 <http://blogs.telegraph.co.uk/news/danhodges/100275086/ newark-by-election-can-we-drop-this-ludicrous-fiction-that-ukip-are-a-real-political-force/> (accessed 23 March 2015).

10. John Hooper, 'Ex-Berlusconi Minister Defends Anders Behring Breivik', *Guardian*, 27 July 2011.

11. 'Borghezio (Lega): "E'un patriota"', *La Repubblica*, 27 May 2011; 'Borghezio: "Idee di Breivik condivisibili", E Calderoli chiede scusa all Norvegia', *Le Repubblico*, 26 July 2011; John Hooper, 'Ex-Berlusconi Minister Defends Anders Behring Breivik', *Guardian*, 27 July 2011; N. Squires and B. Waterfield, 'Ukip Removes Italian MEP for Racist Insult at Black Italian Minister', *Daily Telegraph*, 23 May 2013.

12. Timo Soini remained in the EFDD until 2011, when he was elected into the Finnish national parliament. He was then replaced by Sampo Terho. The Europe of Freedom and Democracy group had thirty-four elected members between

2009 and 2014, which included representatives from the National Front for the Salvation of Bulgaria, the Danish People's Party, True Finns, Movement for France, Popular Orthodox Rally, the Northern League in Italy, 'I Love Italy', Order and Justice from Lithuania, the Reformed Political Party in the Netherlands, United Poland, the Slovak National Party, as well as an Independent (Frank Vanhecke) and Ukip. The Ukip MEP Nikki Sinclaire refused to join the EFD group, Mike Nattrass temporarily left the EFD, Trevor Colman left the EFD, while David Campbell-Bannerman and Marta Andreasen both left Ukip during the 2009–14 parliament to join the Conservative Party.

13. Nick Squires, Menelaus Tzafalias, and Harriet Alexander, 'What is the Golden Dawn Trial about', *Daily Telegraph*, 20 April 2015.

14. Andrew Higgins, 'Populists' Rise in Europe Vote Shakes Leaders', *New York Times*, 26 May 2014.

15. Beppe Grillo, 'Nigel Farage, the Truth', *Il Blog di Beppe Grillo*, 30 May 2014 <http://www.beppegrillo.it/2014/05/nigel_farage_la_verita.html> (accessed 16 February 2015). Translated by the authors.

16. Bruno Waterfield, 'Geert Wilders Invites Nigel Farage to Join Anti-EU Alliance', *Daily Telegraph*, 13 November 2013.

17. Laurence Dodds, 'Nigel Farage: Ukip Won't Unite with France's Front National', *Daily Telegraph*, 27 May 2014. In April 2014 Farage endorsed a small Gaullist party called Debout la République. See Rowena Mason, 'Nigel Farage Rejects Offer of Ukip Tie to French Far-Right Front National', *Guardian*, 18 April 2014.

18. Some of these statements would later be covered in the British press. See, e.g., Emma Graham-Harrison, 'Nigel Farage's New Friend in Europe: "When women say no, they don't always mean it"', *Observer*, 9 November 2014.

19. Ben Riley-Smith, 'Jewish Group Attacks Nigel Farage's Decision to Partner Ukip with Controversial Polish MEP', *Daily Telegraph*, 21 October 2014.

20. George Parker, 'David Cameron Seeks Allies in Keeping Jean-Claude Juncker from Brussels Job', *Financial Times*, 22 May 2014.

21. Tim Dowling, 'Nigel Farage: Ukip's One-Man Band Plays on', *Guardian*, 17 December 2014.

22. Owen Bennett, 'Never Call us Racist Again', *Daily Express*, 8 May 2014.

23. Also elected to the front bench were Margot Parker, Louise Bours, and Jill Seymour.

24. 'Ukip Defends MEP's "Hitler Speech" Advice', *BBC News*, 10 August 2014.

25. Jim Pickard, 'Nigel Farage to Stand for Parliament', *Financial Times*, 8 August 2014.

26. This would remain true. At the local elections in 2015, for example, four wards in Thanet district council returned a Labour councillor, including Margate Central, which is the most deprived ward in Kent. The three other wards where Labour polled relatively strongly but did not win were also in the ten most deprived wards in Kent—including Cliftonville West (Margate), Eastcliff (Ramsgate), and Newington (west of Ramsgate).

27. A former deputy Conservative leader of Thanet council defected to Ukip in 2012, then a Conservative district councillor and member for thirty-five years defected in January 2013, and then another district councillor defected in October 2014. The former Conservative leader of Thanet council had used inside information to buy property.

28. Andrew Pierce, 'Is Elton Coming out for Ukip?' *Daily Mail*, 18 August 2014.

29. Douglas Carswell, *The End of Politics and the Birth of iDemocracy* (PLACE: Biteback, 2012).

30. Douglas Carswell, 'How Direct Democracy has Inspired Many of the Policies of the Coalition Government', Conservative Home website, 9 August 2010 <http://conservativehome.blogs.com/thinktankcentral/direct-democracy/> (accessed 3 December 2014).

31. Charles Moore, 'There's Nothing Swivel-Eyed about Rebuilding Britain's Democracy', *Daily Telegraph*, 16 October 2009.

32. Douglas Carswell and Daniel Hannan, *The Plan: Twelve Months to Renew Britain* (Published by Douglas Carswell and Daniel Hannan, 2008).

33. Douglas Carswell, '"Tory Party is Run like HMV...and Will Go the Same Way", Says Conservative MP for Clacton Douglas Carswell', *Mail on Sunday*, 3 March 2013.

34. Zac Goldsmith MP: 'Clegg's Recall Bill Was a Stitch-up: Cameron Must Keep his Promise to Introduce the Real Thing', Conservative Home blog, 17 February 2014 <http://www.conservativehome.com/platform/2014/02/zac-goldsmith-mp-cleggs-recall-bill-was-a-stitch-up-cameron-must-keep-his-promise-to-introduce-the-real-thing.html> (accessed 16 December 2014).

35. The academic was Matthew Goodwin, who was presenting research at the conference. Douglas Carswell MP asked where his seat was ranked in a list of the most 'Ukip-friendly' seats compiled by Ford and Goodwin for their book *Revolt on the Right*.

36. Ukip Manifesto, *Ukip: Empowering the People* (Newton Abbott: UK Independence Party, 2010).

## CHAPTER 7. THE DEAL THAT NEVER WAS

1. We have taken the average of two polls undertaken by Survation and Lord Ashcroft towards the end of August 2014. In the first poll by Survation, Ukip was on 64%, compared to the Conservative Party's 20% and Labour's 13%. In the second poll that followed by Lord Ashcroft, Ukip was on 56%, compared to the Conservative Party's 24% and Labour's 16%.

2. Labour MPs had majorities of more than 10,000 at the 1997, 2001, and 2005 general elections. At the general election in 2010 the Labour majority declined to less than 6,000. In earlier years, before the creation of the seat, the seat of Middleton and Prestwich (James Callaghan's old seat) had been held by the Conservative Party uninterrupted from 1945 until 1964, while Heywood and

Royton was held by the Conservatives from 1950 until 1959, and then went Labour. The local council has had a more diverse political history, having been controlled at various points by the Liberal Democrats and Conservatives, although Labour was often the dominant party, and especially in recent years.

3. The exact figures reported by the Polling Observatory, which pools together all the available polling evidence, were as follows: 14.9% on 1 June, 14.8% on 1 July, 13.3% on 1 August, and then 14% on 9 Septemberh. 'The Guardian View on Ukip Conference: Nigel Farage's Phoney Flutter', *Guardian*, 26 September 2014.

4. Oliver Duggan, '"A Feral Mob of Subsidised Students": Ukip Leader Nigel Farage Hits out at Protestors', *Independent*, 18 June 2013.

5. Only four days after the referendum in Scotland the *Guardian* reported that the SNP's membership had increased by 18,000 to 43,644. Severin Carrell, 'SNP Poised to Become One of UK's Largest Political Parties', *Guardian*, 22 September 2014.

6. Helen Daniel, 'Parents Told Pupils Could Be Prostitutes', *The Times*, 3 March 2001; 'Web of the Sex Gangs "Reaches across UK"', *Yorkshire Post*, 24 August 2003. Andrew Norfolk, 'Sexual Grooming: The Grooming of White Girls of Pakistani Heritage Is an Issue that Few in the Community Will Address', *The Times*, 5 January 2011; Andrew Norfolk, 'Sexual Grooming: An Abused Teenager and her Mother Have Told Andrew Norfolk how she Fell Victim to a Predatory Gang', *The Times*, 15 January 2011; 'In the Car in the Dark Alley, a Man's Arm Reached Out To Caress a Child', *The Times*, 7 April 2011. The report was the so-called Jay Report. Alexis Jay, *Independent Inquiry into Child Sexual Exploitation in Rotherham, 1997–2013* (Rotherham Metropolitan Borough Council, 2014). The report (p. 35) went on to note: 'In a large number of the historic cases in particular, most of the victims in the cases we sampled were white British children, and the majority of the perpetrators were from minority ethnic communities. They were described generically in the files as "Asian males" without precise reference being made to their ethnicity.'

7. Louise Casey, *Report of Inspection of Rotherham Metropolitan Borough Council* (Department for Communities and Local Government, February 2015).

8. Following the Jay Report, the Local Government Secretary confirmed that five commissioners would take over the executive functions of Rotherham borough council and that 'all-out' elections would be held in 2016.

9. At the 2014 local elections Ukip averaged 44% across twenty-one local wards compared to Labour's 41%.

10. Rowena Mason, 'Nigel Farage Disowns Ukip's Entire 2010 Election Manifesto', *Guardian*, 24 January 2014.

11. Lizzie Dearden, 'Nigel Farage Leaves Notes from Ukip Conference Keynote Speech on Lectern', *Independent*, 27 September 2014.

12. Farage would finish third in Buckingham, attracting 17% of the vote.

13. Carswell, Reckless, and Atkinson would defect to Ukip by the time of the 2015 general election. Ukip provided additional help to Philip Hollobone, Mark

Reckless, and Bob Spink. Only Spink, Janice Atkinson (then Small), and Alex
Story failed to win their seats. It is worth noting that both Atkinson and Story
saw a relatively strong vote for the extreme-right British National Party (BNP),
which polled almost 6% in Story's seat and 7% in Atkinson's. In another seat,
Stroud, the Ukip candidate used his election address to endorse the Labour
candidate, David Drew, having not been convinced about the Eurosceptic cre-
dentials of the Conservative Party candidate (Neil Carmichael), who went on
to win the seat.

14. The campaign job instead went to a former RAF pilot who resigned soon after-
    wards, claiming that Farage had repeatedly blocked his efforts to professionalize
    Ukip. The party, noted the disgruntled former employee, wanted to remain as
    'a bunch of enthusiastic amateurs having a good time'. Insiders responded by
    claiming that the activist's militaristic demeanour had never been suited to life
    in Ukip. James Kirkup and Jon Laurence, 'Nigel Farage Wants Ukip to Remain
    a "Bunch Of Amateurs"', *Daily Telegraph*, 20 August 2013.

15. Stephen Harper (who had been in the Reform movement) and the Conservative
    Party of Canada were still in power at the time this book was published.

16. 'As Long as the Eurosceptic Vote Is Fragmented, the Euro-Enthusiasts Will
    Keep Winning', *Daily Telegraph* blogs, 17 April 2012 <http://blogs.telegraph.
    co.uk/news/danielhannan/100151515/as-long-as-the-eurosceptic-vote-is-frag-
    mented-the-euro-enthusiasts-will-keep-winning/> (accessed 22 January 2015).
    See also 'Nigel Farage Is Surely now a More Attractive Partner than Nick
    Clegg', *Daily Telegraph* blogs, 16 November 2012 <http://blogs.telegraph.co.uk/
    news/danielhannan/100190187/ukip-is-surely-now-a-more-attractive-part-
    ner-than-the-libdems/> (accessed 22 January 2015).

17. Farage quotation from BBC News, 'Nigel Farage on UKIP–Conservative Deal
    over Referendum', 21 September 2012 <http://www.bbc.co.uk/news/uk-pol-
    itics-19676378> (accessed 26 May 2015); Rowena Mason, 'Ukip–Tory Pact:
    "Absolutely No Chance" Says Downing Street', *Daily Telegraph*, 26 November
    2012; Matt Chorley and Jason Groves, 'Eight Tories "in Secret Lunch Plot to
    Defect to UKIP" as Two Parties Go to War over Electoral Pact', *Daily Mail*, 27
    November 2012.

18. Toby Young, 'Why I Failed in my New Year's Resolution to Unite the Right
    against Ed Miliband', *Spectator*, magazine, 3 January 2015 <http://www.specta-
    tor.co.uk/life/status-anxiety/9405232/a-year-ago-i-had-big-plans-to-unite-
    the-right-this-year-im-keeping-my-ambitions-more-modest/>      (accessed
    22 January 2015).

## CHAPTER 8. LEARNING LESSONS

1. 'Mark Reckless Defection Shows his True Character, Says Grant Schapps',
   *Guardian*, 28 September 2014.

2. George Parker, 'Cameron's Conference Speech Gives Voice to Party Optimism',
   *Financial Times*, 1 October 2014.

3. 'Angry Dave's Jibe at "Fat Arse" Reckless', Steerpike, *Spectator* blog <http://blogs.spectator.co.uk/steerpike/2014/09/angry-daves-jibe-at-fat-arse-reckless/> (accessed 23 March 2015); Matt Chorley, 'Furious Cameron Blasts "Fat A★★★" UKIP Defector Mark Reckless and Says he Cares 1,000 Times Less about Leaving EU than Breaking up the UK', *Mail Online*, 30 September 2014 <http://www.dailymail.co.uk/news/article-2774751/Furious-Cameron-blasts-fat-arse-UKIP-defector-Mark-Reckless-says-cares-1-000-times-leaving-EU-breaking-UK.html> (accessed March 2015); Tom McTague, 'UKIP Supporters Are "Elderly Male People who Have Had Disappointing Lives", Says Veteran Tory Ken Clarke', *Daily Mail*, 30 September 2014; Matt Chorley and Matt McTague, 'Ukip Defectors are the Sort of People who have Sex with Vacuum Cleaners', *Daily Mail*, 30 September 2014.

4. Lord Ashcroft, 'What I Told the Tories in Birmingham', Lord Ashcroft Polls, 28 September 2014 <http://lordashcroftpolls.com/2014/09/told-tories-birmingham/> (accessed 30 April 2015). One of the authors was also at the presentation and took notes from the event.

5. Of the remainder defectors in the Lord Ashcroft research, 22% said they did not know whom to support, 12% were moving to Labour, 3% to the Liberal Democrats, and 5% said either some other party or that they would not vote.

6. Of the 22% of Conservative defectors who said their second preference was a party other than the Tories, 9% said they preferred the Greens, 7% said the BNP, 5% said they preferred Labour, and the remaining 1% said the Liberal Democrats, the SNP, or the Plaid Cymru.

7. 'David Cameron's Grand Riposte', *The Economist*, 4 October 2014.

8. George Parker, 'Blairites Sounded out Alan Johnson on Labour Leadership', *Financial Times*, 6 February 2015.

9. Labour, 'Campaigning against UKIP', Labour Party, published November 2014. See Ben Riley-Smith, 'Labour's Secret Ukip Strategy: Full Details of What the Party Admits in Leaked Document', *Daily Telegraph*, 14 December 2014.

10. When Survation interviewed 700 people from across Clacton and asked what they thought about Carswell's decision, 50% saw the decision as 'honourable', while 23% saw it as self-serving opportunism. A problem for the Conservatives was that this was also mirrored in the response of their own voters from 2010, more than half of whom thought Carswell's actions had been honourable and, in answer to another question, 49% of whom saw Carswell as a hero (versus 17% who saw him as a 'traitor'). Survation/*Mail on Sunday* Poll, Fieldwork, 28–9 August 2014 <http://survation.com> (accessed 17 October 2014). Simon Walters, 'Cameron Faces Ukip By-Election Bloodbath', *Daily Mail*, 31 August 2014. The first poll was undertaken by Survation and excluded undecided and refusal voters. When these were included, the poll still suggested a strong Ukip victory, with Ukip on 48%, the Conservatives on 15%, Labour on 10%, and the Liberal Democrats on 2%.

11. Mark Wallace, 'Open Primaries, Caucuses and One Cheer in Clacton', Conservative Home blog, 4 September 2014 <http://www.conservativehome.com/

parliament/2014/09/open-primaries-caucuses-and-one-cheer-in-clacton.
html> (accessed August 9 2015).

12. Nicholas Watt, 'Divisions between Nigel Farage and Douglas Carswell Reinforced in Clacton', *Guardian*, 10 October 2014.

13. The question read: 'Which, if any, of the following reasons played a part in your decision to vote for...?'. 81% indicated that 'Ukip having the best policies on particular issues that you care about' had played a large part in their decision, while 68% said that Ukip 'having the best candidate locally' had played a large part and 56% said that it was 'a general protest to show that you are unhappy with all the main parties at the moment'. Lord Ashcroft, Clacton By-Election Poll, 29 August–29-September 2014 <http://lordashcroftpolls.com> (accessed 18 November 2014).

14. It was announced on 10 September 2014 that the election would be held on 9 October 2014. Unlike the terrain in Essex, the northern seat was not ideal territory for a Ukip breakthrough. Though almost two-fifths of the local population worked in more insecure routine and manual jobs—a proportion not too different from that in Clacton—there were larger numbers of younger and more highly educated people among whom Ukip tended to struggle. While 30% of the population in Clacton were pensioners, in the northern seat the figure was 16%. And, while 40% of people in Clacton lacked qualifications, the figure further north was 28%.

15. The first poll by Survation and *The Sun* put Labour on 50%, Ukip second on 31%, and the Conservative Party third on 13%. The second poll by Lord Ashcroft put Labour first on 47%, Ukip second on 28%, and the Conservative Party third on 16%.

16. John Bickley was the Ukip candidate at the Wythenshawe and Sale East by-election in February 2014, where he finished in second place with 18%, behind Labour on 55%.

17. Tribal loyalty was also the most common motive for those who indicated that they planned to support the Conservative Party. The campaign survey for Heywood and Middleton was the only survey that asked supporters of all parties to give their motivation. The other two surveys asked the question only to those who indicated that they planned to vote for Ukip. When Survation asked voters for their main reason for voting for their chosen party, 61% of Labour voters said it was because they had always voted for them, 15% said it was because they liked their policies, and 13% said it was because they disliked another party/wanted to stop them winning. When Ukip voters were asked the same question, 29% said it was because they liked their policies, 24% said it was because they were different from the other parties/wanted change, and 14% said it was because they disliked another party and wanted to stop them from winning. Survation/*The Sun*, 1 October 2014. In the seat 54% of Ukip supporters said that they were not feeling the recovery and did not expect to, compared to a figure of 42%

among Labour voters. Lord Ashcroft Heywood and Middleton by-election poll, 30 September–4 October 2014.

18. Jennifer Williams, 'Labour Insiders Worried that they Could Lose Heywood and Middleton Seat to Ukip in By-Election', *Manchester Evening News*, 24 September 2014.

19. Data from the Lord Ashcroft Heywood and Middleton by-election poll, Fieldwork, 30 September–4-October 2014.

20. Tolhurst took 50.4% of the votes, beating her rival by less than 1%, although only 5,688 people had participated in the postal ballot that was open to all voters in the constituency.

21. Patrick Wintour, 'Labour Leadership Accused of Defeatism over Rochester By-Election', *Guardian*, 7 October 2014; also Luke Akehurst, 'Labour's Mr Micawber Election Strategy', LabourList blog <http://labourlist.org/2014/10/labours-mr-micawber-election-strategy/> (accessed 6 July 2015).

22. In the Lord Ashcroft poll in Rochester and Strood on 11 November, voters were asked: 'Have any of the main political parties contacted you over the last few weeks—whether by delivering leaflets or newspapers sending personally addressed letters, emailing, telephoning you at home or knocking on your door?' 81% had heard from the Conservatives, 84% from Ukip, 63% from Labour, and 24% from the Liberal Democrats.

23. According to a Survation opinion poll, undertaken for Unite on 30 October 2014, which asked voters what issue was the most important to them and their family, 37% of all voters said that the quality of local hospitals and GP services was their dominant concern and then put immigration in second place on 25%. Among Ukip voters, 51% ranked immigration as the top issue, followed by 22% who identified the NHS. On Tolhurst and immigration, see, e.g., Matthew Holehouse, 'Now Cameron's By-Election Candidate Attacks his Immigration Record', *Daily Telegraph*, 18 November 2014.

24. The three surveys, all conducted by Survation, were fielded on 28–9 August 2014 in Clacton, on 30 September 2014 in Heywood and Middleton, and on 1–3 October in Rochester and Strood. In Clacton and Rochester and Strood, the question regarding motive reads: 'What is your main motive for intending to vote for UKIP candidate XX in the by-election?' Different question wording was used in Heywood and Middleton, where the question read: 'What is your main reason for wanting to vote for XX party?' A larger number of response options was given, but we limit our discussion to only those options that compare to those given in the other two surveys.

25. 'Tory MPs Pour into By-Election Campaign . . . but don't Stay Long', *The Times*, 19 November 2014.

26. A swing of 44.2 points was recorded at the Bermondsey by-election in 1983 when Simon Hughes defeated Peter Tatchell. But a swing of almost 49 points was recorded from Labour to an Independent candidate in Bleaneu Gwent in 2005.

27. 'Polling Observatory 43: Stability Returns with Race Close To Dead Heat', 17 December 2014 <http://sotonpolitics.org/2014/12/17/polling-observatory-43/> (accessed 29 August 2015).

28. In 2010 the BNP polled 7% in Heywood and Middleton and 4.6% in Clacton, while the English Democrats polled 4.5% in Rochester and Strood. A far right group named Britain First did contest the Rochester and Strood by-election but polled only 0.1%.

29. According to the Office for National Statistics, net long-term migration to the UK was estimated to be 260,000 in the year ending June 2014, a statistically significant increase from 182,000 in the previous twelve months.

## CHAPTER 9. TARGETING TERRITORY

1. Nigel Farage, 'Election 2014: Mission Accomplished', *Daily Express*, 6 June 2015.

2. The Liberal–SDP Alliance came in second place in 313 constituencies (191 for the Liberals, 122 for the SDP). They finished second in 39% of seats they contested and lost only six deposits. See Ivor Crewe and Anthony King, *SDP: The Birth, Life and Death of the Social Democratic Party* (Oxford: Oxford University Press, 1995), and Ivor Crewe, 'Is Britain's Two-Party System Really about to Crumble?: The Social Democratic–Liberal Alliance and the Prospects for Realignment', *Electoral Studies*, 1/3 (1982), 275–313.

3. As Rennard told his party after the election, while twenty-five of the twenty-eight gains came in seats that the party had not represented in parliament before 1992, twenty-two of the twenty-five gains were where the party had controlled the council, while in the remaining three it held almost all council seats. Lord Rennard speech to the Liberal Democrats, 1997, provided to the authors by Lord Rennard.

4. Mark Pack, 'The Liberal Democrat Approach to Campaigning', *Journal of Liberal History*, 83 (2014), 6–14.

5. Sophy Ridge, 'UKIP Poll Reveals 12 "Most Wanted" Seats', *Sky News*, 26 August 2014.

6. Tim Shipman, 'Gleeful Ukip on Course for 25 MPs', *Sunday Times*, 12 October 2014. The internal Ukip source was also cited as stating that the party 'ought to win' a number of other seats, including 'Tory seats in Kent and Essex, plus Rotherham, Rother Valley, Great Grimsby, Dudley North and Plymouth Moor View'.

7. Matthew Holehouse, 'Nigel Farage to Target Nine Seats at General Election', *Daily Telegraph*, 10 October 2014. The piece identified Boston and Skegness, Thanet South, Thanet North, Eastleigh, Great Yarmouth, Thurrock, and Rotherham. Simon Walters, 'Record Poll Surge Gives Ukip 25%: Survey would Hand Farage Astonishing 128 MPs…and Puts Ed Miliband on a New Low', *Mail on Sunday*, 11 October 2014; Alberto Nardelli, Rowena Mason, and George Arnett, 'Ukip Could Capture 30 Seats in 2015 Election, New Data Shows',

*Guardian*, 14 October 2014. The piece identifed a further ten seats where Ukip 'is a good contender', including the Conservative seats of Great Yarmouth, Camborne and Redruth, Bognor Regis and Littlehampton, Folkestone and Hythe, Thanet North, and Waveney, plus the Labour seats of Dudley North and Rotherham, the Liberal Democrat seat of Eastleigh, and Rochester and Strood. It also identified seats where Ukip had a 'chance to win'—namely, Heywood and Middleton, Redcar, Walsall North, Eastbourne, Chippenham, Dorset Mid and North Poole, Newton Abbott, Cornwall North, Somerton and Frome, St Austell and Newquay, St Ives, Torbay, Truro and Falmouth, Plymouth Moor View, and Rother Valley. Jason Beattie, 'Nigel Farage Message to Tories: Defect to UKIP or you'll Face Destruction', *Mirror*, 21 November 2014.

8. The Bow Group identified the following seats as Ukip wins: Camborne and Redruth, Thurrock, Newton Abbot, Waveney, Plymouth Sutton and Devonport, and Halesowen and Rowley Regis from the Conservatives, while taking Great Grimsby, Telford, Walsall North, Newcastle-under-Lyme, and Plymouth Moorview from Labour and St Ives from the Liberal Democrats. Nick Hallett, 'Tory Think-Tank: UKIP Could Take Twelve Seats at General Election', *Breitbart*, 25 June 2014.

9. Marcus Roberts, Robert Ford, and Ian Warren, *Revolt on the Left: Labour's UKIP Problem and How it Can Be Overcome* (London: Fabian Society, 2014).

10. Grace Macaskill, 'Tape Recording Reveals Ukip's Internal War over Race Row Candidate Victoria Ayling', *The Mirror*, 22 March 2015.

11. 'Ukip Increases Number of Target Seats in Thrilling Election Campaign', Ukip website, n.d. (October?) <http://www.ukip.org/ukip_increases_number_of_target_seats_in_thrilling_election_campaign> (accessed 10 June 2015).

12. Paul Gallagher, 'Ukip Grassroots Leave in Protest at Selection of Ex-Tories and Celebrities', *Independent*, 19 December 2014; Heather Saul, 'Ukip Warns Members not to Join Facebook or Twitter', *Independent*, 20 December 2014.

13. Alexi Mostrous and Billy Kenbar, 'Ukip's Star Woman Quits after Sex Claims', *The Times*, 9 December 2014; Matt Chorley, 'Couple in Ukip Sex Scandal "Both Look Like F\*\*\*ing Prats" for Airing Dirty Laundry in Public, Warn Furious Party Insiders', *Daily Mail*, 11 December 2014.

## CHAPTER 10. INTO BATTLE

1. The widest gap was found in an Opinium poll conducted on 11 September 2014. It put Labour on 37% and the Conservatives at just 28%.

2. The first poll of the New Year was conducted by Opinium on 2 January. It put Labour at 33% and the Tories at 32%, with Ukip and the Liberal Democrats at 17% and 8%, respectively. 'General Election 2015: 10 Expert Predictions on who Will Win the General Election', *Independent*, 4 January 2015.

3. Net satisfaction scores are taken from Ipsos-MORI. In January 2015 ⌐ ⌐⌐⌐⌐⌐ had a net satisfaction score of −11, compared to −35 for Miliband

fourteen-point lead. This was not as great as it had been in November 2014 (twenty-nine-point lead) but was wider than during the conference season in September 2014 (fourteen points) and at the start of 2014 (eight points).

4. Edward Malnick, 'Ed Miliband More of a Threat to David Cameron than Ukip, says Former Tory Chairman', *Daily Telegraph*, 17 January 2015.

5. James Kirkup, 'David Cameron has Stopped Trying to Wrestle the Ukip Pig', *Daily Telegraph*, 12 January 2015.

6. Desmond donated £1.3 million to Ukip in April 2015. Helen Barnett 'Nigel Farage Vows Ukip will be Major Party by 2020', *Daily Express*, 27 April 2015.

7. Such was the intensity of anger towards him that Hamilton lost his majority of almost 16,000 votes. He was defeated by Martin Bell, an Independent who in his white suit campaigned and won on an anti-corruption ticket. Both Labour and the Liberal Democrats had stood down to give Bell a free run.

8. The poll was undertaken on behalf of Alan Bown, by Survation. In the version provided to the authors, the poll suggested that Ukip would comfortably win the seat with 46% of the vote, compared to 26% for the Conservatives and 21% for Labour. But when Neil Hamilton was mentioned as the candidate, these figures changed to 41% for Ukip, 26% for the Conservatives, and 23.5% for Labour. Survation/Alan Bown poll of Boston and Skegness, 5–9 September 2014. <http://survation.com/new-constituency-polling-for-alan-bown/> (accessed 6 April 2015).

9. 'Two New Ukip Defectors Mooted as By-Election Win Looks Easy', *Week*, 23 October 2014.

10. e.g. Rowena Mason 'Ukip Stands by Candidate Kerry Smith after Offensive Comments', *Guardian*, 14 December 2014.

11. Michael Crick, 'Explain your Expenses: Ukip Demands Details from Neil Hamilton', Michael Crick blog, Channel 4 News <http://blogs.channel4.com/michael-crick-on-politics/explain-expenses-ukip-demands-details-neil-hamilton/4641> (accessed 6 April 2015). Press Association, 'Hamilton Hits out at "Dirty Tricks"', featured on *Mail Online*, Press Association, 11 December 2014.

12. Peter Oborne, 'Nigel Farage must Ditch Neil Hamilton or Ukip will be Destroyed', *Daily Telegraph*, 16 December 2014.

13. Simon Walters, 'Astonishing Leaked Phone Calls Expose Outbursts of Ukip Man Sent in to Replace Neil Hamilton', *Mail on Sunday*, 13 December 2014; Lucy Fisher, 'Farage Defends Ukip Candidate over 'Chinky Slur', *The Times*, 19 December 2014.

14. Hugh Muir 'Will Nigel Farage's hardline rhetoric be the Undoing of Ukip', *Guardian*, 18 January 2015.

15. 'Farage on Friday: Why Multiculturalism Has Failed Britain, France and every other country', *Daily Express*, 16 January 2015.

16. In a bizarre turn, George Galloway also surfaced to reveal that, in earlier years, the Respect Party had deselected Bashir. 'But probably for the first time ever', said Galloway, 'I have to agree with Nigel Farage that there are grave concerns

about things in this guy's past' ('Bashir was De-Selected by Respect', Respect Party, 25 January 2015 <http://www.respectparty.org/2015/01/25/bashir-was-de-selected-by-respect> (accessed 26 January 2015).

17. The Ipsos-MORI poll was undertaken 22–9 October 2014. The topline voting intentions with changes since the general election in 2010 were SNP 52% (+32), Labour 23% (−19), Conservative 10% (−7), Liberal Democrat 6% (−13), Green 6% (+5). The YouGov poll was also released on 30 October and put the SNP on 43%, Labour on 27%, Conservatives on 15%, and Liberal Democrats on 4%. YouGov returned to Scotland on 13 December and reported the topline figures for Westminster voting intention alongside changes from the previous poll at the end of October as SNP 47% (+4), Labour 27% (n.c.), Conservative 16% (+1), Liberal Democrat 3% (−1), Green 3% (−1), Ukip 3% (−3).

18. The first wave of polls was conducted between 5 and 30 January and included 16,007 respondents. The second wave included 12,005 respondents, surveyed between 2 and 26 February. The second wave also included four seats outside Scotland. Full results available at: <http://lordashcroftpolls.com> (accessed 15 July 2015).

19. 'Secret Ukip Labour Meeting this Lunchtime', Guido Fawkes, 25 November 2014 <http://order-order.com/2014/11/25/secret-ukip-labour-meeting-this-lunchtime/#:PsSVSxuFd7TjIA> (accessed 8 August 2015).

20. 'Tim Aker outlines some of our 2015 Policies', Ukip <http://www.ukip.org/tim_aker_outlines_some_of_our_2015_policies> (accessed 30 April 2015); see also J. Elwes, 'What Will Ukip's Election 2015 Manifesto Look Like?' *Prospect*, 20 August 2014 <http://www.prospectmagazine.co.uk/opinions/exclusive-what-will-ukips-election-2015-manifesto-look-like> (accessed 30 April 2015).

21. Figures taken from the Ipsos-MORI Issues Tracker.

22. Adam Withnall, 'Leaked Documents Show Ukip Leaders Approve NHS Privatisation Once it Becomes More "Acceptable to the Electorate"', *Independent*, 21 January 2015.

23. 'Opportunity for the Tories as Ukip Swings Left', *Daily Telegraph*, 6 January 2015.

24. YouGov surveyed 1640 British adults on 21–2 January and asked: 'Thinking specifically about the UK Independence Party, from what you have seen or heard how much do you know about their policies on . . .'. The percentage of respondents who said 'I don't know anything about what UKIP's policy is in this area' was 54% on the NHS, 66% on the economy, 73% on education, 62 per cent in crime, 66 per cent on defence, and 74% on pensions.

25. Inspired by 'Together we can do great things'.

26. Nigel Farage, 'Nigel Farage's Appeal to Britons: Believe in Britain', *Daily Telegraph*, 11 February 2015.

27. Douglas Carswell, 'It's not only Offensive to Dislike Foreigners . . . it's Absurd Says Douglas Carswell Ukip MP for Clacton', *Mail on Sunday*, 27 December 2014.

28. Lucy Fisher, 'Stop Blaming Immigrations, Carswell Tells Ukip', *The Times*, 29 December 2014.

29. 'Ukip Leader Nigel Farage Says Comedian Al Murray's Bid for Thanet South Seat Could Backfire', Kent Online <http://www.kentonline.co.uk/thanet/news/al-murrays-political-stand-could-30365> (accessed 26 January 2015).

30. In 2010 an Independent candidate had finished second in Castle Point with 27% of the vote.

31. Respondents are coded as being anti-immigration if they indicated that they believe immigrants are a burden on the welfare state and that immigration both undermines Britain's cultural like and is bad for the economy.

32. Heather Saul, 'Conservative Chairman Grant Shapps Rules out Ukip Pact after General Election', *Independent*, 30 January 2015.

33. These data are presented in Appendix D. Ukip was on 14% in Camborne and Redruth and 20% in St Austell and Newquay. The Lord Ashcroft polls released on 1 April probed local campaign activity in these seats. The snapshot polls suggested that Ukip was most active in St Austell and Newquay, where 42% of voters said that they had been contacted by the party, as compared to 57% who had been contacted by the Liberal Democrats, 50% by the Conservatives, and 24% by Labour. In Camborne and Redruth Ukip's contact rate was much lower at 29%, well behind the Conservatives and Labour (both on 65%) and the Liberal Democrats (40%). Lord Ashcroft, 'The Liberal Democrat Battleground', 1 April 2015 <http://lordashcroftpolls.com/2015/04/the-liberal-democrat-battleground> (accessed 5 April 2015).

34. Figures are taken from the multivariate analyses presented in Appendix C.

35. Christopher Hope, 'Nigel Farage: The Truth about my Health—I am Being Treated in Hospital Twice a Week', *Daily Telegraph*, 24 April 2015.

## CHAPTER 11. GROUND GAME

1. During the long campaign parties can spend a maximum sum of £30,700 + 6p/9p per elector in a borough/county constituency. During the short campaign this falls to £8,700 + 6p/9p per elector in a borough/county constituency.

2. A YouGov and *Sunday Times* poll taken after the interviews put Labour on 36% and the Conservatives on 32%. But then a ComRes and *Daily Mail*/ITV poll put the Conservatives on 36% and Labour on 32%.

3. The third wave of Scottish polls from Lord Ashcroft was conducted between 9 and 17 April. 10,009 respondents were surveyed across ten Scottish constituencies. Of the ten seats, the SNP was expected to lose out on only one seat—Berwickshire, Roxburgh, and Selkirk, which was predicted to be a Conservative gain. Full results available at: <http://lordashcroftpolls.com> (accessed 17 July 2015).

4. The poll that we refer to here is the Lord Ashcroft National Poll. It put Ukip on 10% of the vote on 30 March.

5. Laura Elvin, 'Ukip Candidate's Secret Life as Porn Star Called Johnny Rockard Is Revealed', *Mirror*, 9 April 2015; 'Ukip Candidate "To Be Questioned" over Sausage Rolls', *BBC News*, 10 April 2015.

6. Some of these data are presented in Appendix D. Lord Ashcroft polled 10,006 respondents in ten Conservative-held marginals between 28 March and 4 April. Full results available at: <http://lordashcroftpolls.com/wp-content/uploads/2015/04/LORD-ASHCROFT-POLLS-Competitive-Con-Lab-constituencies-April-2015.pdf> (accessed 17 July 2015).

7. YouGov and *Sunday Times* poll, 3–4 April 2015. It is worth noting that 62% of Conservative voters supported the ban and that support was strongest among voters aged 40 years old and above, voters from the working class, and those on benefits.

8. Across all four of the 'snap polls' that were taken after the debate, Farage finished joint second with Miliband on 21%, behind Cameron, who was on 22%, and one point ahead of Sturgeon. Nick Clegg, Natalie Bennett, and Leanne Wood lagged well behind the others.

9. The YouGov/*Times* survey included 1,522 British adults and took place following the end of the debate. The question on performance read: 'Leaving aside your own party preference, who do you think performed best overall in tonight's debate?' Full results available at: <https://d25d2506sfb94s.cloudfront.net/cumulus_uploads/document/58cqsor3fx/Debate_for_website_final.pdf> (accessed 15 July 2015).

10. Figures taken from Wave 5 of the 2014–2017 British Election Study Internet Panel. By comparison, three out of four of those who indicated that they were voting for the Tories or the Liberal Democrats had voted for the party in the previous election, while for Labour it was two out of three supporters.

11. The analyses of the 2014–2017 British Election Study data are presented in Appendix C.

12. The question reads: 'Are you satisfied or dissatisfied with the way Nigel Farage is doing his job as leader of UKIP, the UK Independence Party?' Data are available at <https://www.ipsos-mori.com/researchpublications/researcharchive/88/Political-Monitor-Satisfaction-Ratings-1997Present.aspx?view=wide> (accessed 17 July 2015).

13. Ipsos-MORI polled voters' assessments of the leaders three times during the short campaign: 11–12 January, 10–12 February, and 8–11 March. On average, 33% said they were satisfied with how David Cameron was doing his job as prime minister; 33% indicated they were satisfied with how Nigel Farage was doing as party leader, while 27% were satisfied with Miliband as Labour leader, and 25% were satisfied with how Clegg was doing as leader of the Liberal Democrats.

14. Ipsos-MORI ran two surveys where respondents were given a series of favourable and unfavourable terms and were asked to say whether they thought the statement applied to the party. The first survey ran in September 2014, while the second was fielded in April 2015. While the party's image suffered in several areas, it continued to be perceived as 'different from other parties' by nearly three out of four respondents, and perceptions of the party's extremity had not substantially increased. Data available from <www.ipsos-mori.com/research-publications/researcharchive/3509/UKIP-Image.aspx> (accessed 17 July 2015).

15. On 7–8 April YouGov asked 1,871 respondents, 'Imagine that the Scottish National Party (SNP) and Plaid Cymru put up candidates throughout the whole of the United Kingdom, standing against Labour, the Conservatives, Liberal Democrats, UKIP and other parties. Which party would you vote for?' After those who said they would not vote or did not know had been removed, 11% of all voters said they would vote for the SNP. Among Scottish voters, this figured jumped to 43%. Many of those who would consider voting for the party had previously been intending to vote for Labour or the Liberal Democrats. Data available at <http://d25d2506sfb94s.cloudfront.net/cumulus_uploads/document/jjf1thmxbe/JoeResults_150408_SNP_Plaid:if_national_VI_W.pdf> (accessed 26 July 2015).

16. David Cameron, 'The First Votes Are Being Cast: The Choice Is a Better Britain or Sturgeon's Hostage', *Sunday Times*, 19 April 2015.

17. 'A vote for Ukip Puts Ed Miliband in No. 10', *Daily Telegraph*, 15 April 2015. 'The Sun Says: It's a Tory!', *Sun*, 29 April 2015.

18. 'PM Plea to Potential Ukip Voters', *Northern Echo*, 6 April 2015.

19. Thurrock was among six marginal seats Ashcroft polled between 16 and 23 April. Full results available at <http://lordashcroftpolls.com/wp-content/uploads/2015/04/LORD-ASHCROFT-POLLS-Key-marginal-constituencies-24-April-2015.pdf> (accessed 26 July 2015).

20. Survation and Alan Bown poll, 5–9 September 2014; Lord Ashcroft Boston and Skegness poll, 26 January–5 February 2015.

21. The five target seats were among the seats Lord Ashcroft surveyed during the short campaign, but the fieldwork for the seats did not take place during the same period. Information on each poll can be found in the reports available at: <www.lordashcroftpolls.com> (accessed 26 July 2015).

22. The April poll was the first commission in Castle Point, so we are unable to track the party's support in the seat over time.

23. Four by Lord Ashcroft, two by Survation (funded by a Ukip donor), and one by ComRes.

24. Paul Francis, 'Labour's Will Scobie has Urged the People of South Thanet to vote Tactically to Prevent Ukip's Nigel Farage Becoming MP for the Area', KentOnline <http://www.kentonline.co.uk/thanet/news/vote-tactically-urges-labour-34554/> (accessed 5 April 2015).

25. Michael Savage, 'Cameron Urges Defectors to Farage to Come Back Home', *The Times*, 7 April 2015.

26. Nigel Farage, 'If I Lose in South Thanet it's Curtains for me: I will Have to Quit as Ukip Leader', *Daily Telegraph*, 15 March 2015. The article was an extract from Farage's book: Nigel Farage (2015) *The Purple Revolution: The Year that Changed Everything* (London: Biteback, 2015).

27. Rowena Mason, 'Tories Accused of Pork-Barrel Politics in Nigel Farage's Target Seat', *Guardian*, 13 March 2015; see also Julia Collins, 'Minister John Hayes Announces Review over Manston Airport', *Kent Online*, 5 March 2015 <http://www.kentonline.co.uk/thanet/news/airport-decisions-under-review-32961/> (accessed 9 September 2015).

28. Glen Owen. 'Farage Buries "Loser" Poll: Ukip Leader Covers up Survey Spelling Humiliating Defeat to Tories in Thanet Seat', *Mail on Sunday*, 5 April 2015. On the request for support, this was sent via Nigel Farage's Facebook page, but see also Adam Withnall, 'Nigel Farage Asks Ukip Followers for "Personal Favour" of "One or Two Days' Support" in South Thanet after Poll Shows he May not Win Seat', *Independent*, Monday, 6 April 2015.

## CHAPTER 12. COUNTING THE VOTES

1. The Speaker is not included in the count of Conservative seats.

2. On this point it is worth noting that prior to the general election a series of six forecasts had been collected by the influential website, May 2015. All six had forecast a hung parliament, and, while four had the Conservative Party winning the largest number of seats, none had the party on more than 285 seats. One forecast by the Polling Observatory team had Labour winning the largest number of seats. See <http://www.may2015.com/category/seat-calculator/> (accessed 10 June 2015). Prior to the election, the London School of Economics had also hosted a major gathering for election forecasters. Across twelve forecasts the average expected result was for Labour to win the largest number of seats, which was mirrored in the results of an 'expert' survey by the Political Studies Association (PSA).

3. In 1983 Labour won 209 seats and in 1987 it won 229.

4. While the SNP took forty seats from Labour, only thirty-nine were held by Labour politicians by the time of the 2015 general election. Eric Joyce was representing Labour when he was re-elected as MP for Falkirk in 2010, but he left Labour in 2012. He served the remaining years as an Independent.

5. In three seats the SNP share of the vote increased by more than 40%, including by 41 points in Glasgow South West and Glasgow North and by 44 points in Glasgow North East.

6. Moreover, and as Curtice also noted, these figures do not take into account the likely boundary changes that would further damage Labour's prospects ahead of

the next general election. John Curtice, 'A Defeat to Reckon with: On Scotland, Economic Competence, and the Complexities of Labour's Losses', *Juncture* (2015) <http://www.ippr.org/juncture/a-defeat-to-reckon-with-on-scotland-economic-competence-and-the-complexities-of-labours-losses> (accessed 30 June 2015).

7. 'Leaked memo shows Miliband was warned over deficit, immigration and welfare in 2010', Labour List, 5 August 2015 <http://labourlist.org/2015/08/leaked-memo-shows-miliband-was-warned-over-deficit-immigration-and-welfare-in-2010/> (accessed 6 August 2015).

8. Curtice, 'A Defeat to Reckon with'.

9. The four seats (where the Greens finished second to Labour) were Bristol West, Liverpool Riverside, Manchester Gorton, and Sheffield Central.

10. John Rentoul, 'So Much for the Great Fragmentation—It Seems Two-Party British Politics Still Works', *Independent*, 15 July 2015.

11. By this we mean that the effective number of parties had not increased.

12. Farage first attempted to enter Westminster in 1994, when he stood at a by-election in Eastleigh. He has stood as a candidate in every general election since 1997, as well as the 2006 by-election in Bromley and Chislehust.

13. Compared to the by-election in October 2014, Carswell's support had fallen from 59.7% to 44.4%, with his majority falling from 12,404 votes to 3,437. It was also a significant drop from when he had stood as a Conservative MP in 2010, when his majority had been 12,068 votes.

14. In the Lord Ashcroft poll, when voters were asked how they would vote in the election, the Ukip MP trailed the Tories by seven points, and when they were asked how they would vote in their seat, he was behind by three. The poll by Survation was undertaken in the final week of the campaign. It was funded by a Ukip donor. When normal weightings and likelihood to vote were applied, with undecided and refused removed, the Conservative Party candidate was on 42.5%, Reckless was second with 35.9%, and Labour a distant third on 16.9%.

15. The poll was undertaken by Survation and funded by a Ukip donor. When normal weightings and likelihood to vote were applied, with undecideds and refused removed, it put Ukip in second place on 35%, the Conservative Party first on 41.9%, and Labour a distant third on 18.2%.

16. The internal poll was undertaken by Survation and funded by a Ukip donor. When normal weightings and likelihood to vote were applied, with undecideds and refused removed, Aker was on 29.6%, the Labour candidate Polly Billington was second on 34.4%, and the Conservative Party candidate Jackie Doyle-Price was first with 35.1%.

17. The poll was undertaken by Survation and funded by a Ukip donor. When normal weightings and likelihood to vote were applied, with undecideds and refused removed, Harris was in first place on 52.1%, Huntman was in second on 34%, and the Labour candidate was a distant third on 10.4%.

18. David Butler, 'Elections Transformed: Michael Ryle Memorial Lecture 2015', Speaker's State Apartments, 16 July 2015 <http://www.studyofparliament.org.uk/spgmrml15.htm> (accessed 26 July 2015).

19. The most loyal switchers were actually those who had voted for Clegg in 2010. In the month after the European election, 21% of Ukip supporters said that they had voted for the Liberal Democrats in 2010, and Ukip had lost 44% of these switchers by May 2015.

20. Across all British constituencies, Ukip took 14% of the vote in seats that it had also contested in 2010, compared with 10% in seats it was contesting for the first time. However, if we look only at constituencies in England and Wales, we see that the party averaged 14% in both new and previously contested seats.

21. Other examples include Wentworth and Dearne, Sittingbourne and Sheppey, Stoke North, Bradford South, Bolton South East, South West Norfolk, Penistone and Stocksbridge, Romford, North East Cambridgeshire, and Makerfield.

22. David Butler, *The British General Election of 1955* (London: Macmillan, 1955), 2.

23. Rowena Mason, 'Nigel Farage: Ukip Will Be Main Challenger in Nearly Every English Seat', *Guardian*, 12 February 2015.

24. The six Welsh seats where Ukip finished second were Aberavon, Blaenau Gwent, Caerphilly, Islwyn, Merthyr Tydfil and Rhymney, and Swansea East.

25. The exception was Richmond in Yorkshire, where the sitting Conservative MP, William Hague, had announced his decision to stand down ahead of the 2015 election. Ukip also finished second in two London seats, the outer-east Dagenham and Rainham, home of Labour MP Jon Cruddas, and the Conservative-held Hornchurch and Upminster.

26. An alternative means of evaluating change in seats would be to calculate a measure of 'swing' between the two parties (David Butler, 'Appendix III: The Relation of Seats to Votes', in R. D. McCallum and Alison Readman, *The British General Election of 1945* (London: Oxford University Press, 1947), 277–92). Traditionally measures of the 'total-vote swing' or of the 'two-party swing' have been used to capture the change in the relative strength of two parties. However, these measures are more reliable when the nature of the party system remains unchanged over time—that is, the same two parties occupy the top positions in two subsequent elections. Given that there are dramatic changes in the nature of the party system at the national or constituency level between 2010 and 2014, we instead look at the change in the vote share of individual parties. That being said, our substantive conclusions remain unchanged if we look at the swing between two parties.

27. A seat is classified as marginal if the difference between the first and second place vote-receiving candidates is less than 10%.

28. It won more than 20% in four north-eastern seats and failed to recruit at least half that number in only one. Ukip polled over 20% of the vote in Blyth Valley, Hartlepool, Houghton and Sunderland, and South Shields. The party won 9.9% of the vote in Hexham. In Yorkshire, Ukip surged past 20% in sixteen seats.

29. The 'routine and manual occupations' category includes respondents employed in lower supervisory and technical occupations, semi-routine occupations, and routine occupations. While Ukip recruited a higher share of its supporters from this group than Labour, the differences between the parties are modest. Of Ukip's supporters, 30% were employed in routine or manual occupations. For Labour, the corresponding figure was 27%. For the SNP—the party that had the most supporters in routine occupations—the figure was 31%. While Ukip, the SNP, and Labour all have a relatively similar composition, there are striking class differences between Ukip and the Conservative party, which drew just 18% of its supporters from this group. With respect to education, 52% of those who reported that they voted for Ukip left school before the age of 17. The next closest party was Labour, which recruited 36% of its supporters from this group. Among Ukip's supporters, 49% were over the age of 55 years. This was five points higher than the Tories, the next closest party. Finally, 96% of Ukip's supporters were white. In terms of other data, one example is a large-scale survey of 100,000 people, undertaken by YouGov, which explored the extent to which different groups in society supported different parties around the time of the election. The results, shown in Appendix D, suggest that Ukip drew the bulk of its support from voters who will now be familiar to readers— men, pensioners, people with few qualifications and from the more insecure working classes, and those on benefits. Almost one in five of those in work-ing-class occupations voted for Ukip, compared to one in ten of those who worked in more secure middle-class jobs. And, whereas one in five of those whose education had stopped at the GCSE level had voted for Ukip, only one in twenty graduates had done so. Labour was the only party to draw more support from this group than from graduates, but the differences are not nearly as stark as those for Ukip.

30. These analyses can be found in Appendix D.

31. Lord Ashcroft, Post-Vote Day Poll, 7 May 2015' <http://lordashcroftpolls.com/wp-content/uploads/2015/05/LORD-ASHCROFT-POLLS-Post-vote-poll-summary1.pdf> (accessed 1 July 2015).

32. There is a strong, positive correlation between the BNP's vote share in 2010 and 2015 ($r = 0.62$, $p < 0.01$).

33. We define 'low' Ukip performance as seats where Ukip received vote shares that were below average – less than 14%. Seats where Ukip received vote shares above 14% are classified as cases of 'high' Ukip performance.

CHAPTER 13. CIVIL WAR

1. Ivor Crewe and Anthony King, SDP: The Birth, Life and Death of the Social Democratic Party (Oxford: Oxford University Press, 1995), 383.

2. Rachel Sylvester, 'Farage Should not Lead Sceptics in Referendum, Says Party's Only MP', The Times, 23 May 2015.

3. Short money is an annual payment to opposition parties that have representation in the House of Commons to help them with the costs incurred in performing their parliamentary functions. The amount payable to qualifying parties is £16,689 for each seat won at the most recent election, in addition to £33.33 for every 200 votes gained by the party.

4. 'House Divided', *The Times*, 14 May 2015.

5. Laura Pitel, 'Top Farage Ally Turns on "Snarling" Ukip Leader', *The Times*, 14 May 2015.

## CHAPTER 14. REFERENDUM

1. These averages are based on polls between 9 May 2015 and 16 August 2015, collected by Anthony Wells and the UK Polling Report website <http://ukpollingreport.co.uk> (accessed 16 August 2015).

2. David Butler and Uwe Kitzinger, *The 1975 Referendum* (London and Basingstoke: Macmillan, 1976), 279–80.

3. Liesbet Hooghe and Gary Marks, 'A Post-Functional Theory of European Integration: From Permissive Consensus to Constraining Dissensus', *British Journal of Political Science*, 39/1 (2008), 1–23. For an excellent summary of this literature and Britain's relationship with the European Union more generally, see Andrew Gamble, *Britain and the European Union* (Basingstoke: Palgrave, 2013).

4. Figures are calculated using Wave 6 of the 2014–2017 British Election Study Internet Panel.

5. House of Commons, 11 May 1953.

6. In the YouGov poll, the percentage of voters who said that they would opt to remain in the EU versus leave the EU, with leavers being ahead, reached 22 points in August 2011, 23 points in May 2012, and 21 points in November 2012. These same data are used in Figure 14.1.

7. These figures are taken from YouGov. Voters are given the following statement. 'Imagine the British government under David Cameron renegotiated our relationship with Europe and said that Britain's interests were now protected, and David Cameron recommended that Britain remain a member of the European Union on the new terms. How would you then vote in a referendum on the issue?' In May 2015 58% said they would remain, while 24% would leave, and 18% either would not vote or did not know how they would vote.

8. The question reads: 'Do you think Britain's long-term policy should be to leave the European Union, to stay in the EU and try to reduce the EU's powers, to leave things as they are, to stay in the EU and try to increase the EU's powers, or, to work for the formation of a single European government?' Prior to 1997, the question referred to the 'European Community'. Comparable questions were not asked in the surveys run in 2007 or 2009–11. For a more in-depth discussion of these data, as well as other insights from the British Social Attitudes Survey, see John Curtis and Geoffrey Evans, 'Britain and Europe: Are we All Eurosceptics

Now?', in R. Ormston and J. Curtice (eds), *British Social Attitudes: The 32nd Report* (London: NatCen Social Research, 2015).

9. Figures do not take into account those who said they did not know how they would vote. If we include the 'don't know' category, 86% of those who supported Ukip would vote to leave, 7% said they would vote to stay, and 7% said they did not know.

10. Gamble, *Britain and the European Union*, 11.

11. When YouGov asked this question on 6–7 April 2015, 43% of respondents indicated they thought Britain would be worse off economically if it left the EU, while 25 per cent said that the county would be better off.

12. The additional YouGov questions read: 'Do you think Britain would be better or worse off economically if we left the European Union, or would it make no difference?'; 'Do you think Britain would have more or less influence in the world if we left the European Union, or would it make no difference?'; 'Do you think it would be good or bad for jobs and employment if Britain left the European Union, or would it make no difference?'; 'And do you think you personally would be better or worse off if we left the European Union, or would it make no difference?'

13. Sunder Katwala, 'Is Nigel Farage Hurting the Eurosceptic Cause?' *New Statesman* '*The Staggers' Blog*, 3 April 2015 <http://www.newstatesman.com/politics/2014/04/nigel-farage-hurting-eurosceptic-cause> (accessed 4 August 2015). On the evidence in September, see Sunder Katwala, 'How Immigration could Decide the EU Referendum, One Way or Another', *British Future*, blog, 4 September 2015 <http://www.britishfuture.org/blog/how-immigration-could-decide-the-eu-referendum-one-way-or-the-other/> (accessed 6 September 2015).

14. On the specific studies, see Lauren McLaren, 'Public Support for the European Union: Cost/Benefit Analysis or Perceived Cultural Threat', *Journal of Politics*, 64/2 (2002), 551–66; and Sara Hobolt, Wouter van der Brug, Catherine De Vreese, Hago Boomgaarden, and M Hinrichsen, 'Religious Intolerance and Euroscepticism', *European Union Politics*, 12/3 (2011), 359–79. See also Liesbet Hooghe and Gary Marks, 'Does Identity or Economic Rationality Drive Public Opinion on European Integration?', *Political Science and Politics*, 37/3 (2004), 415–20; Lauren McLaren, 'Explaining Mass-Level Euroscepticism: Identity, Interests, and Institutional Distrust', *Acta Politica*, 42/2 (2007), 233–51; Hajo G. Boomgaarden, Andreas R. T. Schuck, Matthijs Elenbaas, and Claes H. De Vreese, 'Mapping EU Attitudes: Conceptual and Empirical Dimensions of Euroscepticism and EU Support', *European Union Politics*, 12/2 (2011), 241–66. It is important to note evidence that these drivers are dependent upon the surrounding economic context. On this point, see John Garry and James Tilley, 'The Macroeconomic Factors Conditioning the Impact of Identity on Attitudes towards the EU', *European Union Politics*, 10/3 (2009), 361–79.

## APPENDIX

1. For all areas in England and Wales, the bivariate correlation between Ukip favourability and vote share in the 2014 European elections is 0.72.
2. The correlation between Ukip favourability and vote share in the 2014 local elections is 0.62.
3. The correlation between Ukip favourability and vote share in the 2015 general election is 0.74.
4. For constituencies that overlap with multiple local authorities we take the party's average vote share across the authorities that overlap with the constituency.
5. We use performance in the European election, as opposed to Ukip's performance in the 2010 general election, because it was a more proximate election, and, therefore, it is arguably a more current measure of the party's strength in an area. However, our substantive conclusions remain unchanged if we use the party's 2010 performance or include the results from both elections.
6. Our substantive conclusions remain unchanged if we use the change in the BNP's vote share between 2010 and 2015.
7. The total effect of demographic favourability is the sum of the direct effect of the favourability and the indirect effect that favourability has on performance via its effect on the party's past performance. The direct effect of demographic favourability is 11.03 points, while the indirect effect is 5.78 points.

# List of Figures

# List of Tables

# Illustration Credits

# Index

Note: The suffix 'f' following a page number indicates a figure, 'n' indicates a footnote, 'p' a photograph, and 't' a table.